HISTORY

OF

DELAWARE COUNTY

AND

Border Wars of New York

New York Classics

A. J. Parker

AMASA JUNIUS PARKER, LL.D.

HISTORY
OF
DELAWARE COUNTY
AND
Border Wars of New York

JAY GOULD

WITH A NEW INTRODUCTION BY
EDWARD RENEHAN

AN IMPRINT OF STATE UNIVERSITY OF NEW YORK PRESS

Originally published in 1856 by Keeny & Gould, Publishers.

This edition was typeset from a transcription originally done by volunteers to the dcnyhistory.org website.

On the cover: Map of Delaware County by Jay Gould, first published in 1856. Library of Congress.

Published by State University of New York Press, Albany

© 2021 State University of New York

All rights reserved

Printed in the United States of America

No part of this book may be used or reproduced in any manner whatsoever without written permission. No part of this book may be stored in a retrieval system or transmitted in any form or by any means including electronic, electrostatic, magnetic tape, mechanical, photocopying, recording, or otherwise without the prior permission in writing of the publisher.

Excelsior Editions is an imprint of State University of New York Press

For information, contact State University of New York Press, Albany, NY
www.sunypress.edu

Library of Congress Cataloging-in-Publication Data

Names: Gould, Jay, 1836–1892, author. | Renehan, Edward, 1956– writer of introduction.
Title: History of Delaware County and border wars of New York / Jay Gould ; [introduction by] Edward Renehan.
Description: Albany : State University of New York Press, [2021] | Series: New York classics | "Originally published in 1856 by Keeny & Gould, Publishers."
Identifiers: LCCN 2020055649 | ISBN 9781438485393 (hardcover : alk. paper) | ISBN 9781438485409 (pbk. : alk. paper) | ISBN 9781438485416 (ebook)
Subjects: LCSH: Delaware County (N.Y.)—History. | New York (State)—History. | New York (State)—History—Revolution, 1775–1783. | Antirent War, N.Y., 1839–1846. | Murphy, Timothy, 1751–1818. | United States—History—Revolution, 1775–1783—Personal narratives.
Classification: LCC F127.D3 G74 2021 | DDC 974.7/36—dc23
LC record available at https://lccn.loc.gov/2020055649

10 9 8 7 6 5 4 3 2 1

CONTENTS

New Introduction   vii
Edward Renehan

HISTORY OF DELAWARE COUNTY AND BORDER WARS OF NEW YORK

Preface	xiii
Contents	xv
Chapter 1	1
Chapter 2	9
Chapter 3	17
Chapter 4	35
Chapter 5	53
Chapter 6	69
Chapter 7	91
Chapter 8	120
Chapter 9	137
Chapter 10	150
Chapter 11	161
Chapter 12	173
Chapter 13	188
Chapter 14	203
Chapter 15	229
Chapter 16	237
Appendix	261

NEW INTRODUCTION

Edward Renehan

JAY Gould (1836–1892) has gone down in history as the consummate Gilded Age robber baron. For more than three decades he astonished and oftentimes outraged Wall Street with his grand schemes for manipulating stocks, bonds, and various derivatives, eventually amassing a fortune that stood at $125 million by the time he died (or $3.5 billion in today's dollars). His impact on the financial landscape of his time cannot be overstated. He owned, at various times, the Western Union Telegraph Company, the Missouri Pacific Railroad, the Union Pacific Railroad, the Manhattan Elevated Railroad, and (briefly) the *New York World* newspaper. His majestic mansion, Lyndhurst, on the banks of the Hudson River at Tarrytown, New York, remains today a landmark and showcase owned by the National Trust for Historic Preservation.* Gould also owned another mansion, on Fifth Avenue in New York, now demolished.† Both mansions were very far away, in miles and in time, from Gould's birthplace, a humble farmhouse in rural Roxbury, New York—the tiny Delaware County hamlet where Gould was raised along with his contemporary, and nearby neighbor, the future essayist/naturalist John Burroughs.‡

Gould had deep roots in Delaware County. His paternal grandparents, Abraham Gould, Jr., and Anna Gould, came from Connecticut and settled in Roxbury in 1789, at a time when the place was known as "West Settlement" and comprised a part of the Hardenbergh Patent. (Settlers paid rent for their lands to the influential Hardenbergh family and their partners, who owned approximately two million acres in Delaware, Ulster,

---

* The National Trust for Historic Preservation inherited the estate in 1961, upon the death of Jay Gould's youngest daughter, Anna Gould. There is a website: http://www.lyndhurst.org.
† 579 Fifth Avenue, at the northeast corner of the intersection with 47th Street.
‡ Late in life, Burroughs (1837–1921) was to comment: "It is a curious psychological fact that the two men outside my own family of whom I have oftenest dreamed in my sleep are [Ralph Waldo] Emerson and Jay Gould; one to whom I owe so much, the other to whom I owe nothing; one whose name I revere, the other whose name I associate, as does the world, with the dark way of speculative finance." John Burroughs, *My Boyhood* (Garden City: Doubleday & Page, 1922), 27. Note that the original Gould farmhouse, in which Gould was born, still stands on Roxbury's West Settlement Road and is in private hands.

Green, Orange, and Sullivan Counties.) On Gould's mother's side, he was the great-grandson of two other Hardenbergh renters, John and Betty Taylor More, who emigrated from Scotland and settled in what became the town of Hobart in 1772. Thus, they became the very first white people to make a home anywhere in Delaware County. The Mores later founded the town that became Moresville, where John operated a prosperous tavern and inn. John More died in 1840, at age ninety-five—leaving four-year-old Jay as one of more than one hundred and twenty great-grandchildren.*

At Jay's Lyndhurst mansion, in the surprisingly small office where he tended to his affairs when at that residence, one sees an ancient transit surveying tool propped in the corner. Gould used this relic as a young man in the 1850s when, not wanting to follow in his father's and grandfather's footsteps as dairy farmers, he tried to make a living doing surveying work for land speculators, railroad developers, road builders, and other clients throughout the Catskills and as far north as Albany.

At the same time that he worked at his surveying, Gould also pursued two separate projects that fit well with his primary trade. One idea was to create a large and comprehensive full-color map of Delaware County, to have various businesses and landowners pay a fee to see their locations and names highlighted, and to then sell copies of the map, which he would publish himself (through the Philadelphia printers Collins and Keeny). His other project was to research and write a full history of Delaware County, which he would likewise publish himself and to which he would sell prepublication subscriptions.

While journeying about the county doing surveys, Gould regularly paused to talk with elderly farmers and other citizens, interview them about historical events and folklore, and earnestly record their words in a series of notebooks. (Whenever possible, he also sold his interviewees subscriptions to his forthcoming book, in which he promised their families would be mentioned.) Many of those families have descendants who remain in Delaware County, many in their original houses. Therefore, one wonders how many first-edition copies of Gould's *History of Delaware County and Border Wars of New York* might lurk on dusty bookshelves in centuries-old farmhouses within the watershed of the Delaware's East Branch. (Interestingly, when I looked through Gould's extensive private library at Lyndhurst, I could not find a single copy of the book. It may be, however, that a few were to be found in the equally large library at Gould's Manhattan mansion, the entire contents of which were auctioned off in the early 1940s.)

By mid-1856, at age twenty, Gould had the map completed—and all

---

* The John More Family Association, consisting of descendants John and Betty Taylor More, calculates the couple as having about sixteen thousand descendants. There is a website: http://www.johnmore.com.

the printing and distribution accomplished. Only a hundred or so copies were run off, and today the few remaining originals are much in demand, commanding high prices among collectors.* That April, he also had his book in good order—in printer's plates, ready to go to press—when disaster struck. A fire completely destroyed the firm that Gould had commissioned to print the book. Not only were the printer's plates destroyed but also Gould's one copy of the original manuscript. Only a few proof sheets remained, preserving small slices of Gould's prose. Undeterred, Gould sat down and rewrote the manuscript during May and June. He issued the book under his homegrown imprint of "Keeny & Gould" that September. Once again, only a hundred or so copies were printed.

Gould's book is invaluable in that, through his fastidious interviews, he was able to assemble the closest thing we have to first-person accounts of the early settlement of the region. Gould's interviewees, some of them in his own family, were only a generation or two away from the first white people to come to the area.† They knew the old stories well. Without Gould's transcriptions of these early reminiscences and tales, a great gap would exist in the historical record of Gould's home region.

The book is considered not only a classic but also highly reliable in its accounts of people and events. As to reliability, Gould says this in his preface: "I do not claim that this work is free from error; perfection, in a history of this character, where much of the information to be relied upon is of an oral and indefinite nature, is an impossibility. I have been careful to weigh all the statements presented—to discriminate between truth and fiction—and have suppressed much apparently interesting matter, which lacked the proper authenticity, or conflicted with truth; still, doubtless, there is room for improvement."

Most notable, perhaps, is the vantage point the book provides for viewing the Delaware County Antirent war of the early 1840s, when many residents—although not, interestingly, Gould's father—successfully rose up against the Hardenbergh Patroons, demanding land reform and an end to their serfdom. Gould spoke to dozens of Antirenters and recorded their tales in painstaking detail, creating a record that remains of great use and importance to historians.

Soon after publishing his book, Gould departed for Manhattan and, more specifically, Wall Street. He rarely returned, although he remained in sporadic touch with old friends and cousins. In 1880, he came home to install a large marker above the simple Gould family plot in the burial

---

* There are several original copies of Gould's map of Delaware County on public display. One hangs in the town hall of Andes, New York, and another in the hall of the Jay Gould Memorial Reformed Church in Roxbury, New York. Among collectors, Gould's map is considered something of a masterpiece of cartography.

† Indeed, Gould's own father—John Burr Gould—was said to have been the first white child born in Roxbury.

ground, at Roxbury's "Yellow Meetinghouse," where his parents lay. He made another brief visit in 1884, and again in 1887. Finally, in July of 1888, only a few months after receiving a diagnosis of tuberculosis—which, at the time, constituted a death sentence—he came back one last time with four of his children, intent on introducing them to cousins and familiarizing them with their roots.

The Goulds came into town by train. They slept several nights in Jay's elaborate private railroad car, Atalanta, which was pulled up on an Ulster & Delaware siding. Dispensing with his usual retinue of Pinkerton bodyguards, Gould walked his children about town and reminisced while, at the same time, greeting old neighbors. He showed his children the small attic space above what was once a tin shop where he'd worked on his map and his book, the little farmhouse in which he'd been raised, the still-smaller one-room school where he'd learned his letters, the graves of their ancestors, and a few of the spots where he and other boys, among them John Burroughs, had always liked to fish.*

When I was researching my book *Dark Genius of Wall Street: The Misunderstood Life of Jay Gould, King of the Robber Barons*, I learned that after Gould's 1892 death members of his family continued to maintain a close relationship with Roxbury and the region around it.† His daughter Helen Gould Shepard established a summer home there, Kirkside, to which she returned every year until her death in 1938.‡ With her brothers and sisters, Helen endowed the building of Roxbury's Jay Gould Memorial Reformed Church, dedicated in 1894. Gould's son George Jay Gould established a summer home in the Delaware County town of Arkville, on the banks of Furlow Lake, which is still owned by the Gould family. George's grandson, my good friend Kingdon Gould Jr., was instrumental in the founding of the Catskills Center for Conservation and Development and in 2013 received the "Spirit of the Catskills" award from the Coalition to Save Belleayer. Kingdon passed away in 2018.

One senses that Jay Gould would probably be gratified to know that, all these years after his death, his family still remains connected to his natal region—also that his book continues to be respected and of use to people interested in the history of Delaware County and the history of the Catskills as a whole.

Edward Renehan
Wickford, RI

---

* The old tin shop in the attic of which Gould worked on his map and his book is now a gallery space, Liberal Arts Roxbury, located at 53525 State Highway 30, in the middle of the town of Roxbury.

† Edward Renehan, *Dark Genius of Wall Street: The Misunderstood Life of Jay Gould, King of the Robber Barons* (New York: Basic Books, 2005).

‡ Helen Gould's summer home, 53865 State Highway 30, is now a senior living facility: the Kirkside Home for Adults.

Entered according to Act of Congress, in the year of our Lord 1856,

BY JAY GOULD,

In the District Court, for the Eastern District of New York.

TO THE

HON. A. J. PARKER,

𝔗his work is respectfully 𝔇edicated,

BY THE AUTHOR.

PREFACE

It is usual for authors, in the preface to their productions, to cite to the reader all the good qualities of their writings, and especially those which their own imaginations suggest, and which, unless mentioned, might otherwise have been passed over unnoticed.

I shall then deviate from this ancient established usage of writers, for various, and to myself obvious reasons, the most prominent of which is, that I esteem that class of persons into whose hands this work may fall, as an intelligent and reading people, better prepared to pass judgment than myself, who, if they utter criticism, will base their opinions upon the merit of the work itself, aside from the self-eulogistic encomiums of the author. I do not claim that this work is free from error; perfection, in a history of this character, where much of the information to be relied upon is of an oral and indefinite nature, is an impossibility. I have been careful to weigh all the statements presented—to discriminate between truth and fiction—and have suppressed much apparently interesting matter, which lacked the proper authenticity, or conflicted with truth; still, doubtless, there is room for improvement.

I claim no honor for having been the *tell-tale* of the past. The having simply told what others have done, is far from implying, that had we been placed in the same situation, and affected by the same circumstances, we would have acted the same noble part. It is one thing to write, another to do:—"Give honor to whom honor is due." And if, after perusing what we have been enabled to glean of the history of the acts and actors of the past, you are enabled to discern in them anything noble—anything worthy of your admiration and emulation, then treasure up for the hardy and industrious pioneer a kind and grateful remembrance—then cherish in sincerity, long after the author has said his say, a fond appreciation of those Spartan sires, whose ashes are now mouldering in the tomb, and whose tongues have become silent and speechless, palsied by death.

I would take this opportunity of returning my sincere thanks to all who have interested themselves in furnishing material for the completion of this work.

THE AUTHOR.

CONTENTS

CHAPTER I.   1

History—Its origin—Causes of its development—Its Influence on a free government—Divisions of history in point of time—Divisions in regard to subject—General history—Particular history—History of Delaware county; a particular history—Early purchases made of the Indians—Their dissatisfaction—Deed of purchase of 1768—Extent of the purchase—Consideration paid—Effects produced by the final adjustment of Indian claims—Commencement of emigration.

CHAPTER II.   9

Indian character—Suppositions of the origin of the race—Enumeration of the Six Nations, who formerly owned a large portion of the State—Their union in cases of emergency—Date of the admission of the Tuscaroras into the confederacy—Power and influence of the Iroquois—Success in battle—Agriculture prosecuted to some extent—Love of war—Torture of their victims—Weapons of warfare—Introduction of fire-arms among the Indians—First settlement at Albany—Estimate of the number of Indians east of the Mississippi at that period—Number of distinct languages—Enumeration of the different tribes—English Settlements in 1664—Conquest of New Netherlands by the English—Its capture—Dutch again obtain possession of it—Its final restoration to the English the following year—English conciliate the favor of the Indians by presents—Early missionaries among the Indians—Information derived of the Indians respecting the Susquehanna country—Indians desire the English to establish trading posts on the Susquehanna—Jealousies of New York in relation to Penn's trading with the Indians—Final adjustment of the difficulty.

CHAPTER III.   17

New York in 1770—Total population of the colony at that period—Tryon and Charlotte counties erected—Their extent—Population of Tryon—First settlement German Palatines—Settlements made by them—Heldeburgh Hills—Origin of the name—Schoharie valley—Its settlement—Settlement at Cherry Valley—Privations of the settlers the first winter—Hair-breadth escape from starvation—Succored by a friendly Indian—Nativity of the early settlers—Harper family—Settle in Cherry Valley—Their influence with the Indians—Harpers found a new settlement—Called Harpersfield—Obtain a patent—Surveyed—Mrs. Harper, the first white woman in the town—Constructs a log-house with her own hands—The first house in Harpersfield—Privations the following winter—Providential relief from starvation—Slow progress of the settlement—Reception of new settlers—Settlement in Middletown, before the Revolution—Death of Dumond, by the Schoharie Guard—Brugher shot by the Indians while threshing buckwheat—His son taken prisoner—Release and return of the son to Middletown—Drowned while crossing the Delaware some years after—Indian villages on the East Branch—Milling stories—Indian hunting-grounds—Beaver; peculiarities of the animal—Ancient apple-trees; anecdotes concerning—Pakatakan, an Indian village—Supposed signification of the name—Tribes of Indians who occupied Papagouck and Pepacton, other Indian villages—Historical communication of Dr. O. M. Allaben.

CHAPTER IV.   35

Revolution—Early conflicts—Eloquence of Pitt in parliament—Advocates the cause of American rights—His efforts unavailing—Provincial Congress assemble—Eloquent appeal of Patrick Henry—Effect of his speech—Resolution of continental congress—George Washington unanimously chosen commander-in-chief of the American forces—His acceptation—Meetings of the inhabitants to express their sentiments—Vigilant committees—Organization of, in Tryon county—Influences brought to bear—Sir Wm. Johnston espouses the royal cause—His sudden death—His successors in office—Patriotism of the inhabitants of Harpersfield and Cherry Valley—First open act of hostility—Organization of a vigilant committee in Harpersfield—Their service to the American cause—The names of members—The chairman—Col. John Harper dispatched by Congress on a mission to the Indians—His apparent success—Reception by the Indians—Great feast and other ceremonies—Harper returns—Intimacy between Brant and Harper—Copy of a letter—Indians prove treacherous—Affidavit of the Rev. Wm. Johnston—Driven with his family from Sidney Plains—Obituary notice of Capt. Hugh Johnston—Effect of the intelligence communicated by Johnston along the frontiers—Letter from Harpersfield vigilant committee—Herkimer's mission—Singular interview between Gen. Herkimer and Brant—Speech of Brant—Failure of the expedition—Evacuation of Harpersfield—John Moore an early settler—Warned of danger—Journey to Catskill—Accident—Enumeration of the inhabitants

before the war—Scotchmen settle in the Valley of Wright's Brook—
Story of the Scotchman and his gold—Capture of a party of Indians by
Col. Harper—McDonald, a tory, invades Schoharie—Exposed situation
of the settlement—Harper volunteers to go to Albany—Procures a
company of cavalry—Marches to Schoharie—Disperses the enemy—
Letter from Harper to Congress.

CHAPTER V.   53

St. Leger Cowley—Contention between himself and a tory—Dispute settled
by his wife—Capture of Cowley and Sawyer on the West Branch—
Indian sports—Journey of the captives toward Niagara—Murder of
their captors—Pursued by the Indians—Miraculous escape—Narrowly
escape starvation in the wilderness—Arrival at a frontier settlement in
Pennsylvania—Recruit and return to Schoharie—Procure a company of
troops to aid in the removal of their families—First grist-mill on the
West Branch—Death of Cowley—Indian revenge—Murder of McKee
family—Capture of Miss Anne McKee—Compelled to run the gauntlet—
Fort Niagara—Retaliatory expedition to the Indian territory—General
Sullivan appointed to command—Detachment under Clinton—March
down the Susquehanna—Union of Clinton and Sullivan near Tioga
Point—Complete annihilation of Indian settlements—Expedition
of Sullivan an expedition of discovery—Minisink an ancient Indian
settlement—Massacre of the inhabitants—Battle of the Delaware—
Defeat of the inhabitants—List of the killed—Burial services performed
in 1820—Statement of Benjamin Whitaker—General outlines of the
campaign of 1779.

CHAPTER VI.   69

Repose of the frontier settlements—Scout under Colonel Alexander
Harper—Sent out to Harpersfield—Harper returns to Schoharie—His
return to Harpersfield—Capture of the party by Brant—Recognition
between Brant and Harper—Death of several of the party—Inscription
on the Hendrys' tombstones in the Harpersfield burying-ground—Young
Lamb attempts to escape—Is overtaken and captured—Questions put
by Brant to Harper—Harper's shrewd reply—Indian Council—Debate
in regard to the fate of the prisoners—Party decamp for Niagara—
Obtain provisions of a miller on the Delaware—Inhumanity of this man
and his daughters to the prisoners—Incidents of the Journey—Murder
of Mr. Brown—Arrival of the party at Fort Niagara—Harper finds
friends—Prisoners run the gauntlet—Expedient of Brant to alleviate
their sufferings—Reception of the party at the Fort—Imprisonment
in Canada—Return of the survivors of the party to Harpersfield .
Punishment afterward inflicted on Beacraft, a tory—Bennett family—
Early settlers—Capture of by a party of Indians—Incursion of the

Indians into Colchester—Capture of Rose—Interesting incident—Correspondence in relation to the war—Indians capture Beach and family—Encounter a scout below Hobart—John Hagidore wounded—Company of troops pursue the Indians—Overtake and release the captives.

CHAPTER VII.   91

Declaration of Peace—Its joyful reception by the colonies—Early Settlements at Sidney Plains and along the Susquehanna—Inconveniences to which the inhabitants were obliged to submit—Ruins of an ancient Indian fort—Sidney Plains—First death that occurred in Sidney—Great famine in 1787—First grist-mill on Susquehanna—First raft of lumber on the Susquehanna—Geographical boundaries of Sidney—Origin of the name—Ouleout Creek—Indian signification—Original land-owners—First settlements in Franklin—Information derived principally of Joshua Pine, in relation to early settlers in Walton—Account of a duel fought in Walton—Early settlements and settlers at Deposit, Chehocton, and in the Western part of the country—Dickinson's City—Hunting stories—Indians who remained after the war—Old Abraham—Canope, Ben Shanks and Haycou—Tragical murder of the former and latter.

CHAPTER VIII.   120

Adventures and final settlement of Timothy Beach in Sidney—Reminiscences of John Wickham, an early settler of Harpersfield—Names of early settlers—Privations to which they were subjected—Adventure of James Gordon with a bear, while crossing the Charlotte River—First Church in Harpersfield—Manner of its erection—Church-raising—Whipping-posts and stocks erected in Harpersfield—Other whipping-posts in the county—How Harper caught his wife—Persons punished by this ordeal—First settled minister in Harpersfield—Maple-sugar-making—Scotchman's idea of making maple-sugar—Information derived from Stephen Hait of Stamford—Settlements made in 1789—Information derived from David Squires—Discovery of and first settlement in Roxbury—Interesting information in relation to—Anecdotes—Information derived principally from Cyrus Burr—Early settlements in Middletown and Andes—Hall's adventure with Mr. Earl—His discovery that he had neighbors—Catamount-killing in Andes.

CHAPTER IX.   137

Increase of population in the interior of the State—Necessary alterations of the civil divisions from time to time—Erection of Otsego in 1792—

Petition for the erection of a new county in 1796—New county erected in 1797—Called Delaware—Number of towns at the erection of the county—Enumeration of the other towns in the order of their erection—Names of the first supervisors—First representatives to the assembly—First court held in the county—First judges—First sheriff—Court-house and jail erected—Murder of Cameron and McGilfry—Arrest of the murderer—Escape of the prisoner from jail—Re-arrested on Cabin-hill—Tried and found guilty—Sentenced to be hung—Execution a public one—Description by an eye-witness of the execution—Execution of Foster in 1819—Burning of the court- house and jail—One man burned—Legislative act—Erection of the Delaware Academy—Its founder—Manner of its endowment—Geological society formed in Delhi—Its short existence—Matter in relation to the formation of the county—Extract from the Diary of Judge Foote—Obituary notice—List of assemblymen since the formation of the county—Surrogates and county judges—sheriffs—county clerks.

CHAPTER X.   150

The lost manuscript—Early organization of religious societies—Report of the first missionary—Summary of report—Different sects in the county—Educational interests of the county, and other information.

CHAPTER XI.   161

Anti-rent difficulties—Early grants of land within the limits of the county—Hardenburgh patent—Dispute in regard to the western limits of the patent—Survey of the patent—Protest of the Indians—Indian deed of the land between the branches of the Delaware to Johanus Hardenburgh—Bradt patent—Enumeration of the other patents in the order in which they were granted—Land monopoly—Early restrictions placed upon grants—How eluded—Views of the early legislatures—Recognition of the grants prior to the revolution—Validity of the manorial titles—Leasehold system—Systematic classification of deeds—Durable lease—Redemption lease—Three life lease—One and two life lease—Yearly lease—Seven year proviso—Claims of the tenants—History of the excitement—Grievances of the renters.

CHAPTER XII.   173

Introduction of the excitement into Delaware county, 1844—Roxbury—First public meeting—Description of the costume worn by an Indian—Molest John B. Gould—Second attempt to enforce submission—Tar and feather H. More—Tar and feather T. Corbin—Sheriff's papers taken and destroyed—First *equal rights' convention*—Legislative proceedings—Passage of an act preventing persons appearing in disguise—Copy of the same—An act of D. W. Squires—Extract from a letter to the adjutant general—Organization of an armed force by the sheriff—Steele in limbo at Andes—His defence—Letter to the sheriff—His release—Antipathy of anti-renters against Steele—His courage—Their threats—Shacksville battle—Particulars of the same—Names of prisoners—Sale in Andes—Painful death of Steele—His last moments—Extract from the correspondence of the Albany Evening Journal—Funeral services—Indignation meetings at various places—Resolution passed—Summerset of anti-rentism.

CHAPTER XIII.   188

Action of the Executive—Proclamation of county in a state of insurrection—Copy of the same—Its reception in Delhi—Arrival of Adjutant General Farrington—Organization of an armed force—Officers chosen—Extract from a letter—Mode of operating—Erection of temporary log-jails—Convening of the court—Grand jury—Judge Parker's able charge—Allusion in the same to the demoralizing influence of the excitement upon the county—Result of the trials—number of convictions—O'Connor and Van Steenburgh convicted of murder—Sentence of the prisoners—Court adjourns—Attempt on the life of a guard—Reprieve of the sentences of O'Connor and Van Steenburgh—Revocation by the governor, of the declaration "declaring the county in a state of insurrection"—Close—Closing remarks.

CHAPTER XIV.   203

The following sketch of the services of the late Timothy Murphy in the border warfare of the revolution, were kindly furnished the author, and although in some respects they deviate from what he conceives to be truth, in the main he has ascertained them to be correct.

CHAPTER XV.   229

The following interesting production, from the pen of a daughter of E. B. Fenn, Esq., is inserted, at the request of numerous friends.

CHAPTER XVI.   237

Obituary notices—Captain Abraham Gould—Aaron Hull—Gabriel North—Rev. Stephen Fenn—Hon. Roswell Hotchkiss—Rev. Daniel Shepard—James Hughston—Hon. Samuel A. Law—Daniel Gould—Col. Adam Shaver—T. H. Rathbun—Simeon McIntosh—Richard Peters—Thomas Hamilton—Major Joseph Duren—William C. Christiani—Abel Gallup—Jacob Every—Pierce Mitchell—Margery Walcott—Edmund

Kelly—Abram Thomas—Gen. Orrin Griffin—Claudius Flansburgh—Levi Hanford—Abigail Marvine—Hon. Selah R. Hobbie—Frederick L. Hanford—George B. Foote—Peter Penet—William Holliday—Col. Amasa Parker—Joel T. Headley.

APPENDIX. 261

Delaware Gazette—The Central Sun—the Deposit Courier—The Deposit Union Democrat—Delaware County Courier—Bloomville Mirror—Weekly Visitor—Delaware Bank—Deposit Bank—Secret organizations; Freemasonry, Odd Fellowship—Iodine Spring—The Delaware Literary Institute—Fergusonville Boarding Academy—The Social League.

HISTORY

OF

DELAWARE COUNTY

CHAPTER I

History—Its origin—Causes of its development—Its influence on a free government—Divisions of History in point of time—Divisions in regard to subject—General History—Particular History—History of Delaware county; a particular History—Early purchases made of the Indians—Their dissatisfaction—Deed of purchase of 1768—Extent of the purchase—Consideration paid—Effects produced by the final adjustment of Indian claims—Commencement of emigration.

HISTORY with the more and more extensive meaning acquired by the advancement of civilization, by the diffusion of education, and by the elevation of the standard of human liberty, has expanded into a grand and beautiful science. It treats of man in all his social relations, whether civil, religious, or literary, in which he has had intercourse with his fellows. The study of history, to a free government like the one in which we live, is an indispensable requisite to the improvement and elevation of the human race. It leads us back through the ages that have succeeded each other in time past; it exhibits the condition of the human race at each respective period, and by following down its pages over the vast empires and mighty cities now engulphed in oblivion, but which the faithful historian presents in a living light before us, we are enabled profitably to compare and form a more correct appreciation of our own relative position.

It is the saying of an eminent historian that "Liberty and History go hand in hand, the health and vigor of the one dependent upon and coexistent with that of the other." And it is certain that the more enlightened and free a people become, the more the government devolves upon themselves; and hence the necessity of a careful study of history, which, by showing the height to which man as an intellectual being is capable of elevating himself in the scale of usefulness and moral worth, teaches that the virtues of the good man are held in sacred emulation by his countrymen for ages succeeding, long after the scythe of time has gathered the earthly remains of the actor to the silent grave. Such thoughts, or rather such reflections as these, inspire within the human bosom an ardent desire to attain that which is good and shun that which is evil, an honest and laudable ambition to become both great and good; or as another has beautifully written, "Great only as we are good." To illustrate more fully, Who would not be a Washington? whose name and virtues are virtually associated with those eventful times, that chaos of the last century, from which sprung what was afterward destined to become the mightiest republic on the globe; "it was the hand of Washington that lit the flame," that flame which baffled the skill and prowess of the engines of the old world to extinguish, and which for seventy-nine years has spread as with a magic wand, North, East, South, and West—spreading and burning still; while kings and haughty monarchs pause, behold and tremble, as they sit upon their tottering thrones, lest a burning spark from the unquenchable fire of freedom should strike root in the stronghold of their own despotism, and deprive them of their titles and their power. One of the great benefits of history to our own Government is by studiously comparing other modes of rule with our own; the defects of both become more visible, and we are enabled thereby to profit by all former times.

The history of the world is divided into three great divisions; Ancient History, from the creation of the world to the Christian era, the Advent of Christ; the History of the Middle Ages, extending to the discovery of America by Columbus, in 1492; and Modern History, which comes down to and embraces the present time. The history of the United States and of the whole Western hemisphere, is embraced within the sphere of modern history. With regard to the subject, history is either general, where a whole nation is treated of, or particular, where a sub-division of the same government is assumed as the basis of a history. Thus, the history of the United States would be general, while that of the State of New York would be particular; and as such, would contain much matter relating to her alone, of the utmost interest and importance; which in the general history, would be put down as improper and out of place. To say that the legislature of the State of New York in 1855, passed the Maine law, with the attendant circumstances of its execution, would, I venture to say, be as much out of place in the general history, as one of the Black Foot Indians of Kansas territory would be in the halls of Congress at Washington.

The territory then which we have chosen as the basis of this history, characterizes it as one of the *particular kind*; and while at the commencement we exhort those into whose hands it may fall, who are perhaps better informed than ourselves, not to be too *particular* in their criticisms, we shall at the same time strive to be *particularly* correct in all our assertions, nor leave any stone unturned, that will add any thing of interest to those who may read its contents.

The American Indians were the original proprietors of the soil. At the discovery of America by Columbus in 1492, the entire American continent was the birthright, and by the universal law of nations, the property of the Indian. The whites then were eminently intruders in founding settlements upon the shores of the western world; but the policy of aggrandizement which characterized the maritime powers of Europe, recognized no other law than "might makes right," and consequently had no conscientious scruples against the acquisition of territory, even by an offensive and unjust war. It was the Spaniards in particular, who have left an indelible stain upon their national character, by their ignominious and cruel warfare waged against the Montezumas of Mexico, and the Incas of Peru. The English, although far from being guiltless, nevertheless pursued for themselves a more judicious, and at the same time a more humane policy. They opened a successful commerce with the Indians—they attempted to introduce some of the arts of civilization from Europe, and *all* the vices, especially that glaring monster, intemperance, which sounded the death knell to so many of the *"tall trees"* of their race. This evil increased with such fearful rapidity, that the Indians at last themselves became startled, and knowing their utter inability to withstand the temptation, demanded of the whites what the whites now demand for themselves,* that no liquor should be brought amongst them. The following speech was delivered by the great Chief Hendrick, at the Congress held at Albany in 1754, of which Benjamin Franklin was a member:

"'*Brethren*—There is an Affair about which our Hearts tremble and our minds are deeply concerned; *this is the selling of Rum in our Castles.* It destroys many of our Old and Young people. We request of all the Governments here present, that it may be forbidden to carry any of it amongst the Five Nations.

"'*Brethren*—We are in great Fears about this Rum. *It may cause murder on both sides.*

"'The Cayugas now declare in their own name, that they will not allow any Rum to be brought up their River, and those who do must suffer the Consequences.

"'We, the Mohawks of both Castles have also one request to make, which is, that the people who are settled round about us, may not be Suffered to sell our People Rum. It keeps them all poor, makes them Idle and Wicked, and if they have any Money or Goods, they lay it all out in Rum. It destroys Virtue and the progress of Religion amongst us. [The lower Castle of the Mohawks has a Chapel and an English Missionary belonging

---

* Maine-law men.

to it.] We have a friendly request to make to the Governor and all the Commissioners here present—that they will help us to Build a Church at Canajoharie, and that we may have a bell in it, which, together with the putting a stop to the Selling of Rum, will tend to make us Religious and lead better lives than we do now.'"

The English early adopted a plan of purchasing by treaty the territory of the Indians, and as early as 1683, the sachems of the Cayugas and Onondagas, to whom the Susquehanna country belonged, executed an instrument, sealed in the presence of Robert Livingston, conveying said territory to the English government.

These conveyances gave rise to unexpected difficulties; the white settlers were continually overstepping the prescribed limits of the purchase, and trespassing upon the hunting-grounds of the aborigines. The Indians were continual in their complaint to the authorities having jurisdiction in the matter, and at last to avert an open rupture between the Six Nations and the Colonies, Sir William Johnson, then Commissary of Indian Affairs, convened the Six Nations and all the tribes that pretended any claim to the territory in question, at Fort Stanwix.

The result of this convention was the formation of a treaty, or rather an agreement to a separating line between the whites and Indians. This document is one of those relics of our dealings with an injured and almost extinct race of people, and for the curiosity of the reader we insert the instrument in full.

"*Deed executed at Fort Stanwix, Nov. 5th, 1768.*

"To all to whom these presents shall come or may concern. We, the Sachems and Chiefs of the Six Confederate Nations, and of the Shawanese, Delawares, Mingoes of Ohio, and other dependent Tribes, on behalf of ourselves and of the rest of our several Nations, the Chiefs and Warriors of whom are here now convened, by Sir William Johnson, Baronet, His Majesty's Superintendent of our affairs, send greeting:—Whereas his Majesty was graciously pleased to propose to us, in the year one thousand seven hundred and sixty-five, that a boundary line should be established between the English and us, to ascertain and establish our limits, and prevent those intrusions and encroachments of which we had so long and loudly complained, and to put a stop to the many fraudulent advantages which had been so often taken of us in land affairs; which boundary appearing to us a wise and good measure, we did then agree to a part of a line, and promised to settle the whole final, whensoever Sir William Johnson should be fully empowered to treat with us for that purpose. And whereas his said Majesty has at length given Sir William Johnson orders to complete the said boundary line between the Provinces and

Indians, in conformity to which orders, Sir William Johnson has convened the Chiefs and Warriors of our respective Nations, who are the true and absolute Proprietors of the lands in question, and who are here now to a very considerable number. And whereas many uneasinesses and doubts have arisen amongst us, which have given rise to an apprehension that the line may not be strictly observed on the part of the English, in which case matters may be worse than before; which apprehension, together with the dependent state of some of our tribes, and other circumstances which retarded the settlement and became the subject of some debate, which Sir William Johnson has at length so far satisfied us upon, as to induce us to come to an agreement concerning the line, which is now brought to a conclusion; the whole being fully explained to us in a large assembly of our people before Sir William Johnson, and in the presence of His Excellency, the Governor of New Jersey, the Commissioners from the Provinces of Virginia and Pennsylvania, and sundry other Gentlemen, by which line so agreed upon, a considerable tract of country along several provinces is by us ceded to his said Majesty, which we are induced to and do hereby ratify and confirm to his said Majesty, from the expectation and confidence we place in His Royal Goodness, that he will graciously comply with our humble requests, as the same are expressed in the speech of the several Nations, addressed to His Majesty through Sir William Johnson, on Tuesday, the first of the present month of November, wherein we have declared our expectation of the continuance of his Majesty's favour, and our desire that our ancient engagements be observed, and our affairs attended to by the officer who has the management thereof, enabling him to discharge all these matters properly for our interest. That the lands occupied by the Mohocks around their villages, as well as by any other nation affected by this our cession, may effectually remain to them and to their posterity; and that any engagements regarding property, which they may now be under, may be prosecuted, and our present grants deemed valid on our parts, with the several other humble requests contained in our said speech. And whereas, at the settling of the said Line, it appeared that the Line described by His Majesty's permission, was not extended to the Northward of Oswegy, or to the Southward of the Great Kanhawa river, we have agreed to and continued the Line to the Northward, on a supposition that it was omitted by reason of our not having come to any determination concerning its course, at the congress held in one thousand seven hundred and sixty-five; and in as much as the Line to the Northward became the most necessary of any, for preventing encroachments at our very Towns and Residences, we have given the Line more favorably to Pennsylvania, for the reasons and considerations mentioned in the Treaty; we have likewise continued it South to Cherokee River, because the same is and we declare it to be our true Bounds with the Southern Indians, and that we have an undoubted right to the country as far South as that River, which makes the cession to His Majesty much more advantageous than that proposed. Now therefore know ye, that we, the Sachems and Chiefs aforementioned, Native Indians or Proprietors of the Lands hereinafter described, for and in behalf of ourselves and the whole of our Confederacy, for the considerations hereinbefore mentioned, and also for and in consideration of a valuable present of the several articles in use amongst Indians, which, together with a large sum of money, amount in the whole to the sum of ten thousand four hundred and sixty pounds seven shillings and three pence sterling, to us now delivered and paid by Sir William Johnson, Baronet, His Majesty's sole Agent and Superintendant of Indian Affairs for the Northern Department of America, in the name and on behalf of our Sovereign Lord, George the Third, by the Grace of God, of Great Britain, France and Ireland, King, Defender of the Faith, the receipt whereof we do hereby acknowledge, we, the said Indians, have for us and our heirs and successors, granted, bargained, sold, released and confirmed, and by these presents do grant, bargain, sell, release and confirm unto our said Sovereign Lord, King George the Third, all that Tract of Land situate in North America, at the Back of the British Settlements, bounded by a Line which we have now agreed upon and do hereby establish, as the Boundary between us and the British Colonies in America, beginning at the mouth of Cherokee or Hogohege River, where it empties into the River Ohio, and running from thence upwards along the South side of said River to Kittanning, which is above Fort Pitt, from thence by a direct line to the nearest Fork of the West Branch of Susquehanna, thence through the Allegany Mountains along the South side of the said West Branch, until it comes opposite to the mouth of a creek called Tiadaghton, thence across the West Branch along the South side of that Creek, and along the North side of Burnett's Hills to a creek called Awandae, thence down the same to the East Branch of the Susquehanna, and across the same and up the East side of that River to Oswegy, from thence East to Delaware River, and up that River to opposite where Tianaderha falls into the Susquehanna, thence to Tianaderha and up the West side of the West Branch to the head thereof, and thence by a direct line to Canada Creek, where it empties into the Wood Creek, at the West of the Carrying Place beyond Fort Stanwix, and extending Eastward from every part of the said Line as far as the Lands formerly purchased, so as to comprehend the whole of the lands between the said Line and the purchased lands or settlements, except what is within the Province of Pennsylvania, together with all the hereditaments and appurtenances to the same belonging or appertaining, in the fullest and most ample manner, and all the estate, right, title, interest, property, possession, benefit, claim and demand, either in law or equity, of each and every of us, of, in, or to the same, or any part thereof, *To have* and to hold the whole lands and premises hereby granted, bargained, sold, released, and confirmed as aforesaid, with the hereditaments and appurtenances thereunto belonging, under the reservations made in the Treaty unto our said Sovereign Lord, King George the Third, his heirs and successors, to and for his and their own proper use and behoof for ever. In witness whereof, we, the Chiefs of the Confederacy, have hereunto set our marks and seals, at Fort Stanwix, the fifth day of November, one thousand seven hundred and sixty-eight, in the ninth year of His Majesty's reign.

	For the Mohawks.
TYORHANSERE ALS ABRAHAM,	[L.S.]
	For the Oneidas.
CANAGHAGUIESON,	[L.S.]
	For the Tuscaroras.
SEGUAREESERA,	[L.S.]
	For the Onondagas.
OTSINOGHIYATA ALS BUNT,	[L.S.]
	For the Cayugas.
TEGAAIA,	[L.S.]
	For the Senecas.
GUARTOAX,	[L.S.]

Sealed and delivered and the consideration paid in the presence of
WM. FRANKLIN, Governor of New Jersey.
FRE. SMYTH, Chief Justice of New Jersey.
THOMAS WALKER, Commissioner for Virginia.
RICHARD PETERS, } Of the Council of
JAMES TILGHMAN, } Pennsylvania."

The territory ceded by this treaty to the English crown, was far more extensive than was then known or supposed. The western line of the present county of Delaware, was the exact limits of the treaty—that county being ceded to the English—while Broome and Chenango, still farther westward, remained in possession of the Six Nations or their dependencies. The consideration paid for this extensive territory, now so valuable in agricultural and mineral resources, was ten thousand four hundred and sixty pounds sterling, or about fifty thousand six hundred dollars.

The honorable and friendly adjustment of the existing difficulties by the Stanwix Treaty, restored the confidence which had been so severely tested by the lawless and inhuman depredations which had been of frequent occurrence for a term of years preceding upon the settlers and their property, for infringements, whether real or imaginary, upon the territory claimed by the Indians.

About the period of 1770, the tide of emigration may be said to have fairly commenced. The two years of uninterrupted peace that had preceded, strengthened by the glittering allurements of the future, had succeeded in burying the inclemency and sufferings of the past in oblivion. The hardy settlers, accompanied by their wives and children, together with the rude accoutrements of civilization, were seen penetrating the wilderness in every direction; and not twenty years elapsed from the time the first settler crossed the North river in the bark canoe, and followed the Indian trial to some desirable location for himself and his family a home—although the scenes of the Revolution are numbered within that period—ere the whole surface of the territory, from the majestic Hudson to those great inland seas, was dotted by innumerable clearings—the homes of honest, industrious, and daring pioneers; where, by dint of hard labor and economy, in most instances, they succeeded in obtaining a comfortable support for themselves and families.

The gigantic forests which had flourished in their majesty and grandeur from age to age, now faded away before the woodman's axe, as the mist of night vanishes at the first rays of the morning sun, and the earth was made to yield from her bounteous stores to contribute to the sustenance and support of man. The wild beasts, startled by the strange, uncouth sounds of civilization, or the sharp click and unerring aim of the hunter's rifle, either fell farther back into the forest, or fled precipitately to some unfrequented hiding place among the hills. The Indian, too, chaunted the sad requiem over the sacred mounds that contained the ashes of his parents—the sepulchre of his tribe—had sped the last arrow upon his favorite hunting ground, where his unerring aim had often brought the timid deer to kiss the dust, and retreating westward, "pauses his steps upon the verge of the distant eminence," to supplicate the Great Spirit, and to behold once more and for the last time, the glorious sun-set upon the broad valley, the bright home of his youth; and for ages past the favorite hunting-ground of his tribe.

CHAPTER II

Indian Character—Suppositions of the origin of the Race—Enumeration of the Six Nations, who formerly owned a large portion of the State—Their union in cases of emergency—Date of the admission of the Tuscaroras into the Confederacy—Power and influence of the Iroquois—Success in battle—Agriculture prosecuted to some extent—Love of war—Torture of their victims—Weapons of warfare—Introduction of fire-arms among the Indians—First settlement at Albany—Estimate of the number of Indians east of the Mississippi at that period—Number of distinct languages—Enumeration of the different Tribes—English Settlements in 1664—Conquest of New Netherlands by the English—Its capture—Dutch again obtain possession of it—Its final restoration to the English the following year—English conciliate the favor of the Indians by presents—Early Missionaries among the Indians—Information derived of the Indians respecting the Susquehanna Country—Indians desire the English to establish trading posts on the Susquehanna—Jealousies of New York in relation to Penn's trading with the Indians—Final adjustment of the difficulty.

> "Swift flee the dark forms on the wings of the wind,
> Nor leave at their castles one soul of their kind."

THERE is something peculiarly interesting—I may say fascinating—in the contemplation of Indian character, to every lover of history. The only written record of the sayings and doings of the red men, is that delineated by his inveterate enemies, the *white men*; but notwithstanding, the brave, generous, and noble characteristics of his race, still shine forth in their unassuming dignity. There is a mystery, an unsolved problem, beneath whose vortex lie concealed the past history and future destiny of his race. The data of his origin is yet—if indeed it ever is to be solved—a mystery. We can trace him back definitely but to a comparatively recent period, and tradition with her fabulous tongue goes not much farther. The most probable hypothesis is, that the Aborigines came over by Behring's Straits, and gradually spreading eastward and southward, until in the lapse of ages they had peopled the whole western hemisphere. Their aggregate numbers cannot definitely be known, as no census has been taken, and there are doubtless many tribes inhabiting the unexplored interior of the Great West, of whose numbers we can form no idea. In North America, at the outbreak of the Revolution, they are estimated to have exceeded three millions. Since that period they have been rapidly decreasing; many powerful tribes have become extinct, while but scanty remnants of others remain. In our own State, but a few hundred souls are left, who are provided for by the State government. They are principally descendants of the Six Nations, but constitute but a meagre representative of the courage, fortitude, and prowess, which has so characterized their ancestors. And the historian, whose duty it is to view with impartial and candid judgment the acts and actors of the past, cannot do less than to pay a passing tribute to the native Indian.

At the time the Dutch landed at Albany, in 1620, New York was possessed by Five Confederate Nations, or tribes, and their dependents. Their names were the Mohawks, who occupied the country westward from Albany, and south of the Mohawk river to the German Flatts, a distance of ninety miles; the Oneidas, still farther westward, through whose territory ran the division line of 1768, referred to in the previous chapter; the Onondagas, the Cayugas, and the Senecas, whose territory lay still farther to the west and south. Although distinct and powerful tribes, and who acted separately in matters pertaining only to themselves, yet, in cases of emergency, a confederacy or congress of the chiefs and braves of each respective nation assembled around the common council fire, where the *great question* was debated in a committee of the whole, and where they listened to, and waxed patriotic, from the harangues of their untutored but truly eloquent brethren. It was this council that declared war and ratified peace.

This confederacy carried terror to all the surrounding nations, none of whom could compete with them in battle, or equal them in fortitude and courage. In the arts, too, they far outstripped their tawny brethren. They did not live entirely by hunting and fishing, but paid a good deal of attention to agriculture. They cultivated patches of Indian corn in the most fertile districts of their territory. Grapes grew in abundance along many of the principal rivers, and hoary apple trees may now be seen in many parts of the State, from whose boughs the Indian, when in the zenith of his power, plucked its choicest fruit to regale his own appetite or that of his simple, confiding sweetheart.

The Indian nature is peculiarly susceptible of excitement—the giddy war-dance and the battle-field are to him theatres of fascination; he seeks rather than avoids them. He takes delight in inflicting torture, and in the excruciating pains of his captives; he makes it his study to inflict the greatest amount of pain before death ensues—the stake, with its slow fire—skinning alive—scalping—and the gauntlet, are all familiar modes of punishment.

Their weapons of defence are the bow and arrow, the war club and the scalping knife. In the use of these messengers of death they are well skilled. With the simple bow and arrow, the wily Indian easily captures the shyest animal of the forest—the faithful arrow speeds with unerring aim, and leaves no report or volume of smoke behind to reveal his hiding-place. In this way he often captures a number of animals, whereas the report of a rifle would give a timely warning, and the otherwise easy prey would make good their escape.

The use of firearms was unknown to the Aborigines. The simple weapons I have described had been their armory for ages. The rifle, therefore, was to him a source of inexplicable mystery and awe—the quick flash—the lightning speed it gave the leaden ball, and the shrill report and smoke that followed, were unsolved problems in his mind. To the celebrated navigator, Samuel Champlain, is the introduction of fire-arms among the Indians accredited. In 1608, Champlain founded a settlement of French upon the present site of the city of Quebec, in Eastern Canada. At that period a fierce and bloody war was raging between the Algonquins, the Montagues, together with the Hurons in alliance, against their powerful enemy, the Iroquois nation. Impelled by his restless spirit, Champlain, in an unlucky moment, joined these tribes against the Iroquois. He furnished the Algonquins with arms and the munitions of war, and it is even asserted that he headed the beleaguered force and mingled in the hottest of the fight. A change now came over the tide of battle, and the Iroquois heretofore uniformly victorious, were now defeated in numerous pitched battles. The booming musketry and the thundering cannon sent their showers of iron hail into their ranks with terrible devastation and death, and disheartened and dismayed, they were obliged to evacuate the ground they had so lately won.

About this time a settlement was made at Albany, on the Hudson, and trading houses were erected to open communication with the Indians. The vanquished Iroquois seized this opportunity with avidity, and bringing their choicest furs, exchanged them for fire-arms and other munitions of war. The contest was now renewed upon equal footing, and the Five Nations soon regained their former ascendancy; and not content with the chastisement they had inflicted upon their combined foes, they turned now to deal out the measure of their revenge upon the French settlements, whose inhabitants and governor had been so instrumental in their reverses four years before. They continued to harass the French settlements, and held the bloody tomahawk extended over Quebec for a period of nearly a hundred years.

The number of Indians east of the Mississippi, although, as we before remarked, not definitely known, are not supposed to have exceeded two hundred thousand at the time the first settlements were effected by the whites upon their shores, and although the various historians have attributed to them a vast number of dialects, yet radically distinct, there are only eight. The Algonquin, which was the language of a vast number of tribes, was spoken in variated forms from the Carolinas on the south to the St. Lawrence on the north. They are thus enumerated by the antiquarian:

The Micmacs, who inhabited Nova Scotia, and a few adjoining islands, and who lived principally by fishing, in Newfoundland.

The Abenakis, who inhabited the upper counties of the Penobscot, Kennebec, and Androscoggin rivers, in Maine.

The Echemins, who had by numerous conquests possessed themselves of the whole Atlantic coast, from Passamaquoddy bay to the mouth of the Kennebec river. They were particularly fond of sailing and other aquatic sports; from which characteristic the neighbouring tribes gave them the appellation of *Canoe-men*.

The Sokokis lay still farther south, principally in the valley of the Saco. Adjoining them on the south and west, were the Pawtuckets, who included within their territory the river Merrimac and most of its tributaries.

The Massachusetts occupied the territory around the bay of the same name. South of them lay the Pokanokets, a branch of which tribe dwelt on the island of Martha's Vineyard; they also occupied Bristol county, in Rhode Island.

The Naraghansetts occupied the part of Rhode Island west of Naraghansett bay, Rhode Island, and a number of smaller islands in the vicinity. The Naraghansetts surpassed in civilization any of the neighbouring tribes.

The Pequods inhabited the eastern part of Connecticut, and acted in conjunction with the Indians on the eastern extremity of Long Island.

The Mohegans, or Mohicans, held their council fires in the valley of the Connecticut and upon the banks of the Hudson.

The Scatacooks, or Manhattans, occupied the interior territory between those rivers. They were also scattered among the Mohicans.

The Lenni Lennape, occupied the greater portion of New Jersey, and in the valleys of the Delaware and Schuylkill. They are subdivided into the Minsi and the Delawares, and constituted a dependency of the Six Nations.

The Nanticokes inhabited the territory around the Delaware and Chesapeake bays.

The Acomacs lived on the eastern shore of the Chesapeake, adjoining the Nanticokes. Some writers have given this tribe a place in the Powhattan Confederacy.

The Powhattan Confederacy, comprising more than thirty different tribes, occupied the entire lowlands of Virginia, a territory of over 800 square miles.*

The Monahoacks and the Monacons occupied the territory west of the Powhattan Confederacy, and together numbered as many as fifteen different tribes.

---

* Mr. Jefferson computed the number of the Powhattan warriors at 2,500, or the total population at 8,000.

The Pamlicoes, Shawnese, Miamis, Illinois, Ohios, Chippeways, Menomonies, Sacs, Foxes, and the Kicapoos, who occupied portions of the territory east of the Mississippi, all spoke the Algonquin language.

The Sioux dialect was spoken principally by the Mississippi Indians.

The Wyandot, next to the Algonquin, was the most common language east of the Mississippi. It was spoken by many powerful tribes, amongst which were the Mohawks, Oneidas, Onondagas, Cayugas, and Senecas, in the north; and by the Chawans, Nottaways and Tuscaroras in the south. The latter tribe having been unsuccessful in a contest with the Carolina Indians, were driven from their territory, and emigrating northward, were kindly received by the Five Nations and incorporated into the Confederacy.

The Cherokee language was principally confined to the southern tribes. The remaining dialects were the Uchee, the Natchez, the Mobillian and the Yamassee, which were spoken only among the southern Indians.

The English settlements in 1664 reached as far north as Maryland on the south, and included Massachusetts and Connecticut on the north. At this period, Charles the second conceived the bold idea of uniting these detached settlements by an offensive conquest. He accordingly made a grant to his brother, James, the Duke of York and Albany, of New York and New Jersey, reaching to the Connecticut river on the east, a part of which territory was then in the peaceable possession of the Dutch.

In August of the same year three armed vessels appeared in the harbor of New York, and demanded the surrender of the town to the English crown. The demand of the English commander was clothed in persuasive and respectful language, offering the most favorable terms to all who were peaceably disposed. As the Dutch were in no condition to offer a successful resistance, and being withal peaceably inclined, they adopted the alternative, and Governor Stuyvesant was obliged to capitulate. Accordingly, Colonel Nichols, the English commander, immediately assumed the government of the colony, and raised for the first time, the colors of his native country upon the island of Manhattan.

This accession of territory gave the British exclusive control of the Atlantic coast, from Maine on the north, to Florida on the south. The English remained in peaceable possession of their newly acquired territory until 1673, when, through the treachery of the English commanding officer,* the Dutch again obtained possession of their territory, but which they permanently restored to the English crown by the treaty of 1674.

The importance of conciliating the favor of the Indian tribes, and of preserving the amicable relations existing between them and their predecessors in power, the Dutch, was not overlooked by the English, who succeeded them in the government of New York. In this scheme they were not unsuccessful. A system of negotiations was established

---

* Captain John Manning. See Documentary History of N.Y.

through agencies appointed by the crown, with the Iroquois and other neighbouring tribes. Valuable presents, implements of agriculture, art, and war, together with articles of clothing, were freely distributed amongst them with the most satisfactory results. Missionaries were sent to instruct and civilize them—to plant the standard of the white man's God in the rude uncultivated soil of the Indian's soul. Traders, with their stores of notions, penetrated far into their territory, and carried on a successful and lucrative traffic, in exchange for their goods receiving furs and other Indian commodities. From these two sources were derived all the information of the vast unexplored wilderness in the interior portions of the State—of its lakes, its rivers, and the mighty ranges of mountains that traverse its surface, except what was gleaned from the natives themselves, until the expedition fitted out by the colonists in 1779, under the command of General Sullivan, which will be referred to in a subsequent chapter. This expedition penetrated several hundred miles into the Indian territory, to inflict a salutary chastisement in retaliation of the depredations and cruelties to which the frontier settlements had been subjected for a long period before. The eminent success of this expedition, fitted out as it was, under the fostering spirit of the great Washington, and the comparative cloak which for a time it threw around the unprotected pioneers, occupies already, as it deserves, an eminent page in our national history.

The earliest missionary to the Iroquois nation, of whom the histories I have perused give any clue, was a Frenchman, Father Simon Le Moine, who commenced, at the instigation of the French Government, in 1674, a journey to their country. The real object of this visit, cloaked as it was, under the guise of propagating the standard of religion, was nevertheless to obtain a knowledge of their strength, of the situation of their strongholds, and if possible, to effect a reconciliation between them and the Indians. He was a Catholic priest, and first planted the standard of his faith on Lake Ontario. He was successful in his negotiations with that powerful confederacy, which, as stated in the previous part of this chapter, had carried on a bloody war against the French settlements in Canada, in retaliation of the fatal error of Champlain. A treaty of peace was concluded, and permission given to found a French settlement on the south side of Lake Ontario.

In 1683, three Indians were examined by the commissioners of the British Government at Albany, in relation to the Susquehanna country, and gave a description of it as follows:

"That it is one day's journey from the Mohawk castles to the Lake whence the Susquehanna river rises, and then ten days' journey to the Susquehanna castles—in all eleven days.

"One and a half's journey by land from the Oneida to the Kill, which falls into the Susquehanna river, and one day unto the Susquehanna, and then seven days to the Susquehanna Castles—in all nine and a half's journey.

"Half a day's journey by land and one by water from Onondaga, before we arrive at the river, and then six days' journey from the river.

"From Cayuga one day and a half by land and by water, before arriving at the river, and then five days from the river.

"From Sinnekas' Four Castles three days by land and two days by water ere arriving at the river, and thence five days from the river—in all ten days, which is easy, they conveying their packs in canoes from the river."

During this interview, the Indians expressed a strong desire that some traders should come and establish themselves on the Susquehanna, to buy their furs. It being, as they represented, much nearer than Albany, as well as much easier of access—as they might then convey themselves and packs by water—whereas they are now compelled to bring every thing hither upon their backs.

About this period, Philadelphia began to attract attention as a trading post. It had been established but the year before (1682,) and now contained one hundred houses, and rapidly growing. The guiding spirit of the miniature colony was the renowned Penn—a Quaker—a man possessing untiring energy of mind; of broad and liberal views—he was eminently calculated to ingratiate himself into the favor of the Indian tribes. To this he paid early attention: he had hardly set foot on American soil, ere he commenced a friendly intercourse through the medium of trade, with the Indians in the neighborhood of his settlement; an intercourse which the following year he attempted to extend to the Iroquois nation, and thereby divert the Indian trade from Albany. To consummate more effectually his intended design, he dispatched a commissioner combining the necessary requisites of sagacity and address, to purchase the Susquehanna territory.

The announcement of Penn's intention, spread the greatest consternation throughout the northern trading posts, particularly at Albany, where it was received with a spirit of marked resentment. Trade with the Indians being their only support, any attempt to divert it away would naturally excite their indignation, and they accordingly exerted themselves to frustrate the plans of the designing *Quaker*. The territory in question was claimed by the Cayugas and Onondagas, who had four years before conveyed it by promise to the Governor of New York, who at this particular crisis, convened the chiefs of these two nations in a treaty at Albany. The result of this conference was the confirmation of the original purchase, by a sealed instrument. Such is a brief sketch of the origin of the Susquehanna titles, and our limits will not in this place allow us to glance at the various controversies and conflicting claims that afterwards proved serious sources of agitation to the early settlers. The reader is referred to an interesting article in the Documentary History of the State, entitled "Susquehanna

Papers;" and also to a small volume published in 1796, by Croswell, in Catskill, entitled "Susquehanna Title Stated and Examined." Both articles are well worth a perusal.

Having glanced at some of the prominent features that stamp the early history of our common country; and rendered a passing notice to the character of the Aborigines, who were the original proprietors of the soil, we are now prepared to enter upon a more limited field of discussion, and although we may at times digress from our prescribed limits, it is to preserve unbroken and unimpaired the common chain that connects us with the past.

CHAPTER III

New York in 1770—Total population of the Colony at that period—Tryon and Charlotte counties erected—Their extent—Population of Tryon—First settlement German Palatines—Settlements made by them—Heldeburgh Hills—Origin of the name—Schoharie valley—Its settlement—Settlement at Cherry Valley—Privations of the settlers the first winter—Hair-breadth escape from starvation—Succored by a friendly Indian—Nativity of the early settlers—Harper family—Settle in Cherry Valley -Their influence with the Indians—Harpers found a new settlement—Called Harpersfield—Obtain a Patent—Surveyed—Mrs. Harper, the first white woman in the town—Constructs a log-house with her own hands—The first house in Harpersfield—Privations the following winter—Providential relief from starvation—Slow progress of the settlement—Reception of new settlers—Settlement in Middletown, before the Revolution—Death of Dumond, by the Schoharie Guard—Brugher shot by the Indians while threshing buckwheat—His son taken prisoner—Release and return of the son to Middletown—Drowned while crossing the Delaware some years after—Indian Villages on the East Branch—Milling stories—Indian hunting-grounds—Beaver; peculiarities of the animal—Ancient Apple-trees; anecdotes concerning—Pakatakan, an Indian Village—Supposed signification of the name—Tribes of Indians who occupied—Papagouck and Pepacton, other Indian Villages—Historical communications of Dr. O. M. Allaben.

> "The noblest men I know on earth,
> Are men whose hands are brown with toil;
> Who, backed by no ancestral graves,
> Hew down the woods and till the soil,
> And win thereby a prouder fame
> Than follows kings and warriors' name."

As we have stated in a previous chapter, in 1770, the tide of emigration received a sudden impetus, and the line of the frontier settlements began rapidly to recede westward. The *river towns*, which lay along or near the noble Hudson, were passed by and left to slumber on in comparative obscurity, while the daring and enterprising citizens were lured by the inducements offered them by the forest beyond. At this period, William Tryon was the principal Governor of New York; his name stands last in the catalogue of the provincial rulers, and it is conceded by both friend and foe, that he was endowed with all the attributes necessary to constitute a wise officer and a useful citizen. It is true that it was during his reign in office, that the yoke of foreign dominion was peremptorily cast aside, and the link which united us to the mother country was severed; but the causes which opened the door to that eventful struggle in which the goddess of liberty rode triumphant over tyranny and oppression, and erected an asylum for the down-trodden subjects of every land, were beyond his or human power to control. It needs but a casual glance at the history of the Revolution and its causes, to convince even the most skeptical that the clouds of political discord had been gathering and accumulating blackness for a long period before the fatal issue came. Wise men of England had descried the star of liberty—the saviour of freedom—rising faintly above the western horizon—dimly at first, but gathering renewed brightness from every wafted breeze—the prophecy had gone forth, and the proud aristocrats of England, jealous of their power, and benumbed to every noble feeling of compassion or justice, like Pharaoh of old, had sent forth their impious decrees to conquer by compulsion and force, what kindness and mutual feeling could alone beget: instead of recognizing their brethren across the water as Englishmen, with the same ancestral blood thrilling through their veins—moved by the same impulses and characterized by the same traits—bestowed upon them the epithet of servile subjects. To England this was a fatal step, but they either saw their error too late, or were too proud to retrace their steps, and the fatal snare they had carefully adjusted for another was sprung literally upon themselves; the same *impromptu* that caused Englishmen in England to usurp an unjust power, caused Englishmen in America to rebel.

In 1771, New York, although it comprised within its limits the whole of the present State of Vermont, was divided into but twelve counties, viz.: New York, Albany, Ulster, Dutchess, Orange, Westchester, Kings, Queens, Suffolk, Richmond, Cumberland, and Gloucester. The total population was but 168,000, of which nearly 20,000 were blacks. Nor was this population anywise evenly distributed throughout the colony. It was in the main confined to Long Island, Richmond, New York, and a half dozen settlements along the Hudson, foremost amongst which were Albany and Kingstown.

In 1772, two new counties were erected, Charlotte and Tryon, both of which have been since divided and subdivided, and are now recognized by other names. Charlotte was composed of the western half of the present state of Vermont, and of the counties of Clinton, Franklin, Essex, and Washington, in this State. Tryon county embraced all the territory west of Charlotte, between that and the St. Lawrence river, and west of a line running through nearly the centre of the present county of Schoharie to Utsayantho lake, which is the source of the west branch of the Delaware river; thence down the west branch to the Pennsylvania line. It embraced the whole State west of these defined limits. From its original extent, the whole or a portion of the following counties have been erected, viz.: Alleghany, Broome, Cattaraugus, Cayuga, Chautauque, Chemung,

Chenango, a part of Delaware, Erie, Essex, Franklin, Fulton, Genesee, Hamilton, Herkimer, Jefferson, Lewis, Livingston, Madison, Monroe, Montgomery, Niagara, Oneida, Onondaga, Ontario, Orleans, Oswego, Otsego, St. Lawrence, a part of Schoharie, Schuyler, Seneca, Steuben, Tioga, Tompkins, Wayne, Wyoming, and Yates.

The entire population of Tryon county at its formation did not exceed ten thousand whites, and these were exclusively confined to the eastern portion; of which it may be said that it contained some comparatively, for that early period, flourishing settlements. But the reader will do well to bear in mind the distinction between what was called a flourishing settlement at that early period and the present time. It needed not then some rich and favoured section of the State, with its railroads, canals, and all the modern improvements of art—with its fine farms, rich farmers, and flourishing mechanics—with its beautiful and stately edifices; its numerous churches, academies, and school-houses, to merit that appellation. It was rather where the first phase from a savage state to civilization had been passed; where a few pioneers had centred together, and where, by dint of unremitting toil, they were enabled to enjoy some of the necessaries and luxuries of life—where, at the close of day, the hardy, toil-weary, care-worn parents assembled with their children around the wide fire-place in the humble log-cottage, in unalloyed enjoyment—there was then no, *the rich* and the poor; no the *high circle* and the low circles; no superb mansion standing out in contrast with the humble cottage of the poor. All was unity and harmony; the same feelings swayed every heart—kindness; the same impulses throbbed every soul—hospitality; every thing beat in unison with the spontaneous sentiments of love. Such is a description of a flourishing settlement in the primitive history of our country; and of such we say a few existed in Tryon county at its formation. The county seat was located at Johnstown, a place of early note, as being the residence of the old baronet, Sir William Johnston, a man of military fame; having distinguished himself in the wars of the northwest, with the Indians. He was also His Majesty's Superintendent of Indians Affairs in America, through whose agency treaties were formed, and purchases consummated with the Aborigines.

The earliest settlement in Tryon County, of which I find any record, was made by a company of German Palatines, in the early part of the eighteenth century. About 1709 or 1710, three thousand Palatines landed at New York, many of whom had served in the army of Queen Anne, by whom they were hired of the princes who ruled over them. A large portion of these emigrants were induced by Penn to settle on his lands in Pennsylvania; many settled in New York, where they erected the first Lutheran church in America—settlements were made by them at East and West Camp, on the Hudson, and the remaining families emigrated to Schoharie county. The journey from Albany occupied four days; they crossed the spur of the Catskill mountains, which extends through the present county of Albany from north to south; and which they named in their native tongue, "Heldeburgh," signifying "Prospect Hill;" carrying upon their backs tools and provisions, with which they had fortunately provided themselves. They located in the beautiful and fertile valley of the Schoharie-kill, more or less of which had been cleared, and to some extent improved and cultivated by the Schoharie Indians, who had located there—tradition says—twenty years before.

These settlements continued to spread until the outbreak of the Revolution, when their comparatively prosperous condition was suddenly and fearfully disturbed; when their homes became the theatre of a dark and bloody war. The comparatively remote situation of the little settlement from the theatre of military operations, surrounded as they were by forests, which formed a shelter and a hiding-place for their savage foe, rendering them the fit subjects of Indian barbarity and wanton cruelty. Devastation and destruction, like meteoric flames, spread in every direction. The happy hearths of the settlers became the scene of bloody assassinations. The unholy savage, with fiendish barbarity spared neither young nor old; the innocent babe and the helpless female were alike sacrificed by the tomahawk or burned at the stake; the well filled barns were given to the mercy of the flames; the cattle butchered or driven away, to furnish sustenance and support to their enemies, presenting altogether a picture surpassing description.

The next settlement made within the limits of Tryon—and which literally speaking, formed the entrance-way to many of the early settlements in the present county of Delaware—was made in Cherry Valley, Otsego county. Glancing over the pages of an ably written work, "Campbell's Annals of Tryon County," we note that in 1738, a patent of eight thousand acres of land was granted to Jacob Lindesay, Jacob Roseboom, Lendert Ganesvoort, and Sybrant Van Schaick, the former of whom having obtained an assignment of the whole patent, the following summer laid the foundation of the future settlement. He was accompanied in the novel enterprise of founding a settlement far beyond the pale of civilization by his wife, father-in-law, and a few domestics only. The season had far advanced when they encamped for the first time upon the spot designated to become their future home. They had scarcely succeeded in constructing a rude tenement to shelter themselves from the storm, and to afford protection during the inclemency of winter, ere the ice-bound monarch became their unwelcome guest.

Imagine to yourselves what must have been the condition of this family, who were not only deprived of the little luxuries of life, but of neighbors and friends; in the midst of a howling wilderness, over which wild beasts and savage Indians disputed proprietorship, with a scanty supply of provisions, and the snow lying upon the ground full three feet deep. Day after day passes; night after night they await in anxious expectation, but in vain, for a cessation of its severity, to enable them to go to the Mohawk for provisions and aid.

Their situation at last became terrible in the extreme, starvation stared them in its most hideous form; and the grim spectre, death, seemed already to have impressed his signet upon his victims. In this extremity a kind providence sent them succor in the person of a friendly Indian, who kindly volunteered to go to the Mohawk for provisions, travelling by the aid of snow shoes, and returning with the provisions upon his back. This faithful child of the forest did not desert them until spring dawned upon their unpleasant situation; his unerring aim supplied them with venison and other wild game, and he frequently visited the Mohawk settlement to procure a fresh supply of meal and flour.

The following year, 1741, the Rev. Samuel Dunlop, who had been prevailed upon by the generous proprietor of the patent to settle in Cherry Valley, induced several families among his acquaintances and friends to locate there also. Among these are the names of David Ramsay, William Galt, James Campbell, and William Dickson, from Londonderry in New Hampshire, to which place they had emigrated from the north of Ireland, some years previously. These pioneers were peculiarly calculated to become the founders of a flourishing settlement—energetic, hardy, inured to toil, and susceptible of endurance. But in their new homes they experienced many privations unlooked for and unprepared for, the story of which deterred many others from following them, and hence, during the ten subsequent years only one or two families came into the valley, and the little germ of a settlement struggled on alone.

In 1754, the enterprising family of Harpers emigrated from Windsor, a town in Connecticut, and purchased a small tract of land in the Valley suitable for the pursuit of agricultural purposes, and immediately commenced improvements thereon. The category of this family included John and Abigail, the ancestors, and nine children; the names and fortunes of most of whom became afterward vitally woven in the frowning struggle of '76, and all of whom fought unexceptionally and unreservedly for liberty.

William, the eldest son, was an active member of the Provincial Congress, and when Otsego county was organized in 1792, he was appointed one of the assistant judges, William Cooper, Esq., being first judge. He died in 1817, at the advanced age of eighty-seven years, at his residence at Milford, Otsego county, New York.

James, the second son, was a vigilant and bold asserter of American independence.

Mary, the eldest daughter, married John Moore, an efficient and fearless member of the "Tryon County Committee of Safety," and who, with her three daughters, were taken prisoners at the massacre of Cherry Valley, in 1778; and compelled, under the savage protection of Brant, to perform the journey to Niagara. Fortunately for her, she found in the person of the commandant of that fort, a relative and friend, to whose kindness and humanity they were indebted for their subsequent restoration to their home.

John, the next brother in lineal descent, held a colonel's commission during the Revolution, and was particularly distinguished for the humanity which he exhibited on every occasion toward those of the enemy who fell into his power, and for that cool, intrepid courage, which several times saved the Schoharie settlements from wanton destruction. It is to him that Harpersfield is principally indebted for its early improvements, and from him that that town derived its name.

Joseph and Alexander, the youngest male members of the Harper family at the above mentioned date, both of whom fought during the Revolution in the protection of Harpersfield and the Schoharie frontiers, (for a more particular account of which reference is had to a future chapter,) and who afterward removed to Ohio, where they obtained a grant of land, and where their descendants now reside. In the words of another—"The approach of civilization was not congenial to them; they preferred the life of a borderer, and sought it amid the boundless forests that covered that beautiful State.

Another member of the Harper family, a younger sister, Abigail, married William McFarland, and who also removed to Ohio, some time subsequent to the ratification of the treaty of peace. He is said to have been an intelligent and respected citizen, as a proof of which, it may be mentioned that he was for several years Supervisor of the town of Harpersfield, while it yet formed a portion of Tryon, or as it was called, Montgomery county.

By referring to the register of this family, we find that their grandsire removed from the county of Derry, in the north of Ireland, and settled at Casco Bay, in the province of Maine, as early as 1720, but subsequently, on the breaking out of a bloody war between the settlers and several tribes of Indians, he removed with his family; leaving however his eldest son, John, who enlisted in the defence of the frontiers, and remained in the service three years and eight months. On his discharge he followed the family to Boston, and from thence a year or two subsequently he removed to Hopkington, where he became acquainted with and married Abigail Montgomery, mentioned above, who died at Cherry Valley the year before their removal to Harpersfield.

Following the history of the family through a later period, in 1729 they removed to Nodell's Island, near Boston, and from thence to Connecticut in 1741, from which place they finally removed to Cherry Valley.

From the period at which the Harpers had taken up their abode in Cherry Valley, their fortunes became an inseparable link in the history of the frontier settlements. Inheriting as they did, a goodly portion of the bold and martial spirit which had conspicuously characterized their ancestors, and profiting by the experience and knowledge of Indian character and its peculiarities, acquired by the elder John during the long campaign through which he had passed in Maine, they were enabled to cultivate successfully amicable relations with the Six Nations, and to exert over them a powerful controlling influence, a consideration of the utmost importance in their exposed situation at that period. Between the afterward renowned Indian sachem, *Jo* Brant, as he was familiarly known, and John Harper, Jr., an intimacy had sprung up while attending school together at Lebanon, Connecticut, where the young half-breed had been placed, through the influence of Sir William Johnston, in July, 1761. This school was at that time under the supervision of the Rev. Doctor Wheelock, afterward President of Dartmouth College, into which this institution was merged at a subsequent date. It is now familiarly known, as it was then called the "Moor Charity School."

In 1768, the Harpers and several other individuals, whom they had associated with them in the novel enterprise, determined upon founding a settlement of their own; but what induced them to decide upon Harpersfield as the theatre for their future operations, it is impossible at this remote day but to conjecture. It might have been at the instigation of friendly Indians, but more probably was the result of their own explorations and observations. The manufacture of maple sugar was then looked upon as a comparative lucrative business, and requiring but a limited capital—a *sap kettle* and a supply of wooden troughs being all that was necessary; as the forests at that early day were considered as of but little consequence. Accordingly, during the winter months small parties of two or three persons would associate themselves together and go out in the forests in various directions, selecting a favorable location where the sugar maple trees were standing thickest, would prepare a sufficient quantity of troughs and fuel, and construct a temporary log-hut, which answered the double purpose of shielding their persons from the storm, and in which they boiled their sap. Having made all things in readiness at the *"camp,"* they repaired to it again at the opening of spring, and frequently remained several weeks making maple sugar, often returning at the expiration of the sugar season with large quantities of delicious sugar. Harpersfield was well adapted to this pursuit, and it is more than probable that the knowledge of this fact induced them to locate there.

Persevering in their determination of founding a new settlement, they purchased of the Indians a large tract of land, stretching from the Charlotte on the north, to the head waters of the west branch of the Delaware river on the south. Accordingly, in conformity to the above purchase, a grant was secured the following year by letters-patent to John Harper, William Harper, John Harper, Jr., Joseph Harper, Alexander Harper, Andries Riber, and sixteen other individuals, of a tract of land containing twenty-two thousand acres, included by the present town of Harpersfield.

In the spring of 1770, Governor Tryon sent out a surveyor to accompany the patentees and locate the limits of the patent. He was accompanied by John Harper, the principal proprietor, and his faithful consort. This heroic woman, whose courage and fortitude entitle her to a conspicuous place among the heroines of those early times, unwilling that her husband should share alone the perils incident to the undertaking, determined to accompany, and if possible, in some degree alleviate their situation. While the men were surveying, she with her own hands constructed a rude log-hut and covered it with bark. In this hut she frequently was compelled to remain alone days, and sometimes-even nights, while her husband and his companions were engaged upon a remote part of the patent. It is a historical fact and one worthy of mention, that this was the first domicile dedicated to civilization, erected within the present limits of the county; and that its fearless architect was unquestionably the first *pale face* of the fair sex whose presence lent a delectable charm to the lonely wilderness.

In the spring of 1771, the survey and division of the patent having been completed, the family of Harpers removed from Cherry Valley to Harpersfield, and made a permanent settlement there.

The following incident was related to me by the Rev. Mr. Boyce, of Harpersfield, who married a niece of Colonel Harper, and who has been for many years intimately connected with the family. The first winter succeeding the removal of the Harpers into Harpersfield, was distinguished for its unprecedented severity. The partial and incomplete arrangements they had been enabled to make, proved hardly sufficient for the unseen privations they were called upon to endure. During the summer and fall preceding this memorable winter they had removed their goods, provisions, &c,. to Schoharie, from which place to Harpersfield there was no road, and they had stored them at the former place—except a few provisions—intending to remove them to the place of destination upon the snow. Winter set in much sooner than was anticipated, and the snow fell upon the ground to a great depth, cutting off all communications, and rendering it almost impossible to reach any settlement of which, the reader must be aware, there was none nearer than Schoharie, over twenty miles distant—Cherry Valley, their former place of residence, lying still farther off.

In the midst of this dilemma their stock of provisions became exhausted excepting a little corn, which was powdered in a mortar and converted into a rude bread, familiarly known as *Johnny cake*. Upon this scanty diet they subsisted for a brief period, in the hope of a speedy cessation of the extreme cold weather. At last the remaining meal was all consumed, and but one small loaf of *Johnny cake* was left to preserve the existence of the members of the new settlement. His faithful partner, who had borne up under all their former privations with becoming fortitude, now began to yield. Cautiously she had concealed from her husband the real state of their provisions, well knowing, as she did, the imminent peril that would surround any attempt to reach the settlements, as well as that bold resolution that would prompt him immediately to undertake the journey, at any hazard. Noble woman, I would fain weave for thee, in this history, a eulogy worthy of such heroism. The fierce contest had raged in her own bosom, between alternate hope and fear—the love with which she cherished her offspring and the plighted affections of her husband—and would that the invocation of the prophet had been there, by his power from above, to have replenished the exhausted "measure of meal." But the urgent claims of hunger and the prospect of starvation, will unnerve the strongest mind and move the firmest purpose.

A sad and painful picture did that little family circle present, as the children, prompted by hunger, gathered around the mother and anxiously presented their urgent demands for bread. The youngest were uttering their cries, while those who were older and better able to realize more fully their extreme situation, but hardly comprehending its fearful reality, were anxiously propounding the inquiry, "Mother, must we starve?"

While the children were gathered around the mother, the father entered; his eyes immediately fell upon the pale and anxious features of his wife; her tearful eyes met his own and revealed to him the reality of their situation. It was useless to conceal the truth from him longer, and she now told him that one small loaf was the last morsel the house contained, and for this even the children were crying, but she dared not give it to them, hardly knowing what they would do when that was consumed.

The father now resolved, as a last resort, to repair to the Schoharie settlement on the morrow, which he doubted not he could do, travelling by the aid of snow shoes; and taking the dainty morsel from the shelf and breaking it, distributed it among the members of the family, giving a portion to his wife and each of his children, but touching it not himself. John Harper was a consistent Christian and a good man, and the trust he reposed in his God sustained him in this trying hour. He consoled his wife, by exhorting her to "fear not, Providence would provide."

We will now turn to the Schoharie settlements; the inhabitants, aware of the scanty supply of provisions of their neighbors at the "Bush," as Harpersfield was usually termed, and conscious that unless they could afford them succor, they must perish with hunger, had fortunately, the same day that the provisions of the family became exhausted, and the affecting scene narrated above had transpired, determined to go to their assistance. Accordingly, early on the day in question, a company set out from Schoharie, travelling by the aid of snow shoes toward Harpersfield, at which place they arrived at midnight, to the joyful surprise of the starving inhabitants.

The little settlement at Harpersfield continued gradually but slowly to increase, during the subsequent years that intervened up to the period of the Revolution. Each year added some new comers to the list of their neighbors, and each was hailed with unaffected joy by the inhabitants. A correspondent, whose grey hairs entitle him to a respectful hearing, and whose memory serves him of by-gone times, says: "It was an invariable custom among the early settlers, that when a new comer made his appearance among them, the most commodious house in the whole settlement was freely offered for his use, until a *bee* could be made, and a house prepared without any expense to himself. Indeed to such an extent were their peculiar sentiments of hospitality carried, that neighbors frequently quarrelled which should have the pleasure of accommodating the new guests."

It is the design of the present chapter to recite briefly the history of the early settlements in the county prior to the Revolution, but of the other settlements made within the limits of the county, and especially of those in Middletown, the description which I shall be able to give, will at the most prove but vague and uncertain. How much ever of interest their antiquity may possess, a great portion of their history is buried in oblivion, and the men who first settled there, and all who might have rendered valuable assistance have passed away; the researches of the antiquarian therefore must prove an almost hopeless task.

From the few reliable reminiscences I have been enabled to gather, it appears that at a very early period, a few Low-Dutch families from Marbletown and Hurley, followed up the Esopus or *Shandaken* creek (the latter being the Indian name, signifying *swift waters*,) and crossing the hills that divide its waters from the east branch of the Delaware, located themselves in a small settlement upon the fertile flats that skirt the latter stream. One of these settlers, a Mr. Van Waggoner, settled near the present residence of Colonel Noah Dimmick, to whom the author is indebted for the above information. Another settled a short distance above, by the name of Kittle—this place was afterward familiarly known as the "Kittle Farm." Several other settlers were scattered along at intervals for several miles down the river, among whom were Hermanus Dumond, about a mile below Margaretville, on the opposite side of the river, who was shot during the Revolution under the following painful circumstances:

Dumond, in company with John Barrow, a neighbor, who occupied and owned the present residence of Warren Dimmick, Esq., in Middletown, had been—as my informant Colonel Dimmick recollects, and which somewhat differs from a subsequent recital of the same event in this chapter—up the river on a hunting excursion, and when returning and while near Arkville on the flat, they unexpectedly fell in with a company of Schoharie guards, who had been sent by Colonel Vroman, of Schoharie, to scour the head waters of the Delaware, and to arrest certain disaffected persons, and to destroy supposed Indian settlements, and who were now on their return to Schoharie.

The Guard perceiving them armed, ordered them to "halt." Dumond and Barrow, from the best authority I can command, were favorable to the cause of the colonies, although from considerations of personal safety they had been prompted to maintain, as much as possible, a neutral position. It is therefore probable, that in their haste they mistook the character of the troops, and supposing them to be tories and Indians, disregarded the injunction, and immediately attempted to flee. Perceiving their retreat, the commander of the troops ordered his men to fire upon them, when Dumond fell mortally wounded, surviving his fall but a brief period, while Barrow, more fortunate than his companion, escaped unhurt and unmolested, to carry the painful intelligence to the family of the deceased. The guard dismounted, and gathering around the expiring man, expressed in heartfelt grief their sympathy at his untimely death; raising him gently upon their locked arms, they conveyed him to a house near by. No physician was at hand to render efficient aid, and indeed none was necessary, for it was apparent to all as they watched the tremulous palor of his countenance, the glazed and fixed expression of his dark eye, and the cold drops of sweat that gathered upon his icy, but manly forehead, revealed in unmistakable language,

"That the golden bowl was broken,"

and that life hung for a time but by a flickering and dissevered thread. It was indeed a time for mourning; that little band of brave men had wives and children and hearth-stones of their own, and it was for these, the dearest and tenderest of all human interests, that they had come forth and taken upon themselves the armor of war, to protect and defend them; and when the expiring man with his last accent breathed sweet counsel to his wife and children, who depended upon him for their daily bread, there arose spontaneous in every bosom, the reflected counterpart of their own homes; perhaps at that instant the ruthless savage has raised the fierce war-whoop, and with tomahawk in hand has passed the threshold of his own domicile to drink the heart's blood of his own kindred, or if they escape death, to be carried into a captivity, if possible, worse even than death. But pass this picture! for already have the eyes of the unfortunate man closed, and he has sunk in the embrace of that sleep which wakes only at the resurrection morn. A rude and shallow grave is prepared, in which, without coffin or shroud, or monument to mark his resting-place, they placed him with his arms slightly folded, and without removing his clothes.

The death of Dumond was an unfortunate circumstance for his family. He was the father of a large family of children, most of whom at that time were small. My informant, Cyrus Burr, Esq., knew three of the sons, John, David and Hermanus, all of whom are now dead, and two daughters, both of whom married men by the name of Yaples. One of them, the widow of Philip Yaple, deceased, resides at present in Plattekill, in the town of Middletown.

There was another pioneer who had located in Middletown by the name of Burgher; of the precise place he occupied I am unable to state definitely, but it lay several miles farther down the river, and within the limits of the town of Andes. This settler, supposing he might remain in safety during the war, by professing to take no part in the issues of the day, was shot by an Indian scout while threshing buckwheat in the open field. His eldest son, then but a lad, who was at work with the father, was taken into captivity, where he suffered greatly during the remainder of the war. After an absence of several years he was finally permitted to return to the family at Middletown. He was drowned many years after, while attempting to cross the Delaware during a freshet, on horse-back.

At the period of the first settlements which were made along the east branch of the Delaware, there were scattered upon that stream several small Indian settlements.* It is not probable, however, that this tribe or tribes made any permanent residence on the Delaware, but only visiting it at certain seasons of the year to prosecute their favourite employment of hunting and fishing, which commodities there existed in great abundance; and it may here be remarked, that beaver were found in abundance along up the river. The first settlers found several huge dams which this ingenious animal had thrown across the stream. One of these dams, near the site of the present village of Roxbury, was the circumstance from which it derived its former name of "Beaver Dam."†

One of these Indian villages was only a short distance above Margaretville, on the opposite side of the stream, where may be seen a

---

* VOL. I., Documentary History of New York.

† A full-grown beaver weighs from fifty to sixty pounds; its length is usually about four feet from the snout to the end of the tail. The tail is about five or six inches wide by one inch in thickness, and what seems peculiar, although the body of the animal is so well covered with fur and hair, the tail is without either, except at its insertion, and is covered with a species of scales. The fore part of the beaver has the consistency of land animals, while the hind legs and tail have not only the smell, but the savor, and nearly all the qualities of the fish.

The food of the beaver is principally vegetable. The bait used by hunters to entice them to a trap is *castoreum*, or bark stone, which substance is obtained from the glandulous pouches of the male animals. The beavers prefer usually to locate their dams in a moderate current, which they substitute as a motive power, to float the trees which they fell into the stream above, to the precise point where they are required. The number of trees which they thus cut is truly surprising, and those unacquainted with the animal, would suppose them cut with an axe.

The dams which they build in a running stream are curved, with the convexity-opposed to the current; the interstices are filled with mud and stones. Their work is all prepared in the night; as soon as any of the material is placed where it is intended to remain, the animal turns round and gives it a smart blow with its tail. The same sort of a blow is struck by them on the surface of the water, when they are in the act of diving. The hut of the beaver is rudely constructed of bushes and mud, which is applied after the water becomes sufficiently cold to freeze it.

couple of ancient looking apple-trees, which are said to have been nurtured by the original proprietors themselves. The oldest living settlers bear witness to the fact, by stating that they were *old trees* when they were boys; they were perhaps at that early date the only bearing apple trees in the county, and those persons are still living who can bear witness to the miraculous disappearance of the fruit.

An intelligent and reliable informant, speaking of these apple trees, related the following anecdote of their early history: Some fifty years ago, the only grist-mill for a large circumference of territory was situated on the east branch of the Delaware, near Arkville. This mill had been built, and for some years owned and occupied, by a man by the name of _____, distinguished especially among the "younger America," who frequently bought grists to his mill, for his generosity and liberality. The apple trees spoken of above were owned by him, and usually, in the fall of the year, hung loaded with myriads of tiny apples, scarcely larger than a small sized hen's egg, but a greater rarity at that time to boys especially, than the delicious fruits of the tropics are now. And it was principally to the liberality with which he allowed his young customers to partake of this fruit, and load their pockets to carry to their mothers and sisters at home, that the miller had acquired his enviable reputation. Several years after, this place was purchased by one _____, who, in contradistinction with the former owner, soon came into notoriety, under the appellation of *stingy*; but the boys, who had come to think themselves as by right entitled to some of the fruit, were not to be outdone, and after several unsuccessful attempts to persuade the proprietor to open his heart toward them, an expedient was put in execution, which proved successful, to the miraculous disappearance of the fruit. Two of the boys were sent to *coax* the old man, who by the way was short of sight, while their companions repaired at the same instant to the trees, which in mock charity to the owner they handled rather roughly, and procured a goodly quantity of his apples.

The same informant states that, when a lad of a dozen years, his father packed him off to this mill—the first he had ever visited—upon horseback, with a small grist to be converted into flour for the consumption of the family. The father, before he left, impressed upon the mind of the young lad the necessity of watching the miller pretty closely, remarking, "that millers sometimes steal." This caution placed the young tyro on his guard, and sure enough, shortly after the grist had been emptied into the hopper he saw the miller go to a small bin near by, and, taking a measure, filled it from the grain in the hopper, and emptied it back into the bin. The boy kept watch, and when a favourable opportunity presented itself, and when the miller's back was turned, he filled the measure out of the bin, and emptied it back into the hopper, replacing what he supposed the miller had intended to steal. To use his own words, he said: "I felt really proud of what I had done, and when I returned home that night I related to my father what had transpired at the mill, telling him that the miller did not get much the best of me, 'for he struck the measure full he took out of the hopper, while I heaped up the one I put in;' that he was a big thief, for there was a large bin full of grain, which I felt sure he had stolen in like manner. My father laughed heartily over the joke, and then explained to me that this was the way they were paid for the use of their mill."

The tribe of Indians who occupied this village near Margaretville, and which, in the Indian dialect, was called Pakatakan, said to signify the union of two streams in one, (an appropriate cognomen, as it was at this place that the Dry-brook stream falls into the East Branch,) according to O. Callaghan's History of New York, were the Wappinger Indians of Dutchess county and Esopus; and according to the same account, this same tribe had a couple of other villages farther down the river in Colchester, one of which they called Papagouck and the other Pepacton.

The following information kindly furnished by Dr. O.M. Allaben, of Margaretville, who has evinced much interest in the compilation of this work, coming to hand too late to become incorporated in the thread of my history, and although some parts are a repetition of the foregoing, we have inserted it in full. We regret to state in this place, that so few persons are found who have evinced the same degree of interest in the collection of historical reminiscences.

"Dear Sir:—The timely appearance of your work, embracing the settlement and early history of Delaware county, furnishes a desideratum, the importance of which has long been felt; and I cheerfully contribute the few historical items which I have been enabled to gather from an intercourse of more than twenty years with the people of this town, for the purpose of rescuing from oblivion what is still matter of veritable history, but which will have become mere tradition, unless speedily placed upon record by the historian. Reliable sources of information have sensibly decreased within the few years last past, and indeed I believe no person is now living who came into this town with the early pioneers, and but few even are left, who have any knowledge of the trials and unforeseen embarrassments which beset the hardy adventurers who first emigrated into this valley."

I am principally indebted for the facts here presented, to Frederick Kittle, who came into the settlement with the first emigrants, by his stepfather, Mr. Hendricks. He spent nearly his whole life in this neighborhood, and died some years since at a very advanced age. He was a boy when the little colony was founded, but old enough to remember many of the incidents attendant upon that event. Also, to Christian Yaple, who at the age of about two years emigrated with his father from Pennsylvania, and settled in Middletown, about six years prior to the Revolution. Also, to Nelly Yaple, the only person now living, who was upon the stage of action when most of the events to be narrated occurred. She is the daughter of Hermanus Dumond, one of the original settlers, and was born in Middletown in 1774. Also, to James Dumond, grandson of Peter Dumond, another early settler, who was born about the close of the Revolution, and who has resided in Middletown ever since. The latter person is, perhaps, as well acquainted with the traditionary history of the first settlements, as any person at present living,—possessing naturally an enquiring mind and a retentive memory, and having been brought up in one of the original families, most of the leading incidents have come within the scope of his research and observation.

Perhaps no settlement in Delaware County, dates anterior to that in Middletown. In the latter part of the year 1762, or early in the spring of 1763, a party was formed in Hurley, Ulster County, for the purpose of exploring the Delaware valley, and if considered expedient, of making arrangements for emigrating thither with their families. Among these adventurers were Hermanus Dumond, his brother Peter Dumond, Johannes Van Waggoner, and a man by the name of Hendricks; each of whom, after having made the necessary explorations, purchased a farm of the patentee, at a place called by the Indians, Pakatakan, and as before stated, near where the present village of Margaretville is located. These four pioneer families, constituted the first permanent colony on the East Branch, but at the period of their arrival in the valley, there still remained abundant evidence of their having been preceded by others, supposed to have been French Canadians, or half-breeds, who had squatted upon these flats previous to, or during the French war, for the purpose of traffic with the aborigines, but who were compelled to retire from considerations of personal safety, during the troublesome times that followed. Mr. Kittle, has frequently asserted that his step-father Hendricks, purchased his possession of one of these squatters, and Mrs. Yaples well recollects from the narrations of her mother, that agricultural implements of various kinds, were found by her parents on their arrival, satisfying them that they had been preceded by others of European extraction.

The land titles of the first settlers, were warranty deeds granted by Mr. Livingston to the purchaser, with a provision allowing the latter to cut wood or quarry stone, upon any part of the patent, for farm or family uses. The date of these deeds is April 6, 1763.

The Indian village of Pakatakan, was a little above the site of the present village of Margaretville, as before stated, and near the junction of the Bush-kill with the East Branch. Mr. Kittle designated it as a Tuscarora village, and informed me that the Indian etymology of the name was, *"The place where the streams come together,"* or *"The meeting of the waters,"* a very appropriate cognomen, as three very considerable streams intersect in that neighborhood, besides three or four smaller ones.

The early settlers were principally Dutch, and both wrote and spoke that language. They lived, so far as I have been able to learn, upon very friendly terms with the Indians, up to the dark period of the Revolutionary war. They suffered all the privations incident to a new and distant settlement, and were for a long period obliged to do their milling, trading, &c., at Esopus, forty-five miles distant, and the greater part of the distance being through an unbroken wilderness.* For a period of more than ten years from the first settlement, and until the breaking out of hostilities, the little colony continued slowly to increase in the valley of the Delaware, and nearly all the alluvial lands along the main stream were occupied, and more or less improved for a distance of more then twenty miles. Several schools were also established, where instruction was given in the Dutch dialect.

But few of the names of those who settled before the war has been handed down to us; among them, we find those of Hermanus and Peter Dumond, Van Waggoner, Hendricks, Kittle, Yaple, Brugher, Slyter, Hinebagh, Green, Blanch, and others. Among the friendly Indians were Tunis and Canope, (the sad fate of the latter of whom is narrated in a future chapter.)

The disputes and strife which preceded the war of the Revolution, took early and deep root among the inhabitants of Pakatakan, attributable doubtless, in a greater or less extent, to the influence which the presence of a savage foe, exerted upon the fears and hopes of a frontier settlement, and consequently, it does not seem strange that a large portion of the settlers should have espoused the royal cause. There were a few whigs however, and among them, were Yaples, Peter Dumond, and Hinebagh. Hermanus Dumond and Peter Brugher, the former of whom was killed by the Americans, and the latter by the Indians, were said to occupy neutral ground.

The first open rupture, growing out of the political troubles of the times, among the settlers of Pakatakan, is said to have occurred at a school house within the precincts of the settlement, between Isaac Dumond, a son of Peter, and a boy by the name of Markle. Markle called Dumond a rebel, whereupon the latter in a fit of resentment, dealt the other a blow. A bout of fist-cuffs ensued, which finally broke up the school.

Early in the spring of 1778, or soon after the burning of Kingston, by the detachment of British troops, under Gen. Vaughn, the hostile Indians, emboldened by the terror which that act produced in the minds of the border revolutionists, advanced to Colchester or Pepacton, as it was then called, where they encamped, and commenced the perpetration of a series of depredations upon the whigs in the vicinity, stealing their cattle, goods, &c., and finally, they formed a plot with the cognizance of some of the tories, to murder or drive them out of Pakatakan.

This intended massacre was prevented by a timely notice from Tunis, a friendly Indian, who informed Yaple of the impending danger, and advised him to leave the settlement. Yaple immediately spread the alarm among

---

* Mr. Kittle informed me, that both the settlers and Indians (who, it seems employed horses,) fastened their horses and cut fodder for them at the Beaver meadows, in Roxbury, distant ten or twelve miles, following an Indian trail or foot-path, from Pakatakan to the meadows.

the whigs, who, after hastily collecting their cattle, and such of their goods as they could conveniently carry, and after burying or otherwise concealing the remainder, took a hasty leave of the settlement. On the same day that Yaple, Peter Dumond, and Hinebagh fled, the Indians made a concerted descent upon the settlement, and after destroying such of their effects as remained unconcealed, and reducing the buildings to ashes, sent a detachment of twenty Indian warriors under the guidance of two well known tories in pursuit of the fugitives, who followed them as far as Shandaken, when they gave up the chase. Yaple subsequently returned after the remainder of his goods, and was taken prisoner by the tories, among whom was Blanch. He was taken to Colchester, where he was detained in custody for several weeks, but finally allowed to return with his goods.

These outrages at Pakatakan, aroused the attention of the Americans, who sent a company of militia from Schoharie to drive the marauders from the frontiers. On the approach of the troops, the tories fled to the older settlements of Hurley, while the Indians retired toward the Susquehanna.

No further attempts were made by the settlers to establish themselves at Pakatakan, until after the close of the war, but occasional visits were made to the place, by the settlers, for the removal of their property, or gathering in of their crops. It was on occasions like this that both Dumond and Burgher were shot. Dumond was killed on the twenty-sixth of August, 1778. He had returned with John Barrow from Hurley, to which place they had fled, as stated above, in order to secure a piece of grain. Having accomplished their purpose, they set out to return again to Hurley, and when about a mile from his place of residence at Pakatakan, they fell in with the Schoharie Guard, who took them prisoners. They were mounted upon a single horse, Burrow behind Dumond, to accompany the troops. Seeing a favorable opportunity to escape, they put spurs to the horse and rode off in an opposite direction. They were fired upon by the guard, and Dumond fell fatally wounded to the ground. He was conveyed to the house or the farm where Col. Dimmick now resides, where he died after suffering excruciating pain for three days. Burrow made his escape, threaded the forest, up Dry Brook, and over the mountains into Shandaken, travelling through the day and lodging in a tree by night. Such is the commonly received opinion in relation to the death of Dumond; but Mrs. Yaple, however, believes that her father and Burrow mounted one of his own horses and attempted to escape before he was taken prisoner, supposing the troops to have been Butler men, and enemies of the colonies.

In the fall of the same year, 1778, Peter Burgher returned with his son, a small boy, and others, to secure his crops. He had incurred the displeasure of the Indians by piloting the troops from Pakatakan, and they sought this opportunity to ambush and destroy him. He was shot, it is said, by a Seneca Indian named Abraham, while threshing buckwheat, and his little son was taken prisoner, carried to Niagara, and sold to a British officer. He afterwards returned, and was drowned while crossing the Delaware, near where his father was killed, in the neighborhood of Mill Brook.

There is, near Margaretville, an ancient grave-yard, supposed to have been used either by the early Dutch settlers before the Revolution, or by the half-breeds who preceded them. It has long been abandoned, and the spot and even the graves of many of them are overgrown with trees and underwood, and little or nothing is now known of its history save its existence. Near the mouth of the Mill brook, and on the banks of the Delaware, are certain remains which bear strong resemblance to works of art. Many suppose them to have been ancient fortifications or works of defence, but when or by whom they were erected is mere conjecture. I am informed by Mr. Dickinson, who resides near them, that in that vicinity were once found what was supposed to have been a stone battle-axe, and that arrow-heads exist in great abundance in that immediate locality, which strengthens the opinion that they were of Indian occupation. They are two in number, each of a circular form, and have been surrounded by a high embankment, protected by a deep ditch.* The one on the east side of the river has been passed over many times with the plow, but much of its original symmetry and form are still visible. The other, on the opposite side, further down the stream, is still surrounded by a deep ditch filled with growing trees and underwood, but has less regularity, and will not so soon attract the attention of the antiquarian.

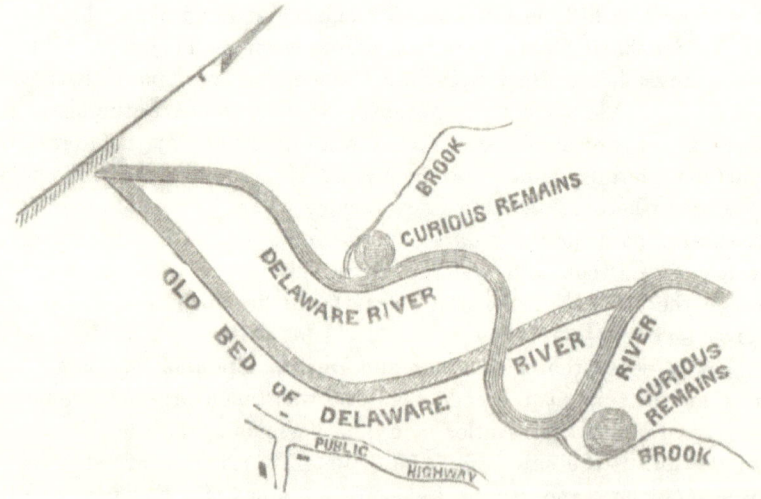

* Gould Map

CHAPTER IV

Revolution—Early conflicts—Eloquence of Pitt in Parliament—Advocates the cause of American rights—His efforts unavailing—Provincial Congress assemble—Eloquent appeal of Patrick Henry—Effect of his speech—Resolution of Continental Congress—George Washington unanimously chosen Commander-in-Chief of the American forces—His acceptance—Meetings of the inhabitants to express their sentiments—Vigilant Committees—Organization of, in Tryon County—Influences brought to bear—Sir Wm. Johnson espouses the Royal cause—His sudden death—His successors in office—Patriotism of the inhabitants of Harpersfield and Cherry Valley—First open act of hostility—Organization of a Vigilant Committee in Harpersfield—Their service to the American cause—The names of members—The chairman—Col. John Harper despatched by Congress on a Mission to the Indians—His apparent success—Reception by the Indians—Great feast and other ceremonies—Harper returns—Intimacy between Brant and Harper—Copy of a letter—Indians prove treacherous—Affidavit of the Rev. Wm. Johnston—Driven with his family from Sidney Plains—Obituary notice of Capt. Hugh Johnston—Effect of the intelligence communicated by Johnston along the frontiers—Letter from Harpersfield Vigilant Committee—Herkimer's Mission—Singular interview between Gen. Herkimer and Brant—Speech of Brant—Failure of the expedition—Evacuation of Harpersfield—John More an early settler—Warned of danger—Journey to Catskill—Accident—Enumeration of the inhabitants before the war—Scotchmen settle in the Valley of Wright's Brook—Story of the Scotchman and his gold—Capture of a party of Indians by Col. Harper—McDonald, a tory, invades Schoharie—Exposed situation of the settlement—Harper volunteers to go to Albany—Procures a company of Cavalry—Marches to Schoharie—Disperses the enemy—Letter from Harper to Congress.

HAVING rendered a passing notice to the early settlements, within the present limits of the county, we now approach that dark period of warfare, strife, and blood—the Revolutionary struggle, which eventually resulted in the immolation and cessation over them of foreign despotism in the colonies. Already have the clashing of steel and the boom of musketry been heard upon Bunker and Breed's Hill. Already have the excited and irritated Bostonians, disguised as Indians, consigned the cargoes of tea of several vessels to the mercy of the waves, as a mark of their just indignation at the infamous *Stamp Act* of Parliament.

It was now evident, that the rupture had become irreparable. The eloquence of Pitt, in Parliament, whose voice had been raised uniformly in behalf of the oppressed against the oppressor, who, at the close of a speech upon an illustrious occasion, in which he had exhorted the House to the exercise of wisdom and moderation in their dealings with America, concluded with the words of Prior the poet:—

"Be to her faults a little blind—
Be to her virtues very kind."

All had proved unavailing. In 1775, the Provincial Congress re-assembled at Philadelphia, to resolve on what steps were necessary in the emergency in which the colonies were placed. It was during this session, that Patrick Henry depicted with his thundering eloquence the history of our relations to the mother country: closing his appeal he remarked *"The war is inevitable!* and let it come!! I repeat it, sir, *let it come!!!* It is in vain, sir, to extenuate the matter. Gentlemen may cry peace, peace—but there is no peace! The war is actually begun! The next gale that sweeps from the north will bring to our ears the clash of resounding arms! Our brethren are already in the field! What is it that gentlemen wish? What would they have? Is life so dear, or peace so sweet as to be purchased at the price of chains and slavery? Forbid it, Almighty God! I know not what course others may take, but as for me," he cried, with both arms extended aloft, his brow knit, every feature marked with the resolute purpose of his soul, and with his voice swelled to its loudest note: *"Give me liberty or give me death."*

This speech had its desired effect; its noble and fearless sentiments found a home in every patriotic breast. On the fifteenth of June, a resolution was adopted by the CONTINENTAL CONGRESS, "That a general be appointed to command all the Continental forces, raised for the defence of American Liberty." George Washington was unanimously called to assume the responsibilities of this station, who rose in his place, being a member from Virginia, and signified his acceptance in a brief and appropriate reply; at the close of which he remarked: "As to pay, sir, I beg leave to assure the Congress that, as no pecuniary consideration could have tempted me to accept the arduous employment, at the expense of my domestic ease and happiness, I do not wish to make any profit from it. I will keep an exact account of my expenses. These, I doubt not, they will discharge, and that is all I desire."

And while their representatives were assembled, the people themselves were far from being idle. Meetings of citizens were called in every village and district; to give expressions to their sentiments, to favor liberty or oppression. Committees of vigilance were organized, whose duty it was to report the names of disaffected persons, to correspond with the General Assembly, and to whom was acceded the power of calling out troops in cases of emergency, to repel invasion; although, I believe, they actually possessed no such power. Such a committee was organized in Tryon county, as early as May, 1775, consisting of members from each of the districts; and we may perhaps with propriety in this place glance at the peculiar political condition of the county, in order to better understand the nature of the forthcoming struggle.

The population of Tryon was a mixed one, composed of Dutch, who lived principally in the Mohawk valley, the descendants of the German Palatines, who had settled in the Schoharie valley, and of Scotch *Irish*, who had settled in Cherry valley, Harpersfield, Laurens, Otsego, and other places. The Dutch and Germans were an exceedingly illiterate people, and had been accustomed to look up to Sir Wm. Johnston for counsel and advice, who, being a man of sagacity and address, it is not strange that, when he declared himself openly opposed to Congress, and favored the cause of that monarch who had heaped upon him emolument and honor, a major portion of the inhabitants within his potent influence should also go over to his standard. But Providence, in the midst of his active preparations for war, and when in the midst of an Indian council at Johnston, called him suddenly away

"To that bourne from which no traveller returns."

He died in June, 1774, and was succeeded in his estates and titles by his son, Sir John Johnston, while the authority of superintendent of the Indian department fell into the hands of his son-in-law, Col. Guy Johnston, who understood the Indian affairs better than any one else, having acted in the capacity of deputy to the old baronet. The successors of Sir William were illy calculated to assume, and fulfil successfully the exalted station vacated by his death, and consequently, quite a number of those least affected, declared unconditionally for the cause of Congress soon after.

But while the larger portion of the inhabitants of the northern and eastern sections declared themselves unconditionally in favor of the authority of the crown, in Cherry Valley and Harpersfield an exactly opposite state of things prevailed; they there openly denounced the position assumed by the Johnstons and their adherents; they denounced the oppressive acts of Parliament, and loudly extolled the measures adopted by the CONTINENTAL CONGRESS. A high state of excitement prevailed,—frequent and angry discussions were indulged in, which strongly tended to neutralize the parties from each other, and prepared them to embrace the actual commencement of hostilities with open arms, with the vain hope of satiating their personal animosities under the all-sufficient *cloak* of war; where they might justify themselves in applying the lighted torch, or the merciless tomahawk,—sacrificing with impunity the property and lives of their nearest neighbors, whose only fault was,—

"They did not think as we."

The first open act of hostility that was committed in Tryon county, was at the meeting of those favorable to the cause of Independence, in May, 1775, at the house of John Veeder, in the Caughuawaga district, for the purpose of raising a "liberty pole." The citizens, unapprehensive of danger, assembled unarmed. In the midst of their deliberations, and while one of their leading whigs* was haranguing the assembled multitude, whose hearts beat in unison with his own, they were suddenly thrown into great confusion by the appearance of an armed body of loyalists, commanded by Sir John Johnston in person. The whigs, indignant at the unceremonious interruption of their proceedings, determined to compel Johnston and his retainers to withdraw: a violent scuffle ensued, which resulted in *black eyes* and *bruised noses* on both sides, but no blood was shed, or other serious injury sustained by either side, when the parties actually withdrew, the loyalists to Johnstown, and the whigs to their respective homes, leaving the "pole" unraised.

The report of these proceedings was immediately communicated to the general committee of safety, and by them transmitted throughout the State, and leading whigs were everywhere vehement in their denunciations of Johnston and his adherents, and overflowing in the emulation of the bravery and resolute spirit evinced by leading patriotic Tryon brethren.

In August, 1775, a meeting of the citizens of Harpersfield was held at the house of John Harper, and a committee of vigilance was appointed to watch the movements of certain disaffected persons, and to gain what information they could of the stealthy movements of the hostile Indians under Brant, who, report had reached them, was then at Oquago, on the Susquehanna. The exposed situation of Harpersfield, and the well known and patriotic character of the leading inhabitants of that section, rendered their communications to the state council of safety, not unfrequently of the utmost importance. They, through intercourse with friendly Indians, and by scouts, were constantly kept reconnoitering the disaffected settlements. Cautiously were the movements of Brant and his host of bloody retainers noted, and when, at last, the storm broke in all its fury,— when the impatience of the savages could no longer be restrained, and they demanded to be led on "to butcher and to burn,"—when Schoharie, and all the frontier settlements of New York were about to become the theatre of predatory warfare, this committee communicated the timely warning to their faithful brethren.

It may be a matter of interest to learn, and certainly it deserves to become a matter of record, the names of the persons who braved every danger, and several of whom sacrificed life, property, and everything dear,

---

* Stone's Border Wars, gives the name as Sampson Sammons

upon the altar of liberty. Their names were John Harper, John Harper, Jr., Alexander Harper, Joseph Harper, Isaac Patchin, Freegift Patchin, Andries Riber, Wm. McFarland, St. Leger Cowley, Sawyer, John More, Jas. Stevens, and several others, all of whom took the prescribed oath, and signed the articles of association.

The following is the oath which was prescribed by the Provincial Congress, and which was administered to every member.

> "You shall swear by the holy evangelist of the Almighty God, to be a true subject to our continental resolve and Provincial Congress and committees, in this difficulty existing between Great Britain and America, and to answer upon such questions as you shall be examined in, so help you God."*

Isaac Patchin, who was afterwards among the prisoners captured by Brant, in the spring of 1780, and the particulars of which will be narrated in a future chapter of this work, was the efficient chairman of the committee during its entire deliberations.

With the hope of influencing a portion of the Indians to join the American standard, or at least of obtaining pledges of neutrality in the forthcoming struggle, in the winter of 1776, Col. John Harper was despatched with a letter from the Provincial Congress, to Oquago, the winter quarters of a large number of warriors of the Six Nations. The success of this mission was considered to be a matter of the utmost importance to the interests of the frontier settlements, and it was one, too, combining imminent hazard and peril, as it was reported that the Johnsons had already stirred them up to hostile movements.

Harper cheerfully undertook the performance of the arduous duties assigned him, and immediately made preparation for the journey, a distance of over seventy miles, through an almost unbroken wilderness.

He was accompanied down the Susquehanna, a distance of nearly fifty miles, to the Johnston settlement, by the regiment of militia under his command, when, deeming it imprudent to march farther into the Indian country, lest the appearance of an armed force amongst them should frustrate the important object of the mission, he stationed his force at this settlement, giving private orders to the captains to hold themselves in readiness, at a moment's warning, to march to his relief, should he be inhospitably detained beyond the appointed time for his return.

He was accompanied the remainder of the journey by a friendly Oneida and one white man, who resumed their route from the settlement, travelling the whole distance to the Indian encampment upon the frozen surface of the Susquehanna. They were received by the Indians with every demonstration of friendship; a council fire was built, and the chiefs and braves assembled around it to deliberate upon the objects of the mission.

---

* Simms' History of Schoharie.

The letter from the Provincial Congress of New York was read to them by Harper, who needed no interpreter, and who, in a few remarks in the Indian tongue, which he *spoke* and *gestured** fluently, represented to them the advantages of an alliance with the colonies; as the inevitable result of the war would be the establishment of their independence. He then distributed some presents among them. In the afternoon they again assembled at the council fire; the Indians having held a discussion in secret, when a principal chief arose: he stated to Harper, that the report that in connection with the Johnsons, an expedition into the frontier settlements had been concerted in the following spring, was untrue—that they deplored the existing difficulties into which their brethren had been placed—that they should take no part in them, and that they desired to remain neutral. Having closed his speech, according to Indian usages he presented Harper with a deer skin, as a pledge of the sincerity of his pretensions.

At night a feast was prepared, and an ox which Harper had brought for the occasion, was killed and roasted. The ceremonies were conducted in all the novelty and pomp of Indian custom, and Harper, painted as one of them, and dressed in Indian costume, mingled freely in all their performances, and partook with a hearty relish of the roasted *viand*. The repast being over, the chiefs and *great* ones assembled around their hostage, when a crown, which consisted of a belt richly decorated with beads, was placed upon his head as a mark of distinction, and which entitled him to a voice in the deliberations of the Six Nations.†

Harper having successfully accomplished his mission, accompanied by his companions, returned to the Johnston settlement, where he joined his regiment, and from thence returned to Harpersfield.

It was, I believe, unusual for the Indians so far to forget their native prejudices as to bestow this mark of distinction upon a *pale face*, and I have never read of any other person excepting Sir William Johnston, upon whom the favor has been bestowed; and although the long struggle which immediately followed, was calculated to place him at enmity with the Indians, his bravery and the humanity he exhibited, still the more endeared him to them. He never took life when he could avoid it, and never suffered himself or those under his command to commit any of those barbarities which placed so dark a stain upon the history of the border warfare of the Revolution.

The following is an exact copy of a manuscript letter found in possession of the Rev. Mr. Boyce, of Harpersfield, who married a niece of Col. Harper, and which goes to show that the intimacy existing between

---

* Gestures are a radical part of Indian oratory—every sentence is accompanied by an appropriate gesture.

† I procured this information of the Rev. Mr. Boyce and others, of Harpersfield. See also Stone's Border Wars, and the Proceedings of the Provincial Congress of New York.

Harper and the Six Nations was kept up for many years, and that he frequently transacted business for them. The communication is in Brant's own hand-writing:

"Head of Lake Ontario, October 2nd, 1804.

"DEAR SIR,—I now send the bearer for those papers you mention in your letter to have obtained for me; it was my intention to have called on you myself on my way out, but the season will be so far advanced before I shall leave home, and being under the necessity to pass through Albany, it will not be in my power to see you until I return, when I will call on you myself, or let you know immediately the success I meet with: if I am fortunate you may depend on my influence with the Oquagos to do you justice, which I believe is their full determination, whenever it is in their power. Another reason why I wish to get the papers before I leave home is, to arrange them with others before I set off. I have not heard anything from Governor Clinton on the subject, and would wish your advice respecting it, as to my calling on him; whether you think he would be disposed to lend me such assistance as would be in his power? In that case I conceive he might be of great service to me, as he was during the whole transaction of the business—executive of the State. As I supposed you might have mentioned something of my business to him about the time you wrote me, and will be able to know his feeling toward me, your opinion in writing to me will direct my calling on him, or mentioning my business to him.

"I am, Dear Sir, your most
"humble servant,
"JOS. BRANT.
"COL. JOHN HARPER."

But however sincere may have been the protestations of the Indians to Harper at Oquago, they were, unfortunately for the colonies, doomed to be of short duration, as will appear from the following affidavit made only a few months after, by the Rev. Wm. Johnston, which I find in the New York Journal of the Council of Safety, dated July 16th, 1777.

"*Ulster County*, ss.
"William Johnston being duly sworn, says that on the second day of June, Joseph Brant came up from Onehoghquaga to Unadilla, with between seventy and eighty warriors; that they came out of the Indian territory and within the division line (referred to in a previous chapter as having been established in 1768,) about one mile; that Brant and his party sent for the officers of the militia company and the minister of Unadilla, and informed them that they were in want of provisions; that if they could not get them by consent, they must take them by force; that

Joseph Brant told the officers that their agreement with the king was very strong, and that they were not such villains as to break their covenant with the king; that they were naturally warriors, and that they could not bear to be threatened by Mr. Schuyler; that they were informed that the Mohawks were confined—that they had not liberty to pass and re-pass as formerly; that they were determined to be free, as they were a free people, and desired to have their friends removed from the Mohawk's river, lest if the Western Indians should come down upon them, their friends might suffer with the rest, as they would pay no respect to persons; that the inhabitants being but weak and defenceless, they let them have some provisions; that the said Brant and his party, after staying two days at Unadilla aforesaid, took eight or ten head of horned cattle and some sheep and hogs, and returned to Onehoghquaga again; that those of the inhabitants who were friendly to the cause of America, removed with their families and effects to places of more security; that the examinant then went to the officers of Tryon county and informed them of the matter; that General Herkimer went with a party of men to Unadilla.

"WILLIAM JOHNSTON, JUN'R.

"Sworn and examined this 16th
day of July, 1777, by me,
"JOHN MCKERSON, Not. Public."

Johnston, together with his family and the rest of the little settlement, deeming their lives unsafe in the exposed situation of Unadilla, repaired immediately to Cherry Valley, as will appear from an obituary notice of one of the party, and which I consider worth an insertion here:

"DIED at Sidney Plains, October 23d, 1833, HUGH JOHNSTON, aged 70 years. Captain Hugh Johnston was born April 10th, 1763, in Duanesburgh, Schenectady county, New York. He, together with his father, the Rev. William Johnston, and other connections, came to the Susquehanna Flats (now Sidney Plains,) in 1775. They were the first settlers in that part of the county, and for two years suffered all the hardships and privations of a new country. In June, 1777, they were obliged to leave their homes and flee before an invading foe—Brant, a chief, with one hundred and ten warriors, came and burnt their buildings and slaughtered their cattle.

"The Johnston family fled to Cherry Valley, where they remained until Nov.11th, 1778, when seven hundred Indians and tories came unawares and burnt the village of Cherry Valley, and murdered twenty-eight women and children. The Johnston family narrowly made their escape. They then removed to Schenectady, where they remained until May, 1784, when they returned to the Susquehanna Flats, their former place of residence."

The ravages committed at the Johnston settlement, and flight of its inhabitants to the Mohawk, exceedingly alarmed the frontier settlements, and gave rise to numberless reports of invasion by a savage foe. A meeting of the Harpersfield vigilant committee was convened, and the following letter addressed to the State Council of Safety:—

"Gentlemen,—The late irruptions and hostilities committed at Unadilla by Joseph Brant, with a party of Indians and tories, have so alarmed the well-affected inhabitants of this and the neighboring settlements, who are now the entire frontier of this State, that except your Honors doth afford us immediate protection, we shall be obliged to leave our settlements to save our lives and families; especially as there is not a man on the outside of us, but such as have taken protection of Brant, and many of them have threatened our destruction in a short time, the particular circumstances of which Colonel Harper (who will wait on your Honors,) can give you a full account of, by whom we hope for your protection, in what manner to conduct ourselves."

It was now resolved to make yet another effort to induce the Indians to adhere to their professions of neutrality, and accordingly General Herkimer was despatched down the Susquehanna to hold a second interview with the Oquagos; a messenger had been previously sent forward with a letter to Brant, requesting him to advance up and meet him at Unadilla, which he accordingly did.

It was not until several days after Herkimer had made a halt at the appointed place of meeting, that Brant arrived. He was accompanied, according to his own statement, by five hundred warriors, to within a mile or two below where Herkimer was waiting, to whom he immediately despatched a messenger to inquire the object of his visit. Herkimer replied, that "he merely wished to hold a friendly converse with Captain Brant." The wily Indian, casting his eye around upon the armed force accompanying him, very sarcastically remarked: "And all these men wish to talk with the chief, too?" The preliminaries of a meeting were now arranged about mid-way, between the two encampments, and each commander was accompanied to the designated spot by a body guard of about fifty men, unarmed. A circle was formed with Brant and Herkimer in the centre. Brant was the first to break the silence, by haughtily inquiring—as the messenger had done before—the object of the visit? In reply to a direct question, as to the intentions of the Mohawks touching the difficulty of Great Britain and America, the chief replied that: "The Indians were in concert with the king, as their fathers and grandfathers had been; that the king's belts were yet lodged with them, and they could not falsify their pledge. That General Herkimer and the rest had joined the Boston people against their king. That Boston people were resolute, but the king would humble them. That Mr. Schuyler, or General, or what you please to call him, was very smart on the Indians at German Flats; but was not at the same time able to afford them the smallest article of clothing. That the Indians had formerly made war on the white people all united; and now they were divided, the Indians were not frightened."

At the close of this harangue, Colonel Cox, a brave but impulsive young officer, who had accompanied General Herkimer, remarked, that if that was their determination the matter was ended. The Colonel, it is said, had had difficulty with Brant before the war in relation to some land, and it is highly probable that the same hard feelings still existed between them, as the Indians are the last persons in the world to make or receive amends, when the link of friendship is once severed. The haughty chieftain became highly indignant at the decided expression of Cox, and sarcastically asked, *if he was not the son-in-law of old George Klock?* "Yes," replied the Colonel, equally sarcastic, *"and what is that to you, you d—d Indian?"** At the close of this dialogue, Brant turned and gave the signal to his warriors, who gave a terrific *whoop*, and fled precipitately to their quarters, but immediately reappeared in hostile array, and discharged a volley of musketry into the air, the booming report of which echoed and reëchoed among the surrounding hills. Herkimer now renewed his declaration, that he had come on a peaceful mission; that they had met as friends, and he desired that they should part as such; but as either party were too highly excited to proceed farther with the business, the preliminaries of a meeting the following morning at nine o'clock were arranged, when the parties fell back to their respective encampments for the night.

Herkimer knew enough of Indian character to appreciate to the fullest extent, the exposed situation in which his person would be placed on the morrow's interview, and being too accomplished a soldier to proceed without any precaution to guard against surprise, in the morning, a short time preceding the appointed time for the interview, he called one of his most fearless and trusty men, Joseph Waggoner, and enjoining upon him *secresy*, he informed him that he wished him to select three other persons whom he could rely upon, and that the four armed with rifles, should secrete themselves in a conspicuous position, where, concealed from observation, they could overlook the interview between himself and Brant, which, should the interview not end amicably, as he hoped it would, they were to sacrifice Brant and his three companions, rather than that he, Herkimer, should be detained a prisoner.† But although we think Herkimer was perfectly justifiable in this precaution of safety, nothing transpired to justify his fears, and consequently the order committed to the *ambush*, was not carried into execution. The parties having met according to agreement, Brant was the first to break the silence. Addressing himself

---

* This dialogue is given on the authority of Simms' History of Schoharie County.
† Stone, and I think rather unjustly, stigmatises this act of precaution in Herkimer, but certainly I think the times justified, if not *demanded* it.

to Herkimer, he said: "I have five hundred warriors with me, armed and ready for battle. You are in my power, but as we have been friends and neighbors, I will not take advantage of you." At the close of the interview, General Herkimer presented the chieftain with a number of fat cattle, which had previously arrived from Otsego lake; for which the chief could not refrain from thanking him, as provisions with them were exceedingly scarce.

Campbell, speaking of this expedition, says: "This singular conference was singularly terminated. It was early in July, and the sun shone forth without a cloud to obscure it, and as its rays gilded the tops of the forest-trees, or were reflected from the waters of the Susquehanna, imparted a rich tint to the wild scenery with which they were surrounded. The echo of the war-whoop had scarcely died away before the heavens became black, and a violent storm of rain and hail obliged each party to withdraw and seek the nearest shelter. Men less superstitious than many of the unlettered yeomen, who, leaning upon their arms, were witnesses of the events of this day, could not have failed in after times to have looked back upon them, if not as an omen, at least as an emblem of those dreadful massacres which these Indians and their associates afterward visited upon the inhabitants of this unfortunate frontier."

The unsuccessful termination of the pacific mission of General Herkimer to the Indians, and which ended June 28th, together with their open declaration in favor of the king, as well as their denunciation of the acts of the Boston people, rendered the situation of the well-affected citizens of Harpersfield still more precarious; and accordingly in July, the month immediately following, it was deemed advisable that all except the male able-bodied part of the inhabitants, who were to remain for a time to harvest their crops and protect their homes, should evacuate the settlement. Some went to Cherry Valley, where they had friends and relatives, but the larger portion decamped to Schoharie, distant about twenty miles, at which place three forts were afterward erected and garrisoned. From Schoharie a number of them removed to the places of their former residences in the Eastern States, and among this number were the female portion of the Harper family, who returned to East Windsor, in Connecticut, where they remained until after the war had terminated.

Among those who left about this time and sought safety in the more populous sections of the country, were John More and his family, consisting of a wife and four small children. Although a member of the association, so precipitate had been the retreat of the inhabitants from Harpersfield, that he, living as he did in a remote part of the town, remained uninformed of their retreat, until made aware of the fact by a visit from a friendly Indian chief, with whom he had been familiar before the war, and who with his men had frequently partaken of their hospitality before the commencement of hostilities, while on hunting excursions in that vicinity. To this chief, although he was known to be avowedly in favor of the king's cause, the sturdy Scotchman unfolded his situation: he hardly knew what course to pursue, or what expedient to adopt. He had considerable property, and it seemed almost an impossibility for him to move. The Indian listened attentively to his story, and in reply to the inquiry, if he thought his family would be safe where they were? replied: *"I am thy friend, and so long as I am with you not a hair of your head shall be injured; but I cannot always be with the men myself, and I therefore advise you to go."* This advice was immediately acted upon, and together with his family he made hasty preparations for their journey.

An able address upon the "Pioneer," thus does justice to the memory of this settler. Referring to the incident related above, he says: "The reminiscences of this old gentleman I have oftened listened to with intense pleasure: had they been preserved and recorded, they would fill an interesting chapter in the history of those eventful times. But I fear, as I said at the commencement, that the record of his battles has never been preserved. Aye, he did battle! He contended singly and alone with foes, before whose formidable front many a valiant hero would have quailed. He had settled in Delaware county ere the Revolution broke forth—ere the fierce tempest of political discord, with its mighty thunderings shook the very sphere to its centre, and the mighty surge of war sent its echo to the remotest *log-cabin* in the wilderness. But he lived far back from the haunts of civilization, a hermit in the wilderness! Surely the home of the pioneer will escape the blood-thirsty vengeance of war. Its solitude will form a shield! But hark! In the still, solemn hour of the night, a chieftain warrior leaves his dusky band in the strong embrace of their midnight slumbers, and by a path unknown to any footstep but his own, he winds his way through the dark frowning forest, until he reaches the little clearing of the pioneer; he approaches the log-cabin. His knock arouses the slumberers from their sleep; and in reply to the demand of the settler, 'Who's there?' the well known voice of his Indian friend is recognised. The mission of the chieftain is speedily performed, and lest his presence from his comrades be missed, he quickly disappears in the dark forest and returns to the camp-fire of his dusky mates, by the same blind trail. But he has made revelations which will banish sleep from the eyelids of the occupants of that house that night. He has told the pioneer that, ere to-morrow's sun shall finish his diurnal course, and sink behind the western hills, this home of his will be marked but by a heap of ashes, and that that loving *partner* in the rugged journey of life, and these merry children who cluster around his knee, and himself, did they remain, would yield up to the tomahawk the price of British bribery. That noble chieftain was none other than the renowned Jo Brant. His generosity saved the white man and his family from a cruel death, but their hard-earned home vanished amid the wreathing curls of the crackling flames, as the chief had predicted, on the morrow."

The rude state of the roads at that period, being for many miles nothing but an Indian trail, prevented even the convenience of a sled, and much less a wagon. They collected a few things, the most valuable of which they contrived to tie in packs upon their horses, and the remainder they buried or concealed in the crevices of a ledge of rocks a short distance behind the house.

A passing description of this family, as they appeared when the arrangements for their journey had been completed—the last box of goods had been carried and secreted—the cattle turned loose into the wilderness, and they, too, equipped and just ready to plunge into a forest for many miles unbroken by a single clearing in the direction they were to pursue. Upon one of the horses was Mrs. More and her two youngest children, one of which, a mere babe in her arms, she carried before her, and the other being large enough, was compelled to cling on behind, although, as he frequently assured the writer, when an old man, I used to sit upon his knee, and for long hours listen with breathless attention to the reminiscences of his childhood, upon which he loved to dwell, that several times during that journey he came near being brushed off by projecting limbs overhanging the way; and that just as they had started the second day, having encamped for the night on the identical spot which, after the country became settled, was reserved as a burying-ground, and where, but a year since, a large concourse of relatives and friends consigned his lifeless remains to the silent chamber of the tomb,* and where, crossing the Bear Hill, a short distance below the village of Moresville, he came near losing his life, in the following manner:—In those early times, the streams were guarded by high banks on either side, which were effectually prevented from yielding to the inroads of the current, by the rooty projections of trees, making the crossing exceedingly difficult for a horse with a heavy burden, as the animal would, in most cases, have to step down full two feet into the stream, and to spring with all his force to attain the bank on the opposite side. It was while the horse was performing this last act of springing up, that he slid off behind, and went over backwards into the water, sticking his head beneath the mire in the bed of the stream, which filled eyes, nose, and mouth—the father, who was immediately in front, perceiving him fall, sprang and rescued him from the unpleasant situation, and carried him to the shore, exclaiming, when he found that he was apparently lifeless, and could not speak, with all the feeling peculiar to his native tongue, "Sondy! Sondy, is thee dead?" He soon recovered, however, after a copious effusion of cold water, which effectually removed

---

* Alexander More was the first white male child born in Delaware County. Born January 5th, 1775.

the mud; and not being otherwise injured, they again proceeded on their journey.

After a short digression from the main subject, we will return and complete our description of the family: across the other horse were slung two baskets, one on either side, and which were fastened together by a rope; they were filled with provisions and clothing. The animal was managed by the elder of the boys, aged about eight years—this person is still living, although bowed down by the weight of years—the venerable John T. More, of Moresville. Behind him clung his little brother Robert, who died at Prattsville, Greene county, a few years since, an aged man. The sire of the family accompanied them on foot, with an axe, to lop the bushes and under-brush, which frequently obstructed their progress. After a tedious journey of four days, they arrived at Catskill, where was then only one or two rude habitations. At this place he resided with his family until 1786, when, peace having been established, he removed and settled at Moresville, and was the first white settler within the present limits of the town of Roxbury.

It is impossible at this late day, to ascertain with accuracy the number of inhabitants within the present limits of the county of Delaware, but it is certain that it could not much have exceeded one hundred souls. In the absence of better authority, I shall assume the liberty of distributing them as follows:—

Harpersfield,	50
Pakatakan,	20
Pepacton,	15
Johnston Settlement,	20
Kortright,	10
Stamford,	5
Total population,	120

There were two or three families of *Scotch*, who had settled within the present limits of the town of Kortright, but who, becoming affected with what is commonly called *toryism*, sought an asylum in Canada. Among them was one, who for those times, was considered wealthy, if indeed gold could have constituted wealth in so isolated a spot. I give the following anecdote upon the authority of several early settlers of that town.

Among the early settlers within the limits of the county, were a few Scotch pioneers, who located themselves in the valley of Wrightsbrook, within a short distance of the site of the present village of Bloomville. After the war broke out, the murders and lawless depredations committed upon the lives and property of the frontier settlers, gave them a timely warning. They saw safety only in flight. Although favorably inclined to the British Government, a heavy bounty had been offered for scalps, and the Indians were as likely to sacrifice friend as foe, and they consequently prepared to leave. The arrangements were soon completed, their goods boxed and buried, or otherwise secreted in places recognised by themselves through the agency of *marked trees*, intending to return and possess themselves of their property, as soon as peace should be restored.

The Scotchman, fearing to take much money with him in his flight, pondered long and earnestly in what manner most effectually to conceal his "pile;" at last he bethought himself to bury it—selecting a spot favorable to his purpose, he sank an excavation at the roots of a hollow tree, in which he deposited the wallet, containing, as he asserted upon his dying bed, five hundred guineas, and carefully replaced the dirt, and designated the spot by a marked line of trees, to the junction of *Wright's* brook with the Delaware river.

The party sought a refuge in Canada, and while there the family of this Scotchman became the fated victims of a contagious disease: one by one were consigned to the grave, until he alone remained. At last he was taken ill himself, and when upon his dying bed, he called the physician who had kindly attended him during his illness, and revealed to him the secret of his hidden treasures, and all the attending circumstances.

Immediately after the declaration of peace, the physician, not doubting from the minute statement of the dying man, but that he could easily discover the concealed treasure, made a journey into the county in search of it. He arrived at the place, then and until recently, known by the appellation of "Four Corners," concealing the object of his mission from every one, and accounting for his strange conduct by pretending to be searching for herbs of rare medicinal properties, which a friendly Indian had told him abounded in that region. He readily discovered the line of marked trees—but alas! he had come too late, and the improvements of the Scotchman were now occupied by an enterprising settler, and upon the identical spot where the treasure was concealed years before, was now waving a heavy crop of wheat. The physician now made careful inquiries of the present occupant, who stated "that in ploughing the field over there, (pointing to the same lot,) the ploughshare had struck and smashed in the end of a wooden box, which, upon examination, he found to have once contained clothing, but of which only a few decayed remnants remained; he had also ploughed up a set of harrow-teeth and an iron wedge, and that these were all that he had discovered." After a futile search of nearly a week, the physician was compelled to abandon the enterprise, and return to meet other engagements. Before his departure, however, he made a revelation of the facts to one Gregory, a merchant at the "Corners;" but to this day the treasure remains undiscovered, although many persons have searched for it since that time.

The following account of a successful enterprise of Colonel John Harper, during the Revolution, was often related by the late Rev. Stephen Fenn, for many years a minister at Harpersfield, who had received the information from the colonel's own lips. It was first published in the Annals of Tryon county.

"In the year 1777, he had the command of one of the forts in Schoharie, and of all the frontier stations in this region. He left the fort in Schoharie, and came out through the woods to Harpersfield, in the time of making sugar, and from thence he laid his course for Cherry Valley, to investigate the state of things there; and as he was pursuing a blind kind of Indian trail, and was ascending what are now called Decatur Hills, he cast his eye forward, and saw a company of men coming directly towards him, who had the appearance of Indians. He knew that if he attempted to flee from them they would shoot him down: he resolved to advance right up to them, and make the best shift for himself he could. As soon as he came near enough to discern the white of their eyes, he knew the head man and several others: the head man's name was Peter, an Indian with whom Col. Harper had often traded at Oquago, before the Revolution began. The Col. had his great coat on, so that his regimentals were concealed, and was not recognized: the first word of address on Col. Harper's part was, 'How do you do, brothers?' the reply was, 'Well; how do you do, brother? which way are you bound, brother?' 'On a secret expedition; and which way are you bound, brothers?' 'Down the Susquehanna, to cut off the Johnston settlement.' (Parson Johnston, and a number of Scottish families, had settled down the Susquehanna, at what is now called Sidney Plains, and these were the people whom they were about to destroy.) Says the colonel, 'where do you lodge to- night?' 'At the mouth of Schenevus creek,' was the reply. Then shaking hands with them, he bid them good-speed, and proceeded on his journey.

"He had gone but a little way from them before he took a circuit through the woods, a distance of eight or ten miles, on to the head of Charlotte river, where were a number of men making sugar; ordered them to take their arms, two days' provisions, a canteen of rum, and a rope, and meet him down the Charlotte, at a small clearing called Evan's place, at a certain hour that afternoon; then rode with all speed through the woods to Harpersfield, collected all the men who were there making sugar, and being armed and victualed, with each man his rope, laid his course for Charlotte: when he arrived at Evan's place, he found the Charlotte men there in good spirits; and when he mustered his men there were fifteen, including himself, exactly the same number as there were of the enemy; then the colonel made his men acquainted with his enterprise.

"They marched down the river a little distance, and then bent their course across the hill, to the mouth of Schenevus creek: arriving at the brow of the hill, where they could overlook the valley where the Schenevus flows, they cast their eyes down upon the flat, and discovered the fire around which the enemy lay encamped. 'There they are,' said Col.

Harper. They descended with great stillness, forded the creek, which was breast-high to a man; after advancing a few hundred yards, they took some refreshment, and then prepared for the contest. Daylight was just beginning to appear in the east. When they came to the enemy, they lay in a circle, with their feet toward the fire, in a deep sleep; their arms and all their implements of death, were stacked up according to the Indian custom when they lay themselves down for the night; these the colonel secured by carrying them off a distance, and laying them down; then each man, taking his rope in his hand, placed himself by his fellow: the colonel rapped his man softly, and said, 'Come, it is time for men of business to be on their way;' and then each one sprang upon his man, and after a most severe struggle, they secured the whole number of the enemy.

"After they were all safely bound, and the morning had so far advanced that they could discover objects distinctly, says the Indian Peter—'Ha! Col. Harper! now I know thee; why did I not know thee yesterday?' 'Some policy in war, Peter.' 'Ah, me find 'em so now.' The colonel marched the men to Albany, delivered them up to the commanding officer there; and by this bold and well-executed feat of valor, he saved the whole Scotch settlement from a wanton destruction."

Shortly after the above successful adventure of Col. Harper, McDonald, with a body of two hundred regulars and tories, had concerted a plan for the destruction of the whole Schoharie settlements. This expedition would doubtless have proved successful, had not their intentions been thwarted by the timely exertions of Col. Harper.

The fort at Schoharie was commanded by Col. Vrooman, a good man, doubtless, but illy calculated for the performance of the arduous duties devolving upon him as commandant. They saw the enemy wantonly laying waste the settlement, destroying everything on which they could lay their hands. The garrisons, from their reduced condition, could spare no men from the forts to protect the inhabitants, or secure their crops. *"What shall be done?"* says Col. Harper. *"Oh, nothing at all,"* says Col. Vrooman, *"we be so weak we cannot do anything."* It was however resolved that a messenger must be sent to Albany for succor, and Col. Harper volunteered his services, and mounting a fleet horse was soon far on his way toward the place of destination. After travelling about five miles, he concluded to put up for the night at a tavern, and having finished his supper, he retired to an upper room, fastening the door behind him.

During the night a party of tories arrived at the tavern, whose object it was to secure the person of Harper, whose mission they rightly conjectured, and thinking to thereby prevent the news of the invasion of the settlement by McDonald, reaching Albany. The landlord stoutly protested against their disturbing the repose of his guest, but all to no purpose. They ascended the stairs, and finding the door was fastened, of the room into which Harper had retired, knocked loudly, demanding admission. Harper, who had only lain down, and who had not been asleep, arose, and with pistol in hand opened the door, and presenting himself in an attitude of defence before his unwelcome and intruding guests, demanded of them their business, but at the same time cautioned them against entering his room, as *"the first man who stepped over the threshold should pay for it with his life."* After a little conversation the party withdrew, and did not again molest him.

The next day he rode into Albany, when he informed the commandant of the exposed situation of Harpersfield. A small body of cavalry was granted him, which left Albany the same evening, and continuing to ride all night, at the break of day arrived at the tavern where he had spent the preceding night. They soon came up with the forces of McDonald, who made but a slight stand and then dispersed and fled, the moment the impetuous troopers charged amongst them. This daring and well- executed feat again restored confidence to the drooping spirits of the Schoharie patriots, and redounded double credit upon the head of this brave commander; who thus recapitulates his success in a letter to the Provincial Congress:

"Schoharie, August 28th, 1777.

"GENTLEMEN,—Since we put Captain McDonald and his army to flight, I proceeded with some volunteers to Harpersfield, where we met many who had been forced by McDonald, and some of them much abused. Many others were in the woods, who were volunteers; and as we could not get hands on those who were active in the matter, I gave orders for all to make their appearance when called on, at Schoharie, in order to give satisfaction to the authority for what they had done; and if they do not, that they are to be proclaimed traitors to the United States of America; which they readily agreed to, and further declare that they will use their best endeavors to bring in those who have been the cause of the present disturbance. I would therefore beg of the Honorable Council of Safety that they would appoint proper places to try those persons, as there are many that can witness the proceedings of our enemy, and are not in ability to go abroad.

"From your most obedient humble servant,
"JOHN HARPER, Colonel.

"P.S. The people here are so confused that they do not know how to proceed, I therefore would beg the favor of your honorable body to appoint such men as are strangers in these parts.

"To the Honorable the Council of Safety of Kingston."*

---

* See Journal of Provincial Congress, page 1053.

CHAPTER V

St. Leger Cowley—Contention between himself and a tory—Dispute settled by his wife—Capture of Cowley and Sawyer on the West Branch—Indian sports—Journey of the captives toward Niagara—Murder of their captors—Pursued by the Indians—Miraculous escape—Narrowly escape starvation in the wilderness—Arrival at a frontier settlement in Pennsylvania—Recruit and return to Schoharie—Procure a company of troops to aid in the removal of their families—First grist-mill on the West Branch—Death of Cowley—Indian revenge—Murder of McKee family—Capture of Miss Anne McKee—Compelled to run the gauntlet—Fort Niagara—Retaliatory expedition to the Indian territory—General Sullivan appointed to command—Detachment under Clinton—March down the Susquehanna—Union of Clinton and Sullivan near Tioga Point—Complete annihilation of Indian settlements—Expedition of Sullivan an expedition of Discovery—Minisink an ancient Indian settlement—Massacre of the inhabitants—Battle of the Delaware—Defeat of the inhabitants—List of the killed—Burial services performed in 1820—Statement of Benjamin Whitaker—General outlines of the campaign of 1779.

AMONG the early pioneers who settled on the West Branch of the Delaware river, was St. Leger Cowley, a native of Ireland, who removed from Albany with his family and located himself below the site of the present flourishing village of Bloomville, and not far from the south corner of the town of Kortright. After the commencement of the Revolution the few *whigs* (as those persons who dared to disown the king were called,) living in the valley of the Delaware, became, as it were, isolated from even what historians have termed the frontier of New York. They were few in number, and beyond the reach of any definite tidings of the victories and reverses of the respective armies. The flying reports which reached their ears, were principally those which had been industriously circulated by the tories and Indians, and consequently they scrupled to believe them. And what rendered their situation still more precarious, was the fact that the valley in which they lived, was, during the Revolutionary war, a principal thoroughfare by which warlike parties traversed their way to the Schoharie settlements on missions of plunder and destruction.*

---

* I am indebted to the manuscript kindly furnished me by Asahel Cowley, Esq., a highly respectable citizen, and a descendant of St. Leger, mentioned in the context, for most of the above information. He resides in Stamford, Delaware County.

These expeditions were usually accompanied by tories, who were the more unprincipled of the two, and much more given to plundering from those they knew or even suspected guilty *of the crime called "Democracy,"*[*] and frequently they took upon themselves the responsibility of plunder, unaccompanied by their less savage allies.

One day, when the wife of St. Leger Cowley—a strong, resolute woman, from the "Emerald Isle,"—came into the house, from which she had been absent but a short time, she found a tory blackened, so as to appear as an Indian, contending with her husband about a pair of breeches, which the former had taken from a chest, and was grasping with both hands, while her husband was holding on to another part of the garment with a grasp equally firm. Having learned the cause of the contention, and thinking it a game which could be better played by three persons—even though the third were a woman—she, by a sudden movement, took the "bone of contention" from their hands, and seizing a wooden poker which was standing by the fire-place, threatened to use it on the tory's head, at the same time suiting the gesture to the word in such a manner as to warn him of the necessity of beating a hasty retreat.

Notwithstanding the dangers to which the settlers were exposed, a number of them remained on the Delaware until 1779. In the spring or early part of the summer[†] of that year, Cowley, accompanied by his eldest son, Jonathan, a lad some twelve or thirteen years of age, had been to the house of Isaac Sawyer, another whig, then living a short distance below the present village of Hobart. On their return, having arrived near home, the father walking, and the son riding on horseback, they were surprised and captured by four Schoharie Indians, Ham Henry, Seth Henry, Adam, a sister's son, and Nicholas, also a relative. Immediately after their capture the Indians fastened a military feather (which they had doubtless procured from the hat of a fallen soldier in battle,) to the front of the boy's cap, and sent him on ahead, while they and their prisoner followed. The family of Cowley, who were anxiously looking for his return, seeing the lad approaching alone on horseback with a military ornament so conspicuous, were filled with apprehensions. They were, however, kept but a short time in suspense, for soon the father made his appearance accompanied by his captors.

The Indians offered no kind of violence to any of the family, but amused themselves by shooting their fowls, exclaiming, *"pidgee! pidgee!"* One of them shot at a churn which was standing out of doors partly filled with water, and expressed his gratification by laughing heartily to see the

---

[*] Quoted from the inscription on the tombstone, in the Harpersfield burying-ground, to the memory of Thomas and John Hendry, who sacrificed their lives and property to the common cause of liberty. See more fully the capture of Colonel Harper and his party at Harpersfield, April 8th, 1780.

[†] Simms' History of Schoharie gives the date as "early in the spring," and as I have usually found his statements correct, I think it more than probable this was the time.

water gush out of the hole made by his rifle ball. After a short time spent apparently in high glee, one of their number was left to guard the prisoner, while the others went up the river to capture Sawyer. It was night when the Indians arrived at his house, and being unapprehensive of danger, and unprepared for defence, they took him with little difficulty. The next morning the Indians returned with their captive, when, contrary to the usual custom, they left the women and children, and took only the men away with them as prisoners.

The party encamped the first night a short distance below Delhi; at which place the Indians, assisted by their willing captives, constructed a rude raft, on which they all floated down the Delaware, a distance of about forty miles, to a place well known in those early times as the Cook-house, (now Deposit village,) where they intersected the *Oquago trail*, leading toward the Susquehanna. From the Cook-house they resumed their journey by land to Fort Niagara, the place of their destination.

The prisoners were far from being ignorant of *Indian character*, and to conceal their original design—which was to escape the first favorable opportunity—would intimate by signs as well as they could (they were unable to converse with the Indians in either the Dutch or Indian language,) that they would rather proceed with their captors than return to the settlements they had left; and they avoided conversing together as much as possible, lest it should excite the suspicions of the Indians, one or more of whom were always watching their movements. They had already proceeded eleven days on their journey without seeing a favorable opportunity of making their escape—the last ray of hope seemed to have sped—they had followed the blind *Indian trail*—had traversed hill and dale—crossed large streams, and were already far beyond any white settlement—all the horrors of a long captivity seemed inevitably their fate; the extremely dangerous feat of running the gauntlet, was presented vividly to their imagination, with its long files of hideously painted Indians ranged on either side, through which the life-race lay. Death seemed preferable to such a scene, and they mentally resolved to make one bold effort to escape, or die in the attempt.

On the eventful night of the eleventh day's captivity, the party encamped near Tioga Point. The captives, on such occasions were ordered to make the preparations for building a large fire, (which they ignited in those *matchless days* by the aid of a large tinder-box,) and also to cut and carry to the encampment a supply of fuel for the night. As they had only one axe, which had been taken from Cowley's at the time of the capture, one would cut, while the other carried it to the spot where it was to be used. "While Cowley was cutting and Sawyer waiting for an armful, the latter took from his pocket a newspaper and pretended to be reading its contents to his fellow, instead of which, however, he was proposing a plan for regaining their liberty."—*Simms' History of Schoharie.*

A quarter of venison that had been shot that afternoon was rudely roasted, and eaten without the wholesome seasoning of salt and pepper, when they all laid down to sleep—a prisoner between two Indians; and the latter of whom were soon wrapped in deep slumber. After waiting till near midnight the mutual signal was given, when the two friends cautiously arose. They shook the priming from the guns of their captors, and removed the remaining implements of death beyond the observation of the savages, then returning, Sawyer, with the tomahawk of Ham Henry—who was thought the most desperate of the four—took his station beside its owner, while Cowley with an axe, placed himself beside another sleeping Indian. The fire afforded sufficient light for the captives to make sure of their victims. At a given signal the blows fell fatal upon two—the tomahawk sank deep into the brain of its owner, but unfortunately, Sawyer drew the handle from the weapon, in attempting to free it from the skull of the savage. The first one struck by Cowley was killed, but the blows which sent two to their final reckonings, awoke their fellows, who instantly sprang to their feet. As Seth Henry arose he received a blow, which he partially warded off by raising his arm, but his shoulder was laid open, and he fell back stunned. The fourth, as he arose, received a heavy blow on his back; he was pursued and fled into a swamp near by, where he died. The two men returned to the fire, and were resolving on what course to pursue, when Seth Henry, who had recovered, and feigned himself dead for some time to embrace a favorable opportunity, sprang upon his feet, dashed through the fire, caught up his rifle, levelled and snapped it at his foes, then ran into the forest and disappeared.—*Simms' History of Schoharie.*

The liberated captives were now masters of the bloody field, and once more free; but after such an exciting scene, no sleep came to their eyes during the remainder of the night. Their first precaution was to arm themselves with the implements of their fallen foes. They took each a gun, a tomahawk and a scalping-knife, together with all the remaining ammunition, and thus equipped, they anxiously awaited the approach of day. At last the luminous orb raised his head from behind the eastern hills, and its rays peering through the overhanging branches of the forest trees, revealed to their eyes more fully the reality of the sad spectacle, and gave the signal for the commencement of their march.

They conjectured, and with truth, that the escaped savage would communicate the fearful tidings of the massacre of his comrades to the nearest Indians, and that they would be immediately pursued. Deeming it unsafe, therefore, to follow the same trail they had lately passed over, they boldly struck out into the forest in a south-easternly direction, knowing that sooner or later, that course would lead to the settlements of the whites. They had not proceeded many miles on their journey when the sound of the piercing *"war-whoop"* saluted their ears, and once during that afternoon, from an elevation they descried a company of Indians in the valley below. They encamped at night without food and without any fire, lest its glaring light should betoken to their foes the place of their concealment—they secreted themselves by crawling under the side of a huge *bass-wood* tree, which had been blown down, and covered themselves with leaves, which effectually concealed their persons from observation. They had been in this situation but a short time, when an Indian approached and seated himself on the identical log beneath which they lay concealed, and immediately gave a piercing *"whoop."* The two friends deeming themselves discovered, now gave up all hopes of escape, and prepared to die. Immediately the savage Indians, who had been scouting the woods in different directions, assembled and seated themselves in a row on the log. They were ignorant of the substance of this Indian council, but heard one of the party, who spoke English in broken accents, propose to build a fire against the log and encamp for the night; but shortly after the party left, following the back track, having given up all hopes of finding them in that direction.

The next day they resumed their course, and the same afternoon Sawyer ventured to shoot a buck, a piece of which they immediately roasted to satisfy the urgent demands of hunger; and at last, after several days' fatiguing travel, during which Cowley was at times light-headed, they emerged into a frontier settlement near Minisink, where they found friends, and procured assistance, as soon as sufficiently recovered, to return to Schoharie, where they were received with exclamations of joyful surprise.

From Schoharie, Cowley went to Albany with a letter to Governor Clinton, and obtained a company of forty men, who returned with him to the Delaware, to remove their families to a place of greater security. They removed first to Schoharie, thence to Albany, and afterward crossed the river to Greenbush, where they resided several years. About 1792, he came back to the Delaware near its source, and erected the first gristmill on that stream, about a quarter of a mile below where the Catskill Turnpike crosses the Delaware. He also purchased a saw-mill situated about half a mile below Lake Ulsayantho. In 1794, he removed his family from Greenbush into a house which he had recently erected near his grist-mill, and where he resided till his death, which took place in 1797.*

It is a prominent trait of Indian character, to measure out revenge for wrongs, whether real or imaginary: it is indeed a custom they venerate—a vital part of their religion; and many of the fatal examples on record of Indian barbarity and cruelty are attributable to this same source. And accordingly it is presumed that a party of Indians were sent out to

---

* Simms' History gives the place of Cowley's death, as Albany, which is doubtless ascribable to the inaccuracy of his informant. Sawyer died many years afterward at Williamston, Mass.

revenge the lives of their three brethren who were sacrificed, as the price of Cowley and Sawyer's freedom. Shortly after the families of those men had been removed to Schoharie, a party of Indians came up the Delaware, and proceeding to near Hobart, followed up a small stream, the outlet of Odell's Lake, where they had been informed a whig by the name of McKee was living, but who had that day gone to Schoharie to learn the news and procure some flour for his family.

It was a dark and dismal night when the war-whoop sounded the death-knell of the inhabitants of that peaceful dwelling. The members of the family rushed out of the house to escape, if possible, the certain doom which awaited them should they remain within. As Mrs. McKee rushed from the house with an infant in her arms, and attempted to reach an out-door cellar, she was shot down. The remainder of the family were butchered and thrown into the flames, with the exception of a girl about 16 years of age. She fled to a swamp near by and concealed her person under a log, and while she thought herself secure from all harm, she ventured to raise her head to look toward the burning buildings, when she saw an Indian of large stature approaching her, wielding a firebrand in one hand and a large knife, smeared with blood, in the other. She immediately sprang from her hiding-place, and with outstretched arms approached the hideous savage and threw herself at his feet. That bold act saved her life. She was led back by her captor to the burning buildings, and putting several pairs of stockings on her feet, they then resumed their course to Fort Niagara.

What must have been the agony, think you, reader, of the husband and father, when the next day he returned, to behold his happy home a heap of ruins, beneath which he found the charred and mangled remains of his family. There was at this time a small fort at Harpersfield, garrisoned by only eight or ten men. By their assistance he collected the remains of the dead, and buried them all in one rude box.

Priest, in his narrative of the captivity of Schermerhorn, and while speaking of his running the gauntlet near Fort Niagara, says: "This dreadful race was also run by a Miss Anne McKee, who was taken prisoner in the town of Harpersfield, New York, during the Revolution, by the Mohawk Indians under Brant. She was a young Scotch girl, who, during the journey suffered incredibly from hunger, the want of clothes, and other privations. When she came to Fort Niagara, the squaws insisted that she should run the race, in order that the *pale-faced squaw* might take a blow from the same sex of another nation than her's. It was a grievous sight to see a slender girl, weak from hunger, and worn down with the horrors and privations of a four hundred miles' journey through the woods, by night and day, compelled at the end to run this race of shame and suffering. Her head was bare, and her hair tangled into mats, her feet naked and bleeding from wounds, all her clothes torn to rags during her march—

one would have thought the heart-rendering sight would have moved the savages. She wept not, for all her tears had been shed—she stared around upon the grinning multitude in hopeless amazement and fixed despair, while she glanced mournfully at the fort which lay at the end of the race. The signal was given, which was a yell, when she immediately started off as fast as she could, while the squaws laid on their whips with all their might; thus venting their malice and envy upon the hated white woman. She reached the fort in almost a dying condition, being beaten and cut in the most dreadful manner, as her person had been so much exposed on account of the want of clothing to protect her. She was at length allowed to go to her friends—some Scotch people then living in Canada—and after the war she returned to the States."

The startling massacres that had been perpetrated the year before in the beautiful and peaceful valley of Wyoming and at Cherry Valley, as well as the almost numberless tragedies similar to the one related above—hardly a week passing but the ears of the public were startled by the tale of cruel murder committed upon the peaceful frontier settler—these, and other important considerations, at last induced Congress to send a sufficient army into their territory to at least cripple the movements of the enemy in future, if not to bring them to terms of peace. The command of this expedition was entrusted to Major General Sullivan. More effectually to carry out the designs of Congress, and to prevent any premature attacks, by clearing the country of the numerous parties of savages who were continually prowling in the secure recesses of the forest bordering on the frontiers, ready to spring out when a favorable opportunity presented itself, and surprise and capture their victims, and thereby to restore the faltering confidence of the settlers along the frontiers, it was determined to march in two divisions, and unite in the midst of the Indian territory at Tioga Point.

General Sullivan, who commanded the southern division, marched from the Hudson through Warwarsing, in Ulster County, crossing the Delaware, and following it down to Easton, and from thence, by a tedious route across the mountains, to Wyoming, then a desolate and deserted place. From Wyoming they conveyed their artillery and stores up the Susquehanna in 150 batteaux to Tioga Point, where they disembarked their baggage, and awaited the arrival of the division under Clinton, which did not come up with them until nearly half a month afterwards.

Gen. James Clinton, with the 1st and 3rd New York regiments, passed up the Mohawk to Canajoharie, from which place a detachment of five hundred troops, under the command of Col. Van Schaick, was sent out to destroy some villages of the Onondagas. They took in this expedition 37 prisoners, and nearly as many were killed of the enemy.*

* Annals of Tryon County.

They were obliged to open a road from Canajoharie to Lake Otsego,* a distance of twenty miles, for the conveyance of their baggage, at which place they launched their boats upon the placid waters of that beautiful lake, and passed to its outlet, a distance of nine miles. The outlet of this lake proved a formidable obstacle to the egress of their loaded boats, as it was both too shallow and too narrow to permit them to pass out; but the fertile genius of Clinton was equal to every emergency. He ordered a dam to be thrown across the outlet, and when the surface of the lake had risen about three feet, the dam was broken, and the boats passed down with apparent ease to the deeper waters of the Susquehanna. They joined the main army of Gen. Sullivan at Tioga Point, on the 22d of August. While awaiting the approach of Clinton, Gen. Sullivan had erected a fort, after whom it took its name, "Fort Sullivan."

Our limits, even were it directly our province, will not permit us to follow this army through the entire campaign. The subject has already been the theme of numerous historians,† orators and poets, who have bestowed upon it time and ardent labor—they wrote, too, when at least a *precious few* of the aged veterans of that campaign were yet survivors of its dangers and hardships—but who, now, after a lapse of over seventy years, have all been gathered to that "bourne from which no traveller returns,"—their tongues are lifeless and silent—their voices hushed—and the countenances which would glow with animation when they dwelt upon those scenes, and in imagination,

"Fought their battles o'er again,"

will be seen by us no more for ever. Suffice it to say that this expedition had the desired effect of crippling the future operations of the Six Nations against the Colonies—but it did not entirely silence them, as will be seen from the perusal of the succeeding chapter, although its successful termination went far toward raising the desponding spirits of the whigs, and restoring their drooping confidence in the final success of our arms.

One of the most exposed of the frontier settlements during the campaign of 1779, was Minisink, an ancient settlement on the Delaware River. Count Pulaski had been stationed there with an armed force until the February preceding, when he had been ordered to South Carolina, thus leaving the settlement without any defence. Of this fact the Indians were

---

* The word Otsego is thought to be a compound which conveys the idea of a spot at which the meetings of the Indians are held. There is a small rock near the outlet of the lake called the "Otsego Rock," at which precise point the savages, according to an early tradition of the county, were accustomed to give each other the rendezvous. In confirmation of these traditions, arrow-heads, stone hatchets, and other memorials of Indian usages, were found in great abundance by the first settlers in the vicinity of the village of Cooperstown.—*Chronicles of Cooperstown.*

† For more particular accounts of Sullivan's campaign, see Annals of Tryon County, Simms' History of Schoharie, Stine's Border Wars, Delafield's History of Seneca County, and also an interesting little volume entitled Sullivan's Revolutionary Campaign in Weston, N. Y.

aware, and accordingly Brant, on the 20th of July, made a descent upon it with a large body of Indians and tories.

An interesting and valuable work, entitled the "Pioneers of the Delaware," has afforded us the following interesting account of the attack and massacre of this settlement, and the battle of the Delaware, fought two days afterward.—"This attack was begun before day-light, and so silently and stealthily did the crafty Mohawk chief approach his victims, that several families were cut off before an alarm was made. The first intimation which the community received that the savages were upon them was the discovery that several houses were in flames. Dismay and confusion seized upon those who had escaped the first onslaught. They were altogether unprepared to defend themselves. They were without leaders and scattered over a considerable area, although, it is to be presumed they were not altogether unarmed. The first movement many of them made was to flee to the woods with their wives and children, thus leaving the enemy to plunder them of their property, or destroy it, as they preferred.* A few of the inhabitants gathered into the block- houses, which were not assaulted.

James Swartwout, whose father and brothers were killed the preceding year, as stated in the note, again escaped narrowly. He was in a blacksmith's shop with a negro, when he discovered the Indians close at hand. He at once crept up the chimney of the shop, while the negro remained below, not fearing the savages, and knowing probably that they would not harm him. When the Indians entered they commenced throwing things about the premises and selecting such as they fancied. Finally, one of them went to the bellows and began to blow the fire at a rate which proved very uncomfortable to Swartwout, who was nearly strangled with the smoke and fumes of the burning charcoal, and had great difficulty in retaining his place in the chimney. The Indian became weary of the sport after a little, or was induced by the negro to go at something else. After they had gone off, Swartwout came down from his uncomfortable quarters and escaped.

---

* Brant made more than one descent upon Minisink. On the 13th of October, 1778, he invaded Peeupack, and the neighboring settlements, with about one hundred followers, and murdered several of the settlers. The alarm was given in time for most of the inhabitants to flee to the block-houses, of which there were three; one known as Fort Gumaer, another as Fort Dewitt, and the third as Fort Depuy. All who were caught out of the block-houses were murdered. They were pursued through fields and woods and shot or tomahawked. A young man named Swartwout, attempted to escape by swimming in the Neversink. Just as he gained the opposite side he was shot. Three of his brothers and his father were killed. One of the brothers reached a block-house near by and escaped. In Fort Gumaer there were but nine men, and the commander, whose name was Cuddeback, caused the women to put on men's clothes and parade around the fort with their husbands, sons and brothers, when the Indians first made their appearance and were at such a distance that they could not detect the *ruse*. The natives, in consequence of this stratagem, passed by the block-house at such a distance that the few shots which were fired at them were harmless. Fort Dewitt was not attacked, and the other fort was unoccupied.

Most of the barns in the neighborhood were burnt and the cattle driven off. It is probable that Count Pulaski was stationed there but a few weeks or months at most.

A man named Roolif Cuddeback was pursued some distance into the woods by an Indian, and found it impossible to outstrip his pursuer. When nearly overtaken, he stopped suddenly, and the Indian hurled a tomahawk at him, which hitting a bush, missed its mark. Cuddeback at once grappled with the supple savage, and they had a furious battle with the weapons of nature. Both struggled for a knife which was in the Indian's belt, and which finally fell to the ground. Neither could safely stoop to pick it up, and so they resumed their struggle for life or death in the natural way. Cuddeback was the most athletic of the two; but the savage had besmeared his limbs and body with grease, so that he could slip from Cuddeback's hands whenever the latter laid hold of him. Cuddeback, however, gave the red-skin such a buffeting that, after a while he was glad to beat a retreat. It is said that he never recovered from the rough handling he received from the white man, but died subsequently from the injuries inflicted by Cuddeback. The latter escaped.

Eager, in his history of Orange County, says, that "The savages visited the school- house, and threatened to exterminate one generation of the settlers at a blow. Jeremiah Van Auken was the teacher, and they took him from the house, conveyed him about a half a mile, and then killed him. Some of the boys in the school were cleft with the tomahawk, others fled to the woods for concealment from their bloody assailants, while the little girls stood by the slain body of their teacher, bewildered and horror-struck, not knowing their own fate, whether death or captivity. While they were standing in this pitiful condition, a strong, muscular Indian suddenly came along, and with a brush dashed some black paint across their aprons, bidding them "hold up the mark when they saw an Indian coming, and it would save them;" and with the yell of a savage plunged into the woods and disappeared. This was Brant, and the little daughters of the settlers were safe. The Indians, as they passed along and ran from place to place, saw the black mark, and left the children undisturbed. The happy thought, like a flash of lightning, entered the minds of these little sisters, and suggested that they could use the mark to save their brothers. The scattered boys were quickly assembled, and the girls threw their aprons over the clothes of the boys, and stamped the black impression upon their outer garments. They, in turn, held up the palladium of safety as the Indians passed and repassed; and these children were thus saved from injury and death, to the unexpected joy of their parents."

Col. Stone, in his life of Brant, says:—"No sooner had the fugitives from Minisink arrived at Goshen with the intelligence, than Dr. Tustin, the colonel of the local militia, issued orders to the officers of his command to meet him at Minisink on the following day, with as many volunteers as they could raise. The order was promptly obeyed, and a body of one hundred and forty-nine men, including many of the principal men of the county, met their colonel at the designated rendezvous, at the time appointed. A council of war was held, to determine upon the expediency of a pursuit. Colonel Tustin was himself opposed to the proposition with so feeble a command, and with the certainty, if they overtook the enemy, of being obliged to encounter an officer, combining, with his acknowledged prowess, so much of subtlety as characterized the movements of the Mohawk chief. His force, moreover, was supposed to be greatly superior to theirs in numbers, and to include many tories, as well acquainted with the country as themselves. The colonel therefore preferred waiting for the reinforcements, which would be sure to arrive, the more especially, as the volunteers already with him were but ill provided with arms and ammunition. Others, however, were for immediate pursuit; they affected to hold the Indians in contempt, insisted that they would not fight, and maintained that a re-capture of the plunder they had taken, would be an easy achievement. Town-meeting counsels in the conduct of war, are not always the wisest, as will appear in the sequel. The majority of Tustin's command were evidently determined to pursue the enemy, but their deliberations were cut short by Major Meeker, who mounted his horse, flourished his sword, and vauntingly called out, 'Let the brave men follow me, the cowards may stay behind!" It may readily be supposed that such an appeal to an excited multitude, would decide the question, as it did. The line of march was immediately taken up, and after proceeding seventeen miles the same evening, they encamped for the night. On the morning of the 22nd, they were joined by a small reinforcement under Colonel Hathorn, of the Warwick regiment, who, as the senior of Col. Tustin, took the command. When they had advanced a few miles to Half-way brook, they came upon the Indian encampment of the preceding night, and another council was held there. Colonels Hathorn, Tustin, and others, whose valor was governed by prudence, were opposed to advancing further, as the number of Indian fires and the extent of the ground they had occupied, removed all doubt as to the superiority of their numbers. A scene similar to that which had broken up the former council was acted at this place, and with the same result. The voice of prudence was compelled to yield to that of bravado."

It was the opinion of some of the officers, that the best way to attack the enemy was to fall upon them at night, while they were encamped and asleep. This project was discussed at the council, but was finally abandoned, because it was thought that in the confusion and uncertainty of a night attack, the Americans would be as apt to destroy each other as to kill the Indians.

"Captain Tyler, who had some knowledge of the woods, was sent forward at the head of a small scouting party, to follow the trail of the Indians, and to ascertain, if possible, their movements, since it was evident that they could not be far in advance. The captain had proceeded but a short distance before he fell from the fire of an unseen enemy. This circumstance occasioned considerable alarm, but the volunteers nevertheless pressed eagerly forward, and it was not long before they emerged upon the hills of the Delaware, in full view of that river, upon the eastern bank of which, at the distance of three-fourths of a mile, the Indians were seen deliberately marching in the direction of a fording-place, near the mouth of the Lackawana. This discovery was made at about nine o'clock in the morning. The intention of Brant to cross at the fording-place was evident, and it was afterward ascertained that his booty had already been sent thither in advance.

"The determination was immediately formed by Colonel Hathorn to intercept the enemy at the fording-place, for which purpose instant dispositions were made; but owing to intervening woods and hills, the opposing bodies soon lost sight of each other, and an adroit movement on the part of Brant, gave him an advantage which it was impossible for the Americans to regain. Anticipating the design of Hathorn, the moment the Americans were out of sight Brant wheeled to the right, and by threading a ravine across which Hathorn had passed, threw himself into the rear, by which means he was enabled to select his ground for a battle and form an ambuscade. Disappointed in not finding the enemy, the Americans were brought to a stand, when the enemy disclosed themselves partially in a quarter altogether unexpected."*

The first shot was fired upon an Indian, who, as the Americans came to the bank of the river, was crossing the Delaware with a portion of the booty, and who was mounted on a horse he had stolen in Minisink. He fell upon the neck of the horse, but managed to keep his place in the saddle until he had reached the opposite bank, and joined such of his friends as had crossed before him. It is said that he died from his wounds not long afterward.

The belligerents soon engaged in deadly conflict; when, above the yelling and whooping of the savages, the hurrahs of the whites, and the report of fire-arms, Brant was heard—in a voice which was never forgotten by those who were present—commanding all who were on the opposite side of the river with the plunder, to return. They at once dashed into the Delaware, and soon fell upon the rear of the Americans, who were thus completely surrounded and hemmed in, except about one-third of their number, whom Brant in the early part of the engagement, had contrived to cut off from the main body. The enemy were several times greater in number than the Americans, who were ultimately driven in and confined to about an acre of ground.

"Being short of ammunition, Hathorn's orders, in imitation of those of Putnam, at Bunker's Hill, were strict, that no man should fire until very sure that his powder would not be lost. The battle commenced about

---

* Stone's Life of Brant.

eleven o'clock in the morning, and was maintained until the going down of the sun; both parties fighting after the Indian fashion—every man for himself—and the whole keeping up an irregular fire from behind rocks and trees, as best they could."*

The militia were completely cut off from water, and suffered greatly during the day from thirst. About sunset their ammunition gave out, and the survivors attempted to escape by breaking through the circle of bloodthirsty savages, but were many of them cut down.

"Doctor Tustin was engaged behind a cliff of rocks in dressing the wounded, when the retreat commenced. There were seventeen disabled men under his care at the moment, whose cries for protection and mercy were of the most moving description. The Indians fell upon them, however, and they all, together with the doctor, perished under the tomahawk. Among the slain were many of the first citizens of Goshen; and of the whole number that went forth only thirty returned to tell the melancholy story. Several of the fugitives were shot, while attempting to escape by swimming across the Delaware."

One of the militia who escaped, was so exhausted he could not run far; he followed in the direction his friends had gone, till he could go no farther; he then got out of the path, near which he remained some time. In a little while he saw the Indians, one after another, running in the direction the whites had taken; none of them looked towards the place where he was, until a very powerful Indian discovered him. The Indian's eye no sooner rested upon him, than the white man fired his last shot and fled; the Indian did not follow, and it was supposed he was killed or badly wounded. The name of the white man, we believe, was Cuddeback.

"There was one (Major Wood,) who, during the battle, saved himself by means which Brant said were dishonorable. By some process or other, though not a Freemason, he had acquired a knowledge of the master mason's grand hailing signal of distress; and having been informed that Brant was a member of the brotherhood, he gave the mystic sign. Faithful to his pledge, the chieftain interposed and saved his life. Discovering the imposture afterward, he was very indignant. Still he spared his life, and the prisoner ultimately returned to his friends after a long captivity."

There is another reason given why Wood's life was spared by Brant. Eager says, that the "sign" was accidentally made by him, and that further, "on the evening after the battle, when Brant was about to tie him lest he should escape, Wood remonstrated, and said he was a gentleman, and promised not to escape. They did not tie him, but directed him to lie down between two Indians, who informed him that if he attempted to escape they would tomahawk him. The blanket on which he slept caught fire during the night, and he dared not move from his position to

---

* Stone's Life of Brant.

extinguish it, lest he should experience the reality of the threat, and be tomahawked. At last the fire reached his feet, and he kicked it out. The blanket belonged to Brant, and Wood was harshly treated by him ever after; and when asked the reason of his conduct, he said, 'D__n you, you burnt my blanket.' Wood resided in the county for many years, and was a very respectable citizen.

"But we are of opinion, from all the circumstances of the case, and the character of Wood, that he was not a Freemason; and from the reason of the enmity of Brant, as expressed in the above anecdote, that Wood was innocent of any fraud upon Brant, and that the suggestion was a slander."

Among the killed was Moses Thomas, second son of the gentleman of that name who was murdered by the savages at the block-house in Cochecton. He was slain by a tory named Case Cole.* For forty-three years the bones of these victims of warfare were permitted to bleach upon the bleak hill-side where the battle took place. But one attempt had been made to gather and bury them—*and that was made by the widows of the slain*—of whom there were thirty-three in the Presbyterian congregation of Goshen. They set out for the battleground on horseback; but finding the intervening country too rough and broken for them to proceed, they hired a man to perform the pious duty, who proved unfaithful to the trust, and never returned. In 1820, the remains of these martyrs of freedom were gathered together and deposited in the burying-ground at Goshen, with appropriate ceremonies. A suitable monument was erected over them, and their names inscribed on it in the following manner; -

INSCRIPTIONS ON THE MONUMENT IN THE CHURCH-YARD AT GOSHEN.

NORTH SIDE

Benjamin Tustin, Col.,	Gabriel Winser, Esq.,
Barahil Tyler, Capt.,	Stephen Mead,
Ephraim Mastin, Ens.,	Benjamin Vail, Capt.,
Nathaniel Fish, Adj.,	John Wood, Lieut.,
John Duncan, Capt.,	Nathaniel Terwilliger,
Samuel Jones, Capt.,	John Lockwood,
John Little, Capt.,	Ephraim Ferguson.
Ephraim Middaugh, Ens.,	

---

* Moses Thomas, second, enlisted during the early part of the war, and was with the army some time at West Point and Newburgh. Becoming dissatisfied with his officers, he hired a substitute, and returned to his family, who were in Minisink. When Brant fell upon that point, Thomas volunteered, and was killed, as stated. His widow married a man named Nathan Chapman, and they removed to the valley of Wyoming, where he was murdered by the Indians. Chapman, and a Mr. Jamison, were in company, on horseback, when some savages, who were in ambush, fired upon them. Jamison fell dead, and his companion, who was mortally wounded, clung to his horse until he reached a house, where he soon after died. Mrs. Chapman subsequently married a Mr. Jesse Drake. Her descendants are among the most respectable inhabitants of Cochecton.

WEST SIDE

Roger Townsend,	Joseph Norris,
Samuel Knapp,	Gilbert S. Vail,
James Knapp,	Joel Decker,
Benjamin Bennett,	Abram Shepherd,
William Barker,	Shepherd,
Jacob Dunning,	Nathan Wade,
Jonathan Pierce,	Simon Wait,
James Little,	Talmage.

SOUTH SIDE.

John Carpenter,	Gamaliel Bailey,
David Barney,	Moses Thomas,
Jonathan Haskill,	Eleazer Owens,
Abram Williams,	Adam Embler,
James Morher,	Samuel Little,
Isaac Ward,	Benjamin Dunning,
Baltus Ninpos,	Daniel Reid.

EAST SIDE.

Erected by the Inhabitants of Orange County,
July 22d, 1822.
Sacred to the memory of forty-four of their
Fellow-citizens, who fell at
The Battle of Minisink, July 22d, 1779

The battle of the Delaware was unquestionably one of the hardest fought conflicts during the Revolutionary war; and Brant afterward informed Squire Whitaker,* that when the Americans gave the order to retreat, he had just resolved to give the same order; and had the soldiers retained their position a few moments longer, they would have been left in possession of the field.

Some slight idea of the fruit of this fight may be gathered from the following statement of Benjamin Whitaker, an aged pioneer of this county, who still lives in the valley of the Delaware, two miles below Deposit.

"I had two uncles in the battle of the Delaware, at Cedar Falls. One of them, Benjamin,† was wounded, and becoming sick and faint from loss of blood, he eluded the vigilance of the watchful enemy, and secreted himself in the crevice of an impeding ledge of rocks, where he succeeded in stanching the blood by tow from his cartridge-box, and binding up the wound with a handkerchief, joined eagerly in the fight. The other was

---

* Squire Whitaker was one of the earliest settlers in the western part of the county. He had lost all of his property at the massacre of Wyoming, and barely escaped with his family to Orange County, where he remained until the declaration of peace, when he removed to Delaware County, in 1785.

† Benjamin afterward lived at Deposit.

John, who mingled in the hottest of the fight, and, strange to say, was almost the only person who escaped uninjured, although he received nine bullet-holes through his hat and clothes."

The campaign of 1779 was principally, on the part of the Americans, of a defensive character; this mode of operation being the least expensive—an important consideration in the then crippled state of the finances. The belligerent operations were carried on during the year in three different quarters; the forces of Washington and Clinton in the north; the British troops sent south to subjugate the Carolinas and Georgia; while the marine of England and France were contending fiercely upon the high seas. The tide of war in the north was marked by various reverses to the American arms. The British had captured the forts at Verplanck and Stony Point, which latter place, however, was shortly after gallantly retaken by the brave General Wayne. The infamous Governor Tryon, with six thousand troops, had made a predatory incursion into Connecticut. His course was marked alike by devastation and blood. Fairfield and Norwalk were laid waste, and his forces were about to fall upon New London, which would have shared the same fate, had it not been for the timely check of Clinton, who ordered Tryon to another quarter. These, together with the expedition of General Sullivan, formed the principal features of the foregoing campaign.

CHAPTER VI

Repose of the frontier settlements—Scout under Colonel Alexander Harper—Sent out to Harpersfield—Harper returns to Schoharie—His return to Harpersfield—Capture of the party by Brant—Recognition between Brant and Harper—Death of several of the party—Inscription on the Hendrys' tombstones in the Harpersfield burying-ground—Young Lamb attempts to escape—Is overtaken and captured—Questions put by Brant to Harper—Harper's shrewd reply—Indian Council—Debate in regard to the fate of the prisoners—Party decamp for Niagara—Obtain provisions of a miller on the Delaware—Inhumanity of this man and his daughters to the prisoners—Incidents of the journey—Murder of Mr. Brown—Arrival of the party at Fort Niagara—Harper finds friends—Prisoners run the gauntlet—Expedient of Brant to alleviate their sufferings—Reception of the party at the Fort—Imprisonment in Canada—Return of the survivors of the party to Harpersfield. Punishment afterward inflicted on Beacraft, a tory—Bennett family—Early settlers—Capture of by a party of Indians—Incursion of the Indians into Colchester—Capture of Rose—Interesting incident—Correspondence in relation to the war—Indians capture Beach and family—Encounter a scout below Hobert—John Hagidore wounded—Company of troops pursue the Indians—Overtake and release the captives.

THE expedition of Sullivan into the depths of the Indian territory the preceding year, and the desolation which had marked his course, had had the effect to lull the frontiers into a precarious repose. It was not deemed probable, or even possible, that the Indians could recover from the severe but just retribution that had been inflicted upon them, in order to prosecute an offensive part during the year 1780; but in what manner their hopes were to be realized will, in a measure, appear from the forthcoming chapter.

On the 2d day of April, 1780, a scout, under the command of Captain Alexander Harper, consisting, in all, of fourteen persons, was sent by Col. Peter Vrooman from Schoharie into Harpersfield, for the purpose of making a quantity of maple-sugar, and watching the movements of certain disaffected persons residing in that vicinity.

The names of the scout were Alexander Harper, captain, Freegift* and Isaac Patchin, brothers, James Hendry, and his two sons, Thomas and John, William Lamb, and son, Ezra Thorp, lieutenant, Henry Thorp, Cornelius Teabout, James Stevens, and two others, whose names I have been unable to learn.

---

* Freegift Patchin settled apart at Patchin Hollow, Schoharie County, after whom the place took its name. He was a worthy man, and once represented the county in the State Legislature. He was familiarly known in his latter days as *General* Patchin. He died in 1830.

Shortly after the party had arrived at the place of rendezvous, a block-house* near the present village of Harpersfield Centre, and distant from the Schoharie forts about thirty miles, where they deposited their provisions, a heavy snowstorm came on, during which the snow fell about three feet in addition to what was already on the ground.

After completing the "camp," as it was commonly termed, and seeing the men fairly engaged in the merry business of making sugar at the different bushes, five in number, Harper returned to Schoharie on some business, and did not come back to them till the 8th. Among the early settlers in Harpersville was one Samuel Cloughston, a tory, who resided on lot No. 13, now owned by James Smith, and situated on the road called Smith street. He had purchased the same of Col. John Harper, sometime in 1776, and had continued to harbor the Indians and tories ever since the commencement of hostilities in that quarter; indeed, so noted had this place become, in this respect, that it was universally known as the "tory house," which name it retained for many years after the cessation of the war, and even up to the time it was demolished. The residence of Cloughston lay directly on the road from the camp to Schoharie; and Harper, when he arrived near the house, and to the place where the ancient trail took a sort of circuit, and came back something like an *ox-bow*, in order to avoid observation, as well as to shorten the distance, determined to go straight across, and while in the act of stooping to adjust his snow-shoes, Brant, and two other Indians, came upon him unawares, and took him prisoner. Harper did not discover their approach until they were too near to allow even the slightest possible chance of escape by flight, and he consequently submitted peacefully. As Brant approached Harper, he swung his tomahawk, as if in the act of finishing his victim at a single blow, and when the instrument of death was suspended by his stalwart arm high in the air, Brant exclaimed, as he recognized in the person of his prisoner an old acquaintance: *"Ah! Col. Harper, is it thee? I am sorry to find thee here!"* "Why," said Harper, "are you sorry, Captain Brant?" "Because," he replied, *"I must kill you, although we were schoolmates in youth."* Harper replied, that *"There was no use in killing those who submitted peacefully."* He was accordingly bound, and taken to Cloughston's house, where he found the rest of Brant's forces, amounting in all to forty-three Indians, and seven tories. This was about 8 o'clock in the morning.

In order to make the surprise more complete, and to allow none an opportunity to escape, the enemy were distributed so as to fall upon all parties at once; and so well was the plan of attack concerted, and so silently did they approach, that not even a signal of alarm was given. A company approached the hut where Stevens was engaged, which was on land owned at present by A. B. Wilcox, Esq. Stevens had been up the greater part of

---

* This block-house was erected as soon as 1778; but the precise time I have been unable to learn.

the night boiling sap, but towards morning, his store becoming exhausted, he laid down in an empty storetrough and fell asleep; he was aroused by the voices of the approaching enemy, and was in the act of springing for his gun, which stood in one corner, when an Indian came to the entrance, and perceiving the movement, instantly hurled his tomahawk, which his intended victim dodged, and it struck in a log of the hut behind him. Stevens was an athletic man, and immediately grappled with the savage; the contest lasted but a moment; with almost herculean strength, in an instant he precipitated the Indian head-foremost beneath the boiler, upon the still unextinguished coals: but the fatal tragedy was not yet accomplished. The deed had scarcely been done, when a second tomahawk, hurled with unerring aim, sank deep into his brain; he reeled and fell dead, when the Indians finished the sad picture, by scalping the unfortunate man.

A second party proceeded to the clearing of Thomas Hendry, who, offering some resistance, he, together with his eldest son James, was immediately tomahawked and scalped, while the youngest son, John, who submitted peacefully, was taken prisoner. A small detachment were sent to capture William Lamb and his son, who were at work alone some half a mile distant; they surprised and captured the father, who was in the hut. The son, who had gone to gather some sap, was just returning with two pails—which he carried with the aid of a yoke, a contrivance much used in sugar-making in those early times—when he perceived the Indians, and was at the same moment observed by them: he dropped his pails, and ran down the hill, closely pursued; being lighter, however, the frozen surface of the snow sustained him, while his pursuers broke through. He was apparently gaining on them, when he commenced ascending the opposite hill, which happening to face the east, the snow had become too much softened to sustain him, he soon became exhausted, and was obliged to yield.*

---

* I copied the following inscriptions from the stones in Harpersfield burying-ground:—

"Sacred to the memory of THOMAS and JOHN HENDRY,
who were sacrificed by the Tory party,
April 8th, 1780,
for the crime called Democracy.

"When the British and Tories o'er this land bore the sway,
A less cruel Indian my body did slay.
"THOMAS HENDRY."

On the same stone:—
"When my brother was murdered I was standing by,
But in Quebec prison I was doomed to die.
"JOHN HENDRY."

Another:—
"In memory of MR. JAMES HENDRY,
who was killed by the Indians and Tories, April 8th, 1780,
in the 35th year of his age.

"While British tyranny o'erspread the land,
I was slain by cruel hands."

After some time spent in plundering the different encampments of all articles of value, including the maple-sugar, the different parties reassembled with their prisoners, when Brant approached Harper in a menacing attitude, and fixing his eagle eye upon him, demanded, *"Are there any troops in the forts at Schoharie?"* Harper perceived in a moment, that his reply would procure their instant death or save their lives; for, if he should say "No," which would have been the truth, the Indians would have instantly killed them all, and then proceeded to the settlements at old Schoharie and cut them all off, before assistance could be procured from any quarter; accordingly, he answered: *"There are three hundred continental troops now at the forts, who arrived there about three days since."* The whole of this statement was untrue, yet who will condemn the Captain, or say the circumstances did not justify him.

On hearing this, the countenance of Brant changed from the fierceness of his peculiar look to a milder expression; a council of war was immediately held, and the eleven surviving prisoners were securely pinioned and confined in a pig-pen until morning. A guard of tories was placed over them, among whom was one Beacraft, a blood-thirsty villain: a large fire was built, around which their captors assembled, and held a long and fierce consultation in the Indian dialect, involving the fate of their prisoners.

"While this question was pending," says Patchin in his narrative, "we could see every act through the chinks of the pen, and hear every word, though none of us understood their language but our captain, whose countenance, we could perceive by the light of the fire, from time to time change to the alternate expressions of hope and fear, while the perspiration stood in large drops upon his forehead, from the labor of his mind, although it was a cold night; and added to this, the bloody Beacraft would every now and then console us with the imprecation, *'You will all be in hell before morning.'*"

In the morning the Colonel was again paraded before Brant and his associate chiefs, who informed him that they were suspicious he had lied to them the night before. The Colonel, with an expression indicating scorn, at having his word disbelieved by them, replied: *"That what he had said to them was wholly true, and if they any longer disbelieved the statement, they should go there and see."*

Not a muscle of the brave man's countenance moved with hesitation or apprehension, and his statements—fortunately for himself, his companions, and the inhabitants of the whole Schoharie Valley, where the savages had determined to act over again the sad tragedies which had engraven desolation in characters of blood upon the beautiful, but unprotected valleys of Wyoming and Cherry, a couple of years before— *were believed.*

The rest of the prisoners were now let out of the pen, when Brant addressed them in English, telling them that the destination of the expedition had been to lay waste Schoharie, and that his men were so highly irritated at its failure, that it had been with difficulty that he had saved them from being scalped: that if they would accompany him to Niagara, as prisoners of war, he would deliver them up to the English; but if any of them failed by the way, they must not expect to live, as their scalps were as good to him as their bodies.* The line of march was now taken up. The prisoners were compelled to carry the plunder in packs, upon their backs. About ten or twelve miles from the settlement at Harpersfield, on the Delaware river, was a grist-mill, owned by one Calder,† at which place the Indians made a halt, to obtain some refreshments. They were received and kindly treated by this man; and while he loaded the unhappy prisoners with the most horrible oaths and imprecations, he observed to Capt. Brant, that *"they might better have taken more scalps and fewer prisoners."* The daughter openly urged Brant to kill and scalp his prisoners, stating as a reason that should they ever return, their own lives might be taken by the whigs, but that *dead men told no tales*. At this mill the Indians obtained about three bushels of corn, which was all the whole party had to subsist on, except what they might accidentally fall in with, during their whole journey to Niagara.

I make the following extract from Patchin's narrative:—

"From this mill we travelled directly down the river; we had not, however, gone many miles, when we met a man who was a tory, well known to Brant, by name Samuel Clockstone, who seeing us, the prisoners, was surprised, as he knew us; when Brant related to him his adventure, and how he had been defeated by the account Capt. Harper had given of the troops lately arrived at Schoharie. 'Troops!' said Clockstone: 'there are no troops at that place; you may rely upon it, Capt. Brant; I have heard of none.' In a moment the *snake* eyes of Brant flashed murder, and running to Harper, he said in a voice of unrestrained fury, his hatchet vibrating about his head like the tongue of a viper: 'How came you to lie so to me?' when Harper, turning round to the tory said: 'You know, Mr. Clockstone, I have been there but four days since: you know, since our party was stationed at the head of the river, at the sap-bush, that I have been once to the forts alone, and there were troops, as I have stated; and if Capt. Brant disbelieves it, he does it at his peril.'

---

* It was an act of the English government, allowing the same stipulated sum for scalps as for prisoners, which we see acted as a direct inducement to the Indians to murder and scalp their victims, thereby being more certain of the bounty; as prisoners, during the long journey to Niagara, had frequent opportunities of escape, which more than one party had improved. There is something so odious and disgusting in this act of parliament, that it is hard to reconcile it with their well known pretensions to an enlightened government.

† The date of the erection of this mill I have been unable to learn; but it is certain that it was standing in 1780. Some with whom I have conversed give the owner's name as Rose; but Stephen Hait, Esq., of Stamford, whose father was an old settler, and who has taken pains to investigate the matter, gave me his name as Calder. This mill is said to have stood on lands owned by John B. Thomas, near Bloomville.

"That Harper had been there, as he stated, happened to be true, which the tory also happened to know; when he replied, 'yes, I know it!' All the while, Brant had glared intensely on the countenance of Harper, if possible, to discover some misgiving there, but all was firm and fair; when he again believed him, and resumed his march.

"There was a very aged man, by the name of Brown, who had not gone off with the rest of the families who had fled the country. This miserable old man, with two grandsons, mere lads, were taken by Brant's party, and compelled to go prisoners with us. The day after our meeting with the party, as above noticed, this old man, who was entirely bald from age, became too weary to keep up with the rest, and requested that he might be permitted to return, and alleged as a reason that he was too old to take part in the war, and therefore could do the king's cause no harm.

"At this request, instead of answering him, a halt was made, and the pack was taken from him, when he spoke in a low voice to his grandsons, saying, *I shall see you no more, for they are going to kill me;*' this he knew, being acquainted with the manners of the Indians. He was now taken in the rear of the party and left in the care of an Indian, whose face was painted entirely black, as a token of his office, which was to kill and scalp any of the prisoners who might give out by the way. In a short time the Indian came on again, with the bald scalp of the old man dangling at the end of his gun, hitched in between the ramrod and muzzle. This he often flapped in the boys' faces, on the journey. The place at which this was done, was just on the point of a mountain, not far from where Judge Foot used to live, on the Delaware, below Delhi. There he was left, and doubtless devoured by wild animals; human bones were afterward found on that part of the mountain.

"We pursued our way down the Delaware, till we came to the Cook-House, suffering much night and day from the tightness of the cords with which our arms were bound. From this place we crossed through the wilderness, over hills and mountains, the most distant and dismal to be conceived of, till we came to a place called Oquago, on the Susquehanna river, which had been an Indian settlement before the war. Here they constructed several rafts out of logs, which they fastened together by withs and poles running crosswise, on which, after untying us, we were placed, themselves managing to steer. These soon floated us down as far as the mouth of Chemung river, where we disembarked and were again tied, taking up our line of march for the Genesee country.

"The Indians, we found, were more capable of sustaining fatigue than we were, and easily out-travelled us, which circumstance would have led to the loss of our lives, had not a singular Providence interfered to save us; this was the indisposition of Brant, who, every other day for a considerable time, fell sick, so that the party were compelled to wait for him: this gave us an opportunity to rest ourselves.

"Brant's sickness was an attack of fever and ague, which he checked by the use of a preparation from the rattlesnake. The rattlesnake he caught on the side of a hill facing the south, on which the sun had shone and melted away the snow from the mouth of their dens, when, it appears, one had crawled out, being invited by the warmth. The reader will also observe that now about a fortnight had elapsed since the time of our captivity, so that the season was farther advanced; and, added to this, the snow is sooner melted on the Chemung in Pennsylvania, being farther south by about three degrees, than the head of the Delaware; yet in places, even then, there was snow on the ground, and in the woods it was still deep. Of this snake he made a soup, which operated as a cure to the attack of the ague.

"The reader will remember the three bushels of corn given us at the mill; this they fairly and equally divided among us all, which amounted to two handsful a day; and that none should have more or less than another, while it lasted, the corns were counted as we received them; in this respect Brant was just and kind. This corn we were allowed to boil in their kettles when they had finished theirs: we generally contrived to pound it before we boiled it, as we had found a mortar at a deserted wigwam, left by the Indians the year before, who had been driven away by General Sullivan. While in the neighborhood of what is now called Tioga Point, we but narrowly escaped every man of us being butchered on the spot; a miracle, as it were, saved us. The cause was as follows: At this place, when Brant was on his way down the Chemung, on this same expedition, but a few days before, he had detailed eleven Indians from his company, to pass through the woods from Tioga Point to a place called Minisink. It was known to Brant, that at this place were a few families, where it was supposed several prisoners might be made, or scalps taken, which, at Niagara, would bring them eight dollars apiece. This was the great stimulus by which the Indians, in the Revolution, were incited by *Butler*, the British agent, to perpetrate so many horrid murders upon women, children, and helpless old age, in this region of the country.

"This party made good their way to the Minisink, when, lying concealed in the woods, they managed to get into their possession, one after another, five lusty men, and had brought them as far as to the east side of the Susquehanna, opposite Tioga Point. Here they encamped for the night, intending in the morning to construct a raft, in order to float themselves over the river, as they had done on their way toward the Minisink, a few days before, and so pursue their way up the Chemung, which course was the great thoroughfare of the Indians from the Susquehanna country to that of the Genesee.

"Here, while the eleven Indians lay fast asleep, being greatly fatigued and apprehending no danger, as the prisoners were securely bound, and also sleeping soundly, as the Indians supposed, before they laid themselves down; but as the soul of one man, the prisoners were ever watching some opportunity to escape.

"But this was not possible, even if they could have made their escape, unless they should first have effected the death of the whole party of Indians. This object, therefore, was their constant aim. In the night, by some means unknown, one of the prisoners got loose, doubtless either by gnawing off his cord, or by chafing it in two as he lay on it, or during the day had managed to hitch it as often as he could against the snags of the trees, till it had become fretted and weak in some place, so that at last he got it in two. When this was effected he silently cut the cords of his fellows, the Indians sleeping exceedingly sound; when each man took a hatchet, and in a moment nine of them received their blades to their handles, in their brains; but the sound of the blows, in cutting through the bone of their heads, awaked the other two, who sprung upon their feet as quick as thought, when one of them as they fled, received the blade of a hatchet between his shoulders, which, however, did not kill him, nor prevent his escape, yet he was terribly wounded. These men, who had so heroically made their escape, returned, as was supposed, to their homes, to relate to their families and posterity the perils of that awful night.

"After they had gone, the two Indians returned to the spot where lay their ruthless, but unfortunate companions, fast locked, not only in the sleep of night, but that of death, never more to torment the ear of civilized life with the death-yells of their sepulchral throats. They took the moccasins from the feet of their slaughtered friends, nine pair in number, and then constructed a float of logs on which they crossed the river, and had proceeded a little way up the Chemung, where they had built a hut, and the well Indian was endeavoring to cure his wounded companion.

"When the whooping of the party of Indians to whom we were prisoners struck his ear, he gave the *death-yell*, which rung on the dull air as the scream of a demon, reverberating in dull echoes up and down the stream; at which the whole body made a halt and stood in mute astonishment, not knowing what this could mean, when directly the two Indians made their appearance, exhibiting the nine pair of moccasins, and relating in the Indian tongue—which Harper understood—the death of their companions. In a moment, as if transformed to devils, they threw themselves into a great circle around us, exhibiting the most horrid gestures, gnashing their teeth like a gang of wolves ready to devour, brandishing their tomahawks over us, as so many arrows of death. But here, let it be spoken to the praise of a Divine Providence, at the moment when we had given ourselves up as lost, the very Indian, who was a chief, and had been the only one of the eleven who had escaped unhurt, threw himself into the midst of the ring, and with a shake of his hand gave the signal of silence, when he plead our cause, by simply saying, 'These are not the men who killed our friends, and to take the life of the innocent, in cold blood, *cannot* be right.'

"As it happened, this Indian knew us all, for he had lived about Schoharie before the war, and was known as an inoffensive and kind-hearted native, but when the war came on, had seen fit to join the British Indians: his words had the desired effect, arrested the mind of Brant, and soothed to composure the terrific storm that a moment before had threatened to destroy us.

"Again we resumed our course, bearing the anguish of our sufferings with considerably more patience and fortitude than it is likely we should have done, had not our lives been preserved from a greater calamity, just described. We soon came to Newtown, where we were nearly at the point of starvation, Indians and all, as we had nothing to eat except a handful or two of corn a day; and what the end would have been is not hard to foresee, had not an amazing number of wolf-tracks remaining directed us to the carcass of a dead horse. The poor brute had been left to take care of itself the summer before, by Sullivan, in his march to the Indian country, being unfit for the service of a pack-horse. Here, on the commons of nature—which, during the summer and fall, it is likely, produced an abundance of pasturage, but when winter came on, and rendered it impossible for the poor worn-out animal to take care of itself—death came to its relief. That it had lived until the winter had become severe, was evident, from its not being in the least degree putrescent, but was completely frozen, it having been buried in the snow during the winter.

"The wolves had torn and gnawed the upper side quite away, but not being able to turn the carcass over, it was sound and entire on the under side. This we seized upon, rejoicing as at the finding of hidden treasures; it was instantly cut to pieces, bones, head and hoofs, and equally divided among the whole. Fires were built, at which we roasted and eat, without salt, each his own share, with the highest degree of satisfaction.

"Near this we found the famous *Painted Post*, which is now known over all the continent, to those conversant with the early history of our country; the origin of which was as follows:—'Whether it was in the Revolution, or in the Dunmore battles with the Indians, which commenced in Virginia, or in the French war, I do not know: an Indian chief on this spot had been victorious in battle, killing and taking prisoners to the number of about sixty. This event he celebrated, by causing a tree to be taken from the forest and hewed four-square, painted red, and the number he killed, which was twenty-eight, represented across the post in black paint, without any heads; but those he took prisoners, which was thirty, were represented in black paint, as the others, but with heads on. This post he erected, and thus handed down to posterity an account that here a battle was fought, but by whom, and who the sufferers were, is covered in darkness, except that it was between the whites and Indians.'

"This post will probably continue as long as the country shall remain inhabited, as the citizens heretofore have uniformly replaced it with a new one, exactly like the original, whenever it has become decayed.

"Nothing more of note happened to us till we came to the Genesee river, except a continued state of suffering. We passed along between the Chemung and the heads of the lakes Cayuga and Seneca, leaving the route of Sullivan, and went over the mountains farther north. These mountains, as they were very steep and high, being covered with brush, and our bodies weak and emaciated, were almost insurmountable; but at length we reached the top of the last and the highest, which overlooks immeasurable wilds, the ancient abode of men and nations unknown, whose history is written only in the dust.

"Here we halted to rest, when the tory Beacraft, took it into his head to boast of what he had done in the way of murder, since the war began. He said that he and others had killed some of the inhabitants of Schoharie, and that among them was the family of one Vrooman. These, he said, they soon dispatched, except a boy about fourteen years of age, who fled across the flat, towards the Schoharie river. 'I took after the lad,' said the tory, 'and although he ran like a spirit, I soon overtook him, and putting my hand under his chin, laid him back on my thigh, though he struggled hard, cut his throat, scalped him, and hung the body across the fence.' This made my blood run cold, vengeance boiled through every vein; but we dared not say a word to provoke our enemies, as it would be useless. This man, however, got his due, in a measure, after the war was over, as will be related at the end of this account.

"Another of them, by the name of *Barney Cane*, boasted that he had killed one Major Hopkins, on Dimon's Island, in lake George. A party of pleasure, as he stated, had gone to this island on a sailing excursion, and having spent more time than they were aware of before they were ready to return, concluded to encamp and remain all night, as it was impossible for them to return to the fort. 'From the shore where we lay hid it was easy to watch their motions; and perceiving their defenceless situation, as soon as it was dark we set off for the island, where we found them asleep by their fire, and discharged our guns among them. Several of them were killed, among whom was one woman, who had a sucking child which was not hurt. This we put to the breast of its dead mother, and so we left it. But Major Hopkins was only wounded, his thigh bone being broken; he started from his sleep to a rising posture, when I struck him,' said Barney Cane, 'with the butt of my gun, on the side of his head; he fell over, but caught on one hand; I then knocked him the other way, when he caught with the other hand; a third blow, and I had laid him *dead*. These were all scalped except the infant. In the morning a party from the fort went and brought away the dead, together with one they found alive, although he was scalped, and the babe, which was hanging and sobbing at the bosom of its lifeless mother.'

"Having rested ourselves, and our tantalizing companions having finished the stories of their *infamy*, we descended the mountains towards the Genesee, which we came in sight of the next day about two o'clock. Here we met a small company of natives, who had come to the flats of the Genesee for the purpose of *corn-planting*, as soon as the waters of the river should fall sufficiently to drain the ground of its water. These Indians had with them a very beautiful horse, which Brant directed to be cut in pieces in a moment, and divided equally, without dressing or any such fashionable delay, which was done; no part whatever of the animal being suffered to be lost. There fell to each man of the company a small piece, which we roasted, using the white ashes of our fires as salt, which gave it a delicious relish; this, Brant himself showed us how to do.

"On these flats were found infinite quantities of ground-nuts, a root in form and size about equal to a musket-ball, which, being roasted, became exceedingly mealy and sweet. These, together with our new acquisition of horse-flesh, formed a delicious repast.

"From this place Brant sent a runner to Niagara, a distance of about eighty miles, to inform the garrison of his approach, and of the number of prisoners he had, their name and quality. This was a most humane act of Brant, as by this means he effected the removal of all the Indian warriors in the two camps contiguous to the fort.

"Brant was in possession of a secret respecting Harper, which he had carefully concealed in his own breast during the whole journey, and probably, in the very first instance, when he discovered that Harper was his prisoner, operated, by influencing him, if possible, to save his life. This secret consisted in the knowledge that there was then in the fort a British officer, who had married a *niece* of Harper, Jane More, whose mother was the sister of Captain Harper. This girl, together with her mother and sister, had been captured at the massacre of Cherry Valley, and carried to Niagara. This information was conveyed, by means of the runner, to the husband of Jane More, Captain Powell, who, when the girl was first brought by Butler and his Indians a prisoner to the fort, loved, courted, and honorably married her.

"Now, if Powell wished to save the life of his wife's uncle, he had the opportunity by doing as Brant had suggested,—that was, to send the warriors of both camps down the lake to Nine Mile Landing, with the expectation of meeting Brant there, whose prisoners would be given into their hands, to be dealt with as the genius of their natures and customs might suggest. Accordingly, Powell told his wife that her uncle was among the prisoners of Brant, who had sent him word, and that the warriors *must* be sent away; to whom he gave a quantity of rum, as they thought, to aid in the celebration of their infernal pow-wows, at the Nine Mile Landing, having obtained the consent of his superior, Col. Butler, to do so.

"Brant had concealed, from both his Indians and tories, as well as from the prisoners, that Powell, at the fort, was Harper's relative, or that he had made the above arrangement. The reader may probably wish to know why the warriors in those two camps must be sent away, in order to save the lives of the prisoners. All persons acquainted with Indian customs in time of war, know very well that the unhappy wretch who falls into their hands, at such a time, is compelled to run what is called the gauntlet, between two rows of Indians, composed of warriors, old men, women and children, who, as the prisoner flies between, if possible to reach a certain point assigned, called a council-house or fort, receives, from every one who can reach him, a blow with the fist, club, hatchet, or knife, and even wadding fired into their bodies, so that they generally die with their wounds before they can reach the appointed place, though they struggle with all the violence of hope and despair.

"We had now, on the fourth day after the runner had been sent, arrived within about two miles of Niagara, when the tories began to tell us the danger we were soon to be exposed to, in passing those two Indian encampments, which, till then, we knew nothing of; this difficulty they were careful to describe in the most critical manner, so that every step, although so near our journey's end, when we hoped at last to have our hunger satisfied, was as the steps of the wretch condemned to die. But on coming to the *first* encampment, what was our surprise and joy at finding nothing there capable of injuring us but a few old women and children, who had, indeed, formed themselves as before described. However, one old squaw coming up in a very friendly manner, saluted *me*, by saying, 'poor *shild!* poor *shild!*' when she gave me a blow which, as I was tied, could not be parried, that nearly split my head in two.

"But now the desired fort, although it was to be our prison-house, was seen through the opening woods. I had come to within about five rods of the gateway, still agonizing under the effect of the old squaw's blow, when a young savage, about twelve years old, came running, with a hatchet in his hand, directly up to me, and seizing hold of the *petumb hi*, or cord by which I was tied, twitched me around so that we faced each other, when he gave me a blow exactly between my eyes on the forehead, that nearly dropped me dead, as I was weak and faint. The blood spouted out at a dreadful rate, when a soldier snatched the little demon's hatchet, and flung it into the lake. Whether Brant was rewarded over and above the eight dollars (which was the stipulated price per head) for Harper, or not, I cannot tell; but, as was most natural to suppose, there was, on the part of himself and niece, great joy on so unexpectedly falling in with friends and relations in the midst of enemies; and on the part of Powell, respect and kindness was shown to Harper, on account of the lovely Jane, who had become a talisman of peace between them.

"We had scarcely arrived, when we were brought to the presence of a number of British officers of the crown, who blazed in all the glory of military habiliments; and among them, as a chief, was the bloated, insolent, unprincipled, cruel, infamous *Butler*, whose name will *stink* in the recollections of men to the latest page of American history; because it was him who directed, rewarded, and encouraged the operations of the Indians and tories all along from Canada to the State of Delaware. This man commenced to question us in a very abusive manner, respecting the state of American affairs, and, addressing me in particular, probably because nearer me than any of the rest, asked, whether I did not think that, by and by, his Indians would compel a general surrender of the Yankees? I replied to him in as modest a manner as possible—not feeling in any mood of repartee, as the blood from the wound in my forehead still continued to trickle down my face, covering my vest and bosom with blood—that I did not wish to say any thing about it, nor give offence to any one. But he would not excuse me, still insisting that I should say whether I did not think so; to which I firmly replied—feeling what blood and spirit there were yet in me to rouse a little—that if I *must* answer him, it was to say NO; and that he might as well think to empty the lake of its waters at a bucketful at a time, as to conquer the Yankees in that way. At this he burst out in a violent manner, calling me a *'dam'd rebel!'* for giving him such an insolent answer, and ordered me out of his sight; but here, when ready to sink to the floor, (not from any thing the huge bulk of flesh had said to me, but from hunger, weariness, and the loss of blood,) a noble-hearted officer interposed, saying to Butler: 'The lad is not to blame, as you have compelled him to answer your question, which, no doubt, he has done according to the best of his judgment. Here, poor fellow, take this glass of wine, and drink.' Thus the matter ended. [Here the old General wept at the recollection of so much kindness where he expected none.]

"We were now given over to the care of a woman, Nancy Bundy by name, who had been ordered to prepare us a soup made of proper materials, who was not slow to relieve our distress as far as she dare, as she was also a prisoner. But taking off the belt which I had worn around my body, as the manner of the Indians is, to keep the wind out of the stomach, it appeared that I was ready to disown my own body, had I not been convinced by my other senses that there was no mistake.

"I will just give the reader a short account of this woman, as I received it from herself. She stated, that herself, her husband and two children, were captured at the massacre of Wyoming, by Butler's Indians and tories, and brought to the Genesee country, then entirely inhabited by the natives.

There she had been parted from her husband, the Indians carrying him she knew not whither, but to some other and distant tribe. She had not been long in the possession of the tribe with whom she had been left, after her husband was taken from her, when the Indian who had taken her prisoner addressed her, and was desirous of making her his wife; but she repulsed him, saying very imprudently, 'she had one husband, and it would be unlawful to have more than one.' This seemed to satisfy him, and she saw him no more for a long time; but after awhile he came again and renewed his suit, alleging that now there was no objection to her marrying him, as her husband was dead; 'for,' said the Indian, 'I found where he was, and have killed him.' 'I then told him that if he had killed my husband, he might kill me also, for I would not marry a murderer. When he saw I was resolute, he took and tied me, and brought me to this place and sold me for eight dollars. But where my husband is buried, or whether he is buried at all, or where my children are, I cannot tell;' but whether she even returned to the States again, is beyond my knowledge.

"From this place, after being sold to the British garrison for eight dollars a head, we were sent across the lake to Carlton Island; from this place down to the Cedars: from the Cedars we were transported from place to place, till at length we were permanently lodged in the prison at Chamblee. Here we were put in irons, and remained two years, suffering every thing but death, for want of clothes, food, fire, medicine, exercise, and pure air. At length, from the weight and inconvenience of my irons, I became so weak that I could not rise from the floor, when my fellow sufferer, Thorp, who was not so badly off as myself, used to help me up.

"The physician appointed to have the care of the prisoners, whose name was Pendergrass, paid but very little attention to his charge, seldom visiting us, and never examining closely into our situation; consequently a description of my horrid condition would afflict the reader, on which account I forbear it. At length, however, this physician was removed, and another put in his place, of an entirely contrary character; he was humane, inquisitive, industrious, and skilful. When he came first to that part of the prison where myself and about twenty others were confined, the captain of the fort came with him, when the doctor proceeded one by one to examine us, instead of giving us a general look only, as the other had done. The place where I sat was quite in one corner. I had chosen it because it was the darkest, and served to hide me from observation more than any other part of the room. I had contrived to get into my possession an old rug of some sort, which partly hid my naked limbs; this I kept over my lap, in the best possible manner.

"After a while it became my time to be examined; when he said, 'Well my lad, what is the matter with you?' From shame and fear, lest he should witness the loathsome predicament which I was in, I said, 'nothing sir!' 'Well then,' said he, 'get up.' 'I cannot, sir,' said I. He then took the end of his cane, and putting it under the blanket which was partly over me, and served to hide me from my waist downward, threw it quite from me, when a spectacle of human suffering presented itself, such as he had not expected to see. I had fixed my eyes steadily on his face to see if aught of pity moved his breast, which I knew I could trace in his countenance, if any appeared. He turned pale; a frown gathered on his brow, the curl of his lip denoted wrath; when he turned round to the captain of the fort, whose name was Steel, and looking sternly at him, said, in a voice of thunder, 'You infamous villain! in the name of God, are you murdering people alive *here?* send for your provost-sergeant in a moment, and knock off that *poor fellow's* span-shackles, or I will smash you in a moment!'

"O, this language was balm to my wounds, was oil to my bleeding heart; was the voice of sympathy—of determined mercy and immediate relief. I had a soldier's heart, which shrunk not; a fountain of tears; I had none in the hour of battle, but now they rushed out amain, as if anxious to see the man, who by his goodness, had drawn them from their deep seclusion. An entire change of situation now took place, and our health was soon recovered, which rendered my imprisonment quite tolerable. From this place, after a while, we were sent to Rebel's Island, or Culoctelack, or Cut-throat Island, where we remained a year, when peace was declared. We were now sent to Montreal, thence to Quebec, and there put on board a cartel ship and sent round to Boston, though before we reached that place, we were driven out to sea in a storm and nearly shipwrecked, suffering exceedingly; but at last we arrived at the desired haven, where I once more set foot on my native land, and rejoiced that it was a land of liberty and independence.

"As fast as possible we made the best of our way to old Schoharie, which was our home, after an absence of three years, during which I suffered much, as well as my companions, for the love of my country; which, under the blessing of Heaven, I have enjoyed these many years.

"The reader will recollect *Beacraft*, the tory, who stood sentry over us during the first night of our captivity, in the sap-bush, who boasted he had cut the throat of a boy of the Vrooman family; this man had the audacity to return after the war to old Schoharie, the scene of his villanies. As soon as it was known, a number of persons, properly qualified to judge his case,—having, during their captivity, tasted a little of his ability to distress and tantalize unnecessarily, and remembering his deeds, which he had confessed boastingly on the mountains of Genesee—hastened there, and surrounded the house where he was. Two or three of the number, who were as greatly indebted to his philanthropy as need be, knocked at the door and were bidden to come in, when the redoubtable gentleman arose, respectfully inquiring after their health, and extending his hand: the compliment was returned by a hearty and determined clench of his shoulders, by which he had the opportunity of making progress, without the aid of *hydraulic* or locomotive power, as far as to a very ominous *staddle*, which stood not far off, in a beautiful grove of hickory. There were ten persons in number, who composed this jury, and although it lacked two of the legal quantum, they understood the case equally well, nevertheless; and as five of them happened to be left-handed, and five who could swing the *right* honorable arm full as adroitly, were an assortment of kind and character.

"Beacraft was stripped of the habiliments that covered a skin which shrouded a heart in which dwelt a spirit as bad as the devil's worst, and tied to this smooth staddle—as fair a one as grew in the forest. Ten fine excoriators (gads) were taken from the generous redundancy of the axe-handle tree (hickory,) and given to each of those right and left-handed gentlemen, who after binding the culprit to save him the trouble of running away from said staddle, began, after dividing themselves in due form, so that a circle was formed quite around him, to do as the spirit of the occasion might lead their minds.

"Fifty lashes were declared by them a suitable expiation, to be placed upon the bare back, and in such a manner as strength and the exigency of the case most rigorously demanded. Now, in the hour of judgment, a tenfold apparatus, that had the *pliancy* of examining subjects quite around, endeavoured to awake into life a *conscience* that had died an unnatural death some years before.

"A very commendable care in resuscitating this valuable principle, was taken at the dawn of its opening life, to inculcate what *particular* crime it was that had operated with such deleterious influence; and now, through the smarting medium of what is esteemed a *corrective*, as well as a *coercive*—an attempt was making not only to enliven the *conscience*, but to fix the affrighted *memory* on the horrible points most prominent in his life of depravity.

"Now commenced the work of retribution. The first ten lashes played around him like the fiery serpents of the Great Sahara, hissing horror, when they said: 'Beacraft, it is for being a *tory*; when your country claimed the services of those it had nurtured on its bosom, *you*, like a traitor, stabbed it to the heart, as far as your arm had the power.' The second *ten* lashes came with augmented violence, as if the arrows of vengeance were drinking deep of life's keenest sensations—'Beacraft, it is for aiding in the massacre of those who were your neighbors, the Vrooman family.' A third series of ten lashes at a time, played around him, as the lightnings of some frowning cloud, streaming its direful fury at one selected victim, tearing anew, and entering deep into the quivering flesh—'Beacraft, it is for the murder of that helpless boy, the son of Vrooman, whom you scalped and hung on the fence.'

"A fourth quantum of ten lashes at a time, lapped their doleful history around his infamous body—'Beacraft, it is for taunts, and jeers, and insults, when certain persons, well known to you, were captives among a savage enemy, which marked you as a dastardly wretch, fit only for contempt and torture, such as is *now* bestowed upon your infamous body.' The fifth and last series of lashes, fell as if the keen sword, hot from the armory of an independent and indignant people, had sundered the wretched body, one part to the zenith, the other to the nadir—'Beacraft, it is for coming again to the bosom of that country, upon which you have spit the venom of hate, and thus added insult to injury, never to be forgotten.'"

Here they untied him, with this injunction—to flee the country, and never more return to blast with his presence so pure an atmosphere as that where liberty and independence breathe and triumph—with which it was supposed he complied, as he has never been known in these parts since. He expressed his gratitude that he had been so gently dealt with; acknowledging his conduct to have been worthy of capital punishment.

The capture of the scout under Colonel Harper, was the last incident of note that occurred in Harpersfield during the war; it was at that time completely destroyed by Brant, and at the close of the war hardly a vestige of the former settlement remained.

Isaac Bennet, of Stamford, says his father was in Stamford before the war, and helped survey the township of New Stamford; that he bought a farm in the township, and afterwards finding a piece of land near the Cook-house that suited him better, he exchanged farms. At the latter place there were a few families just commencing a settlement. Daniel Bennet and Abijah, his son, (the residue of the family being in Connecticut,) joined them some time previous to 1780, and were taken prisoners with others, the same spring that the Harpers were, but not by the same party; were taken to Oneida, and there remained for three months. From thence they were taken to Canada, and were absent four years and five months before they returned to Connecticut, their native place. The elder Bennet was a tailor by trade, and he was employed in making clothes for the king's troops; the younger Bennet was a drummer.

In the winter of 1786, this family of Bennets settled in the township, on the lands now owned by widow Blish, on which farm Mr. John More built a saw-mill before the war. This is said to have been the first saw-mill in this section of country; some remains of the mill were in existence in 1780. The first mill built after the war, in this county, was built by a man named Potter, near where the Hobart furnace now stands, some time between 1782 and 1786. Potter sold this mill to a Mr. Warn, and he sold it to Bears & Foote. Potter then built a grist-mill on Betty's Brook, and in consequence of some difficulty with one Mills, an agent of the Kortright patent, Potter moved his mill in the night, down on the west side of the river, (about two miles,) on land now owned by James Wetmore.

During the same season, and shortly after the capture of the Bennets, a party of Indians made an incursion into Colchester, then known by its Indian name of *Papagouck*. The families composing this settlement had for the most part sought safety along the Hudson—a man named Rose, had, however, remained with his family unmolested in this exposed situation, during the whole war. The father of the family, at the time of this incursion was absent on a scouting excursion, which fact doubtless, had it been known to the Indians, would have proved a source of mischief to his family, but as it was, they did no injury, except appropriating whatever they chose, to themselves, without asking leave.

At the time the Indians approached the residence of Mr. Rose, his son William was engaged in constructing a canoe on the bank of the river, a short distance from the house. He was shortly afterwards surprised and taken prisoner, and was informed that he must accompany them to the home of the *Red men* in the west. He protested stoutly against accompanying them, but all in vain. The Indians also took three cows belonging to his father, which they drove before them, together with whatever the house contained which seemed to them valuable. The first night, the Indians with their prisoner, encamped but a short distance from the residence of Mr. Rose, and in the morning one of the cows was found to have strayed for home. Young Rose was sent back after the missing cow alone, but with the injunction, "That if he did not return immediately with the cow, they would return and murder them all, and burn their buildings." The boy related to his mother all that had happened, and showed very little inclination to return to his captors; but knowing how well the Indians were apt to execute their threats, she insisted with heroic fortitude, upon his immediate return into captivity with the missing cow. He accompanied the Indians to Niagara, and after a prolonged captivity of three years, was once more permitted to return to his friends at Colchester, where he spent the remainder of his days: he died many years since. We have been favored with the following correspondence, which, although unconnected with the history of the county, except in a general sense, is, nevertheless, worthy of preservation.

The following are copies of the letters:

"Middle Fort, Schoharie, July 19th, 1780."

"Dear Colonel:—By express just now received, yours of the 17th inst. came—am sorry to understand that the enemy have burnt Germantown, but at the same time am glad to hear that the serjeant's party of your regiment behaved so well as to oppose those *infernal* wretches against that fortification. Last night received information from Colonel Wimple, of Schenectady, that a party of tories were gathering at one Captain Pall's, Beaver-dam, in order to go off and join Butler and Brant at Niagara; accordingly we have dispatched this morning a party in pursuit of them—

just now received information that three of the *tory party are taken* by a detachment of Colonel Wimple's regiment, this morning at three o'clock.

"If anything extraordinary should offer, you may be assured I will communicate it by the first. Scouts are continually kept out in order to guard against surprise. Old Mr. Harper, together with your other good friends, desire to be remembered.

"I am, with great respect, dear sir,
"Your humble servant,
"ISAAC BOGERT.

"To COL. HARPER,
    (Superscribed) "On public service,
      "To COL. JOHN HARPER,
        "Fort Harris."

"Poughkeepsie, 25th August, 1780.

"DEAR COUSIN:—I embrace this opportunity to inform you I am still in high spirits. We shall see New York this fall.

"The second division of the French forces has not arrived, but expected soon. The weather has been so uncommonly hot, that it would have been imprudent to fatigue men in the business of besieging, even were we ready in other respects. The French and Spaniards are masters of the West India seas—have had three engagements with the English this summer in that quarter, in all of which the latter have come off second best; and we hourly expect to hear of Jamaica being attacked by our allies.

"In North Carolina, no less a body than one thousand tories had the other day formed themselves and set off to reinforce their friends in Charleston, when a Colonel Rutherford dispatched four hundred militia to watch their movements; they drawing near them, and perceiving them employed in feeding their horses, fell upon them, killed seventy, took four hundred prisoners and all their baggage, with seven hundred horses; the remainder of the thieves dispersed through the woods. Our *cause gains ground* amazingly among the nations of Europe—Russia, Denmark, Sweden, and the States of Holland, have all agreed to afford England no succor, though pressingly demanded; but on the contrary, have entered into a league of armed neutrality. They have invited England to join, but have yet received no answer. The ostensible object of this league is a free unlimited trade to all the world, even to towns besieged; but the real object is to embarrass Great Britain, and make her sick of the war.

"The aforesaid powers have agreed to fit out immediately, for their mutual defence, fifty-two ships of war, which are to defend their ships from being searched, and support their claim to an equal right to the sea. On the 2nd, 3rd, and 4th of June last, there were the greatest disturbances in London known for one hundred years past. Lord George Gordon, at the head of fifty thousand men, marched through Westminster six men deep, crossed over London bridge, and went to the Parliament house, about 12 o'clock on the 2nd of June, and handled all the members they could get at, who were our enemies, in the roughest manner, tearing off their bags, breaking their coaches, &c. They then went to burning their houses up and down throughout the city; they seized the Archbishop of York and several of the Lords, tore their gowns from their backs, and squeezed them almost to death. The King's Council have offered a reward of £500 for the discovery of the ringleader, but I believe they are afraid to find him out, for Lord George Gordon publicly avowed what he had done, and we hear of no notice having been taken of him; it seems that the mob also demolished several ambassador's houses, who belonged to some of the petty princes who are not our friends. This is a good beginning—may they go on and prosper.

"In Dublin, they have also been at the same work; and in Drogheda, twenty-two miles from Dublin, the English soldiers have killed ten of the inhabitants in the street, upon which the volunteer companies there have put the soldiers in jail, and mount guard at the prison, determined to have them brought to trial and execution.

"All this you may depend on for truth, as it has been intercepted in a ship taken a few days ago, bound from England for New York.

"I have no more to add but my sympathy for the distresses of your suffering county, and hope that you will be able to give us a good account of some of those villains. My best respects to the old gentleman and your brothers.

"I am, dear sir, your friend and servant,

"ROBERT HARPER.

(Superscribed) "To COL. JOHN HARPER, of Tryon county.

"Per favor of Mr. Boone."

For the following particulars, the author is indebted to the History of Schoharie, and the narratives of John L. More and others.

In the latter part of July, Seth Henry, of whom we have spoken in the narrative of the capture of Cowley and Sawyer, succeeded in capturing William Bouck, together with a female slave belonging to him, and her three children, two sons and one daughter. Mr. Bouck was captured about two miles from the upper fort, where he had gone to do some work on his farm. The prisoners were all bound, and started with their captors for Niagara. The first night they encamped on the Delaware river, and were entertained by one Hugh Rose, a Scotchman, who was favorable to the king, and who furnished them with several days' provisions for their journey to Canada.

Shortly after the Indians had left the house of Rose, which was about eight o'clock in the morning, and were pursuing their way down the river, a scout, consisting of Wm. Bouck, jr., son of the prisoner, John Hagidore, Bartholomew C. Vrooman, and Barthlomew Hadigore, who had been sent out from the upper fort to anticipate any hostile movement of the enemy, arrived at the residence of Rose, where they halted. They inquired of this man, "if he had seen any Indians in that vicinity?" He replied, "'Yes, the woods are full of them!" and instead of sending them from, he directed them to take the same route pursued by the Indians. The scout proceeded but a short distance when they overtook the party, who had been made aware of their approach, and had awaited them in ambush. As they approached the eminence on which the enemy were concealed, Bouck saw his father's slave, who waved her bonnet at him in such a manner as to warn him of their danger, and they turned and beat a hasty retreat.

The Indians perceiving the backward movement of their foes, fired, when John Hagidore fell, wounded in the hip, but instantly springing up, followed his companions. The Indians did not see fit to pursue, and the scout returned to the house of Rose, where Hagidore's wound rendering him unable to proceed further, they were obliged to leave him with this tory, assuring him that if their friend was not well cared for, or if harm befel him, his own life should be the forfeit.

But to return to the fort at Schoharie—Bouck not returning as was expected, Captain Hager dispatched a company of twenty men, under the command of Lieutenants Joseph Harper and Ephraim Vrooman, to pursue their captors, and if possible, retake the prisoners. They luckily pursued the same route taken by the Indians, and when near the house of Rose they met the scout on their return to Schoharie, who immediately, however, joined in the pursuit.

After arriving at the place where Hagidore was wounded, they struck the trail of the enemy, which ascended the mountain toward the Little Delaware, which course the Indians had evidently taken to avoid further pursuit. They proceeded cautiously but expeditiously up the mountain, near the summit of which, upon an open plain, they discovered the party, who had halted to refresh and rest themselves. Seth Henry, who was chief, had ascended to the summit, from which point he obtained a view of the country for many miles around, and perceiving no indications of pursuit, had returned to his companions with perfect assurance of safety; but that instant the troops gained a fair sight, and within rifle-shot, he having overlooked them from his elevated position. The first impulse was to discharge a volley of musketry into the midst of the Indians, which was timely prevented by Lieutenant Harper, who remarked the exposed situation of the prisoners. But one of the men, having a fair shot at an Indian, raised his rifle and snapped it, but unfortunately it missed fire. The Indians hearing the click, and that instant, for the first, perceiving that they were pursued, seized their weapons, and leaving their packs and prisoners behind them, fled down the mountain and escaped. They then unbound the prisoners, who were overjoyed at so unexpected a deliverance, and proceeded down the mountain to the house of Rose. At this place a litter was made, and one of the tory's best beds was unceremoniously appropriated to add to the comfort of the suffering man during his journey. On this litter Hagidore was placed, and carried on the shoulders of the men to the upper fort, where, with skilful treatment, he soon recovered.*

---

* John Hagidore, for many years after the war, spent much of his time in Roxbury, and John L. More, my informant, stated that he had frequently hired him to work on his farm, and had heard the above narrative from the hero's own lips. The place where he was shot, he designated as on the flat below Sackrider's.

CHAPTER VII.

Declaration of Peace—Its joyful reception by the Colonists—Early Settlements at Sidney Plains and along the Susquehanna—Inconveniences to which the inhabitants were obliged to submit—Ruins of an ancient Indian Fort—Sidney Plains—First death that occurred in Sidney—Great Famine in 1787—First grist-mill on the Susquehanna—First raft of lumber on the Susquehanna—Geographical boundaries of Sidney—Origin of the name—Ouleout Creek—Indian signification—Original land-owners—First settlements in Franklin—Information derived principally of Joshua Pine, in relation to the early settlers in Walton—Account of a duel fought in Walton—Early settlements and settlers at Deposit, Chehocton, and in the Western part of the county—Dickinson's City—Hunting stories—Indians who remained after the war—Old Abraham—Canope, Ben Shanks and Haycou—Tragical murder of the former and latter.

THE long looked for, and anxiously expected declaration of peace at last resounded among the hills and dales of the American Continent, and never was peace more acceptable to any country or people. The colonies had become prostrated by the extravagances, reverses, and collateral evils of a long and disastrous war, their finances had become crippled and exhausted, their credit abroad dwindled away and lost, with want and starvation staring the masses of the poorer classes in the face. That peace, too, was alike honorable as it was acceptable to the American people. They had boldly asserted their rights, maintained them with fortitude and courage, and their exertions had been ultimately crowned with success—the God of battles had graciously smiled upon down-trodden America, *"for she was free."*

The din of battle is now hushed—hostilities have ceased—the remnants of scattered families again gather together, and prepare anew to seek the homes from which they had been compelled to flee before the tomahawks of the ruthless savages, or the machinations of the more inhuman tories; but to which they now returned with feelings of security. And it shall be our task, in this and the following chapters, to narrate, as far as we have been enabled to glean, the history of the early settlements within the limits of the county.

I have been permitted by the author, to make the following extract from *Johnston's History of the Susquehanna Country*, (a work soon to be published) in relation to the town of Sidney.

Rev. Mr. Johnston, with an Indian guide, first explored the Susquehanna Valley, with the view of making a permanent settlement, in May, 1772. They crossed from the Mohawk to Otsego Lake, where they procured an Indian batteau or canoe, in which they descended the Susquehanna river as far as Oquago, now Windsor. During this voyage, he landed at Sidney Plains, at which place he determined to locate. He then returned to Schenectady, sought out the owners,* and purchased a tract of 600 acres of land, situated at the flats, one mile east of the Unadilla Forks.

Early in the following year, Mr. Johnston moved with his family, consisting of his wife, three sons, and four daughters. This was the first white family that emigrated to the Susquehanna Valley, although others speedily followed them. One can hardly conceive the inconvenience and hardship to which they must have been exposed in this remote situation, being 84 miles from a grist-mill, the nearest being on the Mohawk river, and Doctor White, of Cherry Valley, 56 miles distant, was the nearest physician. His neighbors and associates were the red men of the forest; and at Sidney Plains there was an ancient Indian fort, which, according to the tradition of the aborigines, had been built more than five hundred summers ago; its location was on the plain west of the burying-ground, containing about three acres of land, enclosed by a mound of earth, and the whole surrounded by a ditch, provided with suitable entrances. In the early settlements it was known by the appellation of *Fort Ground*. There were also Indian forts at Oxford and Green, on the Chenango river, whose existence is still preserved also by tradition.

The first death of which we find any account, in the town of Sidney, was that of a young Indian, in the year 1775, who became enamored with a beautiful young squaw of the Mohawk tribe, and who was on a visit to the Susquehanna. The Indian made his proposals of marriage, which met with a formal rejection, the fair object of his love having been previously betrothed to another. Unable to brook so sad a disappointment, the young man proceeded to Johnston Cove, where he obtained a poison, the musquash, or wild parsniproot, of which he took and ate in her presence, and survived but one short hour. He was also the first person entombed in Sidney burying-ground.

The year 1787 will long be remembered as the year of the great famine among the early settlers of the Susquehanna, and it was only through the instrumentality of General David Bates, who succeeded in procuring two boat loads of flour from Northumberland, Pennsylvania, that they were saved from actual starvation.

The first grist-mill on the East Branch of the Delaware was erected

---

* This territory was included in the grants made by the King to sundry proprietors, in 1770.

by Abram Fuller, in the year 1778, near the Unadilla Forks; he was his own mechanic—millwright, carpenter, and blacksmith. Judge Courtney, of Sidney, is a grandson of old Mr. Fuller.

The first raft of lumber that ever descended the Susquehanna, was run by Captain David McMasten and others, to Harrisburg, in Pennsylvania, in the year 1795.

The location of the town of Sidney is in the north-west corner of the county, and its boundaries are thus enumerated: on the north by the Susquehanna, which separates it from Otsego; on the east by Franklin; on the south by Masonville, and on the west by the town of Bainbridge, Chenango county. It was first organized in 1801, and derived its name from Sir Sidney Smith, a British admiral, who had gained much notoriety for his victories at that period. The author of this name was a school teacher, John Mandeville, who was an Englishman by birth, and who at the time resided at Sidney Plains. Masonville was formerly comprised in Sidney, and was not set off into a separate township until 1811.

Sidney comprises an excellent township of well watered and fertile land; on the north it has the winding and beautiful Susquehanna, which, in the Indian dialect signifies *"Crooked River;"* on the east, with its fine mill seats and water privileges, is the Ouleout, which name is also of Indian origin, and said to signify *"rapid waters;"* on the south-east runs Carr's creek, so called in memory of Johnny Carr, a tory, who built a saw-mill upon it at an early period. It has one flourishing village, with a number of fine dwellings, two stores, a hotel, and two churches. The population, according to the census of 1850, was 1,807.

The original land-owners were Alexander Wallace Goldsbury, Banyard, John Mason Livingston, and Lawston. The town has sent six representatives to the State legislature, viz: Sluman Wattles, (1799,) Wm. Dewey, Samuel Rexford, James Hugston, J. M. Betts, Reuben Lewis, and Charles S. Rogers.

The following valuable historical information was first published in a series of articles in the "Weekly Visitor:"—

It may be proper to premise for the information of many of the present generation, that this region was included within the territory of the Five Nations—sometimes called Six Nations—inhabiting the greater part of New York, and a portion of Pennsylvania and Ohio. Their names were Mohawks, Onondagas, Senecas, Oneidas, Cayugas, and Tuscaroras, the sixth, and a small tribe that emigrated from the south, and was admitted into the confederacy, the Onondagas giving them land, and they enjoyed equal privileges with the other tribes. These tribes were also in alliance with others of Canada, Ohio, and elsewhere. There was a small number of Indians, from different places, settled on or about the Susquehanna or Delaware rivers, on lands allotted them by the Six Nations, and living under their immediate direction. The names of some of these were Nanticokes, Conoys, Tutecoes, Saponeys, Delawares, &c., &c.

FIRST WHITE PROPRIETORS OF THE SOIL.

Patents were granted in 1770 for the tract of country, beginning one mile west of the river Susquehanna, and thence to the west ('Mohock') branch of the Delaware, which includes the present town of Franklin, to the following named individuals, viz: Henry White, John De Berniere, Robert and John Leake (or Lake,) Jas. Clark, Chas. Babington, and August Provost.

Several of those grants were of from twenty to forty thousand acres each, and were afterwards surveyed, sub-divided and sold to different proprietors, or divided among the different heirs of the original proprietors, so that when sold to actual settlers, very little of the land was conveyed in the name of the grantees. The line between Franklin and Davenport is the north line of the Henry White tract, and it is upon the same that the village of Delhi is situated. The Leake (or Lake) tract occupies the central part of the town, the junction of the two branches of the Ouleout being nearly equally distant from the north and south lines of the patent, and which are very nearly, if not quite, the north and south lines of the western part of Hamden. Franklin village is situated upon the Clark tract; the Provost, or better known as the Livingston tract, occupying the south and not far from a fourth part of the area of the town. So much for the original land-marks of ownership of the soil of the town. At some future time some further observations may be made as to the manner in which most of the grants were made, and by whom.

FIRST SETTLEMENT.

It is about seventy years since the present town of Franklin was an unbroken wilderness, the undisturbed abode of wild beasts, except as the place of annual resort of the Aborigines in their various fishing, hunting and predatory excursions. At that period, (1785,) and as late as 1790, their wigwams, or cabins, were standing at several places along the Ouleout (Indian name *Oleout*) above and below where the west village of Franklin is situated; but the Anglo-Saxon was upon their track, and it is believed, in the summer of 1785, the first white settler, Mr. Sluman Wattles, (afterwards Justice of the Peace and a Judge of the County Court,) erected a log-cabin upon the farm now owned by Mr. William Taylor, and near where the present dwelling stands.

Perhaps this chapter cannot be concluded more acceptably to the general reader, than by attempting a brief account of the pioneer settler, his family, and the circumstances attending their removal to their 'new' and romantic home, in the—as it was then called—western wilderness.

And here the writer begs leave to digress so far as to state, that, in this, as in most instances of the history of the early settlers, many, very many things are involved in doubt, and often in such uncertainty as to render it extremely difficult to be sure that no injustice is done to individuals, or what is of equal if not greater importance, to history, and that in this as in other instances, *mistakes* may and probably will occur; and while it is hoped every one will overlook any such errors, it is suggested that were individuals aware of the difficulties in the way, they would in their criticisms exercise that charity which is meet in cases where the error is only one of the head and not of the heart.

Mr. Wattles, or Judge, as he was commonly called, was born in 1752, but the place of his birth is unknown. He was of Scotch descent, and died in Sidney, Del. Co., N. Y., in 1837, aged 85 years. He resided in Lebanon, Conn., and that town, or region, was probably his native place—married there and had several children, when with his family, he removed to New Canaan, in N. Y.; from there to a place upon the West Branch of the Delaware, supposed to be at, or near what is now called Bloomville, in Kortright. This was near the close of the Revolutionary war, and the place upon the Delaware where he stopped with his family, had been occupied by several Scotch families, who had made some little improvements, and there were two or three log-houses standing, into one of which Mr. W. moved his family—all being vacant, the former occupants living there during the Revolution, left or were driven away by the Indians and tories. During the two years the family remained there, the youngest daughter, Betsey, and afterwards the wife of Col. William Dewey, of Sidney, was born, (1785,) and it was the impression of Judge W., in his latter years, that she was the first white child born in the now county of Delaware, but in this he was evidently mistaken.

It appears that Mr. Wattles had contracted with one or more proprietors of the lands between the Susquehanna and Delaware to survey the same into small tracts, suitable to be sold for farms to those who might desire to settle upon the same; but whether this was before or after he came to the Delaware is unknown; probably after, and it is supposed that while engaged in this undertaking, he, from some cause, made a selection of the land upon the Ouleout, and upon which he removed his family. Previous to moving his family, he had made some improvements, as putting up a log-house, (near Mr. Taylor's,) the covering, or roof, as well as the under and upper floor of which were composed of elm bark. This is believed to have been in 1785.

THE WATTLES FAMILY, ETC.

The narrative of the Wattles family, and other incidents in the present number, are substantially as received from Col. Dewey and Mr. Sluman Wattles, of Sidney, one of the surviving sons of Judge W.

Col. John and Alexander Harper, after the war, bought of the Indians their right and title to a large tract of land—they sold their contract, or part of it, to a company. This company, consisting it is believed of four partners, Livingston and one or two Harpers, the others not recollected. They petitioned the State for a grant of a patent of land, and obtained it. The patent was granted to Peter Van Brugh, Livingston, and others—known as the L. patent, or better for a long time as the 'Wattle's patent'—the Judge having bought out one of the four proprietors. Judge W. superintended the survey, which was intended to be made into lots of 243 acres each. They then made a division of the lots to each—and it is thought drawn by lottery. The survey and division were then filed in the office of the Secretary of State, and each proprietor had separate deeds made out for each of their lots, called "Patent Deeds," or from the State. According to the contract, the sum of money due to the State, was to be paid at a specified time, or forfeit their grant. They depended upon one of the Harpers to pay this at the time, but it not being paid, Judge W. went to him and told him "he (H.) had ruined him, as he had been at great expense in the survey and otherwise, and he should lose the land." What to do he did not know. Fortunately the Legislature was then sitting in New York city, and thinking it might consider his situation, he went to Gov. Clinton and related the circumstances. The Governor asked him if he had the money due the State, and learning he had, said "he would assist him all he could." They went before the Legislature, or a committee: the Governor stated the situation and business of Judge W., and an act was passed, reinstating them in the contract. This is confirmed by the "patent deeds," bearing date *prior* to the time of the visit of Judge W. to New York.

This is probably the manner in which Judge W. became owner of the farm where he first located, instead of receiving it, as some have believed, as a certain share in consideration for his making the survey. It is also believed to explain the cause and means of his coming to the Ouleout.

It appears that after receiving their title from the State, the Indians were also to receive something more, and after his return from New York they came to get their pay. It is said that they met for the purpose of ratification of the treaty, under a large Elm tree, near Mr. Wm. Taylor's. Judge W. had made arrangements for them—that is, had furnished provisions and rum—at his house. They had a "good time," and what is worthy of note—as showing that even savages in those days, were so well acquainted with the nature and effects of intoxicating liquor, that as they began to feel merry from the effects of the rum, they gave up their knives, &c., to Judge W. to keep, so they should do no harm!! They received their money, or pay, and left—believed to be the "Delaware" tribe.

At the time of removal from the Delaware to the Ouleout, there was only an Indian path, or marked trees to direct their course. They went down the river, thence it is thought, up Planter or Walton Brook, across

Hamden-hill and down West Handsome Brook to where Deacon Bowers resides, and from there across the hill, striking the West Walton road a little distance from the present tannery. In after years the Judge and one of the surviving sons, Sluman, who was then eight or nine years of age, have often pointed out the route, in relating the circumstances. They came on horseback—at least Mrs. W.—and moved goods in those days, by packs upon horses.

It may interest all, and particularly the ladies, to hear how arrangements were made for Mrs. W. and the children—five at that time. First, a bed and such other things as could be put on, were placed upon a horse, and then Mrs. W. got upon the horse and took one child before her and one or two behind her. In this way they started on through the forest. They encamped one night in the woods, arriving upon the Ouleout next day. A brother of Judge W., "Uncle John," came with them, and brought Mrs. Col. Dewey, than an infant, a considerable part of the way in his arms.

Judge W. had two brothers, John and Roger, and two sisters, Sarah and ——. John settled upon the farm lately owned by Mr. Abm. Squires, at the junction of the north and south Ouleout roads. Removed to Steuben county, where he died some twenty years since—had one daughter, who married a man by the name of Goodrich, and lives in Chemung county. Roger, youngest brother, first settled upon East Handsome Brook—went to Genesee, Livingston county, and died there in 1848—had two sons and four daughters—"a very worthy family." Sarah, married Daniel Bissell, of Unadilla, and died there—was the mother of a large family. The other sister, Caroline, (?) married Judah Bartlett, and had two children, Sluman (Deacon Bartlett) and Caroline.

The following are the names of the children of Judge W., viz: Caroline, Sluman, John, Simon, Sally, Betsey, Chandler and Nathaniel, (elder,)—of all these, Sluman and Nathaniel alone survive—both reside in Sidney.

Sluman settled in Franklin, and it is believed once resided where Mr. Abner Loveland now lives. A large willow tree standing in the street near the house, and from which the limbs have been cut within a few years past, grew from a cane which he walked home with from Philadelphia, after going "down the river" upon a raft in the spring, and stuck into the ground after his return! When a small boy, he used to be sent on horseback to Harpersfield, if not to Schoharie, "to mill" with grain and for provisions. Wolves were numerous, and used to render night hideous and often frightful, by their howling, especially to the lone residents of the forest, and those so unfortunate as to be obliged to encamp, or remain in the woods at night, as was no uncommon occurrence when upon long journeys; it being impossible to advance or recede without danger of losing the way, owing to the slight trail or paths.

Like his father, his life has been marked by vicissitudes of fortune, and notwithstanding he has attained to nearly fourscore years, and his head has already blossomed, yea, that he is fast ripening for the grave, neither these nor the condition of infirm health from the ravages of a wasting and painful disease, can conceal the fact that in his organization he has been a noble specimen of a man—one who with only ordinary advantages of education would be a leader in society, and leave his impress upon the age in which he lived.

The first wife of Judge Wattles was a native of Lebanon, Connecticut; her maiden name was McCall. She was the cousin of Ephraim McCall, the father of the present deacons, Ira and Elihu. Little is known of her, further than that she faithfully shared the toils and privations of her husband, and such burdens as would necessarily fall upon the mother of a large family under such circumstances, and who succeeded in giving such a direction to the minds of her children as to render them an honour to their parents, an ornament to society, and a blessing to the world. The fruits of her labors alone are conclusive evidence that she must have been at least, in character and life, a devoted and christian mother, whose works still "rise up to call her blessed."

A few incidents in her life have been preserved. After the removal of the family to their home upon the Ouleout, it was about six months before she again saw the face of a white woman. At that time a family was moving past, and she went out to see them, "so as to again see a white woman." She used often to relate the circumstance in after years.

Previous mention has been made of the visit and business of Judge W. to New York. Whether this was the first year after he came, is uncertain; but it was very soon, as he found it very difficult for him to leave, as he had no one to do any thing in his absence but his son Sluman, then quite a small boy. He however made the best provision for his family that he could, and left for New York, expecting to be gone but a short time: this was in December. While there he took the small-pox, and did not recover from it and complete his business, so as to return to his family, until about the first of May following.

About the year 1800, Judge W. sold his farm to Aaron Dewey, Esq., of Westfield, Mass., with the view of "going west," and removed his family some two miles above Unadilla, until prepared to go. While there, Mrs. W. took the small-pox, as did all of her family except her husband. She and her son, Chandler, died with it in 1802. Her age was 52. To prevent contagion, she was buried at night in a lone place near where she died, and without any monument to mark the place of her rest—which to this day remains unknown. Subsequently Judge W. married again, and (what is quite unusual for a man of his age who had become reduced in his property,) he acquired a handsome competency before his death. His remains were deposited in the grave-yard near where he died, and a respectable marble tombstone has been erected to his memory.

For a length of time before the organization of the town of Franklin, Judge W. was one, if not the only acting justice of the peace, in this portion of the then town of Harpersfield; and at the first town meeting ordered by the legislature "to be held at the house of Sluman Wattles," in April, 1793, for the organization of the town of Franklin, he was elected Supervisor, and was often chosen to that and other offices of trust in after years.

After the organization of the county of Delaware in 1797, he also held the office of county judge.

During the active period of a long life, though much engaged in public and private business, his integrity was seldom called in question; and his public duties requiring so much of his time and attention, that he could hardly be expected to amass property except by unfair means, and his failing to do so, and having been at times in reduced circumstances, a fair inference is, that in his day there may have been such a thing as an individual being *too honest to be rich!*

For a long period he was the local agent of different proprietors of wild lands in this region, and no doubt his sympathy for, and the lenity of his disposition towards actual settlers upon the same, who were commonly poor, may have been, and was one, if not the chief cause of the serious pecuniary embarrassments and losses which he afterwards suffered.

As the pioneer settler, and one who for so long a time occupied a conspicuous position in the public business and political affairs of this town and region, the life and character of Sluman Wattles are deserving the careful attention of every resident of the town—his own and the early history of our town being most deeply and intimately interwoven.

He was in many respects a remarkable man—kind-hearted and benevolent—a popular man—an ingenious man—emphatically a man for the times—a genuine specimen of a backwoodsman, or one who in case of necessity could turn his head and hands to almost anything—from the business of a cobbler (which an old resident has informed the writer "he took up himself, being a very ingenious man,") or when in his seat upon the judge's bench—in all stations, at all times and in all places, he was "at home"—in action believing that

> "Honor and shame from no condition rise,
> Act well your part, there all the honour lies."

For the following information the author is indebted to Joshua Pine, and others, of Walton:

In the year 1784, Platt Townsend, a surgeon in the army of the Revolution, contracted with Mr. Walton, the owner of a large tract of land, granted by letters-patent in 1770. The country had been recently explored and the boundaries fixed, extending from the Cooquago, or West Branch of the Delaware river, to near the Susquehanna, and containing several thousand acres. Those persons who had been sent out with the surveyors to spy out and examine the land, had returned with a most favorable report. They stated that the flats or bottom lands, where now stands the village of Walton, were, they should judge, about four miles wide and comparatively free from timber of heavy growth, and indeed nothing, excepting now and then perhaps a thorn-bush; also, that they thought it would be dangerous to build within at least two miles of the river, on account of the annual inundations of its banks, similar, indeed, to the far-famed inundations of the Nile.

Based upon these high-colored descriptions, given of this seemingly *El Dorado* of the Delaware, a river supposed at least to be navigable for sloops, an effort was made, which proved partially successful, to organize a company to emigrate and form a colony or settlement upon the patent. Those who had property, converted it into money as fast as they could, even though at a sacrifice, being desirous of being among the first that moved, in order to secure a choice location upon the patent, while others, more prudent perhaps, chose to send on persons to make a more careful examination, the result of which was that out of a company of about thirty persons, only four or five families concluded to remove; these had all suffered by the war, and were consequently peculiarly calculated to become the hardy pioneers of a new soil, having become accustomed to hardships and privations during that ordeal that "tried men's souls."

They were principally natives of Long Island, but some of them had resided in Westchester county previous to the Revolution, during which they had been driven from place to place; but at the ratification of the treaty of peace with Great Britain, they returned and gathered up the fragments of their fortunes, and assembled the scattered members of their families, and many of them houseless and homeless, prepared to emigrate to new sections of the country.

We shall not, in this place, attempt to follow the miniature colony through all their preliminary arrangements, however replete they may be with interest to the reader, or dwell upon their varied hopes and fears. The parting of friends, and the final adieus are exchanged—they arrive in New York, and take passage on board of an Esopus sloop, which weighed anchor from the foot of Peck Slip, and were soon, with a favorable wind, rapidly making sail up the Hudson.

They left New York about the first of March, 1785, rounded the battery just as the luminous orb of day was sinking behind the western hills; the last glimpse they caught of the great metropolis, as it gradually receded from their view, was in the soft twilight that preceded the darkness of night, and they all retired to commune with their own thoughts. With the indulgence of the reader. we will glance for a moment into the cabin to which the party repaired, and indulge in an impertinent glimpse at those brave men, the *"avant couriers"* of the future prosperity of a large section of Delaware county.

On the right hand bench sat Doctor Townsend, apparently buried in a deep reverie, leaning slightly forward, with a neatly-wrought cane in his hand, which he held suspended, gently tapping the floor, as if to keep time with his wandering thoughts. His looks bespoke an active, an energetic business man, which he was, and just in the meridian of life; he was accompanied by one of his sons, Isaac, the other, William, having previously gone up to Poughkeepsie to collect some money, and was to rejoin them at Marbletown. Opposite him sat Joshua Pine, whose care-worn countenance would have indicated him as the patriarch of the little party: he had been Captain of a Company of Guides in the American army, and had discharged his arduous duties with honor and courage; his family consisted of his wife and two daughters, Hannah and Deborah. Robert North, wife, and infant son, Benjamin; William Furman, wife and two children, twenty-one souls in all, composed the party. They were safely landed at Swart's landing, or Kingston point, and going ashore, took refuge in an old dilapidated warehouse, without windows or fire to shelter them from cold and rain. They proceeded to Marbletown, where they procured a home for their wives and children; while the men went forward to grapple with the forest and prepare a place for their reception, and the land for planting corn. This journey was performed in March, and part of the way on snow-shoes, amidst many privations and difficulties.

At Pepacton they procured a guide by the name of Joseph White, and by whose aid they marked a road over the Colchester mountain, very near where the present road is laid; this road they afterward cut out and succeeded in getting their wagons across. From the overhanging summit of these mountains they caught the first view of the promised land. On the north and west side it appeared to be one dense mass of pines of gigantic growth, and as they descended the mountain and wound down the valley, grove after grove of these huge trees opened to their view, which drew forth from the party many an exclamation of wonder and amazement. At the base of Pine-hill, and near where now stands the beautiful mansion of White Griswold, Esq., they found and immediately took possession of a small hut, in which they deposited their provisions and goods, and made themselves as comfortable as the circumstances would admit of, and far happier than they had been since they left New York. This hut had been built the year before by some men from Neversink, who had come up to cut timber for masts and spars; they had cut over about one acre, on what is now familiarly known as Pine-hill, slid the timber into the river and formed it into rafts, without even the assistance of a team. But little of the lumber, however, ever reached the market—as the rafts, not being suitably constructed, were stove to pieces and lodged along the banks of the Delaware far below, and one large spar lay where it had lodged on an island, about nine miles below Walton, from which fact raftsmen gave it the appellation of Long Mast Island, which name it retains to the present day.

After having spent the summer in making the necessary arrangements for their families, they returned in the latter part of autumn to conduct their families to their new homes.

The second journey of our pioneer settlers with their families and substance, could it all be written with each night's encampment, and incidents by the way, would form an interesting page in this history; but we can only note a few particulars. On leaving Marbletown they followed up the Esopus creek to Shandaken, where they made a short halt to cut out a wagon-road over Pine-hill. This accomplished, the young men went on in advance, marking and mending the road down the East Branch to Pepacton. At this place canoes were procured to transport their goods and part of the company down to the forks of the Delaware, and up the West Branch to the place of settlement. The remainder of the party opened a road over Colchester mountain, and brought over the wagons and horses, and pitched their tents at the foot of Pine-hill, in full view of the river. The Norths and Furmans lived in their tents till September.

Mrs. Robert North, who lived to a good old age, often spoke of this journey as not only very interesting in itself, but by way of rebuking the pride of the present generation. She said she came all the way from Marbletown on horseback, with her bed and all her furniture lashed on behind her, and her son Benjamin in her arms before her. She often boasted that she was the first woman that ever made a foot-print on the soil of Walton. It is seventy years ago this month of June, that these five families commenced the settlement; they had penetrated the wilderness about eight miles, and there were only a few scattered families within the circle of that distance, and of these none could give them aid. For flour and meal, the nearest places they could be procured was at Mohawk, Cherry Valley, Schoharie, and Marbletown, and all except the latter conveyed on horseback over Indian trails. Boards and plank, for building, were made by splitting free rifted pine, and smoothing them with the axe and knife. For the want of nails, the gimlet and wooden pegs were used, but industry, courage, and perseverance overcame all obstacles, and the colony sustained themselves, and were soon prepared to aid those who followed after.

Among those who came before 1790, with their families, we may mention Alverson, from Nova Scotia; the Goslins, Storckten's relatives of the Norths from Long Island, who settled over the river on the Hardenburgh patent, then Ulster county; next Beers, Bradley, and Wakeman, followed on down the river on the same patent; Goodrich, Johnson, Hyde, Eells, Seymour and others, who settled on the Provost or Livingston patent; accessions were annually made to the colony, chiefly from Connecticut. Nor must we omit to mention the inducement offered by Mr. Walton to the first settlers, for growth and increase of the colony. A lot of land was offered for the first-born male child, on condition that he should be named William Walton. The prize was won by Mrs. Robert North, but she had set her heart upon calling him Samuel, and in those days a lot of land could not alter a woman's wish. To pursue the history of Samuel: he was educated in Albany, and was elected clerk of the Assembly, in which capacity he acquitted himself with great efficiency, and we believe he was reëlected under Governor Lewis; he soon after died of consumption.

We have no certain dates by which to mark the exact progress of improvement made by the first settlers. Saw-mills were erected at a very early day, and the manufacture of pine lumber for the Philadelphia market, became the main business by which the inhabitants obtained their support and maintained credit abroad, while the raising of flax and manufacture of linen formed the chief occupation of the women. It is said to have been quite common to take the spinning-wheel with them on making an afternoon visit; and the amount of linen made by some of them seems almost incredible.

Fish and game where plenty. Shad were, if reports were true, near Pine-hill, in quite large numbers; and trout, those delicious fish, the river is said to have been full of them—we being a regular disciple of Isaac Walton, it fairly makes our mouth water to think of them; the women would go out with a pole and line, and in a few minutes catch enough for tea or breakfast; and to use their own expression, some of them would make a pan-full. Those were indeed the days of *women's rights*, when they were allowed to catch fish and manufacture their own clothes; and we should like to be transported back to those good old times, were it only for a day or two, just to breakfast on those delicious trout, dine on samp-porridge, and sup on choice bits of dried elk-meat. Of wild animal, panthers, bears, and wolves, elk and deer, were plenty. Of beaver, otter, and marten, there were a few left, and they gave occasion for a few Indians to linger about the Delaware for the purpose of trapping. Thirteen elk were seen one day fording the river, near the village of Walton, and as they were all adorned with horns five or six feet long, we may well suppose it was a sight worth seeing.

The first grist-mill in the town of Walton was built in 1793, by Captain Samuel Johnson and Michael Goodrich; its location was near or on the site of the mill at present owned by Abram Silliman, of that town. The millstones for this mill, (said to have been the first imported into the county,) were brought from Kingston on the snow, as far as Benjamin Barlow's, in Stamford, from which place to Walton there was then no road, and they were compelled to leave the stones until the river opened in the spring, when the stones were lifted upon two canoes, which were placed side by side and lashed firmly together. In this manner they were floated to within two miles of their destination. This mill, as stated above, was erected in 1793, and a year or two afterward, Daniel Robison built another mill at the place at present occupied by Moses Wakeman, in the *"Den."*

Robert North built the first frame house erected in the town-of Walton; the boards and timber (there being no saw-mill in the town,) were floated down the river on a raft, from Paine's mill at Hobart.

The first wedding which occurred in the town, took place in 1790; the parties were Bartram Olmstead and Savory Goodrich, daughter of Michael Goodrich, spoken of above. The ceremony was performed by Dr. Townsend*

The following anecdote was related by several early settlers of that time:—

A man by the name of Burroughs, residing somewhere in the vicinity of Walton, had been out upon a hunting excursion, and returned with a quarter of venison, which he hung in an unfinished apartment of the house. In the night Mrs. Burroughs, who happened to be left alone, her husband being absent on business, was aroused by a strange noise in that part of the house in which the venison was hanging; she arose and proceeded cautiously to open the door which led to the apartment, when she perceived the dim outlines of some animal, in the act of devouring the saddle of venison. With a coolness worthy of eulogy among the other sex, she stepped back, and taking her husband's rifle, with deliberate aim she put a ball through the animal, which proved fatal. In the morning she examined her prize, and found it to be a panther of huge dimensions.

The manuscript of the following amusing anecdote was kindly furnished by White Griswold, Esq., an aged and highly respected citizen of Walton. It was, so far as I have been enabled to learn, the only adventure in duelling to be recorded in the annals of the county, which I trust will prove a sufficient apology for its insertion. He says:

"The principal hero of the following narrative was Benjamin Tanner, teacher of a district school, two and a half miles from the village of Walton, about fifty years since. Tanner is described by those who knew him, as in bodily shape exceedingly tall, lank, and sharp-featured, and of a very jealous and excitable disposition. He was, indeed, one of those peculiar characters that idle and designing persons love to annoy and play tricks upon. Being in the village one day, he fell in with a number of his acquaintances, who, as the sequel illustrates, were notorious alike for their shrewd tricks and meddlesome dispositions. While in their com-

---

* The following is a list of the Supervisors of Walton since its erection, and the date of their first election:—Robert North, (1797;) David St. John, (1805;) John Eells, (1809;) Gabriel North, (1811;) Isaac Ogden, (1813;) Bennet Beardsley, (1815;) William Townsend, (1823;) Thomas Merwin, (1827;) Alan Mead, (1829;) Samuel Eells, (1832;) Peter Gardiner, (1836;) John Townsend, (1839;) Abraham Ogden, (1843;) John Mead, (1844;) David More, (1845;) Gabriel G. Mead, (1848.)

pany, Tanner expressed a desire to join the masons, which movement was at that time exceedingly popular. The persons to whom he addressed himself were all freemasons, (of which he was aware,) and had a lodge in the same district in which he was teaching. This lodge was then in a flourishing condition, a majority of its members being amongst the most respectable citizens of that vicinity.

"The idea flashed upon the minds of the party that they might enjoy some fun at the schoolmaster's expense; he was accordingly informed that a branch of the lodge existed in the village, and that a meeting should be called that evening to initiate him.

"Frederick Hocty, one of the leading actors of the farce, was at the time a merchant of the village, and had a room in his house, in which himself and companions frequently met to carry on their frolics. These meetings had already come into notoriety, as the *'Croppy Lodge,'* from the circumstance of its members having shaved the heads of some of their *subjects* very closely, contrary to the custom of other lodges, who usually wore it rather long.

"The 'Croppy Lodge,' together with our hero, assembled at the appointed hour, and in due form fastened the doors; when, professing the utmost solemnity, as members of that ancient and venerable fraternity, the meeting was opened. After the preliminary forms were over, Tanner was called forward and several questions propounded to him, in relation to his obligations to the society of which he was about to be honored with a membership. His answers being satisfactory, a vote was taken of the members, which was unanimous, that he be admitted after passing through the rites and ceremonies required of all the members at their initiation, and which they then proceeded to administer.

"Poor Tanner was requested to strip himself stark-naked, and march around the altar in the centre of the room, accompanied by vocal music from the members and the mystic signs of the order. And lastly, a hot gridiron, which was in readiness for the purpose, was brought into the room, with which he was branded. These ceremonies over, the W. Master of the lodge declared the brother a free and accepted mason.

"Whether Tanner suspected any imposition at the time is unknown, but it was said he never betrayed any distrust to his tormentors during the whole performance, and that at its close they had a most jolly time, drinking each other's health and beautifying the glories of masonry, in which Tanner took the lead. Thus the matter ended for the evening.

"A few days subsequent to the above occurrence, (during which Tanner had discovered the cheat which had been practised upon him,) Elnathan Goodrich, who had been one of the party at the initiation, meeting with his new brother, cordially reached out his hand, saying *'How do you do, brother Croppy?'* This was too much for the already excited schoolmaster to brook, and he immediately sent a challenge to Goodrich, to meet him and settle the affront according to the 'code of honor,' which challenge was accepted."

The meeting of the parties, accompanied by their seconds, took place in the field belonging to Isaac Townsend, about a mile above the village of Walton. The field was at the time but partially cleared. It will now attract the attention of the traveller as a spot of surpassing beauty.

"The pistols were presented to the combatants, who exchanged the first shots without effect. At the second discharge, Goodrich threw up his pistol, gave a shriek of agony, and fell heavily to the ground, appearing to be mortally wounded. Tanner immediately left the field, apparently unnoticed, as they were all gathered around the dying man. Reaching his boarding place* in great agitation, he requested the woman in much haste to give him his clothes, saying 'that he must leave the country as soon as possible, having shot Mr. Goodrich in a duel.' He took his bundle of clothes, and crossing the river, disappeared in the woods, on the opposite side; since which time he has not been heard from, and if living, still doubtless carries the impression of having shot a man in a duel."

By a previous arrangement between Goodrich and the seconds, Tanner's pistol was only loaded with powder, while Goodrich's, to render the deception still more complete, was loaded with a ball, which, for effect, he shot in a tree near by where his opponent was standing. Of course his appearing to be wounded was only a pretension.

The field where the duel was fought, has since, in commemoration of the event, received the memorable name of "Hoboken Lot," which name it still retains.

Many of the pioneers who emigrated to the western sections of Delaware county, came by the way of Minisink, which, as we have stated in a previous chapter, was one of the earliest settlements in the State. From Minisink the settlements rapidly spread up the valley of the Delaware, each new comer overreaching the location of his neighbor. In 1783, Abram Rusk came up the river with his goods on a *flat-boat*, and located a short distance above Equinock, in Pennsylvania; and about the same period William Parks took up Equinock Island. The succeeding year, (1784,) Ezekiel Samson came up the river and pitched his tent a short distance below Chehocton Cove, and immediately afterward Richard Jones removed with his family to Chehocton Point.

In 1786, Squire Whitaker also came up the river, and settled at the place where George Debar now lives, about one and a half miles below the rail-road crossing at Chehocton;† and Richard Jones, Travis and Sands,

---

* He was boarding at the house of the father of my informant.

† Chehocton is of Indian origin, and the meaning it conveys is both beautiful and appropriate. To give a just idea of the peculiarity of its location, and of the advantages thence resulting, it is proper to give some account of the place and the surrounding country. It will be perceived, by inspecting the map of the county, that the two branches of the Delaware rise near each other, in the north-east part of the county, and run thence with a very tortuous course, generally

settled in the vicinity the same year. In 1787, Conrad Edict, a single man, came into the settlement and partook of the hospitalities of Squire Whitaker, whose daughter he shortly after married. At the wedding the bride appeared in a *linsey-woolsey* short-gown, and the bridegroom in a new suit of "tow-cloth shirt and trousers."

Although Mr. Edict, at the time of his removal to the settlements on the Delaware, was barely twenty-six years of age, his previous history was woven in the struggles of the Revolution, and his character had been stamped by usefulness to his country's cause. He was born of German parents, on German Flats, in the then county of Albany, September 15th, 1763. At the early age of sixteen years, he enlisted in the service of his country in a company of rangers, and served nine months. He then enlisted in the service of the militia of the State of New York for three years, in which he remained until the close of the war. He was in the battles of Ariskany, Stone, Arabia, Johnstown, and East Canada Creek, where the notorious Colonel Butler was killed, and in many other skirmishes with the Indians and tories. His last expedition was to Oswego, on Lake Ontario, in the dead of winter, in which great numbers of the party died of hunger and cold. He afterward removed from Chehocton and settled at Deposit, where he lived for more than half a century, until his death.

In 1786 Jesse Dickinson came up from Philadelphia to locate himself on a tract of land which he had purchased of Colonel Bradstreet, and which tract contains the present village of Cannonsville. This tract, as well as much of the adjoining land, was thickly covered by a growth of stately pines. And so captivated was the owner with his new purchase, that he conceived the bold project of building a *city,* which, in his ideal vision, contained "stately edifices and lofty spires," and which was to immortalize his own name by styling it *"Dickinson City."* Having become enamored with his new project, he returned to Philadelphia to procure men and building material, which was conveyed to the place of destination in *Durham boats.* He caused a tract of land of sufficient size to be surveyed and laid off into streets and lots, and immediately commenced improvements thereon. He erected a large three-story grist-mill on Trout creek,* near where it empties into the Delaware; on the side next the creek, were rows of tackles projecting out over the water, for the purpose of unloading boats which should run between the two cities, Philadelphia and Dickinson. He also built near by, a building for a hotel, in which was a large arched room,

---

south-westerly, until the West Branch reaches Deposit, (formerly Cook-house,) whence it takes a south-easterly course, until near its affianced bride, at Chehocton Neck; then more southerly, the twain recede and again approach to their wedding union, one and a half miles below, giving occasion for the Indian appellation of Chehocton or Shehawkan, which interpreted in English, is "The Wedding of the Waters."

* This stream took its name from the circumstance that large quantities of trout were annually caught in wooden troughs prepared for the purpose, and placed immediately behind the sheet of water falling over Dickinson's dam. The trout, in attempting to make their way up the falling sheet to the dam, fell through in great numbers into these troughs.

styled the *"City Hall,"* and in which public meetings were actually held for many years. He also opened an avenue from Trout creek to the river, and on either side built a high board fence.

Dickinson failed in business, and returned to Philadelphia in 1795, but for many years thereafter, and until recently, the place retained the name of *"Dickinson's City."* John, a brother of Jesse Dickinson, was also an early settler on a creek near by, which, after him, took the name of *Johnny's Brook.*

It is a fact worthy of note, that Jesse Dickinson run the first raft of lumber that descended the West Branch of the Delaware.

In 1796, Wait Cannon removed from Connecticut, and renewed the purchase of a part of the tract formerly owned by Dickinson, where he resided until his death, which took place in 1803 or 1804, and after whom the place took its present name of Cannonsville. The widow of Wait Cannon afterward married a cousin of her former husband, by the name of Benjamin, the father of our present efficient county-clerk, Benjamin Cannon, Esq.

Before the erection of Dickinson's mill, the settlers were obliged to go to Minisink, distant nearly one hundred miles, to get their grain ground. The river was for many years the only highway, and people and produce were conveyed up and down the same on *"Durham boats,"* or batteaux.

Passing in chronological order, from year to year, we note that in 1790, Martin Hulse came from Goshen, Orange county, and settled at Deposit. He was the grandson of the brave General Herkimer, whose lamented death is recorded by Campbell, in his narrative of the battle of Oriskany. The place upon which he settled is at present occupied by his grandson, Marshal R. Hulse, Esq., near Deposit village, which place was then and for many years afterward, known as the Cook House.* His brother Joseph

---

* Cook House is the corruption of the Indian appellation of *Coke-ooze,* signifying or imitating the hooting of owls. Its pronunciation is like the English coo-coo, the emphasis being placed upon the last syllable. In the early settlement of the country there were two places thus appellated, the other being about three miles below, on the Pennsylvania side, and which was distinguished from the former, as *"Coke-ooze-Sapoze,"* or "Little Owl's Nest." The name doubtless originated from the mountain south of the Laurel Hill Seminary, which is wooded with thick hemlock, giving it a dark and dismal appearance, and from which at frequent intervals, is emitted the hallooings of the hoot-owl. The place did not take the name Deposit until 1814, when the village was laid out and incorporated. It had for many years been a point to which the neighboring mills drew their lumber and deposited it for rafting, and hence the latter name.

Simms, in his History of Schoharie, thus refers to the orthography of the Cook House: "I make the following extract," says the author, "from a letter from the Hon. Erastus Root, of the New York Senate, in answer to several inquiries, dated Albany, April 11th, 1843. 'You ask whence originated the name of Cook House? Various derivations have been given, but the one most probable is this: That on the large flat bearing the name—being on the way from Cochecton, by the Susquehanna and Chemung to Niagara—there was a hut erected, where some cooking utensils were found. It had probably been erected by some traveller who had made it his stopping place, and who had cooked his provisions there. It has been stated to me, as part of the tradition, that the hut remained many years as a resting-place to the weary traveller, and that the rude cooking utensils were permitted to remain, as consecrated to the use of succeeding sojourners.' Gen. Root went to reside in Delaware county, in 1796."

came in the same year, and took up the lot on which the present village is principally built, but after examining the lot, he concluded to abandon his contract, and the same year returned to Orange county.

In 1813, Henry Drinkert caused the village to be surveyed, and sold lots (as appears from an old record of the matter, which has fallen under our observation,) to the amount of $844, and which lots have since increased in value over five hundred per cent.; and the succeeding year, Silas Crandall, William Wheeler and William Butler, purchased lot No. 43, of the Evans patent, adjoining the above, and caused it to be laid off into lots, which they offered for sale upon reasonable terms, to those disposed to build upon the same.

Among the many inconveniences to which the early settlers were obliged to submit, was their great distance from mechanics and tradesmen, being compelled to endure a journey to Minisink, to purchase even the smallest article of merchandise. The journey usually employed a week. The first merchants in Deposit were Captain Conrad Edict and Captain John Parker; the next store was owned and occupied by Henry M. Gregory and Abel Downs, (afterward of Colchester;) and the third was owned by Silas Crandall and Peter Butts, as the firm of "Crandall & Butts." This latter store is still standing; it is owned and occupied by M. R. Hulse, Esq., near the Deposit bridge.

The first school established in Deposit was in 1794, in which a few urchins were instilled in the rudiments of a common education, by Hugh Compton. The school-house is said to have been constructed of slabs, in the most uncouth manner.

Charles Knapp, Esq., an estimable friend and a highly respectable citizen of Deposit, has favored us with the following incidents. He says:—

The following authentic accounts are extracted from the Cabinet of Natural History, and will convey a good idea of the manners and habits of some of the wild animals in the middle States. Both these events transpired in Delaware county.

On the day of the present hunt, I was joined by a very particular friend and a great huntsman, and we took with us, for our day's sport, nine dogs, and two men to assist, leading the dogs. Five of these animals were experienced and well broken, but the other four were young, and about, for the first time, to range the forest after a bear.

It may, perhaps, be worthy of remark, for the information of those who know but little of these animals, that old bears seldom tree, to clear themselves of dogs, if there is any possibility of escape without it; and when necessity compels them to this course, they will, on the approach of a human creature, in despite of every obstacle which may oppose, descend to the ground and take to flight; young bears, however, will climb trees immediately, and often suffer hunters to approach beneath them and shoot them. Knowing the present animal to be an old and formidable antagonist, and judging from the noise of the dogs that he was in a tree, my companion thought it most advisable to destroy him at once, lest he should kill more of our dogs, as by this time he had killed one and disabled two others; he accordingly approached with much caution, until within about eighty yards of the tree in which the bear had taken refuge, when, with much deliberation he fired at his head, and being a first-rate shot, I felt confident that the animal would have fallen dead; but to our great surprise the shot did not take effect, owing to the ball having struck and glanced from a small dead limb, which was immediately in front of the bear's head, but completely unnoticed by my friend. At the report of his rifle, the bear descended backwards for about ten feet, then doubled himself in the form of a hoop and fell to the ground.

It is well known among hunters, that should an old bear be surprised on a tree, he will never descend by sliding down, but, like this bear, roll himself up and fall, sometimes from a most astonishing height, even forty or fifty feet; in which case he always alights on his rump, and when on the side of a hill, will roll like a hoop to the bottom. I have, in several instances, shot them after such falls, and found the extent of injury received, was a few slight bruises near the root of the tail. Experienced dogs are well aware of this stratagem of the bear, and so soon as he lets go his hold, they will run from under the tree to avoid his fall. This plan, also, the bear adopts to clear himself of dogs, as he knows that should he descend the tree gradually, he must encounter a host of enemies the moment he reaches the ground. In the present instance the dogs knew the character of their antagonist, and run so far from under the tree, that the bear had recovered from his fall and ran three hundred yards, ere they could overtake him.

The battle now began to rage most furiously, and we were alarmed for the fate of our dogs, and endeavored to shoot him, but found it impossible to do so, without endangering some of the dogs. He then laid on his back, and would frequently drag some of the dogs to him, in order to squeeze them to death, but being broad across the chest, failed to effect his purpose. This the old dogs knew well, and the moment he would seize them, they would close in with his breast and slip out backwards from him.

Our presence excited the dogs to fight with the utmost ferocity and exceeding courage, for half an hour, but the bear was an overmatch for them, and we were fearful that he would bite them in pieces, and escape at last without our being able to get a ball in him. Amongst our dogs was a favorite old one, we called "Drive," and without exception, the best dog to hunt, I ever saw, and withal the most courageous. He had been our companion in toil and pleasure for several years, and his encounters with wild animals were so numerous, that often has been the time we have carried him from the field of battle helpless and mangled, for miles to our houses; but always, on recovering, he was anxious to engage in deadly strife with any monster of the forest. This old dog, in the present battle, had seized the bear by the back of the neck with so firm a hold as to disable him, in some measure, from injuring the other dogs. This bear, however, endeavored to rid himself of "Drive" in every possible way, but to no effect; thinking now it would be a good opportunity to dispatch him, I resolved to try the virtue of my hunting-knife, and approached him with a view of stabbing him; but the bear immediately broke away from the dogs, and then threw himself on his back again, and when in this position, I set my rifle against a tree, and attempted to make the fatal stroke. The bear anticipated my intention, and met my blow with a stroke of his paw, with so much force as to knock the knife from my hand to the distance of thirty feet, and then arose and made a bold push at me, but I showed him a light pair of heels, and being again seized by the dogs, he was deterred from any farther pursuit.

We then thought of other means, and commenced cutting large clubs; but whilst engaged at this, the bear, disrelishing his new enemies, cleared himself of the dogs, which were so disabled by this time that they could scarcely fight any more, and made off at full speed: I seized my rifle, and just as he was springing over an old hemlock log I fired at him, and being afraid of shooting the dogs, I shot too high, and only cut him across the rump, as he pitched over the log. This put him to a stand, and he ascended a tree, to the height of about forty feet, when I approached and shot him through the heart.

The following is a part of an account given of a wolf, which was run down by some hunters who resided in the village of Deposit, in Delaware county, New York. This animal had lost three toes from one of his feet, and on this account was called the "three-legged wolf." He was particularly famous for his depredations among the sheep, and had been frequently pursued, but from his great sagacity had hitherto escaped. No less that forty-five persons had originally started in the chase on the present occasion, but it was now the third day, and two only had sufficient perseverance to continue the pursuit.

By this time it was fairly light—we were at the spot where we had left the wolf the night previous, and we had not proceeded more than three hundred yards up the hill, before we found his bed. This he had left of his own accord, and walked to the top of a hill, which was about half a mile distant, and then took to another road which led direct to Walton, and continued till he came close to Judge Pine's farm, a distance of fifteen miles, where he had a few weeks previous killed so many sheep, and there, at the foot of another hill, he had reposed the remainder of the night. We soon aroused him, and he took directly up the hill, which was exceedingly steep, but up which we clambered with slow progress until we had gained the top. We had walked fifteen miles, and as I was first on the summit of the hill, I looked down, and saw W—— about thirty yards from me. The wolf kept his course on the brow of that hill for three miles, and then left it, and crossed the road which leads from Walton to Franklin, on the Susquehanna; here I stopped and waited for my companion; W—— was immediately by my side. The wood before us was open for six miles, and gradually ascending, but not so much as to prevent our taking rapid strides; as I neared the top, I waited for W—— to come up. "Now," says W——, "if the wolf keeps this course, we will have a regular descent of nine miles."

I then started at full speed, guarding always against jumping into holes, in which case, probably, my legs would have been broken, until I came within two miles of the foot of the hill, when I saw the rascal about three hundred yards ahead, and he saw me at the same time. We now had it as hard as we could lay to, and I saw that I gained on him but slowly, and being within one hundred and seventy-five yards of me, I fired just as he was quartering on me, but he kept his course, and rose a high mountain before us. I reloaded and proceeded, and found that he had dropped in the snow so often as to evince the greatest fatigue, and nothing but his very life stimulated him on. On this mountain were many wind-falls, and other difficult places, almost impassable for man; and had we been in pursuit of any other animal beside the "three-legged wolf," the number of difficulties at this time, would have disheartened us; but we were intent on victory, and our infatuation blinded our difficulties, and made us callous to suffering.

Our antagonist kept his course on this hill for seven miles, but it being covered with underbrush we could not gain on him; the sun was gliding behind the western hills, and the wolf having so much start of us, we concluded to look out for quarters for the night; we accordingly ascended a high point on the mountain, and in a valley, two miles distant, we saw a house, whither we proceeded, and were immediately recognized by a young man, an inmate of the dwelling: he inquired of us, what brought us there in our hunting-dress, and with our rifles? We told him we "were after the three-legged wolf." "Ah!" says he, "I know him well. I hope you will not leave him here, for only three weeks since, he killed eleven sheep in one night for us, and last winter he killed eighteen others for us: has he not lost a part of his fore-foot?" We told him we were satisfied he knew him, as that was his description, and that we should never give him up until we had destroyed him, unless a snow should fall so as to obliterate his track. This was fifty-two miles from our homes in a direct line, and I have no doubt we had run that day sixty miles, as we were then near Delhi, in the upper part of the county.

We were treated with great hospitality by this family, whose name was Wilson, and every thing was done to make us and our dogs comfortable, that could be devised. After drinking some tea, and eating but little, we found that sleep was more desirable than anything else, and we retired to rest. Our dogs did not reach the house for some time after our arrival, and then they were in a wretched condition; but the family exercised great humanity towards them, especially the children, who had taken them into the parlor, and were rubbing them with dry napkins. When we arose, we found a repast prepared for us, with some dough-nuts to eat through the day. This, generally, was our daily food, and for drink, we could catch up a handful of snow, not allowing ourselves sufficient time to quench our thirst at a brook.

Before light we started, and tracked our way up the mountain; and I can confidently say, I never felt better than at that time; my spirits were buoyant, and I trod with lighter footstep than any day previous; this was the fourth day of our hunt. I asked Capt. W—— how he felt; he said, "I feel well; victory to-day; to-day the wolf must die." But we felt keenly for our dogs, for although they had been so well used, yet they could not move a step, scarcely, without crying; and thus they continued yelping till they had followed us some miles. We would have left them at the farm-house, but they howled so terribly, we were obliged to let them follow us.

About light we got on the wolf-track again, and within three hundred yards, found he had lain down, but had risen again in the night, voluntarily, and walked not more than ten yards, before he made another bed in the snow. It was evident his time was drawing to a close, for in the last bed he had laid until we surprised him in the morning. His former plan was, after we had ceased chasing him, to run a few hundred yards, then lie down for half the night, and rising again, travel off fifteen or twenty miles into the neighborhood of his depredations, and then rest preparatory to the next night's havoc among the sheep; but now it was pretty certain that we had tired him too much to waste any time after sheep, and that he did not possess power to travel much farther.

When we aroused him this time, he led right off from home but we cared not whither he went, so long as he left a track for us to follow him; but this mountain was covered with underbrush, and he appeared to be well acquainted with every inch of ground he ran over, therefore, we could not push him to the extent we desired; this he was well aware of, and he would choose the most dense and difficult part of the wood; but he omitted it now, making his usual circuits about the wind-falls, as he had no time to spare, and could not continue his course direct. We followed him with renewed speed for about seven miles, when he left the mountain and directed his course across a valley six miles, to another mountain. Through this valley was clear open wood, and we pressed him so hard that he began to lengthen his jumps, and made no more beds in the snow, until he reached the above mountain, where he had opportunities again to rest, as the side on which he ran was so perpendicular that we made but slow progress. We found that he would drop himself to rest every five minutes, and just keeping so far ahead as to keep out of our sight, although we were confident he saw us continually. On arriving at the top of the mountain, we found he had made a start for a thicket, on the same mountain, before we could overtake him; but the course he was going was a gradual descent for about fifteen miles, until it terminated at the foot of another mountain, which was in that range, called *Pine Hill*, on the head waters of the West Branch of Delaware River.

I started off at full speed down this side of the mountain, making long jumps; I never felt better, and with ease to myself, I could run a mile in five minutes; my limbs felt invigorated, and my speed was superior to any of the former days. I continued so for nearly thirteen miles, and then came within sight of the wolf. He was then but two hundred yards in advance of me, and he had yet two miles farther to go before he could reach the mountain, and this through open wood. He used every effort to quicken his pace, but in spite of his exertions I gained on him. I had run but a mile since I got sight of him, and when I was within forty yards of him, he looked behind at me, and seeing no possible chance of escaping, dropped his tail between his legs and stopped; I ran within twenty yards, and shot a ball immediately through his body,—he fell and rose again,—crack went Captain W.'s rifle, and down he dropped *dead*. In a moment my foot was on his neck, but we were at a loss to express our joy. We were in the midst of an extensive forest, and we knew not where; we charged our rifles, and gave four rounds in commemoration of the four days' chase. Our difficulties were not yet at an end, for we were determined to take him home; we accordingly took a small stick, and twisting one end, fastened it to his upper jaw, and while one carried the rifles, the other dragged him on the snow.

It appeared, on examining the wolf, that I had struck him on the flank the day previous, when I fired at him, to about the depth of the ball, cutting the flesh, but not so as to retard his progress. We continued dragging him, and followed down a small branch, which we were convinced would lead us to the Delaware or Susquehanna. After proceeding about eight miles, we came to a farm-house occupied by a Mr. Sawyer; he soon recognised us, and seeing us dragging a wolf, asked if we had the "three legged wolf?" and when we answered in the affirmative, says he, "I will hold a day of rejoicing, for I have but few sheep left from last winter, as he then killed nine, and eight of them were my best ewes, and I suppose he came here for more mutton. Tell me," continued he, "what I can do for you, and it shall be done." We asked him if he would take us in his sleigh towards home, or until we could find some one of our neighbors who would take us the balance of the way. We were then eighty miles from the village of Deposit, in a direct line, and he without hesitation agreed to do so.

The number of persons assembled at Walton, out of curiosity, to see the result of the chase, was about one hundred, as every farmer appeared to be deeply interested in the destruction of this wolf; and making a calculation, we found the number of persons assembled there alone, had sheep destroyed by him to the amount of one thousand dollars. When, therefore, they saw our success, it appeared as though they could not do too much for us; they escorted us home with fifteen sleighs, a distance of thirty miles, and our fame resounded through the whole country.

There were but few Indians remaining along the Delaware as late as 1784, having principally emigrated to the hunting-grounds of the Susquehanna, or still farther to the west.

There was an aged scion of the Tuscarora tribe, however, who remained for a number of years in the vicinity of Deposit, by the name of "Old Abram" His hut was on the bank of the river, between the village and the present residence of Benj. Whitaker, near by a large cold spring, which raftsmen to this day call "Old Abram's Spring."

Among those who remained on the hunting-grounds of the Delaware, were Canope, whose tragical end I am about to relate, and Huycon, or Ben Shanks. The following account of the transaction, is taken from the Republican Watchman, of Sullivan county.

Previous to the war, they had been frequently at Minisink, particularly Canope, who was a fine specimen of his race, and had been highly esteemed by his white neighbours.

Ben Shanks, it is said, was the tallest Indian ever seen on the Delaware, and probably from this circumstance received his name. During hostilities, they had taken an active part in favor of King George, and had accompanied several of the ruthless expeditions of the tories and savages against the whigs of Warwarsing and Minisink.

Huycon, as has already been shown, was bold, crafty, and cunning; and, on one occasion, had penetrated Warwarsing, and nearly succeeded in taking prisoner Colonel Jansen, a noted patriot. Shanks was distinguished for his barbarous murders, and was very obnoxious to the whigs, on account of the part he had taken in the murder of John Mack, and the two young ladies who were killed on the Shawangunk.

At the time the circumstances detailed below occurred, the few white families who had located themselves in Cochecton previous to the war, had returned, and again lived on their farms. Some of them were old acquaintances of Canope and Huycon. The Indians stopped on their way down to renew the friendly relations which had existed previous to the late troubles. One of the men they called to see was Joseph Ross, who lived near the mouth of the Calicoon, and some of whose descendants still reside in Cochecton. Ross appears to have been an honest and humane man, and now that hostilities had ceased, felt no longer unfriendly to the Indians, notwithstanding their cruelties during the war. He advised Canope and Shanks to go no farther, and told them it was dangerous to go below, as there were some desperate characters there—Tom Quick among the number,—who would rejoice in an opportunity to kill them: Mr. Josiah Parks gave them the same advice.

The two chiefs were experienced and brave warriors, however, and knew not what fear was. They had lurked about the houses of the whigs when war existed, and they imagined it would now be cowardly to turn back through fear. Saying that it was "peace time," and that they did not think the whites would hurt them, they went to the ponds in the vicinity of Handsome Eddy, where they fished and hunted, but carefully avoided the settlers and others. While they were thus engaged, they were discovered by a man named Ben or Benjamin Haines, who lived at the Eddy. He professed to be friendly, and told them if they would go with him to the river they might make his house their home. They declined at first, but he promised to protect them, and finally they were induced to accompany him.

This Haines, as the result will prove, was a dastardly wretch. He was as barbarous as a savage, but did not possess a single trait which partially redeems the Indian character. The murders of Quick may shock us; but the mean treachery of Haines can elicit no other feeling than abhorrence and contempt.

While the Indians were at his house, Haines pretended that it was necessary for him to go to Minisink after rum and ammunition. The real object of his journey was to see Tom, and induce him to go to the Eddy and murder his guests. It is said, that he wished to get possession of the furs which the Indians had brought with them, and which were of considerable value. He found the old Indian-slayer, who was yet wild with rage, on account of having been robbed of his skins, at the cabin on the Lackawaxen. Tom readily listened to Haines, and agreed to kill the savages, provided he could get any one to help him, for he thought it not advisable to cope with Huycon and Canope alone, as it was well known they were each nearly equal to him in cunning and bravery.

Among Tom's friends was a man named Cobe Chambers, or Shimer, who had formerly lived in Shawangunk, and who was an acquaintance of the two young ladies who had been so barbarously slain by Shanks and his party. It is not too much to suppose he was a lover of one of them, or a near relative, as he readily agreed to assist Tom in killing the guests of Haines, although, as the event proved, he was unused to scenes of blood. If this were not so, why should he, who had never before engaged in any affair in which the life of an Indian was involved, now, in a time of profound peace, engage in an attempt to destroy two of the hated race, and one of whom was regarded with so much abhorrence, because he had shed the blood of two innocent and inoffensive girls?

After conferring with Tom, Haines returned home, with the understanding that the Indian-slayer should follow in a day or two, and bring Shimer with him. Haines found Canope and his companion still at his cabin when he returned. Quick and Shimer reached the Eddy a day or two after Haines got there. They found the latter and the Indians in the cabin waiting for their morning meal to be cooked by the "woman of the house." Ben professed to be surprised at their coming, and greeted Tom as an old acquaintance, but gave him a fictitious name, so that the Indians, who had never seen him before, would not know who he was. After inquiring where they were going, &c., he invited them to eat breakfast with him, which after a little urging, they agreed to do.

While Ben's wife was "putting the dishes on the table," he filled a bowl with water, and taking it out of doors, put it on a stump a rod or two from the house. He then returned and told the Indians to wash themselves. They went out of doors for that purpose, and Haines had a brief opportunity to confer with Tom and Shimer. He told them that he would get the savages to go with him to the "fishing- rocks," to catch fish, and that the opportunity to shoot them from that place would be good, as there was a convenient clump of bushes close by, from which to fire. Tom expressed his satisfaction with what Haines had said—the Indians came back into the house, and all sat down and ate a hearty breakfast. Tom and Haines seemed to be perfectly at ease all the time, as if nothing more than usual was on their minds, while Cobe appeared to be somewhat disconcerted.

After breakfast, the new comers apparently renewed their journey up the river. They were soon in ambush, however, near the place where Ben said he would entice his *proteges*. It was not long after, that Huycon, Canope, and Haines, and a little son of the latter, came "to the rocks," and began to fish. Before Tom and his companion fired, it occurred to Haines that his son might be injured in the affray, and he ordered him to go home. Something in the manner of Haines caused the Indians to suspect his fidelity; but he quickly quieted their suspicions, and they then continued to fish as before. Canope, having broken his hook, and none of the party being in possession of one to give him, laid down on the rocks near Shanks, with his head resting upon his hand and elbow. This was considered a favorable opportunity by Tom and Shimer, and they "took aim." Cobe, who was not used to such business, was greatly excited, and Tom declared afterwards, that his (Cobe's) hand trembled so, that he heard the barrel of his gun rattle against the log on which it rested.

They fired: Tom's ball passed through the hand and lower part of the head of Canope, wounding him dangerously. Shimer, as might have been safely predicted, did not hit Shanks. The wounded man ran to Haines and claimed the protection which had been promised; but instead of granting it, the wretch seized a pine-knot, shouting, "Tink! tink! how you used to kill the white folks. 'Pent! 'pent! I'll send your soul to hell in a moment!" and then dispatched him by beating him on the brain.

Even Tom, familiar as he was with scenes of blood, was shocked at the perfidy of Haines. He came up as the latter was dealing out his blows, and exclaimed, "D—n a man who will promise an Indian protection, and then knock him on the head!"

Shanks, when he heard the report of the guns, jumped into the river, and pretended to be wounded and drowning, until the current had carried him down stream a short distance, to a place where the bank was covered with bushes. Here he scrambled on the shore, and ran off limping, hallooing, and groaning as if in great agony. The *ruse* did not deceive Tom, however; who, finding that Shanks was travelling pretty fast for a man who was apparently so badly wounded, started in pursuit, loading his rifle as he went, and soon got sufficiently near to fire. At the moment he snapped his gun, Shanks looked back, and as Tom shot, fell. The Indian afterwards said that he dodged at the flash of his gun. Be this as it may, Tom did not hit him. A ball-hole was afterwards found through his blanket, but whether made by Cobe or Tom could not be ascertained.

After the last discharge of the gun, Huycon took to his heels in earnest; and Tom found that *his shanks* were neither active nor long enough to overtake him. He returned to the "rocks," saying, "if ever legs did service, it was them."

Two weeks had elapsed since the Indian chiefs passed through Cochecton, when Shanks returned alone, "damning the Yankees for killing Canope," and swearing that they should suffer for what they had done. He was first seen at a house a short distance from Cochecton bridge, where he stopped to rest and get something to eat. While he was there, Mrs. Drake, whose father-in-law and first and second husbands were killed by savages and tories, came into the house. Almost immediately after seeing the savage she fainted, so great was her dread of those who had slain so many of her near and dear friends. He was next seen by Mr. Joseph Ross, who invited him to tarry a while at his house; but he refused to come near Ross at first, the bad faith of Haines having caused him to suspect every pale-face. He finally consented, however, to stay with Mr. Ross a short time. He was kindly treated by Mr. R. and his neighbors.

While here, his conduct afforded much amusement to the juvenile members of the family. Mr. Ross and his "hands," were hoeing corn, and every time they went to their work, Shanks accompanied them. As soon as he got to the field he selected the highest ground in it, and after glancing rapidly and suspiciously over the surrounding country, he seated himself *a la Turque*, among the waving and rustling corn, where he remained out of sight fifteen or twenty minutes. He would then get upon the tip of his toes, "stretch his neck" upwards as far as possible, look around, as if expecting to see Tom, and then squat upon his haunches again. As long as he remained in the field he acted in this way. The boys could compare him to nothing but a rather vigilant and somewhat alarmed turkeycock.

After remaining a day or two, he continued his journey homeward, to relate another great wrong committed by the white man. He left Ross, breathing threats of vengeance, and was ferried across the Delaware, at Equinunk, by Mr. Parks, who has already been mentioned.

The death of Canope was regretted by most of the frontier settlers, for many reasons. His murder was brought about by the blackest treachery, and in violation of a solemn treaty of peace, the strict observance of which was necessary to their safety. Nothing could justify the murder. It was known that others beside Tom were engaged in the transaction, and there was good ground for fear that the Indians would avenge his death, and in doing so, not discriminate between the bloody perpetrators of the outrage, and those who would have sheltered him from harm.

The Indians made a formal complaint to the government against Shimer, Haines, and Quick; but it does not appear that the offenders were apprehended, or that any attempt was made to punish them. After waiting a reasonable time, the savages did what was quite natural on their part: they fell upon a couple of white men in the vicinity of Fort Pitt, and murdered them. A gentleman named Skinner, whose ancestors settled at Cushetunk nearly one hundred years ago, and whose possessions were extensive during the early days of the settlement of Cochecton, styles the murdered men "Uncle Ross and Cousin Cyrus." By this we are given to understand that the vengeance of the Indians fell upon men who had never treated the natives unkindly.

After this event, the fears of the pioneers gradually wore away; and finally they continued to fish, and hunt, and cultivate their lands without apprehension.

CHAPTER VIII

Adventures and final settlement of Timothy Beach in Sidney—Reminiscences of John Wickham, an early settler of Harpersfield—Names of early settlers—Privations to which they were subjected—Adventure of James Gordon with a bear, while crossing the Charlotte River—First Church in Harpersfield—Manner of its erection—Church-raising—Whipping-posts and stocks erected in Harpersfield—Other whipping-posts in the county—How Harper caught his wife—Persons punished by this ordeal—First settled minister in Harpersfield—Maple-sugar-making—Scotchman's idea of making maple-sugar—Information derived from Stephen Hait of Stamford—Settlements made in 1789—Information derived from David Squires—Discovery of and first settlement in Roxbury—Interesting information in relation to—Anecdotes—Information derived principally from Cyrus Burr—Early settlements in Middletown and Andes—Hall's adventure with Mr. Earl—His discovery that he had neighbors—Catamount-killing in Andes.

AMONG the early pioneers to this county after the close and successful termination of the Revolutionary struggle, was Timothy Beach and family, of whose toil and suffering, Priest, in his narrative, gives a life-like picture from the hero's own lips. Speaking of their removal, he says, Mr. Beach partook of the general impulse which at that period pervaded the several New England States, sold his farm which he had acquired after abandoning a sea-faring life, and prepared to remove to the wild banks of the Susquehanna-the hunting-grounds of the Delawares. But before he actually removed his family, he took the precaution to go and explore the lands of that river. On this journey, his eldest son, a lad of twelve years, accompanied him.

After crossing the broken and wild region of country lying between the North River and the sea, they came to a place on the Hudson called Catskill, where a few families had already settled. At this place he entered the woods, with a view of crossing the Susquehanna to a place then known by the appellation of Wattles' Ferry, a distance of nearly one hundred miles. It was, however, considered dangerous to penetrate that distance without a guide, as there was scarce a trace of human industry to mark the way through an almost unbroken wilderness. He was so fortunate as to find a half-breed Indian, who knew the way, and was willing to become his conductor, appearing to be a fleet, shrewd, and intelligent native.

The land which he wished to examine in particular, belonged to Colonel Harper, who had, it is well known, taken an active part in the border warfare of Tryon County, and was situated somewhere near what is still called Oquago, an ancient Indian town. To this place the guide was to accompany him for a stipulated price.

They left Catskill and pursued their way on horseback amid the woods as far as Cairo, where were also a few families scattered along beneath the mountains, who had returned after, or been suffered to remain during the war, as all that region had been traversed by the depredating Indians and tories. From this place they pursued the *Patawa trail,* which lay through a wilderness of the most hideous description, but which is now thickly settled with enterprising farmers, mechanics, and merchants.

The first day after leaving Catskill they advanced to somewhere near the present flourishing village of Osbornville, and, as near as can be calculated, a distance of twenty-five miles. Here they encamped for the night, having gathered grass for their horses on the margin of the headwaters of the Schoharie creek. Along this stream, from thence even down to a place called Break-a-bin, extended a gloomy gulf, then the haunt of wolves, bears, and panthers, as well as an abundance of deer and some elk. Beneath a huge clump of hemlocks near the creek they scraped away the bush, built a fire, refreshed themselves from the contents of their provision-sacks, and drank from a small, green glass bottle filled with *West India Jamaica,* a necessary *help-meet* in those early times. They now addressed themselves to sleep beneath Heaven's canopy, so much of it as could be seen bending over the narrow opening between the hills which embrace the head-waters of that stream. It was near midnight, and the fire had gone out, excepting a few coals amid the ashes; when the shrill, but loud and terrifying scream of some animal, awoke the slumberers from their dreams. They listened, when again the sound struck the ear, though from another quarter, and somewhat nearer. The guide being an Indian, instantly knew what kind of an animal it was, and whispered, *"a painter, a painter,"* meaning a *panther.* With its ferocious disposition, and the best manner of encountering the animal, he was well acquainted, and therefore, seizing his rifle, examined the loading, and bid his companions be silent, but to cover the fire. During this time, the screams of the creature continued at short intervals, but still nearer. He said it was calling its mate on account of the scented game—themselves and horses—with the view of an attack by a leap from the projecting limb of some tree, or some favorable position from the ground. The agility of this animal is not equalled by any other that is known, being able to spring, when hard pushed, or frightened, nearly forty feet on a level. Its strength is amazing, as well as its ferocity and untameableness of disposition.

The Indian had directed Beach to have his rifle in order, as he might have use for it, although not much acquainted with its powers as a hunter. This being done, they listened in almost breathless silence with the expectation of hearing more yells, but in this they were disappointed, as no sound of the animal could be heard. As to this the Indian said in a whisper, so much the greater was their danger, as the animal was creeping towards them on its belly for a leap, unless it had entirely gone off. They waited, however, but about fifteen minutes, when there came suddenly on the stillness of the night, the continued *bleat* of a deer, together with the suppressed yells of some animal which had the mastery of it, and was rending it to pieces. Now was the time for the Indian, who instantly bent low down, and glided off in that direction, as silently as a spectre of darkness; while Beach, in the same manner, and as near as he could, followed after, but rather shyly, as he felt very reluctant about approaching too near the scene of action.

But a few moments had elapsed, while the feeble cry of the deer, still struggling with his enemy, was heard, when the flash and quick report of a gun gave notice that the crisis had arrived. There was a rustling amid the leaves and dry brush, and the Indian stirred not till all was still, when he gave a yell such as the Indians give when a battle is won, and at the same time returned to the fire and reloaded.

They now gathered from the shaggy trunk of a yellow birch, which was growing near, an armful of its dry and pendant bark, of which they made several torches, and lighting one, ventured boldly to the spot, being assured by the Indian that all danger was over, and adding that he had put a bullet between the eyes of the creature. But this proved not exactly correct, as, on coming to the place, there lay stretched beside the deer, which was still bleating faintly, a *panther* of the largest description, having a shot exactly opposite the heart, which was found, on examination, to have pierced the lungs. The deer they now put out of its pain, by dispatching it in as quick a manner as possible; they then dragged the animal to the fire, but delayed skinning him till morning. Being so thoroughly roused by the incident just related, they felt no inclination to sleep, and so kept up a huge fire during the remainder of the night, and kept their courage strong by frequent draughts from the green bottle of *Jamaica*. In the morning they skinned the panther, which measured eight feet from the tip of his nose to the end of his tail, and carried the skin with them as a trophy of the adventure; but the deer they left as it was, except they cut a steak from its haunches, which they easily cooked over the coals for their breakfast.

But after the panther was killed, the remainder of the night was far from being silent, for the wolves had scented the blood of the conflict, and ran howling about till near daylight, and also the screams of another panther were heard, but at a greater distance. These voices were but sport for the Indian, which he often imitated at the top of his voice, but effectually prevented their too near approach by the brightness of the fire, and the frequent shots of their guns.

Thus passed the first night of their journey in the woods. No other incident worthy of record occurred during the remainder of their wilderness trip, although out several nights, except the sight of plenty of deer, and the howling of the wolves. When they were first awakened by the screams of the animal, they could easily have frightened it away, by firing their guns and rousing the fire, but the Indian wished an encounter, as he had no fears about its issue.

They at length came out at the desired place on the Susquehanna, where the river is now crossed by the Unadilla bridge, which place was for a long time before and after, known by the appellation of Wattles' Ferry, from Sluman Wattles, an early settler, who kept a skiff for the accommodation of those who wished to cross or recross the Susquehanna.

From Wattles' ferry they pursued their way down the Susquehanna, toward the land of Harper; at sunset they encamped for the night on an eminence near the bank of the river, not far from Bainbridge. While preparing a place to sleep among the leaves and brush, they heard below a splash in the water, which very much frightened them, not knowing from what cause it might proceed. But presently a small batteau made its appearance, owned and manned by a man named Herrick, who had been down the river on an exploring tour. Here they all encamped for the night, and in the morning an exchange was made of one of Mr. Beach's horses for Herrick's boat and provisions, Herrick paying the difference. In this boat, himself and son glided swiftly down the stream, while the guide, mounted upon the remaining horse, kept pace along the shore.

The second day after their encampment at Bainbridge, the guide proved treacherous, not meeting him according to agreement. This circumstance, and a singular dream in which his father appeared to him two nights in succession, saying to him in an earnest and impressive manner, *"Timothy, go back, go back!"* induced him to give over the project of settling at Oquago, and locate farther up the river. He accordingly commenced setting his skiff up the river with a pole, on his return towards the ferry. The second day had nearly worn away in toiling up the rapid stream, when all at once the guide presented himself upon the bank of the stream, and uttered a loud and horrid yell, which reverberated up and down the shores of the river with the most dismal echoes; but no Indians appeared with him. It was desirable, however, to ascertain if he had seen any during his absence, but to all of their inquiries the wily Indian gave surly and evasive answers. The truth now flashed upon the mind of Mr. Beach, that his life was premeditated, which was confirmed by questioning his son, of whom the Indian had learned that his father had a large sum of money in his possession.

The Indian, at the request of Mr. Beach, now hitched his horse to a tree, and came to assist in pulling the batteau up a steep rift, and when in the most rapid part, while struggling hard against the current, the Indian gave a loud *whoop,* which Beach knew to be a signal of some kind, according to the custom of the Indians. In a minute or two, no less than six Indians rushed from the woods with drawn knives, and leaping into the water, which was not more than waist deep, nor that in many places, came wading toward the boat.

At this occurrence, the guide pretended to be much frightened, and urged Beach to take up his gun and fire among them, well knowing that one shot would not kill them all, and that the survivors would make short work of him, when the money would sooner or later be obtained by himself, as he had not acquainted the Indians with this part of the booty. But there was his horse, his gun, ammunition, his clothes, and a keg of rum they had purchased of Herrick with the boat. These were inducements of sufficient magnitude to persuade the Indians to commit the robbery, and, if necessary, a murder, while the guide had his eye upon the money alone. But Beach perceiving all this at a glance, instead of firing at them, met them at the side of the boat with a bottle of rum in his hand, saying in the most *conciliating* manner he could assume, "The war is now over—we will all be brothers—we will not fight, but be friends." "So we will," shouted one of their number, while the others appeared bent on mischief. He now instantly proposed that they should help push the boat up the swift current, without getting into it, then he would go on shore with them and have a good frolic all night. He, however, was inwardly much terrified, not knowing how to escape. He tied the batteau to a convenient spot, filled a tin tea-kettle with rum and gave it to one of the Indians to carry, who marched off toward the spot selected for an encampment, followed by the rest of the Indians, guide and all, the boy excepted, who curled down in the boat and kept himself still, and as much as possible out of sight.

The guide now, no doubt, considered his prize perfectly safe, as during the night his purpose could easily be effected, either by himself or some of the others. They now sat down in a ring on the ground, while the tin tea-kettle went rapidly round, as they each took deep and long draughts of the rum; the effects of which soon began to show itself by their yelling and leaping. At this moment, when they appeared to be wholly occupied with themselves and their freaks, he stepped to the boat as if to fasten it better, when he gave it a violent push out into the river, and leaping into it as he did so, shot over to the other side.

It was now nearly dark, as the whole transaction had taken place between sunset and twilight, and during the whole time a dense black cloud had been coming up from the south, which, just at the moment of his leaping into the boat, burst forth in a tremendous thunder shower, producing almost instantly, a total darkness. This, it is likely, was the only opportunity in which he could have made his escape, for in the uproar of their drunkenness and the thunder of the coming storm, they did not perceive his intention soon enough to prevent him, as they had no guns, or at least none had been brought to view as yet.

The storm increased, the lightnings flashed around, the thunder rattled terribly among the mountains—the darkness was almost palpable, while the rain poured down in torrents—all of which aided him exceedingly in his flight. They, however, soon perceived that he had escaped, and as soon attempted to follow; this they did a mile or two along the shore, which he knew by their yells, heard between the claps of thunder, but which soon died away, overcome by rain and rum. All night he continued to push his boat up the river, and at daylight found himself at the mouth of *Carr's creek,** in the present town of Sidney. From this place he travelled through the wet and dripping woods to the place where Unadilla bridge now is, where at first a Mr. Wattles had made a settlement. Of this man he obtained help to get his boat up to that place, as the river during the heavy rain, had become so deep that the strength of one man could not push it up the stream.

A few days after his arrival at this place, the Indian, who had given so much trouble, was taken up in the woods in possession of the horse, by two men, Richard and Daniel Ogden, who had been out on a tour of hunting and exploration. These men knew the horse, having seen it when Beach was at the ferry a few days before, and compelled the fellow to come in with them and give an account of himself. But, Indian-like, he answered nothing to the charges brought against him, and here the matter ended, as no further measures were taken against him. At this place Mr. Beach determined to locate himself, and accordingly selected a farm in an entire wild state, which place is now known by the name of *Ketchum farm,* in Sidney, Delaware county, New York. He then returned through the same woods, carrying his boy behind him on the horse, till he arrived at Western, his place of residence, in old Connecticut, but then known by the appellation of *Down Country,* by all such as had removed from that place to the westward.

On the 11th of November, 1784, Mr. Beach and his family commenced their journey to their new home. In order to transport their goods, they were obliged to follow a different route from that taken by himself while exploring the wilderness. They passed through Albany, then up the Mohawk valley, and finally arrived at the outlet of Otsego lake; this was

---

* So called, from a tory by the name of Carr, who built the first saw-mill in Sidney, on this stream.

the end of the road, and they were compelled to dismiss their teams, and embark with their effects on a batteau. This was the same route travelled by the Northern division of Sullivan's army under Clinton in 1779, by whom, as before stated, it was first opened. Gliding down the lake, a distance of nine miles, to its outlet—the head waters of the mighty Susquehanna—for the first time they encamped in the open air, and on the very spot where the village of Cooperstown now stands. At the close of the second day they had descended the Susquehanna as far as the outlet of Cherry Valley creek. Here the female portion of the family first had a sight of the native Indians, who had also encamped at this place, on their journey down the river to their ancient hunting-grounds. They had built a monstrous fire, around which they were merrily preparing their supper from a buck, which had been shot during the afternoon, every now and then uttering a horrid yell of joy, which reverberated fearfully among the hills.

On the evening of the third day from the lake, they arrived at the end of their journey, very much wearied. Here they discovered the remnants of a few log-houses crumbled to ruins, said to have been the habitations of a few Scotch settlers, who had penetrated the wilderness before the Revolution, (see a previous chapter,) at the outbreak of which they were compelled to fly for safety to Cherry Valley, and commit their homes to the mercy of the ruthless savage. One of these Scotch settlers, the Rev. Mr. Johnston, had returned the same year that Mr. Beach settled in Sidney. They had but barely arrived at their new home, when winter, with its deep snows and fierce driving winds, set in. The miserable hovel in which they sheltered themselves, but illy supplied the place of the comfortable home they had left in Connecticut. There were but five families in all that region, none of whom had been there over a few months, and consequently provisions of every kind were very scarce, and could not be procured nearer than Schoharie, a distance of seventy miles.

Mr. John Wickham, an early settler of the town of Harpersfield, informed me that in 1790 his father, in company with a man by the name of Butts, came into Harpersfield, which then constituted a part of Montgomery county, and purchasing a lot of land, erected a log hut upon it. In February, 1791, Mr. Wickham, wife, and three small children, moved from Dutchess county with an ox team, and after a fatiguing journey of one hundred miles, sixty of which lay through a dense forest, with only now and then a small settlement, they arrived at their place of destination. Nothing of interest occurred during the journey, except the falling of a tree, which was blown down by the wind across their sled. No one was hurt, and after some delay in removing the obstruction and repairing the broken sled, they were enabled to proceed. There were but few families in Harpersfield at the time Mr. Wickham settled there—the following are their names: Col. John, Col. William, Col. Alexander, and

Joseph Harper, who had returned in 1785; Hon. Roswell Hotchkiss, who had removed from Guilford, New Haven county, Connecticut, about the same time; Josiah Seley, Matthew Lindsley, Samuel and John Knapp, two by the name of Hamilton, Washburn, Isaac Price, Stephen Judd, Samuel,* Eliab and John Wilcox, Richard and John Bristol, Abijah Baird, Byron McIlvain, David and John McCullough, Isaac Patchin, William Lamb, Caleb Gibbs and family, and William McFarland.

The Harpers who owned the patent, and were at that time the principal men, were kind and generous to the poor, and ready at all times to succor the distressed, and to do anything in their power to make all around them happy.

In 1790, there was no settlement of any account nearer than Schoharie, a distance of thirty miles, and there being but rude improvements in Harpersfield, the people labored under all the disadvantages which can well be imagined; indeed it was not uncommon for those in the best circumstances to be driven to extreme suffering for want of some kind of provision to sustain life, and at times when a little corn could be procured, which was pounded fine in a mortar and made into *"Johnny Cake,"* it furnished a luxurious repast. Schoharie might at that period with propriety be termed a *"Modern Egypt"*—the inhabitants raising large quantities of corn, and those who could possibly raise a few shillings, would go there, usually on foot, to procure a little of the *precious commodity*.

Some of the more wealthy among the inhabitants usually fatted a pig for their year's supply of meat, and were frequently called upon to mourn in consequence of a bear having entered the pen in the night and deprived them of meat for the ensuing year. Bears were very plenty, and when a neighbor shot or captured one, a general distribution of the meat was made, and many a rich repast have those hardy pioneers enjoyed at the expense of Old Bruin. Wild animals were numerous, as late as 1810, and were frequently driven by hunger to attack even men, and many incidents might be related of encounters, where it would be far more desirable to be a looker on than a participant. In the year 1810, as James Gordon was crossing the Charlotte river on a log which had fallen across the stream, and as he stepped on the log on one side of the river, a large bear came up on the other side and made towards him. Gordon was an athletic man, and having an axe on his shoulder, proposed to give battle—the two antagonists met about midway over the stream, when, with almost herculean strength, he aimed a blow at the monster, which the bear warded off by knocking the axe from his hand with his paw. A hand-to-hand contest now ensued, and they both went into the river together. Gordon barely escaped with his life, and not without becoming

---

* Alonzo B. Wilcox, an enterprising farmer of Harpersfield, is a son of Samuel, and occupies the old homestead.

sensible of the amorous embraces of bruin, which cost him an arm and hand horribly mangled, crippling him for a long time.

It was not till 1796 or 1797 that a church was erected in the town. It was built from contributions made by the inhabitants, each one furnishing material of some kind, such as hewn timber, boards, shingles, &c., being so very poor at the time, but few could furnish any money. The same year a place was built called *stocks,* and a whipping-post prepared by Isaac Pierce, for the purpose of inflicting punishment on any who had been charged with crime, and found guilty of the same by a jury. A good deal of curiosity was exhibited, especially among the fair sex, to get a glimpse of the ordeal, and after they were completed, Alexander Harper, who was fond of an innocent joke, invited his wife to accompany him and examine the stocks, which were so arranged, that by placing the criminal's foot in and making it fast, he could not escape. He therefore requested his wife to put her foot in, telling her that *"That fool of a Pierce had made them, and they would not hold any one."* She put in her foot and he let down the block, locked the same fast, and walked off amid the hearty laugh of the spectators and her own earnest entreaties, but soon returned and released her. It was however, regarded as a rich joke for many years afterwards. But one person was ever whipped at the post, and he soon left the county. It may be remarked in this place, that three whipping-posts were erected in Delaware County at about the same period; the one already mentioned in Harpersfield, one on the place now owned by ex-sheriff Thomas, but then in possession of Silas Knapp, who kept a grocery there for several years, and the other near Col. Dimmick's, in Middletown.

There was but one person whipped, as I have been able to learn, at either of the last named whipping-posts. This person was one Turner, a carpenter by trade. The charge which was brought against him, and which he finally confessed, was stealing some fifty pounds of flour belonging to Ezra Hait, from Esq. Rose's mill. After sentence was passed, he was fastened in the stocks, which were constructed of heavy plank, hollowed out above and below sufficiently to contain a man's legs when the planks were shut together. They were secured by a lock. He was left in the stocks for a day, furnishing a good mark for the boys, who showered him with rotten eggs. The next day he was taken out and fastened to the whipping-post, when the remainder of his sentence, fifty lashes, were inflicted, when he was allowed to leave the county, which he was not long in doing.

At the raising of the church, a great portion of the men and women in the town assisted. Some of the women came a distance of six or eight miles, barefooted and bareheaded, and it was considered extravagant for boys not more than 15 or 16 to have hats on their heads, or shoes on their feet. This church was burned in 1831, up to which time it was not only used as a place of public worship, but for the holding of town-meetings and elections.

The first settled minister in the town of Harpersfield, was the Rev. Stephen Fenn, who died in 1833. He graduated at Yale College, in 1790, and came into the county in 1793. He was ordained in 1799, and took pastoral charge of the church. He remained in this situation until 1829, a period of 36 years. He probably attended and officiated at more weddings than any other person in the county, either before or since. In 1823, after he had preached 30 years, he came into possession of a piece of real estate, and received a title in due form from the trustees of the church, in conformity with the desire of Colonel John Harper, then deceased.

The chief employment of the settlers, during a portion of the first year, was making maple-sugar, and indeed, I believe at the present time, that in no town of its size in the county is there so large a quantity, or fine a quality of maple-sugar manufactured. Richard B. Gibbs, Esq., of Harpersfield, the present president of the County Agricultural Society, informed me that he had made 3,000 pounds in one season.

I believe in Europe the sugar-maple does not abound, at least in Scotland; and it seems strange what ideas some of the early emigrants entertained of the manner in which it existed. While some imagined the whole tree to be solid sugar, others had an idea of warm sugar, instead of sap oozing from the tree. An anecdote has been told me of one of Scotia's sons, an early pioneer to the county, and whose descendants are still numbered among her inhabitants, which, although not strictly historical perhaps, nevertheless illustrates the idea suggested above. When questioned as to what would be his employment in his new wild home, he replied: *"The making of maple-sugar, and if I find it a profitable business I intend to follow it the year round."*

The following reliable information in relation to the early settlements of Stamford, was furnished me principally by Captain Stephen Hait, of that town:—A few of the Scotch settlers along the West Branch of the Delaware, having experienced so much vexation from the Indians, after the breaking out of the Revolution, removed to Albany, Catskill, and other places on the Hudson, where they remained undisturbed until the termination of the war. Before leaving, they buried their pots, kettles, and other things they could not carry with them. They took pains to mark the places of their hidden treasures, so that they might find them again should they ever be so fortunate as to return.

Those who were tories, or friendly to the King, (Geo. III.) and opposed to the revolt of the colonies, removed to Canada. One portion of Canada was quite thickly settled by the tories, many of whose descendants are still living. A few tories remained to harbor the Indians, and aid them in killing and troubling those in favor of liberty and independence.

About 1783, the portion that had moved eastward began to return, some by way of Schoharie, Patchin Hollow, and the old Indian trail through Break-a-bin, others by way of Cairo, Windham, Schoharie kill, Moresville,

&c., to the head waters of the Delaware river, now known as Stamford. This latter route was, for a great part, through a dark wilderness of pines and hemlocks, with nothing for their guide but an imperfect foot-path, in many places entirely obstructed by trees that had been blown across it. There were no bridges, and the travellers had to cross the streams on logs, rafts, or canoes, and get their things along as best they could. If they happened to have horses with them, they forded the streams with these. One mode of moving the women and children, was by making large baskets and fastening them together,—placing one on each side, for the children to ride in, while the mother rode and guided the horse. Those who had more baggage than they could carry on horseback, formed an ingenious *carry-all*, by taking two long poles and fastening the smaller ends to some old collar, one on either side in the form of thills, and letting the larger ends drag on the ground, connecting them with some cross-pieces, and with an upright stake in each to fasten a board to; then boards across these thills formed what they called a *dray*. On this they fastened their provisions and other articles necessary to make their condition comfortable during their journey, and maintain them in their new homes, until they could raise the necessaries of life.

In 1789, a company, consisting of twenty heads of families and two single men, principally from Fairfield county, Connecticut, came into Delaware to examine the country and fix upon a favorable situation for a permanent settlement.

The names of the company, so far as I have been able to learn, were Josiah Patchin, Captain Abraham Gould, Colonel John Hubble, Aaron Rollins, Isaac Hubble, Talcott Gould, Isaac Gould, George Squires, Walter and Seth Lyon, John Polly, Stephen Adams, Peter and Eben Jennings, Joseph Hill, and one by the name of Gibson. The two single persons were David Gould and David Squires.* The journey at that period was one of imminent danger, the roads were awful beyond description, and it was frequently necessary to clear them of obstructions in order to proceed. After leaving Catskill, there was not a single bridge for their whole journey. The party, after passing several small settlements, arrived at the house of Benjamin Barlow, in Stamford, who had commenced his improvements the preceding year. He had erected a small log-hut, about twelve feet square, and also a barn, in which, as the house was too small, the party received the kind attentions of their host, while, in the absence of pasturage, the teams and horses were turned into the surrounding woods to browse. The third day after the party had arrived at Barlow's, it was discovered that the horses had strayed off in the direction of home; Abraham Gould, George Squires, and Josiah Patchin, were dispatched with three days

---

* David Squires, my informant, lives in Stamford, and is the only survivor of the company. He is now over seventy years of age.

provisions to follow up and retake the missing animals. After following the trail a short distance, the animals had taken an unexpected turn, and instead of going toward the North River, had followed up a gulf now known as Rose's Brook, and thence across the mountain, near where the present road is located. The sun had passed the meridian ere the party arrived at the height of land; a short distance down the mountain they met a hunter by the name of Israel Inman, who had settled the preceding year on the fertile flats now owned by Jacob C. Kealor, Esq., of Roxbury, and who had the day before taken up the animals, and was now following up their track to discover their owners, if possible.

Inman immediately conducted the weary travellers to his own home, where he entertained them with a repast of *venison steak,* and with all the hospitality common to pioneer settlers. Having ascertained that they were in search of a favorable situation to settle, and being well acquainted with the country, he volunteered his assistance. They examined the lands in the valley of Fall Brook, (now West Settlement,) and having decided upon making a permanent location there, they returned again to the party with the missing horses. They could prevail on but two other persons of the party to join them, Nehemiah Hayes and David Squires, making in all five persons. They were obliged to return toward Catskill, as far as John More's,* at Moresville; from which place to Roxbury, Inman had informed them there was an ancient trail, over which he had passed the year before, carrying his movables on his back.

After a laborious journey they succeeded in reaching the clearing of Inman, where they deposited their goods, until they could prepare a rendezvous of their own. The lots were measured off with a rope, when they agreed to decide by cuts who should have the middle lot, which fell upon George Squires. On this lot they erected a shelter of the rudest material; four crotched poles being firmly driven in the ground, one at each corner of the building, across their tops horizontally were laid the plates, while two other crotches of greater length were driven to support the ridge-pole: this rude frame was covered with strips of elm bark. The floor was also of bark, and a huge maple was felled just in front of the tent, against which they built their fires, and did their cooking in a kettle suspended over the coals. In this tent they passed the remainder of the summer, assembling at night and preparing their supper in their own rude style, of which they partook with a hearty relish, and then, without a covering or a pillow, they laid themselves down upon the hard floor to sleep.

The remainder of the party located themselves in the town of Stamford, principally on Rose's Brook, where many of their descendants now live, and

---

* John More moved to Moresville and settled there in 1786, and was the first settler in the town of Roxbury.

are numbered among the most respectable and enterprising inhabitants of the county.

In the winter of that year they returned to Connecticut for their families, and to bid adieu to their native State. They were soon joined by others, and the settlements grew with almost unparalleled rapidity. It was only a few years before the forests began to disappear, and the music of the blacksmith's hammer, mingled with the buzzing of saw-mills, might be heard in every valley, and the rude log-hut began to give place to the handsome farm-house.

Many incidents might be enumerated in regard to the early settlers, to illustrate more fully the prominent traits of their character. Man is emphatically a being of custom; his nature possesses all the elasticity that enables him to conform to any society or rank in life, or to any age in the world.

We have examples in history, of fond children, who have been torn from their mothers' arms and carried into captivity, where they were subject to the hardships and privations of a savage mode of existence. As they grew up the scenes of early childhood were gradually worn away, and by degrees they became accustomed to the associations and wild sports of their savage companions; indeed, they have thrown around them the most powerful fascinations, and when the boon of civilization has been freely proffered them, the ransom paid, and friends and parents ready to embrace them, they have turned gloomily away and buried themselves again in the forest, and sought their accustomed haunts.

Allowing the influence, then, of early customs on the passions, the appetites, and propensities, which make up the character and control the destinies of men, we are prepared more correctly to form a true estimate of the *avant couriers* of civilization. When we remember that they had just emerged from a long Revolutionary struggle, which had been pregnant with hope and fear, inlaid with peculiar privations—that eventual success had crowned the efforts, not of numbers, but of courage and susceptibility of endurance—we will then very naturally attribute to them *determination, fortitude, courage,* and *perseverance,* and what four attributes are more important to the pioneer than these. It was determination that prompted them to seek a home in a boundless forest—it was fortitude that enabled them to endure privations—it was courage that upheld them in the hour of fear—and it was perseverance that enabled them to toil month after month, and year after year, for the bare maintenance of life. But we have thus casually wandered from the strict matter of fact, to enable the reader more fully, if possible, to form a correct realization of the men and times of which we write, and we will now return to the original design of one or two authentic anecdotes.

Two men, by the name of Hotchkiss, who resided on Rose's Brook, near where Cillick Gould now lives, nearly, if not quite, excelled old Putnam, of

Connecticut, by their daring adventures after wolves. These two hunters one morning discovered a fresh wolf-track on the snow, and immediately determined to go in pursuit. They prepared their guns and ammunition, and started on the track. After following it part of a day, they found that the wolf had crawled into a hollow tree that had broken off near the ground, and fallen directly down a steep hill. Into this crooked tree there was no way of leveling their guns, so as to fire at the sheep-stealer with any chance of success. Being very anxious to secure their game, and having no axe to cut the tree, one of the hunters entered head foremost, with his gun to pilot the way; after getting to a crook in the tree, he made room enough to admit a little light, and when he saw the glaring eyes of the wolf before him, in this position he levelled his gun and fired, and then retreated to the open air as fast as possible. After reloading, he again entered the tree and felt his way before him with his gun; finding that all was still, he returned near enough to touch the wolf with his rifle. As he gave no signs of life, the hunter reached forward with his hand, got hold of his ears, and dragged the dead wolf out after him. This beats "Old Put," as he dared not enter a den of wolves without a rope tied to his legs, to pull him out in case of danger; but this man relied on his trusty rifle and his own exertions, to extricate himself from all trouble.

My informant also relates another incident, which I give in his own language:—"In 1790, there were quite a number of settlers that had located on Rose's Brook, from Connecticut. The names of some of them were Gould, Rollins, Hubble, Jennings, Sturges, Webster, Blish, and the Lyons, the latter of whom, together with Webster, were the mighty hunters of the party. Whether they had acquired this art in their native State, or not, we cannot say, but it is certain that it came very easy for them. The old Mr. Webster would just as soon shoot a good buck, as to eat a good dinner or say his prayers, as the story we are about to relate will illustrate.

"At that early period ministers in Delaware county were a rarity, and these Connecticut people were brought up in a strict Sabbath-day keeping; and before they had stated preaching, the inhabitants would meet on Sunday at some central house in the neighborhood, and the deacon of the settlement would read some old sermon they had brought with them. On one occasion they had met for this purpose at Deacon Webster's; he had read the text, and was proceeding with the sermon, when his black man, by the name of Amos, suddenly appeared at the door, showing his ivory, and addressing his master, the deacon: *'Massa, massa, dar is a fine fat buck in the barn-yard, with the cattle;'* The old deacon took down the rifle, (an old chunk rifle,) stepped to the door and raised it to his eye. Bang! went the rifle, and down went the deer. The deacon told Amos to keep his eye on him a little, and then replaced his rifle and resumed his sermon.

"But this was not all—old Mrs. Rose happened to be out herding the cattle, and hearing the report and seeing the deer fall, she went immediately to her husband, who was justice of the peace, and said, 'Esquire Rose, what do you, think Esquire Webster has been doing?' 'I don't know,' said he, 'my dear, what has he? 'Why, he has been shooting a deer on the Lord's day!' Next morning Esquire Webster received a *polite note* from Justice Rose, setting forth the charge against him, and inviting him to call up and pay the fine."

The following information in relation to the early settlements, was derived principally from Cyrus Burr, a highly respectable citizen of Andes, and formerly, and for a number of years, supervisor of that town.

The family of Mr. Burr moved into the county in 1794, and settled in what was then called Middletown, Ulster County, but now Andes, Delaware County, at which time the entire town, except a few farms along the river, was one unbroken wilderness. The first farm bordering on the river below the Middletown line, was owned by James Phenix, who was among the first that emigrated after the Revolution. He had occupied the place before the war, but had retired for safety during that period. A man by the name of Olmstead, who came in about the same time, possessed the second farm. The third farm had been originally taken up by a man named Burgher, whose unfortunate end we have related in a previous chapter. The next farm was occupied by Joseph Erksine, an English soldier, who was taken prisoner and afterwards enlisted in the American service. The next in course, following down the river, were Silas Parish, from Dutchess County, who had emigrated at an early day, E. Washburn, from the same place, and a few years later, Eli Sears, father of T. B. Sears, of Tompkins County, delegate to the state convention in 1846.

At Shavertown, were several families, among whom were Jacob Shaver, Adam Shaver and John Shaver, from Dutchess County, and Philip Barnhart from Schoharie County, all of whom had located there about the same time. Mrs. Barnhart, was a sister of the father of Ex-Governor Bouck, and quite a number of her descendants remain in that neighbourhood yet. The first settler back from the river was Robert Nicholson, who located about three miles up the Tremperskill, which empties into the Delaware river at Shavertown. He moved with his family, in 1793. Philip Shaver, located himself on the same stream the following spring, and Thomas More, about a mile above, sometime during the same season.

In the spring of 1797, Mark Summers settled about half a mile still farther up, and Jonathan Earl, shortly after, one and a half miles above Summers, and within half a mile of what is now Andes village. About the same time Aaron Hull, afterwards, and for several years, Justice of the Peace of Middletown and Andes, settled about one and a half miles north of the village of Andes. He reached his new home by an entirely different route, (the West Branch and Little Delaware,) from those settlers whom we have already enumerated, and consequently it is not strange that he should have been unaware of his proximity to them. It was nearly a year before he became aware of the fact, and then by simple accident.

Hull had a horse which he was obliged to turn into the woods to pick its living, and it was while in search of his horse that he unexpectedly met Earl, who was also looking for a yoke of oxen that had strayed into the woods. The place of meeting was near the village of Andes.

Early in the summer of 1794, John Burr, Henry J. Bevans, and John Thomas, with their families, moved into what is now the easterly part of the town of Andes, about one and a half miles from Phenix's, above mentioned. Burr and Bevans were from Fairfield County, Conn., and Thomas was a Welshman, direct from his native country. John Jones, another Welshman, settled within the limits of Andes, one mile west of Clark's factory, the same year—where his son and a number of his grandchildren now live. In 1795, Samuel Barlow settled in that neighborhood. During 1794, '95, and '96, settlements commenced along the western line of the town bordering on Hamden, by Patterson, Terry, Holmes, Barnes, and others, and from these points the settlements gradually spread into the westerly and southerly portions of the town.

We have been favored by a valuable correspondent, and an esteemed friend, with the following authentic account of a catamount-killing in Andes, a long time ago, that makes "Old Put.'s" adventure seem a small affair, more especially, when we recollect that the Andes catamount, like catamounts in general, was a fearless and ferocious animal—while Putnam's wolf, like all other wolves, was a cowardly and *sheepish* fellow.

The panther had made great ravages, and a party of young men resolved to kill him. Daniel H. Burr, brother of Isaac and Cyrus, and the first supervisor of the town of Andes, Moses Earl, since painfully associated with the Andes tragedy, and one Samuel Jackson, now deceased, were of the party.

Early one morning the animal was followed by his well known track, from the scene of one of his usual nightly raids, to his den, which was located in the mountain, about one mile from Clark's factory. The dogs were sent in, but refused to proceed nearer than about twelve feet, at which point the den, or rather narrow clift in the rock, turned obliquely to the left, and all that lay beyond was shrouded in complete darkness. The savage beast finding himself disturbed in his chosen retreat, sent forth, at intervals, loud and angry growls. All efforts to dislodge him having proved unavailing, Samuel Jackson resolved to enter the den, and shoot him there.

After having loaded his rifle, and permitted his anxious friends to tie a rope to one of his legs, that might be used, if necessity required, in hastening his exit, he entered the cavern. A lighted candle, thrust into the opening of a split stick, gave just light enough to make the surrounding darkness visible, and with this and his trusty rifle, Jackson entered the cave, into which, he was compelled to creep upon his elbows and knees. When at the point where the cavern's course took a new direction, he discovered the furious animal sitting upon its haunches some twelve feet distant from him, gnashing its teeth, and by the usual motions, evincing its excited ferocity. Jackson with difficulty got his rifle in a position for use, and after a deliberate aim at the panther's head, discharged it. His anxious friends hearing the growl of the wounded animal, mingled with the roar of the rifle, pulled lustily and rapidly at the cord made fast to Jackson's leg. They drew him out, but the sharp angles of the rock tore alike his clothing and his skin; he came out of the cavern almost a naked man, and astonished his anxious friends, while

"The hollow aisles of the dim wood rang,"

with his incontinent hard swearing! It was difficult to tell which was the most furious, the panther at one extreme of the cavern, or Jackson at the other.

The growling of the panther continued, and after an interval of time had elapsed sufficiently for the smoke to clear away, Moses Earl followed the knee-prints of his predecessor Jackson, and entered the cave. His shot was more effectual, and the panther gave no signs of life; Earl's exit, too, from the cave was less expeditious, and far more pleasant than Jackson's. The dead animal was drawn out from the den with little difficulty, and proved to be a full grown female, which like many another female, made up in spunk what was wanting in size.

CHAPTER IX

Increase of population in the interior of the State—Necessary alteration of the civil divisions from time to time—Erection of Otsego in 1792—Petition for the erection of a new County in 1796—New County erected in 1797—Called Delaware—Number of towns at the erection of the County -Enumeration of the other towns in the order of their erection—Names of the first Supervisors—First Representatives to the Assembly—First Court held in the County—First Judges—First Sheriff—Court-house and Jail erected—Murder of Cameron and McGilfry—Arrest of the murderer—Escape of the prisoner from jail—Re-arrested on Cabin-hill—Tried and found guilty—Sentenced to be hung—Execution a public one—Description by an eye-witness of the execution—Execution of Foster in 1819—Burning of the Court-house and Jail—One man burned—Legislative Act—Erection of the Delaware Academy—Its founder—Manner of its endowment—Geological Society formed in Delhi—Its short existence—Matter in relation to the formation of the County—Extract from the Diary of Judge Foote—Obituary Notice—List of Assemblymen since the formation of the County—Surrogates and County Judges—Sheriffs—County Clerks.

THE steady and rapid increase of inhabitants in the frontiers, or the central portions of the State, rendered the formation of new counties and towns necessary from time to time, to enable the more ready administration of government. In 1770, as before stated, the county of Albany contained by far the larger portion of the present county of Delaware; indeed, it comprised the whole, excepting a part of the towns of Hancock and Colchester. Latterly, I think in 1786, the boundaries of Ulster were increased so as to contain the whole of Delaware county east of the Pepacton, or East Branch of the Delaware; and in 1772, a new county by the name of Tryon, was organized, which included the balance, or northern frontier of the county, and the West Branch was made the dividing line, the whole of said river belonging to Ulster county.

These civil divisions remained unaltered until 1792, when Otsego county was formed from Tryon, and the southern boundary was fixed as the West Branch. It now became obvious that another county was necessary from portions of Ulster and Otsego, as those who resided north of the West Branch were obliged to go to Cooperstown to transact their business, and those who attend court, while those on the south side of the same stream did their business at Kingston; and accordingly, in 1796, the following petition was presented to the legislature, signed by the most respectable citizens of Otsego county, including the supervisors of the respective towns:

"To the Honorable the Legislature of the State of New York—the petition of the subscribers, inhabitants of the County of Otsego, humbly showeth:—

"That the Legislature of this State did, in the year one thousand seven hundred and ninety-four, contemplate the erection of a county by the name of Delaware, composed of part of the counties of Otsego and Ulster. Your petitioners, after due consideration, do think it reasonable that the said county of Delaware should be set off according to the boundaries advertised for public consideration. We, your petitioners, do therefore humbly solicit that your honorable House would pass a law for erecting the said county of Delaware.

Benjamin Gilbert,	William Cooper,		
Benjamin Griffin,	Griffian Craft,		
Russel Bartlett,	William Averill,		
Eleazer Robins,	David Ferguson,		
William Cook,	Nathaniel Golt,		
Thomas Fuller,	James Harper,		
A.H. Ten Broeck,	Elihu Phinney,		
Wm. Abbott,	Samuel Huntington,		
Joseph Holt,	Joseph Griffin,		
Israel Guild,	Sluman Wattles, Supervisor of Otsego Co.		
H. Farnsworth,	Benajah Beardsley,	"	"
James Gardiner,	David Goff,	"	"
James White,	William Beekman,	"	"
Stephen Ingalls,	Christopher Colwell,	"	"
Norman Sandon,	Joshua Dewey,	"	"
Wm. French,	Roswell Hotchkiss,	"	"
Oliver Ingalls,	Jas. Strong and Eli Parsons."		"

From the above and other petitions, it appears that in the session of 1794, a plan with boundaries was agreed upon by the Legislature, and by a concurrent resolution it was resolved to defer the erection of the new county until a coming session, "that the same be published in the public papers, with leave to any person or persons affected thereby, to appear at the bar of either house, and show cause (if they have any,) against the passage of such a bill." Accordingly, at the session of 1796, the opponents of the new measures had arrayed themselves fiercely against the proposed boundaries, and had prepared themselves fully for the contest. While the inhabitants of Walton, Cannonsville, and Deposit, petitioned to be annexed to Tioga county, those of the East Branch petitioned to remain in Ulster county, and to do their business at Kingston. As they were compelled to go there once or twice a year to transact their ordinary affairs, they might at the same time do their county business, with little expense or trouble. They also set forth, that between them and the proposed county-seat lay a hideous and almost impassible mountainous wilderness, without roads, and the people too poor to build them. The last remonstrance was signed by one hundred of the most respectable citizens of that section.

It appearing, however, from the remonstrances, that the petitioners were actuated by selfish motives, it had no other effect than to hasten the action of the Legislature, and accordingly on the 10th of March, 1797, the bill passed and became a law.

At its formation, Delaware county contained only seven towns, viz.: Colchester, Middletown, Franklin, Harpersfield, Kortright, Stamford and Walton, and with the exception of the latter, they had all existed previous to 1797. The local interests of the inhabitants, together with the steady increase of population, rendered the erection of new, and the subdivision of old towns necessary, from time to time; and in 1798, Delhi was erected into a town, from territory taken from Kortright and Walton. The village of Delhi was incorporated by an Act of March 16th, 1821; Roxbury was taken from Stamford in 1799; Meredith was taken from the towns of Franklin and Kortright in 1800; Sidney was taken from Tompkins in 1791; Hancock was taken from Colchester in 1806; Tompkins, originally called Pine-field, was erected in 1808; Masonville was erected from Sidney in 1811; Davenport from Kortright and Maryland, Otsego county; Andes was taken from Middletown in 1819; Bovina was taken from Delhi and Stamford in 1820. The name was given by the late General Root, and is of a latin origin, signifying cattle or oxen—it is both beautiful and appropriate. Hamden was taken from Walton in 1825, and was the last town organized in the county.

The Supervisors convened for the first time in the county, May 31st, 1797, for the purpose of canvassing the votes taken in the county. The following is a list of their names and the town they represented:

> Benjamin Milk, of Middletown,
> William Horton, of Colchester,
> Enos Parker, of Franklin,
> John Lamb, of Stamford,
> Roswell Hotchkiss, of Harpersfield,
> Benajah Beardsley, of Kortright,
> Robert North, of Walton.

Annexed is a list of the total personal and real ratable property in 1798, the basis of the first assessment made after the erection of the county:

Walton,	$7,197 50
Middletown,	6,366 50
Kortright,	15,399 54
Stamford,	14,375 00
Colchester,	14,803 75
Harpersfield,	7,896 00
Delhi,	7,835 62
Franklin,	11,169 84
	$85,043 75

The first representatives to the Assembly were Nathaniel Wattles and William Horton. The first sheriff was Elias Butler. The first court was convened at the house of Gideon Frisbee, on Tuesday, the 3rd of October, following the erection of the county. Before proceeding to ordinary business, it was resolved that the seal of the court should be a "stream of water issuing from a high mountain, round which shall be the words, 'Seal of the Court of Common Pleas of the County of Delaware,'" as emblematic of the surface and general features of the county.

Patrick Lamb, William Horton and Gabriel North, were judges, assisted by Isaac Hardenburg and Alexander Leal. The names of the attorneys who were admitted and sworn, were Conrad E. Elmendorf, Philip Gebhard, Erastus Root, Anthony Marvine, Cornelius E. Yates, and David Phelps.

The courts, and all other public gatherings, were held at the hotel of Gideon Frisbee, until the completion of the courthouse and jail, which was in the summer of 1799. Although the county had been to the expense of erecting a jail for the confinement of prisoners, it seems to have been an unnecessary appendage, for we note that in 1813, the Legislature passed an Act "authorising the commissioners of excise of the town of Delhi, in their discretion, to allow an inn or tavern to be kept in the building occupied as a jail;" and considering the extent of the county, Delaware has ever had, comparatively, but a small ratio of crime.

In the early part of the year 1814, the citizens of Bovina and Delhi were thrown into the greatest excitement, by the inhuman murder of two citizens and neighbors. These two men, Hugh Cameron, and Alexander McGilfrey, had been at a logging-bee on a neighbor's premises, and were murdered while passing through a piece of wood on their way home. Suspicion immediately rested upon James Graham, an Irishman, who had had an angry dispute with the men during the afternoon, and who had left for home a short time previous to their departure, pursuing the same route. He was accordingly arrested and confined in Delhi jail, from which he succeeded in making his escape a short time afterwards, in company with another prisoner. After a few days search he was recaptured and returned to jail, where he was locked in a cell, until some irons could be forged to confine him more securely. While in this situation he bethought himself of fortifying his cell in such a manner as to prevent the ingress of any one, and for this purpose he wedged the bedstead firmly between the door and the partition; he then broke the hearth of the stove into suitable pieces, and prepared to defend himself to the last minute. A large crowd of persons assembled around the outside door and in the jail, but none dared to approach the door of the cell, with the exception of one Smith, who made strong pretensions of friendship to the prisoner, and protested his willingness to aid in his escape. After having won his confidence, and when about to take his leave of the prisoner, Smith reached out his hand, which was cordially grasped by Graham, not doubting for a moment his sincerity. He was soon undeceived, however, for Smith seized his arm with a firm hold, pulling it through the door and calling for help. The prisoner was held in this position until a hole was made in the back part of the cell large enough to admit the body of a man, when the officers crawled into the cell and succeeded in securing and ironing him. The weight of the irons was forty pounds.*

The grand jury found a bill against him on the 16th of June, and the following day he was tried, and pronounced *guilty* by the jury.

I make the following extract from the records of the county clerk's office:—"June 20.—The prisoner, James Graham, being arraigned to receive the sentence of the court, was asked if he had any thing to say why judgment should not be pronounced according to law. The court therefore ordered and adjudged that the said James Graham be returned to prison from whence he came, and there to remain until the 29th day of July next, then, between the hours of 12 o'clock and 2 o'clock, to be taken from thence and hung by the neck until he be dead, and his body delivered to Asahel E. Payne and Ambrose Bryan, surgeons, for dissection."

The execution of Graham was to be a public one, and consequently great numbers of men, women and children prepared to witness the proceedings. The following information was furnished me by Isaac Burr, Esq., an eye witness.

"The people commenced pouring into Delhi from all points, the day preceeding that fixed for the execution, so that before night every house in and around the village was filled, while hundreds could get no lodgings at all. A considerable number passed the night in Meredith and that vicinity. More or less kept arriving during the night, and even up to the hour for execution. Probably such a number of people had never before been collected together in the county. The gallows had been erected at some distance in a north-easterly direction from the jail—the place was well chosen to give spectators a chance to witness the execution.† The hills rose on every side somewhat steep, and in a circular form, presenting an amphitheatre of considerable extent, in the centre of which the gallows was erected. The people commenced occupying the ground some hours before the time fixed for the execution, and a dense mass of human beings seated themselves on the hill-side, covering several acres of ground. A battalion of militia had been called out to protect the sheriff in the discharge of his duty. They paraded near the jail, and when the time arrived for the procession to move, the military marched to the ground, followed by the sheriff, Robert Leal, and the prisoner, arm in arm, together with the clergy, judges, and other officers. The militia formed a hollow square around the gallows, while the sheriff, clergy, and others occupied the

---

* I obtained the above information of Robert Leal, Esq., sheriff at the time, and who is still living, aged 77 years.

† See map of Delaware County for the exact location, in the plan of Delhi village.

platform with the condemned man, who walked with a firm step. Prayer was offered, when Graham addressed a few words to the people, declaring that 'he never murdered or stole.' The rope was then adjusted and all things made ready, when leave was taken of the prisoner, and the sheriff and clergy descended from the platform; the sheriff mounted his horse and took his station, telling Graham from time to time, the number of minutes he had to live—and at last that he could live no longer. He drew his sword and with it struck a latch: the next moment the unhappy man was suspended breathless in the air—he made but a slight struggle, and all was over.

"The people immediately commenced leaving the ground, and before night most of the vast multitude were many miles away from the place. The weather was warm, and there were one or more showers during the day, making it very muddy, which somewhat soiled the white dresses of the ladies, although I believe no serious accident took place. To finish the sentence, his body was given to the medical society for dissection, and doubtless his bones are still preserved."

The *iron-wood* handspike with which the two men Cameron and McGilfrey were knocked down, and which was found and produced at the trial, is still preserved in the Albany Museum.

The other prisoner who escaped from the jail with Graham, was named Kinney, and was a resident of the town of Sidney. He was charged with having passed counterfeit money. Expecting that search would be made, he determined, if possible, to deceive his pursuers; for this purpose, he cut his shoes so as to tie them on heel foremost, to give the impression of his having travelled in an opposite direction. He was, however, followed to Sidney and re-arrested—was afterwards tried and sentenced to the state prison for two years.

Only one other execution has ever taken place in the county, that of Nathan Foster, for poisoning his wife, in 1819. Martin Van Buren, Esq., the Attorney General, assisted the District Attorney, on the part of the people, and Erastus Root and Samuel Sharwood, were the prisoner's counsel. Judge Martin Keeler, of Kortright, was then sheriff.

Foster was a tory during the Revolution, and is reported to have been the identical person who inhumanly murdered Col. Alden, at the massacre of Cherry Valley, in 1777. Priest, in his narrative of the capture of David Ogden, who died a short time since in Franklin, Delaware County, thus refers: "This act of barbarity was perpetrated by a man named Foster, a tory at that time, and the same, who a few years since (1819) was hanged for the murder of his wife, by poison, in Delaware County, N. Y., at Delhi. That the same Foster did murder Colonel Alden, was ascertained by a certain *James Campbell,* another tory, who stated to David Ogden, that he had heard this Foster boast of the act, while they were both with the British at Niagara. He was at length overtaken by justice, and ended his miserable life on the gallows, although at the advanced age of __ years. He died without a confession of his guilt."

The spring following the execution of Graham, a fire broke out in the court-house and jail, which were then all included in one building. The following extract is from the Gazette:—

"On the 17th of April, about half-past 3 o'clock in the morning, the fire was discovered by some person, and the alarm given, but all attempts to save the building proved fruitless. What added to the horror of the scene, a young man from the town of Andes, by the name of Abraham Coon, who, but three days before had received the sentence of the court to a short confinement for the petty theft of three yards of cotton cloth, was extricated from the ruins of the building—his arms and legs completely burned off. His mangled remains were interred in the village burying ground. At this time no family resided in the building, and it was supposed the fire originated in his own room."

A meeting of the citizens was immediately called, and it was determined to apply to the Legislature for a loan to enable them to erect new buildings, without resorting to the expedient of directly taxing the people for the whole amount. The limit of the legislative session was about closing, and no time was to be lost. The late Amasa Parker, Esq., was dispatched to Albany to lay the case before Gen. Root, then a member of that body, and to co-operate with him in procuring the loan. Col. Parker did not arrive in Albany until the 10th, when he had an immediate interview with Root, who expeditiously drew up a bill covering the whole ground, and having called upon and secured the co-operation of the leading members of both the Senate and Assembly, the next morning introduced the bill, which passed rapidly through both houses, and before night became a law. The following is a summary of the bill:—The State loaned the county $8000, to be redeemed in four years, at six per cent. interest; that the jail of Greene county should be used in criminal cases, and for debtors who refuse to give bail, and that courts should be held at the house of Jesse C. Gilbert.

I am indebted to Isaac Burr, for the following information:—

"I succeeded Mr. Keeler in the office of sheriff, and the burning of the court-house and jail took place the night before I qualified and took upon myself the responsibilities of the office. I was placed in rather embarrassing circumstances. Mr. Keeler delivered over to me ten or twelve prisoners who were on the limits, and I had not so much as a 'Log Pen,' to confine them in. I, however, succeeded in getting bail for the limits in every instance. In a few days we had a law authorizing me to use the jail of Greene county. And it is a singular fact, that while we were without a jail, for several months, no case occurred that rendered it necessary to take a prisoner to Catskill, and that within two or three hours after we had a prison room in the new jail so far completed as to hold a prisoner, it was necessary to use it."

The same year that the new court-house and jail were put up, the Academy building was also constructed, and it may be interesting to some to learn the history of its origin, and to whom it is indebted for its liberal endowment. In 1770, before the Revolutionary war, John Leake, Daniel Stiles, Roger Richards, and twenty-four other associates, obtained a grant of 27,000 acres of land, comprising what is now commonly called the Beddington Patent, which lies in the towns of Franklin and Walton. In 1820, Gen. Root discovered that a large portion of this tract of land had escheated to the State, its proprietor having died intestate. He accordingly introduced a bill appropriating the proceeds of the sale of these lands to the construction and endowment of an academy at the county seat of Delaware county. The bill, after an exciting debate and a good deal of opposition, finally passed.

The Delaware Academy was one of the first incorporated institutions of learning in the interior of the State, and the first in the county, and has since maintained a high literary reputation. Connected with the institution is a valuable and well-selected library, containing several hundred volumes, and a fine collection of mineralogical specimens, principally collected by the County Geological Society.

This Society was formed in 1821. The meeting for the purpose of organization, was held at the hotel of G. H. Edgerton, on the 6th of September. Charles A. Foote, Esq., was elected president; Rev. James P. F. Clark, vice-president; Charles Hathaway, Esq., receiving secretary; Doctor Calvin Howard, corresponding secretary; and Selah R. Hobbie, Esq., treasurer; Cornelius R. Fitch, Esq., R. W. Stockton, and Ebenezer Steele, were elected directors.

Colonel Henry Leavenworth, of the U. S. Army; Edwin Croswell, then of Catskill, but afterward, and for many years, senior editor of the "Albany Argus;" and O. Rice, Esq., of Troy, were unanimously elected corresponding members.

The main object of the institution was to promote inquiry with reference to the geology, mineralogy, and the natural history of the county, although I believe the researches of the society in the county for specimens, were very limited. "The Autobiography of the Delaware Gazette" thus alludes to this Society:

"This Society had but a short existence—neither it nor any other association making us familiar with the geology or mineralogy of the county. Some years since the State expended large sums in making geological surveys of its territory, which, so far as Delaware county is concerned, was as complete a humbug as ever was known. I think the learned professor condescended to ride through our county—possibly he even slept one or two nights within our territory—but for all practical purposes, the passage through our county of a blind fiddler and his dog, would have been as promotive of public good, as the Professor's journey. Delaware county, geologically and mineralogically considered, is *terra incognita*. We know nothing of our mineral resources, notwithstanding nature hints strongly of treasure lying dormant in the bosom of our mountains."

Our limits—even did it not trespass upon the patience of the reader—will not permit us to indulge in all the minute details of the history of the county since its formation, and we shall therefore content ourselves by glancing at the most prominent features. It may with propriety be stated, that the erection of Delaware county, in the face of such decided opposition, is mainly due to Joshua H. Brett, at that time member of the Assembly from Otsego county, an eminent physician of Harpersfield, and one of its first settlers; John Burr, of Middletown, and Ebenezer Foote, merchant of Newburgh, the latter two being members of Assembly from Ulster county. Joshua H. Brett was appointed first judge, and Ebenezer Foote obtained the appointment of county clerk,* and shortly after removed into the town of Delhi, where he resided until the time of his death.

The following extract is from a manuscript journal of Judge Foote:—

"April 28th, 1828.—I was appointed first judge of Delaware county for the third time. Under my first appointment I served until I was sixty years of age—a term beyond which I could not constitutionally hold the office. I was then appointed judge, and served in that capacity until the new constitution was adopted, when I was again appointed as above stated; and what is rather unusual, my three last appointments have been made by men of different political sentiments from myself."

In 1798, the new town was erected which contained the county seat. There was some dispute as to what should be the name of the new township: General Root and others proposed calling it Mapleton, while Judge Foote and his associates wished to call it Delhi, which name finally prevailed. An anecdote is told of General Root, who was at that time young, but possessing the same impulsive, ardent, fearless disposition, which so conspicuously marked his after life, that when the decision was announced of calling it Delhi, he expressed himself in the following words to Mr. Foote, or some of his associates; "Delhi, *hell-high*—better call it *Foote-high!*" It is hardly necessary, and perhaps out of place, to predict, that were the choice now to be made, Mapleton would be the decision—Delhi being rejected, from its known *Hindoo* origin.

We are indebted to a highly respectable correspondent for the following biographical sketch of the life of the late Judge Foote—a life covering more than half a century of the most interesting period of our county—full of incident and usefulness, which affords abundant matter, would our limits permit, for a more enlarged notice.

---

* Anthony Marvine, father of Charles Marvine, Esq., President of Delaware Bank, recorded the first deed in the county clerk's office.

"Honorable Ebenezer Foote died at his residence in Delhi, on the 28th, (1818,) at the advanced age of seventy-four. Few men have been called to act as many parts in the drama of human life as the subject of this notice, or have sustained themselves as well. Judge Foote became a volunteer in the Revolution at the first beat of the drum, and continued as an intrepid soldier and active officer, until near the time of disbanding the army, in 1783. He participated in the toils and danger of the battle of Bunker's-hill, and shared in the privations and sufferings of his fellow-soldiers at Valley Forge. He escaped from the enemy by swimming the Hudson river, near New York, in December, 1777. The vigilance and ability of young Foote did not escape the observation of the commander-in-chief, from whom he received an appointment in the staff department, and finally left the army in the rank of major. His conduct during the war, won for him the badges of the order of Cincinnati, of which society he was an active member until his death; and perhaps no event of the latter part of his life afforded him more pleasure, than on the 4th of July in each revolving year, joining this little band, the remnant of his Revolutionary compeers, in celebrating the independence which they contributed to achieve.

"At the close of the war, Major Foote had little left but his title and his friends; of the former he was tenacious, and to the latter he was true. He commenced the dull round of his civil life by embarking in mercantile business, in Ulster county, in which he continued with varied success, until 1797; when, upon the organization of this county, he was appointed its clerk, and shortly afterward came to reside upon the spot where his remains are now deposited.

"Judge Foote was a member of Assembly several years, from the county of Ulster; represented the old Middle District four years in the Senate of this State; sat in the Council of Appointment with Governor Jay, and enjoyed his confidence. Upon the resignation of Judge Brett, in 1810, Mr. Foote was appointed to fill the vacancy of first judge of this county, and has ever since remained a distinguished member of the Common Pleas bench.

"Mr. Foote having been identified with party politics in 1800, fell a victim to its retribution when at its utmost height, in 1801, and was deprived of the office of clerk, upon which he relied for the support of himself and family. This event, connected with an indiscreet selection of a successor, gave rise to considerable newspaper discussion of the day, and as the case gained publicity, it secured to Mr. Foote friends who soon obtained for him an extensive and profitable land agency, which he retained during his life. Without the advantages of an early education, Judge Foote nevertheless possessed a liberal share of literary attainments. To an original and strong mind, he united peculiar amenity of manners, a high sense of moral propriety, and unyielding integrity."

The following list contains the names of the members who have been sent to the Legislature from the county, since its erection:

1798. William Horton, Nathaniel Wattles,
1799. Elias Butler, Erastus Root,
1800. Patrick Lamb, Sluman Wattles,
1801. Gabriel North, Erastus Root,
1802.   "   "   "
1803. John Lamb, Elias Osborn,
1804. Gabriel North,   "
1805. Adam I. Doll, Anthony Marvine,
1806. Gabriel North,   "
1807. John T. More, Joshua Pine,
1808.   "   Gabriel North,
1809. Daniel Fuller, David St. John,
1810. John T. More, Elias Osborn,
1811. Daniel Fuller, David St. John,
1812. Daniel H. Burr, Isaac Ogden,
1813. Robert Clark, Andrew Craig, Jr.,
1814. John T. More, Isaac Ogden,
1815. Robert Clark, Asahel E. Paine,
1816. William Dewey, Henry Leavenworth,
1817. Martin Keeler, Asahel E. Paine,
1818. William Beach, Erastus Root,
1819. James Eells, Erastus Root,
1820. Peter Pine,   "   "
1821. John H. Gregory,   "
1822. Benjamin Benedict, Asa Grant,
1823. Samuel Rexford,   "
1824. James Eells, Peter Pine,
1825. Jabez Bostwick, Harman I. Quackenboss,
1826. Erastus Root, William Townsend,
1827.   "   John Thompson,
1828.   "   Edward Doyle,
1829. William S. McCrea, James G. Redfield,
1830. Erastus Root, Matthew Talcott,
1831. David P. Mapes, Peter Pine,
1832. James Coulter, James Hughson,
1833. John Edgerton, Stoddard Stevens,
1834. Samuel Gordon, Amasa J. Parker,
1835. Dubois Burhaus, William B. Ogden,
1836. John Griffin, James W. Knapp,
1837. Jesse Booth, Thomas J. Hubbell,
1838. Cornelius Bassett, Darius Mapes,
1839. Ichabod Bartlett, Jonas More,
1840. Orsen M. Allaben, Nathan Bristol,
1841. Stephen H. Keeler, Charles Knapp,
1842. Samuel Eells, Orrin Griffin,
1843. Milton Bostwick, Nelson K. Wheeler,
1844. Edward J. Burhaus, Jesse Palmer,
1845. John McDonald, Linus Porter,
1846. Orrin Foote, Reuben Lewis,
1847. John C. Allaben, Donald Shaw,
1848. Platt Townsend, John Calhoun,
1849. James E. Thompson, Luther Butts,
1850. George H. Wisner, Richard Morse,

1851. Samuel Doyle, William Gleason, Jr.,
1852. Hezekiah Elwood, Lewis Mills,
1853. Charles S. Rogers, Daniel Stewart,
1854. Samuel A. Miller, Daniel Rowland,
1855. William B. Smith, William Miller,
1856. Haxtun.

Annexed is a list of the first Judges of the County Court, with the respective dates of appointment or election, for which the author is indebted to the New York Civil List, by F. B. Hough, Esq.:

Joshua H. Brett, March 20, 1797.
Ebenezer Foote, March 27, 1810.
Isaac Ogden, March 26, 1816.
Ebenezer Foote, Feb. 10, 1823.
Jabez Bostwick, Jan. 22, 1830.
Charles Hathaway, Feb. 12, 1840.
Nelson K. Wheeler, Feb. 12, 1844.
Edwin More, (elected) June, 1847.
William Gleason, Jr., (elected) Nov. 1851.
Jesse Palmer, (elected) Nov. 1855.

COUNTY CLERKS OF DELAWARE COUNTY.

Ebenezer Foote, March 30, 1797.
Philip Gebhard, Aug. 17, 1801.
John Doll, March 29, 1803.
Homer R. Phelps, March 6, 1809.
Asahel E. Paine, Feb. 26, 1810.
Homer R. Phelps, Feb. 12, 1811.
Ambrose Bryan, March 30, 1813.
Asahel E. Paine, Feb. 16, 1815.
Homer R. Phelps, Feb. 12, 1821.
" " (elected) 1822.
John E. Burhaus, " 1825.
Crawford B. Sheldon, (elected) 1828.
Wm. McClaughry, " 1846.
Benjamin Cannon, " 1852.
" " " 1855.

SHERIFFS OF DELAWARE COUNTY.

Elias Butler, March 20, 1797.
James J. White, Feb. 11, 1799.
Clark Lawrence, May 8, 1801.
Roswell Hotchkiss, March 29, 1805.
Nathan Edgerton, Jr., March 6, 1809.
Jabez Bostwick, Feb. 23, 1811.
Robert Seal, March 13, 1813.
Jabez Bostwick, Feb. 13, 1815.
Martin Keeler, March 6, 1819.

Isaac Burr, March 28, 1820
Martin Keeler, Feb. 12, 1821.

Roger Case,	(elected)	1822.
Martin Keeler,	"	1825.
Gurden H. Edgerton,	"	1828.
John H. Gregory,	"	1831.
Duncan I. Grant,	"	1834.
John M. Betts,	"	1837.
John Edgerton,	"	1840.
Green Moore,	"	1843.
DeWitt C. Thomas,	"	1846.
Daniel Rowland,	"	1849.
Duncan McDonald,	"	1852.
A.H. Burhaus,	"	1855.

CHAPTER X

The lost manuscript—Early organization of religious societies—Report of the first missionary—Summary of report—Different sects in the county—Educational interests of the county, and other information.

THE reader who has glanced at our preface, has already been made aware of the almost total destruction of this work by fire. And this misfortune appears nowhere more evident than in the present chapter. Several of the first pages of the manuscript, containing much valuable and important historical information, are thus irremediably lost. The information too was of a character which cannot be replaced. The index to the chapter having been burned, also containing the different points of observation, coupled with the interval of time with its moving world of other projects, have almost totally obliterated from my mind a definite idea of its contents. A general outline is all that remains.

In the first pages we had remarked the gradual march of improvement from the organization of the county, at which point the preceding chapter had reached, and the development of its moral and social resources. We had extracted from a little pamphlet the report of the first missionary to the county. His visits to the various localities, his remarks on the state of society in the different towns, forming, as they did, interesting themes of instruction and grateful comparison, we are now compelled to omit.

Speaking of the town of Middletown, the missionary thus remarks: "In this town, God appears to have made your society instrumental to the good of many souls, particularly in the settlement of Platte-kill, where the divine spirit was poured out in a remarkable manner.

"At the close of the first sermon, ten or fifteen persons came forward as if impelled by the Spirit, and seated themselves near me, with countenances marked with great anxiety. The first that answered my questions, said with a big tear upon her cheek, that she could scarcely refrain from approaching me till the sermon was closed. Soon many were in tears. I appointed a lecture in the evening, and spent the intervening time till I rose to lecture in conversing and weeping with about twenty persons; and after lecture, till late in the evening, the people appeared unwilling to leave the house. Three days afterward I returned to this place, and after preaching eight times and visiting families, found about thirty persons under conviction, and left three or four of these enjoying hopes of pardon through Christ."

In taking a cursory review of the territory over which he has passed, the pioneer missionary thus refers: "The region through which your missionary was directed to pass, is widely desolate. Two out of the five counties explored, are almost wholly destitute of Presbyterian preaching. A great part of Delaware county seldom enjoys preaching of any kind. Those living on the Delaware and its branches are famishing for the Word.

Having submitted to you this brief sketch of my labours, and the missionary field before you, allow me to drop a few suggestions relative to the direction and future prosperity of your society and its missionaries.

"The strength of your institution depends much on the zeal and energy of your officers. Let such as possess these qualifications be selected; and let them and the members be continually exhorted to unremitted exertion, remembering *Him* that denied himself even to the very death for our sakes.

"Let females also bear offices, particularly that of a committee to enlist new members, solicit donations of the rich, inspirit the society, and to visit and instruct the poor and ignorant. Select young and active missionaries, and assign them stations or limits within which to itinerate.

"As such stations, I would take the liberty of selecting—1st. Meredith and its vicinity, together with the desolate region of Charlotte.—2d. A circuit including the city, Deposit village, the Forks of the Delaware, and a part of Colchester, demanding immediate aid.—3rd. A district of country including Middletown, Roxbury, and perhaps Delhi, with settlements adjacent.—4th. Without pointing out any particular station of it, I shall mention all Sullivan county, as a missionary field, containing three Presbyterian churches, which would probably nearly support a missionary.

"The towns of Sidney, Bainbridge, Masonville, &c., should be frequently visited by your missionaries.

"I would advise that the people you design to supply, be instructed to assist in supporting your missionaries, and that they be encouraged to expect preaching in proportion to the pecuniary aid they furnish.

"Let further attempts be made to form more societies in other counties. Great exertions and more ample funds are necessary to supply that portion of the district already specified.

"You perceive, friends and brethren, you have merely entered upon the threshold of a great work. Let me urge you to press forward zealously and resolutely in the cause of humanity and religion, on the plan you have adopted. Having put your hands to the plough, after the example and injunction of our glorious pattern, never think of looking back."

Up to the introduction of this system of missionary preaching, the moral resources of the county were of the most indefinite character. Indeed, as appears from the extract of the above report, in many localities the inhabitants had not had preaching for years. Society, under such depraved and improper influences, presented but one vast gulf of moral degradation. And at this late day, when we are permitted to draw so favourable a comparison—the past in contradistinction with the present—how grateful a tribute ought we to ascribe to the pioneers of our social and moral improvement. Their peculiar hardships and privations, the ingratitude frequently bestowed upon their ardent labors for the good of others, without emolument or profit to themselves, are fitting themes for discussion in these modern times.

The establishment of churches commenced about 1816, and has kept pace with the gradual increase of population to the present time.

The different sects or denominations which exist in sufficient numbers to support stated preaching, are the Baptist, Congregational, Christian, Dutch Reformed, Episcopal, Methodist, Presbyterian, and Union.

The Methodist denomination is the most numerous: The whole county is comprised in the Delaware, now Prattsville district of the New York conference.

The county is subdivided into twelve circuits, and each circuit is filled by two preachers appointed by the conference at their annual meeting, with a limited period, not to exceed two years.

The Methodist Episcopal Church, was first regularly organized in the United States, December 25, 1784, by John Wesley and his associates, to whose laborious and energetic perseverance the church in the new as well as old world is in an eminent degree indebted for its present high degree of prosperity. The doctrines and beliefs of the society are found elsewhere, but a brief history of the origin and progress of the institution, may not prove uninteresting to the general reader.

In 1729, Mr. Wesley, A.M., Fellow of Lincoln College, in the University of Oxford, a regularly ordained minister of the Church of England, became affected by the general apathy exhibited in that body, and associated himself with a few college associates of like opinions.

A series of weekly meetings, was established for prayer and other religious vocations, and so strict was their outward deportment in comparison with that relic of aristocratic religion from which it had sprung, the Church of England, that the public, either out of compliment or derision, gave to the new organization, the appellation of "Methodist," which name it still retains.

The limits of the present sketch will hardly permit us to dwell in detail upon the gradual increase of Methodism in England, or its introduction into the other civilized countries of the old world. It was introduced about the middle of the Eighteenth century (1766,) into the United States, by a company of Irish emigrants, who landed in the city of New York, and founded the first Methodist society in the new world. The society gradually

DELAWARE COUNTY 153

The following Statistical Table, exhibiting the number of members, Sunday Schools, and collections for benevolent purposes for the entire district, is compiled from the Conference report.

Circuits and Stations	Mem.	L. Pr.	Prob.	S. SCHOOL STATISTICS.					Missionary Society.	Bible Society.	S. S. Union.	Fifth Collection.	Ten cent Collection.	Delegates.	Wes'n Univer.	Ratio.
				No. of Sch'ls.	Offi. & Teac.	Schollars.	Vols. in Library.								
Prattsville	255	1	56	3	36	150	350	$60 31	$5 00		$14 32	$5 04	$5 88		6.2
Gilboa	293	7	101	5	30	100	400	42 00	32 00	$2 80	9 00	3 00	2 00		3.3
Coeymans	350	1	5	4	25	110	400	43 90	30 00	3 00	3 30	4 43	2 30		2.2
Catskill	292		97	3	44	164	832	54 96	4 28	10 27	12 73	26 45	5 58	$2 04	9.7
Durham	310	5	55	3	29	125	370	21 66	108 57	4 00	7 97	7 61	3 00		4.
Livingstonville	201	2	20	5	40	198	321	12 00	7 41	1 50	1 55		0 60		.7
Windham	365	1	79	5	40	181	700	83 26	9 10		8 95	11 18	2 32		4.6
Lexington	202	5	14	2	15	60	260	21 41	2 50	2 82	1 00	1 00			.9
Middletown	220	2	15	3	23	95	213	23 00			3 29	1 00			1.8
Colchester	329	2	89	12	65	310	700	20 00	0 80	5 62	1 60	9 13	2 35		1.3
Beaverkill	134	2	32										2 71		
Kortright	293		37	4	24	100	125	30 84	13 42	8 71	11 65	5 49	4 16		6.
Delhi	189		74	3	25	100	220	32 96	19 46	1 70	5 27		3 80		2.3
Walton	117	1	18	2	9	35	120	10 64	5 83	1 57	1 00	1 36	1 18		1.5
Hancock	125		35	5	46	158	600	7 17	13 21		4 20	2 75	2 59		4.3
Deposit	64		24	1	11	49	160	2 75	25 67		2 50		3 00		2.9
Cannonsville	154	3	50	2	9	70	225	3 00			1 00	1 25	1 00		1.1
Jefferson	570	3	150	9	70	370	1000	84 81	17 00		16 72	20 00	4 61		3.7
Charlotte	390	6	110	8	86	462	740	90 08	30 00		5 57	22 26	2 10		5.5
Franklin	260		26	5	45	193	450	42 18	5 00	5 70	2 33	2 91	2 25		1.8
Total	5113	41	1087	84	672	3030	8186	$686 93	$329 25	$48 69	$114 19	$124 61	$51 43	$2 04	

increased prior to its regular organization, and the churches in some sections of the country had become quite numerous. These churches existed in an isolated and detached form until 1773, when the first conference was held in America. The number of churches represented was ten, who reported in total 1,160 members.

Strange as it may seem, the church, instead of decreasing during the Revolution, which immediately succeeded the first conference, met with an almost incredible increase, so that the conference in 1783, reported fourteen thousand members. At the Annual Conference in 1792, some internal dissension led a large number of members to secede, who styling themselves "Republicans," formed the germ of another denomination, since become quite numerous, as the Christian, or Unitarian Baptist Church.

In 1830, another secession took place, which resulted in the formation of the Protestant Methodist Church. At a still later period (1843,), a third secession from the radical organization was effected, which contributed the elements for the formation of another church, styled the Methodist Wesleyan Church. The succeeding year (1844,), the dissolution of the Methodist Church was brought about, the result of angry dissensions and contentions in relation to slavery, which resulted in the formation of two distinct organizations, the Methodist Church North, and the Methodist Church South.

The next religious denomination, and the only one besides Methodism, having a sufficient number among the citizens of the county, to render an article of general interest, is the Presbyterian Church. Under this head are included all the churches formerly represented in the General Assembly, viz.: Congregational, and Old and New School Presbyterian.

Presbyterianism as well as Methodism owes its origin and introduction in America to Irish emigrants. As early as 1705 or 1706, a Presbytery was convened in Philadelphia, by seven ordained ministers, four of whom were Irishmen, two were Scotchmen, and the seventh, a native-born American.

Rev. P. Douglass Gorrie, in his interesting work on *"Churches and Sects,"* says: "In 1788 the General Assembly of the Presbyterian Church was duly organized, and two years afterwards the Assembly invited the ministers of the Congregational churches to renew the Annual Convention (which had existed prior to the Revolution but had been broken up by internal dissensions,) in connection with the ministers of the Presbyterian Church."

This conciliatory feeling evinced on the part of Presbyterians, met with a mutual return on the part of Congregationalists, and resulted in 1801, in the adoption of a plan of union between the two bodies, which existed with the best of consequences for more than thirty years. Among the questions on morals, which have at different periods, disturbed the harmony of the Church, is the one respecting slavery. The Presbyterian

Church in its earlier history bore decided testimony against slave-holders and slave-holding, but foreseeing that sooner or later these dissensions would result in a dissolution of the church similar to that effected among the Methodists in 1844, they wisely resolved in future to pass that subject in silence, and since 1816, to at least a recent period, all discussions of the subject of slavery have been excluded from the General Assembly.

The work above referred to, adverting to the dissolution of the church, says, after discussing some doctrinal points which had become the issue between what were afterward styled the Old School and the New School churches: "What with complaints, decisions, protests, appeals, reversals, suspensions, restorations, &c. &c., a crisis was evidently at hand, and the notes of preparation for the Assembly of 1837, which were heard in every part of the church, gave fearful evidence of an approaching conflict. Immediately before the session of the General Assembly of 1837, the opposers of Mr. Barnes and his doctrines held a convention in Philadelphia, wherein they prepared a statement of their grievances, and drew up a memorial, with a method of reform. In the memorial they protested against sixteen errors of doctrine, ten departures from Presbyterian order, and five declensions in discipline; and as a means of reform they proposed a severance from the Presbyterian Church of all local churches, presbyteries, and synods which were not organized on strictly Presbyterian principles, and the separation also from the Presbyterian Church of such presbyteries and synods as were known to be composed chiefly of unsound or disorderly members. On the meeting of the Assembly, it was found that the Old School party, as the opposers of Mr. Barnes were called, had a small majority in the body, and finding themselves possessed of sufficient numerical strength, they proceeded, among other things, to abrogate the Plan of Union which had been formed between the Presbyterian and Congregational Churches, and to declare that the Synods of Utica, Geneva, Genesee, and Western Reserve, containing about five hundred ministers and about sixty thousand members, where the supposed heretical opinions prevailed most, were not consistent parts of the Presbyterian Church. After the close of the session, and during the year prior to the next session of 1838, the time was busily employed in preparing for a renewal of hostilities. At length the General Assembly of 1838 met. The commissioners from the different bodies appeared, and among the rest the commissioners of the four excluded synods. The Moderator of the Assembly refused to recognize a motion that these members be received; whereupon the rejected commissioners, with those who advocated their claims to a seat in the Assembly, united in disclaiming the authority of said moderator to refuse to recognize the above motion, and subsequently elected a new moderator and clerk, and organized themselves into what they claimed to be the Constitutional Assembly of the Presbyterian Church. While the latter body was transacting their business in the First church, (Mr. Barnes's,) the old body remained in their seats and transacted their business also as the General Assembly of the Church. Among important acts of the Assembly at each session, is the election of trustees to represent said Assembly as a corporate body. The two Assemblies accordingly elected two sets of trustees to fill vacancies, who subsequently claimed seats in the board; but a majority of the sitting members of the board decided in favor of those elected by the Old School Assembly. As there was considerable church property held by the trustees for the Assembly, it became a matter of importance to know to which Assembly the property belonged. The discarded trustees accordingly commenced a suit in the courts of Pennsylvania, and their claim to the property or trusteeship was allowed by the decision of the Judge. The case, however, was appealed, and the Superior Court granted a new trial. But as the Chief Justice had advanced legal opinions adverse to the claims of the New School party, the suit was very properly discontinued. Since the above period both Assemblies have met statedly, and transacted their business, each as the representatives of the Presbyterian Church in the United States. All that need be added, is, that since the above separation, greater amity and peace have prevailed, not only among the ministers and members of each branch, but between the ministers and members of both branches in their intercourse with each other."

Annexed is a list of the Presbyterian Churches in the county:

CONGREGATIONAL CHURCHES

LOCATION.	NAME OF MINISTER.	NO. OF MEMBERS
1. Franklin,	Rev. Mr. Morgan,	140
2. Harpersfield,	vacant,	84
3. Meredith,	Rev. Charles Chapman,	70
4. Deposit,	O. H. Seymour,	129
5. Hancock,	J. D. Cornwell,	36
6. Walton,	J. S. Pattengill,	150
7. Davenport,	H. Boies,	46
8. New Road,	C. S. Smith,	60
9. Hamden,	vacant,	38
		753

PRESBYTERIAN, NEW SCHOOL

10. Shavertown,	Thomas Larcom,	30
11. Cannonsville,	S. J. White,	40
12. Delhi,	Rev. D. Torrey,	145
13. Hd. of Delaware,	W. Mayo,	80
14. Colchester,	Edward Orton,	105
		400

PRESBYTERIAN, OLD SCHOOL

15. Delhi,   C. B. Smyth.
16. Hamden,   Charles Brown.
17. Stamford.
18. Hobart.
19. Bovina.

Next in importance to the establishment of churches for religious worship, and the promotion of a healthy moral tone among all classes of citizens, and nearly allied to it, as an agent in bringing about the most desirable results, is the diffusion of education throughout all grades of society.

The committee appointed by Gov. Tompkins in 1811, in presenting their report, speaking of the importance of education, thus refer:

"The commissioners think it necessary to represent in a stronger point of view, the importance and absolute necessity of education, as connected either with the cause of religion and morality, or with the prosperity and existence of our political institutions. As the people must receive the advantages of education, the inquiry naturally arises, how is this end to be obtained? The expedient devised by the legislature, is the establishment of common schools; which being spread throughout the State, and aided by its bounty, will bring intellectual improvement within the reach and power of the humblest citizen. This appears to be the best plan that can be devised to disseminate religion, morality, and learning throughout a whole country. All other methods, heretofore adopted, are partial in their operations, and circumscribed in their effects. Academies and universities, understood in contradistinction to common schools, cannot be considered as operating impartially and indiscriminately as regards the country at large. The advantages of the first, are confined to the particular districts in which they are established; and the second, from causes apparent to every one, are devoted almost exclusively to the rich. In a free government, where political equality is established, and where the road to preferment is open to all, there is a natural stimulus to education, and accordingly we find it generally resorted to, unless some great local impediments interfere. In populous cities, and the parts of the country thickly settled, schools are generally established by individual exertion. In these cases, the means of education are facilitated, as the expenses of schools are divided among a great many. It is in the remote and thinly populated parts of the State, where the inhabitants are scattered over a large extent, that education stands greatly in need of encouragement. The people there, living far from each other, makes it difficult so to establish schools, as to render them convenient or accessible to all. Every family therefore, must either educate their own children, or the children must forego the advantages of education."

The subject of universal education was one of the earliest matters of interest which drew the attention of our State Legislature. At the first meeting, after the ratification of the constitution, Gen. Clinton, then governor, called the attention of the legislature to the subject of education. He says: "Neglect of the education of youth, is one of the evils consequent upon war. Perhaps there is scarce any thing, more worthy your attention, than the revival and encouragement of seminaries of learning; and nothing by which we can more satisfactorily express our gratitude to the Supreme Being for his past favors; since piety and virtue are generally the offspring of an enlightened understanding."

In 1795, April 9th, the legislature took the first action on the subject of education, and "An act for the encouragement of schools" was passed, appropriating $50,000 annually for five years, to the establishment of and support of common schools. There were defects in this act, which its practical workings served to demonstrate, and accordingly, on the 5th of March, 1801, the attention of the legislature was again called to the subject, and the following resolution adopted: "*Resolved* That the Act for the encouragement of schools, passed April 9, 1795, ought to be revised and amended, and that out of the annual revenue arising to this State from its stock and other funds, the sum $50,000 be appropriated for the further encouragement of schools, for the term of five years.

In 1811, up to which time no fixed system had been established, Gov. Tompkins adverted to its necessity in his annual message, and an act was passed by the legislature in accordance thereto, authorizing the Governor to appoint a committee of five, to report a system for the permanent organization and establishment of public schools upon a durable basis. This committee submitted their report on the 14th of February, 1812, accompanied by a bill which subsequently became a law, comprising substantially the main features of our common school system, as it existed up to the year 1838.

The main features of the bill are comprised in the following extract from their report: "The outlines of the plan suggested by the commissioners are briefly these; that the several towns in the State be divided into school districts, by three commissioners, elected by the citizens qualified to vote for town officers; that three trustees be elected in each district, to whom shall be confided the care and superintendence of the school to be established therein; that the interest of the school fund be divided among the different counties and towns, according to their respective population, as ascertained by the successive censuses of the United States: that the proportions received by the respective towns be subdivided among the districts, into which such town shall be divided, according to the number of children in each, between the ages of five and fifteen years; that each town raise by tax annually, as much money as it shall have received from the school fund: that the gross amount of moneys received from the State, and raised by the towns, be appropriated exclusively to the payment of the wages of the teachers; and that the whole system be placed under the superintendence of an officer appointed by the Council of Appointment."

We have thus briefly drawn the outlines of the origin and development of our admirable common school system. Its history since that period, is vitally connected with that of the State, and it remains for us but to add, that under the control of a liberal and enlightened legislature, the system has realized the most magnificent results.

In 1827, at the opening of the session, Gov. Clinton, in his annual message, called the attention of the legislature to the expediency of providing "small and suitable collections of books and maps," to be attached to the common schools. No definite action was taken upon the subject at the time, but subsequently, April 13, 1835, an act was introduced authorizing the taxable inhabitants of the several school districts to impose a tax not exceeding twenty dollars the first year, and ten dollars for each subsequent year, "for the purchase of a district library, consisting of such books as they shall in their district meetings direct." In 1838, Gov. Marcy recommended that a portion of the revenue of the United Sates' deposit fund "be devoted to the purchase of DISTRICT LIBRARIES, in such of the several school districts of the State, as should raise by taxation an equal amount for that object." And the legislature, in accordance with the suggestion of the Gov., passed an act appropriating $55,000 from the annual revenue of the United States' deposit fund, "to be expended by the trustees in the purchase of suitable books for a district library."

The number of school districts in the county in 1840, was two hundred and eighty-four, viz., Tompkins 18, Sidney 11, Masonville 11, Delhi 17, Davenport 15, Hancock 8, Franklin 25, Kortright 17, Meredith 14, Bovina 13, Andes 17, Colchester 16, Hamden 13, Harpersfield 20, Middletown 20, Walton 17, Stamford 14, Roxbury 18. The total number of scholars attending these schools, as reported in the census returns for that year, was 10,651. During the ten succeeding years up to 1850, the number of school districts had increased to 302, with a total number of students 12,597, showing an increase over the preceding report of nearly two thousand students, while the total increase of population in the county during that period was but about four thousand, a more favorable report than can be exhibited by any other county in the State, and which argues strongly the gratifying advancement of the county in intellectual development. And it is upon the extent and permanency of this feeling, that the friends of education rely; and this spirit to which they appeal, in looking forward to the just appreciation and judicious improvement of those means of moral and mental enlightenment, which the beneficent policy of the State has placed at the disposal of the inhabitants of the several districts. The renovation of our common schools, distributed as they are, over every section of our entire territory, their elevation and expansion to meet the constantly increasing requirements of science and mental progress, and their capability of laying broad and deep the foundations of character and usefulness, must depend upon the intelligent and fostering care they shall receive, at the hands of those to whose immediate charge they are committed. There is no institution within the range of civilization, upon which so much, for good or for evil, depends— upon which hang so many, and such important issues to the future well-being of individuals and communities, as the common district school. It is through that alembic that the lessons of the nursery and the family fireside, the earliest instructions in pure morality, and the precepts and examples of the social circle are distilled; and from it those lessons are destined to assume that tinge and hue which are permanently to be incorporated into the character and the life.

Ought we not, then, in drawing this brief chapter to a close, to impress upon all good citizens the necessity of devoting their undivided energies to the advancement and improvement of these beneficent institutions. Resting as it does upon their support, indebted to them for all its means of usefulness, and dependent for its continued existence upon their discriminating favor and efficient sanction. The district school must become the central interest of the citizen, and the parent, the clergyman, the lawyer, the physician, the merchant, the manufacturer, and the agriculturist, each must realize that there, under more or less favoring auspices, as they themselves shall determine, developments are in progress which are destined at no distant day, to exert a controlling influence over the institutions, habits, modes of thought and action of society in all its complicated phases; and that the primary responsibility for the results which may be thus worked out, for good or for evil, rests with them. By the removal of every obstacle to the progressive and harmonious action of the system of popular education, so carefully organized and amply endowed by the State, by a constant and methodical and intelligent co-operation with its authorized agents, in the elevation and advancement of that system in all its parts, and especially by an infusion into its entire course of discipline and instruction, of that high moral culture which can alone adequately realize the idea of sound education, results of inconceivable magnitude and importance to individual, social, and moral well-being, may confidently be anticipated.

CHAPTER XI

Anti-rent Difficulties—Early grants of land within the limits of the county—Hardenburgh patent—Dispute in regard to the Western limits of the patent—Survey of the patent—Protest of the Indians—Indian deed of the land between the branches of the Delaware to Johanus Hardenburgh—Bradt patent—Enumeration of the other patents in the order in which they were granted—Land monopoly—Early restrictions placed upon grants—How eluded—Views of the early legislatures—Recognition of the grants prior to the Revolution—Validity of the manorial titles—Leasehold system—Systematic classification of deeds—Durable lease—Redemption lease—Three life lease—One and two life lease—Yearly lease—Seven year proviso—Claims of the tenants—History of the excitement—Grievances of the renters.

IN presenting to the public the history of the late anti-rent difficulties in the county, it shall be our aim, as it certainly is our duty, to narrate it truthfully, and if we err, judgment must be pronounced accordingly. We disclaim the intention of reviving in the minds of any, painful or unpleasant reminiscences connected with the past, and so far as we can do so consistently, we shall avoid any immature conclusions, or hasty expressions, that will not extenuate our determination. Those scenes of excitement, "those times that tried men's souls," are numbered among the things that were. The reign of discord is broken, and terror-stricken he has flown to parts unknown, while the gentle zephyrs of union and harmony, of good feeling and brotherly love, have spread their benign influence over the thousand hills and valleys that mark the surface of old Delaware, and as of old, peace and prosperity, with their attendant blessings, are over all diffused.

With the view of presenting the whole case more fully to the reader, we may be pardoned for drawing aside the curtain of time, and glancing at those early grants which indirectly proved the source of after disturbance.

The first of these grants was made to Johanus Hardenburgh and others, of the county of Ulster, on the twenty-third of April 1708. The defined limits of this patent, now familiarly known as the Hardenburgh patent, were, owing to the unexplored state of the interior or western part, vague and uncertain. An ancient settlement had been made at Minisink, on the Delaware—above which place no white settlement existed. The idea of the source of the Delaware, or as it was then appellated, "Fish-kill," had been gathered from the friendly Indians, who resided upon that stream, or from traders who had boldly penetrated into the wilderness to traffic with them. From these sources of information it had been established that the source of the stream lay many days' journey to the north-east, and hence the description in the original grant—"to the main branch of the Fish-kill or Delaware river;" whereas the two streams are so evenly poised at their junction, that even the more practised eye of the engineer, cannot without elaborate investigation and computation, detect the larger.

It is not strange, then, that the question should at an early day be agitated, "which is the main branch of the Delaware, or Delaware river proper?" and consequently the western limits of the Hardenburgh patent. It was urged by those who assumed that the Hardenburgh title extended only to the East Branch, that it was so understood by the patentees themselves, and that the original survey extended only to that boundary line. The facts relating to this controversy, so far as I have been enabled to glean them, are these. In 1749 Ebenezer Wooster run up the East Branch, and the same year, or the year succeeding, Robert Livingston, also in the employ of the proprietors of the patent, surveyed and located the West Branch. The Indians, who still held peaceable possession of the territory between the branches, either from a misunderstanding on their part, or other motives, availed themselves of the technical misapprehension of the language of the instrument they had executed, and protested in a body to the agents of the government, that the owners of the patent had reached beyond the limits of their purchase, and were trespassing upon their territory. Hence it is obvious that while this matter remained unadjusted, the surveys on the disputed part of the patent should have been suspended, while they were prosecuted upon the other sections. The final result of these disputes between the patentees and Indians was a compromise on the part of the patentees, and the consummation of a second purchase, as will appear by the following instrument:

"To all christian and other people whatsoever to whom these presents shall or may come or concern, we Sandervatheverander, Anough, Hendrickhokeau, Swathekeen, Able, Renp, Shenck, Mounau, Jacobus, Mathesso, Benjamin, and others, All lawful owners and proprietors of a certain tract or parcel of land lying in the county of Ulster and Albany; sendeth greetings: know ye that the abovesaid Indians, for divers good causes, and considerations, them thereunto moving, but more and especially for and in consideration of a certain sum of one hundred and forty-nine pounds, nineteen shillings, current money of the colony of New York, to them or some of them, in hand paid, before the ensealing and delivering of these presents by Johanus Hardenburgh, of Rosendall, in the county of Ulster, and province of New York, hath given, granted, bargained, sold, released, ratified and confirmed unto the said Johanus Hardenburgh, all that certain tract or parcel of land, situate, lying and being, between the Fish-kill and Papagouck river, in the county of Ulster and Albany. Beginning at the head of the Fish-kill, and from thence running with direct line, to the head of Catricks-kill, and from the head of Catricks-kill with a direct line to the head of Papagouck river, and thence down the east side of the said river Papagouck to a certain place called Shokakeen, where the Papagouck river falls in the Fish-kill, and then up the said Fish-kill, including the same, to the head thereof or the place of beginning, together with all the lands, hills and valleys, mines and minerals, whatsoever, contained within the bounds of the said tract of land, together with free fishing, fowling, hawking, hunting, and all other profits whatsoever. To have and to hold the above said tract or parcel of land and premises, with the appurtenances thereunto belonging or in anywise appertaining, unto him the said Johanus Hardenburgh, his heirs and assigns forever, and to the only proper use benefit and behoof of him the said Johanus Hardenburgh, his heirs and assigns forever."

"In witness whereof, we the said Indians, have put our marks and seals, this third day of June, Anno Domini, one thousand seven hundred and fifty-one."

"Signed by
"SUPPAU, JAN PALLING,"
"and twenty other Indian proprietors.

"Sealed and delivered in presence of
"EVERT WYNKOOP, and
"CORNELIUS ELMENENDORF."

The above deed was acknowledged on the third day of June, 1751, before A. Gaasbick Chambers, Judge of the Court of Common Pleas of Ulster county. The receipt for the consideration expressed in the deed, is endorsed upon the back of the instrument.

The next grant was made to Arent Bradt and others, on the third of June, 1740. The grant was contained in four distinct parcels; three of them lay upon the Susquehanna, or its branches in Otsego county, the other tract lay in Delaware, upon both sides of the West Branch, near its source. The whole patent contained ten thousand five hundred acres.

In 1769, Dec. 8, John Harper, and twenty-one other associated individuals, obtained a patent of a tract of land containing twenty-two thousand acres.

In 1770, Lawrence Kortright and his associates, obtained a patent of a large tract of land, principally contained within the limits of the present town of Kortright. The same year the following tracts of land, which, together with those already specified, comprised nearly all the territory of the county, were granted to various associations.

The Goldsborough patent, of 18,000 acres, to Alexander McKee, and others.

The "Franklin patent,"* of thirty thousand acres, to Thomas Wharton, Rees Meredith,† and others, situate in the towns of Delhi, Meredith and Davenport.

The Adaquaintance, or Charlotte river patent of twenty-six thousand acres, in the valley of the Charlotte river, in the counties of Otsego, Delaware and Schoharie, was granted to Sir Wm. Johnston and others.

The Bedlington patent, containing twenty-seven thousand acres in the towns of Franklin and Walton, was granted to John Leake, and his associates‡

John Clark obtained a patent for two thousand acres in the town of Franklin. Charles Babington, also procured a grant for a like quantity.

The Walton patent, was also granted to Wm. Walton and his associates.

In 1775, John Rappalja and others, obtained a patent of thirty thousand acres of land, situate in the towns of Sidney, Masonville, and Tompkins.

The vast compass of the Hardenburgh patent, when its limits had been surveyed and located—a grant of something less than two millions of acres to a single individual,—was a species of monopoly, which, even the British government, with her aristocratic notions, failed to relish, and an order was issued preventing grants of more than a thousand acres to single individuals, or when associated together, of a number of thousand equal to the number of associates.

This act, although beyond dispute it put a restraining check upon land monopoly, yet it did not entirely attain the desired object of preventing them "in toto." It was cunningly eluded by scheming speculators, by substituting either fictitious names, or privileged to use those of their friends, who upon the granting of the patent, executed their respective assignments to the individual for whom the grant was obtained.

It was under these modified restrictions that the public domain became the easy prey of the consummate land speculator, up to the period of the dismemberment of the colonial government. But when the jurisdiction of territory passed from the yoke of a foreign prince to the direct control of the people themselves, it was then made subservient to the promotion of the best interests of the State, by more stringent modifications.

The attention of the legislature, was directed at an early day to the theory and results growing out of these land monopolies. Their eventual tendency seemed too much toward the laying a foundation of a future aristocracy, to comport with the republican spirit of the fearless and energetic statesmen of those times—its results could hardy harmonize with the end desired to be attained by the institution of a new and novel

---

* Called Franklin patent, after Wm. Temple Franklin, who became proprietor of a portion in 1785; hence, also, the origin of the town of Franklin.

† Rees Meredith, after whom the town of Meredith took its name.

‡ This was the patent which escheated to the State, the proceeds of which were appropriated by the legislature to the use of the Delaware academy.

form of government. It could but centre in single individuals a mighty controlling influence, not only over those who became their tenants, but indirectly it might extend to and control the machinery of government. It would give to the capitalist the reins of weal or woe to republicanism, and the high hopes centered upon it, by the annihilation of that social, moral, and political freedom, guaranteed and established by the declaration of our independence, which had emanated from the old congress-hall in Philadelphia, with the unanimous acquiescence of that venerable body, and had been given to the world, a marked epoch in her history and certain omen of future good.

Accordingly we note, that while the State in all good faith acknowledged the validity of previous grants, in 1777 John Jay introduced the following preamble and resolution, which was acquiesced in by the legislature:

"Whereas it is of great importance to the safety of the State, that peace and amity with the Indians within the same, be at all times supported and maintained: And whereas, the frauds too often practised toward the said Indians, in contracts made for their lands, have in divers instances been productive of dangerous discontents and animosities:

"Be it ordained, that no purchases or contracts for the sale of lands, made since the fourteenth day of October, in the year of our Lord 1775, or which may hereafter be made, with, or of the said Indians, be deemed valid unless made under the authority and with the consent of the Legislature of this State."

All these early grants, were made prior to the Revolution. The parties who owned them resided in New York, Philadelphia, and other cities. The titles of those who embraced the cause of American liberty were afterward ratified by the home government, while those who abetted the English suffered the confiscation of their property. The Adaquaintance patent was the only one confiscated in the county.

This much I have premised in relation to the origin of the early grants, but the immediate consequences which grew out of this mistaken policy, demand a more particular notice.

In relation to the validity of these titles; I find in the XXXVI. section of the first constitution of the State, which was ratified at Kingston, April 20th, 1775, the following declaration:—"And be it further ordained, that all grants of land, within this State, made by the King of Great Britain, or persons acting under his authority, after the fourteenth day of October, one thousand seven hundred and seventy-five, shall be null and void; but nothing in this constitution contained shall be construed to affect any grants of land, within this State made by the authority of the said King, or his predecessors, or to annul any charters, or bodies politic by him, or them, or any of them, made prior to that day." And in 1822, when the present constitution was adopted, this same clause was incorporated with all its original force. So far, then, as our present system of legislation has had aught to do with grants made under the colonial dispensation, it has been but to ratify and confirm them under a restricted and modified form—in which the principle of confiscation was not recognized.

The closing scenes of the revolutionary struggle, were succeeded by bright prospects of future prosperity. Its favorable termination could have been attained but by the aid of a higher Power, and in that circumstance gleamed in the dim future the guaranty of our prospective prosperity. But the condition of the country was sadly prostrated. A long and momentous struggle had exhausted the resources of the community—that social and moral degradation ever the accompaniments of war—the financial crises, the partial bankruptcy of the State, by their refusal to redeem the national currency to the amount of several millions, produced a powerful reaction, even more threatening in its consequences than a continuation of war.

Out of these hard times, coupled with the universal poverty that prevailed among the early settlers, sprung up of necessity, a system, the *leasehold system*. A system at that time to a great extent optional with the tenant. It offered the poor man a chance, by economy and industry, of supporting his family and enriching himself without the investment of any capital but his time and labor, and consequently the tenant accepted the proffered bonus regardless of the pregnant future. Under this system of populating the soil a large portion of Delaware county was occupied and improved. "These tenures have been leases, seldom conveyances of the fee, either by warranty or quitclaim; and they can be resolved into four general classes, though there may be slight differences between individuals under each of these kinds."

There will be sufficient uniformity, however, among those but slightly differing to warrant this arrangement.

The first kind is the *durable lease,* given for "as long as grass grows and water runs," or "forever." Under this lease the lessee, his heirs and assigns, are entitled to retain possession of the premises described therein, using and improving the same, as his interest or judgment may dictate, with full knowledge and confidence, that as long as he abides by the terms of his contract, and pays the yearly rent—a stipulated sum or quantity for the use of his farm—he or they can occupy and hold, and forever. In leases of this kind, given on some of the estates, there is reserved, upon every alienation of the premises, otherwise than by last will or testament, a certain proportion of the consideration, usually one-fourth, whence the term quarter-sales; the tenant covenanting to pay such proportion upon every sale. And, connected with this reservation, there is sometimes this privilege, that the lessor, or landlord, shall be permitted, himself, to purchase from the tenant, where a sale at any given sum is contemplated, at the proposed price, if desirous to do so. But aside from these reservations, and such others as may have been agreed to, as well by the tenant as by the landlord, it rests entirely with the tenant whether he will have a constant and lasting home, or surrender it. Holding possession of his landed estate under a contract, in which the rent, whether in kind or amount, is particularly mentioned and specified, fulfilling *his* part of the agreement, he need have no fear that the avarice or hostility of his landlord can place any other burthen upon him, than what he himself has consented to bear. Claiming and exercising only such privileges as he has covenanted to receive, and giving in return therefore, such equivalent as he has agreed, the growing population of the country, the increased productiveness, and consequent enhanced value of the land, can make no addition to the sums he has to pay for occupancy. If the products of his toil and the beasts of his field bring a more than usual return, no cupidity can demand a proportionate increase in the amount due from him for the soil he cultivates. The farm he tills, he knows its bounds, the rent he pays he knows its present sum, and the amount for any future time. Here is a stability beyond the possibility of variation, provided he so wishes, and so determines.

The second kind is the *redemption lease*, uniting the peculiarities and benefits of a lease, with the vested right to become the owner of the fee. Under leases of this character, the tenant may pay, for the use and occupancy of the soil, the stipulated rent, or he may purchase, at a specified price, the fee, and in very many cases, upon whatever part of the purchase-money he pays, legal interest is allowed him, which is applied as so much towards the agreed rent. Two alternatives are offered him, either of which he may adopt; or he may hold under both at the same time, as in the case of part payment of the purchase money, and payment of rent, exceeding the interest of the purchase-money, thus part paid. But accepting either, or holding under both, *his* choice becomes that of his landlord. He must be bound and governed by such conclusions and determinations as his tenant approves and adopts. If preferable to pay the rent, which seldom equals a seven per centum interest upon the actual worth of the land, the lessor cannot take away the privilege: and if unpleasant, and as he may imagine, degrading reservations attach to him as a lessee, he has but to decide and to act, and his is the pleasure of being a fee-owner. Two ways being marked out before him in which to act, no one but himself can be in fault, if he prefer to tread the one most rugged and toilsome, as he alone can select the easier and more agreeable. In many cases, particularly where the lessee has no capital but his wits, and no labor-machines but his own strong hands, redemption leases are much more desirable than a contract for sale. For such, it is much easier to pay the rent, even when the highest pay the annual interest, and a certain portion of the principal, than to make a down payment of the whole. In this kind of lease, also, the tenant finds the same desideratum we have noticed in the first class mentioned, that no changes or circumstances can increase his yearly rent, as long as he maintains his covenanted contract, while in addition, he has the power to change, at any moment, his estate from leasehold to freehold. Surely, no one can fail of observing, that such tenants have great and peculiar privileges, and that any one must be unreasonable who seeks to rid himself of both alternatives.

The third kind is the *three-life lease*, which remains in force during the lives of any three persons, whose names are inserted in the lease, or until the death of the last survivor. From the necessity of the case, such leases being compulsory on the landlord, and available for the tenant, only during the lives of the persons selected, and the uncertainty of life being so great, there can be none of that stability which characterizes the other kinds mentioned. The insertion of the name of a child as one of the lessees, may prolong the leasehold estate through two generations, but can hardly extend it to a third. In most instances, they will but little exceed the duration of a single generation. Viewed in the most favorable light, they are marked by a great degree of uncertainty; an uncertainty, moreover, entirely independent of the parties to them, and one which the tenant cannot by the most prudent and careful watchfulness, obviate. In this respect, at least, they must prove themselves very objectionable.

Nearly allied to this class are the *one and two life leases*, which we shall here consider, because they depend upon, and are characterized by the same uncertainty. The individual name of each of these varieties marks their differences. Each from its precariousness, would seem to be adopted with hesitation, and if adopted, to prevent the lessee from complaining at any event which might happen.

The fourth and last kind is the *yearly lease*, the name of which gives its character. It runs only for a twelvemonth's time, and expires on a given day and date, neither party being bound on a future agreement, to adopt or follow the terms of a former one. Future rent or use must be arranged as the parties in interest can agree, each having the privilege of acting with perfect freedom. In the familiar instances of a yearly lease of a dwelling or a wareroom, the same principles are involved, and the same laws govern. To both, the lessor and lessee, they can neither be desirable nor beneficial; to the one as furnishing a home and habitation for only a little while, and consequently weakening his desire to become a thrifty farmer, and deadening his ambition; to the other, as affording only a poor prospect of any valuable improvements, and increasing the chances of deterioration.

Under leases belonging to some one of the above described classes, these lands, and many other tracts, have been held and occupied, from a time anterior to the organization of our State institutions. Under this leasehold system, the tenants were prosperous. By a great and gradual change the forest had given way to cultivated fields, and the rude hut to splendid or at least commodious mansions. Yet amid numerous gratifying and beneficial changes, at a time when general depression was far removed from the mass, and when prosperity was waiting upon the people, a surmise crept in among them, that the tenures under which they lived were onerous, anti-republican, and unjust, and that as individuals and citizens a strenuous opposition was demanded of them. A feeling extremely radical and consequently highly dangerous, seemed to have pervaded the general mass, seeking some escape. This local excitement discovered a way, and the pent up spirit rushed forth and assumed the name of the local cause which produced it. Some, the calmer and more worthy sort, who honestly believed their leases highly objectionable, and, of right, ought to be modified and corrected, adopted the new name, under which in a legal, honorable way, they meant to combat the error and gain the right. Others again, the larger portion, who fancied they saw a new and easy way to pay their debts, which, like an incubus, were pressing them down, and who stopped not to inquire whether justice and law were with them, provided they could gain their wished for ends, rallied under the gathering word of anti-rentism, and uncouth disguises, and called themselves "Indians," assuming the high-sounding titles of the sons of the forest, and by their actions gave all to understand, that they were determined to prosecute to success their treasonable designs, by force, if necessary, and that they were firmly resolved to pay no longer any rent, or acknowledge a landlord's title. Still another class, followers of Fourier and Owen, world-conventionists, who give a ready support to every scheme, however wide from nature, or wanting in common sense, joined themselves to the two former, and gave them their sympathy and assistance. And dishonest and designing politicians, who could pierce the future, just far enough to see that this excitement, if properly managed, would become a popular doctrine with the great body of those living under such tenures, eagerly seized hold of it, and with brazen lungs trumpeted it to all around, not forgetting to laud their own patriotism in thus coming forth in the support of right, and determined, like many others called honest and pure, to ride into office and gather the spoils.

To all these classes anti-rentism has been as it were a magic word, and under it, they have attempted to repudiate solemn contracts, and defraud the landlords of their honest dues. We are well aware that this position will be denied; but in support of it we refer to facts, now well established, and familiar to all cognizant of the machinery and contrivances of anti-rentism. As a general thing, all the tenants have claimed the protection of associations, have paid a specified tax per acre for such protection, and under the instructions of such associations have refused to pay the yearly rent. That they have so done, is proved from acknowledgments in familiar conversations, and from their own confessions made before legal tribunals, under the sanctity of an oath.

With such objects in view, many counties have rallied under the same standard, and seem determined that it shall be triumphant, even at the expense of law and order. And as the flag of "equal rights" is thrown to the breeze, and misguided and frenzied men are gathering around it, and designing demagogues are driving them on, a duty is placed upon us to inform ourselves of the grievances, under which they imagine they are suffering, and to understand the means adopted for their removal, so that we may be enabled to judge and act correctly, like honest men and honest citizens.

The complaints of tenants are various, but they generally take some or all the following forms—either that the claim of those who assume to be lords of the manor, is unfounded and fictitious; or that the leases contain provisions opposed to the spirit of our republican institutions, or unjust and oppressive in themselves; or that they are precluded from inquiring into and disputing the right of the lessor, though he had no right to lease to them the lands. As a remedy for what they then feel unjust and unequal, they ask such a modification of the law, that the landlord should be bound legally to establish his title, or fail to enforce the conditions of the lease, and also that the right to distrain may be taken away. These charges are supported in part, by those, who from their inability to learn the facts in the case, are necessitated to obtain their information from secondhand sources, and who are unwilling to believe any person would bring forward such grave and weighty accusations, without, at least a fair and plausible foundation; and they also receive countenance from another class, who stifle reason's voice when she speaks not in accordance with their passions, and will not be convinced of the fallacy of the arguments they advance, or if convinced, are like those who—

> "Convinced against their will,
> Are of the same opinion still."

But however supported, it becomes us calmly to investigate the charges, and learn their falsity or correctness.

The terms of many of the original leases, were seven years rent-free, and thereafter a yearly rent of one shilling per acre. So great an inducement was this specification, that even those who could have purchased and paid in full for their land preferred the other alternative.* At the expiration of the seven years, many were still too poor to meet their yearly demands, which through the forbearance of the proprietors, were suffered to pass unpaid, and accumulated from year to year. These *back-rent* demands, which on some places accumulated to several hundreds of dollars, was one of the principal moving causes of the commonly styled "anti-rent war."

That the people had just claims for the revision of existing laws, in relation to distraining for rent, and of ejecting tenants from their farms for

---

* David Squires, and many other original settlers.

the non-payment of rent, when there is unencumbered personal property enough on the place to satisfy the demand, none will deny. And further, if they doubted the validity of the title, the interest of the tenant involved gave him a perfect right to demand an investigation. It was a duty they owed themselves and their posterity to have the matter tested, and the validity of the title established, or declared null and void.

But to speak more definitely; the excitement first showed itself in the form of a mass meeting; accompanied by strong resolutions, and followed up by the refusal of tenants to pay the annual rent, within the manors of Rensselaer and Livingston; and to oppose more effectually the officers in the administration of the law, by screening themselves from observation and detection, masks and disguises were substituted.

The following are what the original anti-rent association claimed as the grievances of the tenants or rent-payers, as published sometime prior to the period when the excitement assumed so popular a form.

"First, It is held by this class of community, that they are under an unequal ratio of taxation, they paying all, and the Patroon none, for the support of either the county or State government.

"This taxing them for lands owned by somebody else, they hold to be an unjust and exorbitant demand.

"Secondly, They consider it wrong, legally, as well as wicked, that the lessor has power to collect rents, while the lessee has no power to contest that right.

"Thirdly, It is believed that this system of things, as practised on the renters of Rensselaer and Livingston manors, has an improper bearing on the elective franchise, through fear of oppression.

"Fourthly, The right and power of *ejecting* tenants of their farms for the non-payment of rent, when there is personal property enough on the premises to pay it, is held to be extremely arbitrary, and is often done to favor a friend.

"Fifthly, They declare against the injustice of being exposed to *ejections* from their farms and homes, merely on account of failing to pay the rent every year. It is the *principle* or *power* of this trait of the leases, that they object to; though it were never put in force. And also, from being exposed to *forfeit* their leases if they failed to live up to every requirement in those instruments.

"Sixthly, But it may be said, that men ought to abide by their bargains, and that they need not to have taken such leases. To this it is replied, that those leases were in a manner forced upon all families who now live upon leased premises, which was done as follows: At first, when the country was new, the Patroon was very good and indulgent, to such as would settle on his manor, even sometimes giving the use of the land for seven years for nothing, with the promise of a good and indulgent lease at the end of that time. During this period, be the same longer or shorter, considerable improvements were sure to be made on the land. But now comes the pinch: a lease is made out, which the renter sees at once is in a considerable degree subversive of his own natural rights as a free citizen. What can he do? He must either accept of it, or lose several years' labor. Thus it is asserted, that these leases were in a manner *forced* upon the rentees.

"Seventhly, The rentees hold that the land they occupy is their own, on account of what is called *legal* possession: that is, being actually on the land, and by enclosing it, while the Patroon's possession is by *proxy* only. But if it is neither the Patroon's nor the rentees', then they hold that the manor belongs to the State, as they abjure the claims of the pretended owners altogether.

"Under the idea of statute prohibitions, it is known that men cannot sell their lives, their liberties, their children, their wives, nor their servants. A man cannot burn his own house, nor even abuse a dumb beast, although the animal may be his own. He cannot sell his vote, nor buy one at elections. The statute prohibition goes against all frauds and usurpations of every nature; on which account it is believed that the requirements of many of the leases do in many particulars infringe on these wholesome principles,* and ought, therefore, to be shorn of these hateful traits of ancient feudalism, by the shears of legislative authority, which would go far to tranquillize the minds of the manor rentees, if nothing *more* can be done in their favor."

---

* On the Rensselaer manor, the proprietors reserved all water powers, mines, ores, and mineral beds, of every name and nature. They reserved the right to make roads, to cut wood and timber for various purposes, and to convey it on, over, and through any of the lands of the manor, except such as the patentees sold.

CHAPTER XII

Introduction of the excitement into Delaware county, 1844—Roxbury—First public meeting—Description of the costume worn by an Indian—Molest John B. Gould—Second attempt to enforce submission—Tar and feather H. More—Tar and feather T. Corbin—Sheriff's papers taken and destroyed—First *equal rights' convention*—Legislative proceedings—Passage of an act preventing persons appearing in disguise—Copy of the same—An act of D. W. Squires—Extract from a letter to the Adjutant General—Organization of an armed force by the sheriff—Steele in limbo at Andes—His defence—Letter to the sheriff—His release—Antipathy of anti-renters against Steele—His courage—Their threats—Shacksville battle—Particulars of the same—Names of prisoners—Sale in Andes—Painful death of Steele—His last moments—Extract from the correspondence of the Albany Evening Journal—Funeral services—Indignation meetings at various places—Resolutions passed—Summerset of anti-rentism.

IN the early part of the summer of 1844, through the co-operation of some leading anti-renters in Schoharie county, where the excitement had taken hold the preceding year, the agitation was introduced into Delaware, first into the town of Roxbury. Before any publicity was given to the proceedings, the articles of association had received the signatures of something more than fifty voters of the town, most of whom had provided themselves "As knights of old, with coats of mail." Report, it is true, with her pliant tongue had diffused her thousand rumors of the characters, manners and customs of the pretended aborigines of the forest; an intense interest had been awakened to learn who, and the "why and wherefore" of the new party; but like the celebrated know-nothings of the latter day, "they knew each other, knew others, but were not known." Soon, however, the excitement assumed a more public form, and the adherents of anti-rent principles became more bold in the confidence of their strength, and by the co-operation and adhesion of some of the leading and most prominent citizens of the town, a great majority of her population were eventually drawn within the meshes of anti-rentism.

The first public proceeding on the part of the Indians in Roxbury was a meeting at the public house of Thomas Keater, a respectable citizen of the town, attended by a large concourse of citizens, and the *elect* in full uniform. The excitement carried with it a novel aspect, which presented itself particularly to the young and inexperienced. Many young men of respectability and promise, entered the ranks, and embraced it ardently, but the great majority were those whose habits and reputation would hardly warrant so pleasing an encomium; who brought with them and incorporated an element in anti-rentism, which however high-toned and worthy of consideration the original aims of that organization might have been, was doomed to place a dark stain upon its future history, and defeat eventually its dearest interests.

A description of the costume worn by those who appellated themselves Indians, although appropriate here, yet nevertheless it would be a delicate task even for the pencil of the artist. The covering which concealed the head was usually of *sheepskin*, with apertures through which the wearer might discern what was going on in the world without—another corresponding to the mouth, and yet another for the accommodation of the nasal organ, through which he inhaled a portion of the aerial element necessary to support the human system. The exposed or outer surface of this mask was usually painted in divers shapes, to accord to the wearer's fancy as to making an impression, just as some men wear their hair long or short, curled and tastefully combed, or careless and unassuming. Some, even more given to the wonderful, went so far as to substitute the necessary appendages of some quadrupeds, and imagined themselves elevated above the generality of the human species, in the capacity of sporting a huge pair of *horns* or a *horse's-tail*.

A calico dress, furnished by the patriotism of the fair sex, and sometimes to the discomfiture and inconvenience of members of the family at home, through the scarcity of that commodity, encircled around the waist by a belt usually ornamented by a profusion of tassels and other fantastic ornaments, together with the implements of warfare, completes the cabinet of an *artificial Indian*.

During the summer of this year parties were frequently seen in disguise, and several peaceable citizens who had chanced to think differently from themselves, belonging to what was termed the *up-rent*, or law and order party, had been molested and severely threatened with rewards for their perverseness. The first open act of hostility was perpetrated on the sixth of July, upon the premises of Mr. John B. Gould, who, regardless of the threats and the timely warning of the association to desist from blowing his horn, had continued to use it as a signal to call his workmen to dinner. Upon the day in question, he had as usual blown his horn at noon, when five Indians, equipped and armed for fight, presented themselves at his door, and demanded redress for the insult he had given to the authority of the association. A spirited and angry discussion ensued, when they were compelled to retreat from the premises, to the tune of the "old king's arm and shell."

Smarting under their unwelcome defeat, a second company was dispatched the following Tuesday to enforce submission, and with instructions to seize the gun and horn, and if necessary mete out to Mr.

Gould a salutary coat of tar and feathers. The sun had just arrived at the meridian, when a favorable opportunity presenting itself, the signal whoop was given, and the savage horde sprung from their hiding places, and with demonlike yells rushed up and surrounded Mr. Gould, who was standing with his little son in the open air in front of the house.

We were that son: and how bright a picture is still retained upon the memory, of the frightful appearance they presented as they surrounded that parent with fifteen guns poised within a few feet of his head, while the chief stood over him with fierce gesticulations, and sword drawn. 0, the agony of my youthful mind, as I expected every moment to behold him prostrated a lifeless corpse upon the ground. His doting care and parental love had endeared him to his family. But he stood his ground firmly; he never yielded an inch. Conscious of right, he shrank from no sense of fear—and finally, when a few neighbors had gathered together, a second time they were driven from the premises without the accomplishment of their object. The Indians marched off the premises and down the road in *single file*. About three miles below they overtook and tarred and feathered Hiram More. In September following, Timothy Corbin was *tarred* and *feathered* at Daniel W. Squires', in the same town, on general training day, while assisting the sheriff, Greene More, Esq., in the service of some official papers. The sheriff's papers were also taken and destroyed.

The following is copied from "The voice of the People," a paper established at Delhi, as the organ of the new party. "On the first day of Oct., 1844, a little band of true patriots assembled in Bovina, at the house of James Seacord, and united in holding the first *Equal Rights Convention* ever assembled in Delaware county. At that convention, John McDonald, of Kortright, and George Thompson, of Andes, were nominated to the assembly." This ticket was defeated in the main, although one of the candidates, having been endorsed at the Delhi convention, was returned to the legislature.

Early in the session of the legislature of 1845, an act, entitled "An act to prevent persons appearing disguised and armed," passed rapidly through both houses of the legislature, and receiving the support of the Governor, became a law.—*Hammond's Political History of New York.*

The following is a copy of the act: The people of the State of New York, represented in Senate and Assembly, do enact as follows:—

§ 1. Every person, who, having his face painted, discolored, covered, or concealed, or being otherwise disguised, in a manner calculated to prevent him from being identified, shall appear in any road or public highway, or in any field, lot, wood or enclosure, may be pursued and arrested, in the manner hereinafter provided; and upon being brought before any judge or other officer, hereinafter designated, of the same county where he shall be arrested, and not giving a good account of himself, shall be deemed a vagrant, within the purview of the second title, of chapter twenty, of the first part of the revised statutes; and on conviction, as provided in the said title, shall be committed to, and imprisoned in the county jail, of the county where such person shall be found, for a term not exceeding six months; and all the magistrates authorized in and by the first section of the second title, in the second chapter of the fourth part of the Revised Statutes, to issue process for the apprehension if charged with any offence, are authorized and required to execute the powers and duties in relation to the offence created by this act, which are conferred and imposed on justices of the peace, by the said second title of chapter twenty, and all other powers and duties conferred and imposed by this act.

§ 2. Every sheriff, deputy sheriff, constable, marshal of a city, or other public peace officer, or other citizen of the county where such person or persons shall be found disguised as aforesaid, may, of his own authority, and without process, arrest, secure, and convey to any such magistrate, residing in the county where such arrest shall be made, any person who shall be found having his face painted, discolored, covered or concealed, or being otherwise disguised as aforesaid, to be examined and proceeded against, in the manner prescribed in the said second title of chapter twenty; and it shall be the duty of any sheriff, deputy sheriff, constable, marshal, or other peace officer, whenever any of them shall discover any person with his face so painted, discolored, covered or concealed, or being otherwise disguised as aforesaid, immediately to arrest, secure and convey, such person to any such magistrate, to be proceeded with according to law; and whenever any such officer shall receive credible information of any person having his face so painted, discolored, covered or concealed, or being otherwise disguised as aforesaid, it shall be the duty of every such officer forthwith to pursue such person, and arrest, secure and convey him to any such magistrate.

§ 3. In the execution of the duties prescribed in the last foregoing section, any sheriff, deputy sheriff, constable, marshal, or other peace officer, shall be authorized to command any male inhabitant of his county, or as many as he shall think proper, to assist him in seizing, arresting, confining and conveying to any such magistrate, and committing to the common jail of the county, every person with his face so painted, discolored, covered or concealed, or being otherwise disguised as aforesaid, and any inhabitant so commanded, may be provided or provide himself with such means and weapons as the officer giving such command shall designate.

§ 4. Every person so commanded, as provided in the last preceding section, who shall refuse or neglect, without lawful cause, to obey such command, shall be deemed guilty of a misdemeanor, and be subject to a fine not exceeding, two hundred and fifty dollars, or to imprisonment not exceeding one year, or to both.

§ 5. Any magistrate to whom complaint shall be made, that any person has appeared in a public highway, or in any lot, field, wood or enclosure, with his face so painted, discolored, covered, or concealed, or being otherwise disguised as aforesaid, may in his discretion, by warrant under his hand, depute and empower any elector of the county, to arrest, seize, confine, and bring such person before such magistrate, to answer such complaint. And in any such warrant, or in any other warrant, or process against any person charged with having his face so painted, discolored, covered or concealed, or being otherwise disguised, as aforesaid, whose name shall not be known, it shall be sufficient to describe the offender by some fictitious name.

§ 6. Every assemblage in public houses, or other places, of three or more persons disguised as aforesaid, is hereby declared to be unlawful; and every individual so disguised present threat, shall be deemed guilty of a misdemeanor, and upon conviction be punished with imprisonment in the county jail, not exceeding one year.

§ 7. Every person convicted upon any indictment for a conspiracy, or upon any indictment for a riot, or for any other misdemeanor, in which the offence shall be charged to have been committed by such person, while armed with a sword, dirk, fire-arms, or other offensive weapons, and while having his face so painted, discolored, covered or concealed, or having his person so disguised as aforesaid, shall be punished by imprisonment in the county jail, for a term not exceeding one year, or by fine, in a sum not exceeding two hundred and fifty dollars, or by both such fine and imprisonment, or by imprisonment in the State prison for two years, in the discretion of the court before whom such conviction shall be had.

This act shall take effect immediately.—*Passed Jan.* 25, 1845.

Several charges having been prepared against D. W. Squires of Roxbury, and the grand jury having found an indictment, an order for his arrest was placed in the hands of the under sheriff, Osman N. Steele, who repaired to that town on the eleventh of February, and in conformity with the third section of the above act, warned out a sufficient number of persons to co-operate with him in the performance of his duty. The party arrived at, and surrounded the house in the middle of the night, when the inmates were supposed to have been in the strong embrace of sleep. But contrary to the expectation of the officer of the law, their approach had been suspected. An entrance was forced, and after considerable search Squires was found concealed between the two ticks of the bed in which his wife and mother were sleeping, and taken into custody.

The following extract from a letter dated Delhi, February 12, 1845, to the adjutant general, thus refers to the arrival of the party at that place the following day after the arrest.

"About 10 o'clock this morning, our under sheriff brought to jail Daniel W. Squires, of the town of Roxbury, in this county. It was said that Squires was engaged in the tarring of Mr. Corbin last summer, and in forcibly taking the papers of Sheriff More at the same time.

"During the day, many of the citizens of this village have volunteered their services to aid the sheriff in the discharge of his duties, and have placed themselves under his command. A guard of twenty men was selected to defend the village and jail, inasmuch as many threats have been made, that if any 'Indian' should be placed in our jail, he would not remain there twenty-four hours."

The day following the same correspondent again writes:

"There has been considerable excitement to day amongst our quiet people, in consequence of Captain North's company of volunteers having received orders, from the sheriff of Delaware county, to repair immediately to Delhi, and hold themselves in readiness to obey orders. The order was read this morning, and at this time (2 P.M.) about forty are here. The companies from Franklin, Meredith, and Walton, have been called upon, and are on the ground. There has been no serious difficulty in Delaware county as yet. Big Thunder, *alias* Mr. Squires, was arrested yesterday by force. The anti-renters have made serious threats, and the sheriff is afraid he cannot do his duty, (namely, serving process and making some arrests,) without this extra force.

"It is said that the companies from the above-named places, are the only ones in Delaware county, but what the disaffected have a-majority in."

It had been reasonably hoped that the prompt and efficient action of the sheriff and his assistants, in conjunction with the timely action of the legislature, by the passage of the preceding act, would completely annihilate all further spirit of revolt, and that those who had been thoughtless enough to convoke themselves in open violation of the established principles of law, would become convinced of the error into which they had fallen, and return again peaceably to the quiet occupation of their homes. And it seemed for a time that these hopes had been realized, but that period proved to be of short duration, and the quiet and heretofore peaceful county was destined yet again to become disturbed by the angry spirit of discontent, and the character of its citizens to be stained by the perpetration of still darker scenes.

Nothing further worthy of note occurred until the eleventh of March, when the excitement again broke forth, as will be gathered by the following letter from a prominent citizen of the county to the editor of the Albany Evening Journal.

"Delhi, March 11, 1845.

"Dear Sir—I write hastily amongst a crowd to inform you of the state of affairs here. The following copy of a letter just received from O. N. Steele, a deputy sheriff, now held in duress at Andes, a village about ten miles from this place, will explain itself:—"

"Andes, March 11.

"To The Sheriff: Sir,—We left Andes yesterday about five o'clock, for Delhi, but were stopped on the road, and, compelled to return to this place. We are now at Hunting's. The house is now surrounded by men in disguise, about one hundred strong. They intend, as near as I can ascertain, to take my papers, tar and feather me, and pass me over to the Middletown tribe. I shall never be able to reach home unless you come over with all the force you can raise. Let every man come armed, and determined to do his duty or die on the spot. Lose no time, but get here as soon as possible."

"Yours,   O. W. STEELE."

"9 o'clock, A.M."

"The messenger whom Steele fortunately obtained to bring his letter with all possible speed, informed me that he left Steele, with Charles Parker, another officer whom the anti-renters have taken, in a small garret in the house, into which they had been driven, retaining possession of the pistols with which they were armed. This outrage is in consequence of Steele's having lately arrested Squires on a bench warrant. The sheriff, immediately on the receipt of the letter, commenced summoning a party to go in pursuit of the rioters. Every man in the village who can procure arms, will leave within half an hour. I have no time to describe the outrages that are daily committed. The country is in a state of actual rebellion."   Yours &c."

The receipt of this intelligence completely electrified the entire village, and although the travelling under foot was exceedingly muddy, in an incredibly short time the posse were on their march from Delhi to Andes. It was a motley group of lawyers, physicians, merchants, tradesmen, mechanics, and citizens—some on horseback—some on foot, and all armed with warlike weapons of some kind,

The Indians, however, becoming aware of the approach of so formidable a foe, dispersed and fled upon their approach, leaving Steele and Edgerton masters of the field.

The Indians had cherished a strong antipathy against Steele, as may be inferred from the above correspondence, in consequence of his having been chiefly instrumental in the arrest of Squires on a bench-warrant, the preceding February. He was well known too, to be a fearless and faithful officer—ever ready and obedient in the performance of his duties, regardless of smiles or frowns. His life had been repeatedly threatened, yet filled with the firm conviction of right, he taunted at their imprecations, and told them that they were disobeying the laws, and as the reward of that disobedience, the claims of justice would sooner or later overtake them. How well his own prophetic words were verified, and how well the dire threats of his life so often thrown in his face were executed, will more fully appear in the progress of the narrative.

A few days after Steele had been in limbo at Andes, he was dispatched upon a second expedition to Roxbury, for the account of which, the author is indebted to the following correspondence 1of the Albany Argus:

"Delhi, March 15, 1845, 10 o'clock P. M.

"DEAR SIR,—Yesterday morning, being the day after the return of the sheriff's posse from Kortright, another posse of about eighty mounted men, in two detachments, under the command of deputy sheriff Osman N. Steele, and Erastus S. Edgerton, started from Delhi for Roxbury, by different routes, for the purpose of making arrests. As that town is the most turbulent part of the anti-rent district, where large numbers of disguised men are frequently collected, and as the roads are exceedingly bad, some anxiety has been felt to-day as to the success of the expedition.

"The party has just entered the village with twelve *Indians* whom they have taken prisoners, disguised and armed.

"The particulars of the skirmish, which showed skill and intrepidity on the part of the officers and men, I cannot at present fully relate. After they had last evening arrested Preston on a bench-warrant, the blowing of horns, and other movements in the neighborhood, announced great preparations for an attempt to rescue the prisoner, who was strictly guarded during the night.

"In the morning, after some reconnoitring, a party of about one hundred and thirty Indians, well armed, were discovered, and immediately charged upon by Steele and Edgerton, and about forty of the mounted men, and they fled to the woods. During the skirmish, there was some firing by the Indians, one of whose shots narrowly missed E. S. Edgerton, who grappled the Indian, and disarmed him of his pistols, which were found loaded with balls. Officer Steele also closed in with another Indian, who was armed to the teeth, and on stripping off his sheepskin mask, found he had captured a constable and collector of Roxbury. The eight Indians, with the prisoner apprehended on the bench-warrant in Roxbury, and four others taken at Bloomville, on their return, are now lodged in jail. The sheriff is now at the court house, detaching men to guard the jail and the village during the night. At the same time horns are blowing, and guns are firing on the mountain opposite the village, informing us of what we may expect, if the insurgents can muster in sufficient force to put their threats in execution."

Among the prisoners were Messrs. Burrill, Tompkins, Osterhout and Knapp, who were severally convicted and sentenced to Sing Sing for two years. Gov. Wright, however, restored the unfortunate men to the rights of citizenship in September, 1846, a short time previous to the expiration of their sentences.

The arrests made in Roxbury in March—the trial and sentence of the prisoners, if anything, had a tendency to add fuel to the flame. The excitement assumed a far more angry and threatening aspect than it had hitherto presented, but no blood had as yet been shed on either side, until the seventh of August, when the public ear was startled by the lamentable death of Steele.

The following are the particulars of the painful tragedy, which put the climax on anti-rentism, as sworn to by Peter P. Wright, before the coroner's inquest, held over the unfortunate man:

"On the fourth of June last, I was called upon professionally to draw a warrant of distress for John Allen, the agent of Charlotte D. Verplanck, to collect sixty-four dollars, the arrears of rent due from Moses Earle, on the premises occupied by him, in the town of Andes. The levy was made, and the sale had been postponed until the seventh of August, at one o'clock. I went at the request of Mr. Allen, from this place in company with sheriff More, in a one-horse wagon, and arrived on the premises of Mr. Earle about ten o'clock in the forenoon. A number of spectators had then assembled.

"Our first business was to see Mr. Earle, to whom we proposed a settlement of the rent; his reply was, 'You will have to go on and sell, I shall fight it at the hardest.' Something was then said about his having written a letter to the sheriff in regard to it, and he stated in substance that he had since altered his mind, and should make no settlement. We discovered from appearances, such as killing of sheep, &c., that preparations had been made to meet us, and we apprehended that there might be some difficulty. About eleven o'clock we discovered a company of six Indians, armed and in disguise, cross the road from the north side above the house, and pass through the pasture lot where the cattle were, and enter the woods near where the cattle were pasturing.

"I told the sheriff that he ought to command every spectator to assist in arresting them, and he did so. In the course of fifteen or twenty minutes I observed another company of about as many more pass into the woods, in the same direction. I observed nothing further until about twelve o'clock, when I discovered a party of forty or fifty come from the woods on the east side of the pasture lot, and pass, in single file, to the woods on the south side, where the others had congregated. At the same time I observed another company of fourteen coming off the side hill on the north side of the road, and were passing in the direction of the others above mentioned; I went up the road about thirty or forty rods east of the house, and came within three or four rods of them as they crossed the road, and passed a few rods into the pasture lot, where they halted at the command of the chief, and looking at me as I stood in the road, cried *'tory, tory.'* The chief then motioned with his hand in the direction of the others, who were passing through the lot, crying *'tory, tory.'* The only remark, I made to them, was to ask them what they wanted of me.—The fourteen immediately turned, and coming towards me, recrossed the road nearly in the same place. As they passed me I observed that several of them had their faces but imperfectly disguised, and I pursued them ten or fifteen rods on the north side of the road, endeavoring to ascertain who they were; they passed up the hill, and I left them and returned again in the road.

"In about one-half or three-quarters of an hour, we observed the Indians coming out of the road, on the south side of the pasture lot, and marching in single file, they passed up near the bars about fifteen or twenty rods east of the house, on the southerly side of the road, when they formed in sections of four each, and passing through the bars, formed in single line in the road, the lower end reaching about opposite Mr. Earle's house. I stationed myself at the bars as they passed, and endeavored to count them. In observing their disguises I lost the count, but should think from the estimate I then made, they were about one hundred strong, all disguised and armed; I saw not one unarmed, most had rifles; there were some muskets, and in addition, several had small pistols, some tomahawks, bags of feathers, &c., &c,. I passed from the bars down along the line of Indians, from four to six feet in front, and on arriving at the centre of the line I met one of the chiefs, who, raising his sword, told me to stand back twenty feet; I stopped, and maintaining my position, told him I should not stand back one inch for him or any of his tribe; he then placed his sword upon my breast, and again ordered me back: I instantly placed my hand upon my pistol, and told him to withdraw his sword from my person, or I would make a hole through him; he then withdrew his sword and drew a pistol; I then told him to violate my person again and I should defend myself to the last, against him and the whole of his tribe; that I should offer no insult or injury to any of them, but that they must let me alone, that I did not fear the whole of them; that I came there on lawful business, that their's was unlawful; they came there to violate the law, and were all outlaws, and liable to be punished in the State prison, every one of them; that they were not ignorant of the fact, for they knew what the law was.

"This was said in a loud voice, so that all could hear, and they responded, 'damn the law, we mean to break it.' I told the chief that I knew him well, and that I should remember him; he replied, 'you can't swear to me.'- The Indians then asked me if I intended to bid upon the property; I told them that I came there for that purpose, and that if I had an opportunity I should. I was then told that if I bid upon the property I would 'go home feet foremost in a wagon.' To this one of the spectators responded, 'that's the talk.' A pail of whiskey was brought from the house of Mr. Earle, and carried along the line, from which they drank. A horn was blown, and some accession was made to their ranks. I remained in the same position about half an hour, during which time I was blackguarded and my life repeatedly threatened, to which I made very little or no reply. Officers Steele and Edgerton then came in sight, and rode up on horseback about two o'clock. The Indians then marched forward against the stone wall on the north side of the road, and about-faced. The sheriff then announced that he would proceed with the sale, and that he would go down and drive up the property, and proceeded with one or two citizens into the pasture lot for that purpose. After he had gone fifteen or twenty rods, the chief called for twelve volunteers to accompany him to see that the property was not sold down in the lot, that he might sell it down there, and that they must prevent it.

"The property was driven by the sheriff with some difficulty up near the bars, where the Indians prevented him from driving the property into the road. The line of Indians by the stone wall, then marched through the bars into the lot and formed a hollow square around the bars, enclosing the property and the sheriff; Steele, Edgerton and myself, took our position by the bars, and Steele told me to stand between him and Edgerton, and they would protect me. Considerable conversation then took place in regard to driving the property into the road. A Mr. Brisbane, an anti-rent lecturer, wanted to know what right we had to drive the property into the road: I told him we had a right to sell it any where on the premises, and we wanted it in the road for the convenience of the bidders. Something was then said about the notice of sale on the barn, when Steele and Edgerton rode down to read it; at this time ten or fifteen of the Indians ran from the lot, and crossing the road on the north side, as if they wished to head them off, supposing they had started for home.

"Steele and Edgerton returned to the bars, and the Indians again to the lot. I then called the sheriff out of the lot, and told him that he might say to the Indians, that unless they would permit the property to be driven into the road, he might adjourn the sale. The sheriff then went back into the lot, saying he thought he should be able to drive the property into the road, and was followed by Mr. Brisbane, about fifteen feet from the bars, a little to the right, where they were surrounded by a number of Indians, and considerable conversation ensued with the sheriff, which I cannot now relate. In a few moments I attempted to pass through the bars into the lot where the sheriff was, and a platoon of Indians guarded the bars, forbidding my passage, and an Indian raised his gun before me. Holding a cane in my hand, I placed it with both hands against his breast, and forced a passage into the lot, the file of Indians at the bars closing in behind me. Steele and Edgerton, apprehending my danger, then rode into the lot about two lengths of their horses. I maintained about the same position near the horse's head. The file of Indians at the bars fell back, forming a semi-circle of fifteen or twenty feet radius around Steele, Edgerton and myself. The crowd around the sheriff formed in the same circle, and some came from the hollow square. The chief then gave the command: 'shoot the horses—shoot the horses:' 'shoot *him*, shoot *him*:' the spectators at the bars moved away at the motion of the Indians, and thirty or forty rifles were pointed at us, and we then supposed death was our portion. Steele and Edgerton then commanded the peace, and Edgerton, in a loud voice, called upon every citizen to assist in preserving the peace. A volley of rifles was then fired upon us, and I saw instantly the blood flow freely from the breast of Edgerton's horse, upon my right, and I should think Steele was wounded in the arm at this fire; in the course of a very few seconds, a second volley was discharged, which came like a shower bath upon Steele and the horses, taking effect in the body of Steele, and also in both horses. Steele fell bleeding upon the ground, three balls having pierced his body, and others gone through his clothes. Edgerton's horse fell dead near Steele, another ball having passed through the saddle into his side.

"Sheriff More appealed to the Indians 'for God's sake to desist; they had done enough.' Edgerton and myself ran and took hold of Steele, and asked him how badly he was hurt: he replied that "two balls had passed through him, and that his bowels were all shot to pieces." We carried him into the house of Mr. Earle, where he survived between five and six hours, enduring the most excruciating pain. He fired once, *and once only, and that was after he was wounded in his right arm*. Edgerton drew his pistol but did not fire, mine was not drawn; I am sure that the Indians fired first, there can be no doubt about it. Drs. Peake and Calhoun were called, who rendered all the assistance in their power.

"While lying upon his bed in the agonies of death, Steele told Mr. Earle, that if he had paid his rent he would not have been shot; and Mr. Earle replied, he should not pay it if it cost forty lives. Mr. Steele was on the ground only about half an hour before he was shot, during which time the Indians used towards him the most insulting and abusive language, as well as threats upon his life, to which he made not the least reply, maintaining that cool temperament and presence of mind for which he was so much distinguished.

"The Indians remained upon the ground some two or three hours, holding an Indian pow-wow around the horses, and exulting in the blood of their victim. Thus has fallen a faithful and fearless officer of the law, who died at the post of duty, suffering martyrdom for no other reason than because he was faithful in executing the laws of his country."

Steele had fallen bravely at his post of duty: he suffered the most excruciating pains, and it seemed evident to all that he could at farthest survive but a few hours. A messenger was dispatched in all haste to carry the painful intelligence to his family and friends, and his wife arrived barely in time to witness the untimely death of her husband, which took place about 8 o'clock in the evening. His remains were taken to Delhi, where the coroner's inquest was held. The funeral ceremonies were performed on the tenth. It was attended by a large concourse of citizens—about two thousand, who had assembled from all parts of the county, and who manifested the deepest feeling at his untimely death.

A monument has since been erected in commemoration of his memory by the citizens of this county, in acknowledgment of his worth as a citizen and his integrity as a public officer.

A correspondent of the Albany Evening Journal writes as follows:—

"Delhi, Sunday Evening, August 10, 1845.

"DEAR SIR,—I arrived at this village last evening, and found a deep gloom hanging over it. This day the remains of Deputy Sheriff *Steele*, were committed to the grave. The funeral services were performed by the Presbyterian, and Episcopal clergymen of this place, assisted by the Rev. Mr. Adams, of the Episcopal Church, at Unadilla. There was a very large concourse of people, so much so that the largest church would not begin to hold them. The clergymen addressed the multitude from a piazza. The clergyman of this village impressed on the minds of his hearers eternal vigilance, until the murderers are brought to punishment, and the majesty of the law sustained.

"The citizens of the village held a meeting last evening, and organized a patrol to guard the village and public buildings. Many persons did not close their eyes for fear of incendiaries. There is a horrible state of things in this county. I found to day that a posse went out last night, to arrest six men living in Roxbury, the town adjoining Andes, where Steele was murdered, who were supposed to have been present, if not implicated in the murder. The posse had just returned bringing in three men, who are confined in jail. An express left here on Friday afternoon for Albany, to confer with, and bear dispatches to the Governor. The inhabitants say that the laws are insufficient. The grand juries will not find bills against anti-renters in this county. They further say, that, if the Governor does not act promptly, and provide relief, they, the people of this county, will take the law into their own hands.

"Steele had many very warm and ardent friends, who are determined to avenge the taking of his life. I presume there are a thousand men waiting anxiously to be led into the disaffected towns, if the laws can have no effect. Much is said here about certain prominent men of this village, who are said to have thrown firebrands by encouraging the anti-renters.

"Men are pouring into the village, from different towns, to protect the public buildings. The anti-renters say that the jail will never again hold any of them long. They will endeavor to destroy the State arms, that are here, by burning them. I am told that the Governor will be requested to declare the county in a state of insurrection, and to proclaim martial law."

Immediately upon the receipt of the intelligence of the death of Steele, meetings of the citizens were convened in various sections of the county.

On the eleventh a meeting of the citizens of Moresville, was convened, and the venerable John T. More presided.

On the fourteenth inst. a meeting was held at the head of the Delaware, at which A. M. Babcock presided. Isaac D. Cornwall, Charles Griffin, Calvin C. Covil, Joshua Draper, Hiram Fredenburgh, and Adam Grant, were appointed a committee of five to draft resolutions, condemning the late outrage, and sympathizing with the widow and relatives of the deceased.

A numerous meeting of the inhabitants of the town of Andes, convened at the house of E. B. Hunting, on the sixteenth inst., for the purpose of taking into consideration the late events which have transpired in that town: the following gentlemen were selected as officers of the meeting; Cyrus Burr, president, Samuel McCabe, vice president, John Dickson, secretary.

The meeting was addressed by several gentlemen in strong and energetic language, denouncing the whole course of proceedings in the late anti-rent excitement—showing the unpolitic course pursued to obtain redress for any grievances they may have, and depicting in glowing terms the consequences which must follow.

The following persons were appointed to draft resolutions, expressive of the sense of the meeting, viz. M. T. Peake, H. Dowie, Jr., Ezra Waterbury, D. B. Shaver, and Luther Jackson, including the president and secretary of the meeting.

The committee after retiring reported the following preamble and resolutions, which were unanimously adopted:

"Whereas, we, the inhabitants of the town of Andes, in consideration of the awful tragedy enacted in our town, resulting in the death of our faithful public officer Osman N. Steele, who fell on the seventh inst., while endeavoring to sustain the laws against an infuriated mob unanimously:

"Resolved, That we hold in horror and detestation those cowardly assassins who have stained our land with innocent blood, and brought a reproach upon our character, as lovers of law and order.

"Resolved, That we deeply sympathize with the widow and relatives of the deceased.

"Resolved, That while we sympathize with the afflictions of our neighbors who are implicated in this transaction, we tender to the law and its officers our faithful allegiance and support.

"Resolved, That those political demagogues who have decoyed a confiding community into this vortex of crime and misery, deserve the execrations of an injured people."

The same day a meeting was held in the school-house at Bovina Centre, and the Hon. James Cowan, was chosen chairman. A preamble and resolutions were unanimously passed, among which was the following:

"Resolved, That the only safety we have for our lives or property, is to be found in the steady and inflexible administration and maintenance of the laws."

Meetings expressive of the indignation of the inhabitants were also held at Hobart, Delhi, Middletown, and several other places in the county. Nor was this exhibition of obedience to law confined to the limits of the county. Even the citizens of adjoining counties held numerous meetings of this character. And I perceive by a reference to a file of Kingston papers, that a large and respectable body of citizens assembled at the courthouse in that village, "to express their indignation at the recent outrage in Delaware county." John Van Buren was called to preside. The meeting was addressed by Messrs. H. M. Romeyn, and Gen. J. G. Smith, in their usual forcible style. The preamble and resolutions were responded to with great applause.

These numerous assemblies, with the strong and emphatic language of the resolutions, in every instance unanimously passed, is sufficient of itself to illustrate the wonderful summerset anti-rentism had taken. The novelty of a calico dress, or a sheepskin face, lost all its magic fascination to those who had become the unfortunate dupes of its flattering pretensions, when it came in contact with the dark realities of an unpromising future. Even those who had secretly aided, and abetted the organization, now came out openly in its opposition, while those, who trembled at the revelations which a court of inquiry would draw out, fled degraded outlaws to evade the vigilance of the officers of the law. Some settlements were almost entirely deserted by the male portion of the population, crops were left unharvested, farms and farm work were neglected, and a sad picture, far surpassing any thing which distrainment for rent could ever produce, was everywhere presented.

CHAPTER XIII

Action of the Executive—Proclamation of county in a state of insurrection—Copy of the same—Its reception in Delhi—Arrival of Adjutant General Farrington—Organization of an armed force—Officers chosen—Extract from a letter—Mode of operating—Erection of temporary log-jails—Convening of the court—Grand Jury—Judge Parker's able charge—Allusion in the same to the demoralizing influence of the excitement upon the county—Results of the trials—number of convictions—O'Connor and Van Steenburgh convicted of murder—Sentence of the prisoners—Court adjourns—Attempt on the life of a guard—Reprieve of the sentences of O'Connor and Van Steenburgh—Revocation by the Governor, of the declaration "declaring the county in a state of insurrection"—Close—Closing remarks.

WOULD that with the closing up of the preceding chapter, we might have dropped the curtain over this painful narrative. But it remains for us to follow out and delineate the restoration of equilibrium and order.

In the latter part of August, Governor Wright issued the following proclamation, declaring the county in a state of insurrection. This document, both for its decided language and intrinsic worth, as having emanated from the pen of that celebrated statesman, as well as for the recital of the disturbance, its rise, progress and results, characterizes it as an indispensable link in the history of that period. And although its great length might have induced us to pass it by, yet we trust its careful perusal may avail us as a timely warning to shape our course in future.

The following is the proclamation:

"The Sheriff, District Attorney, Judges of the County Courts, and other officers of the peace, and citizens of the County of Delaware, have laid before me a body of evidence, to satisfy me that the execution of civil and criminal process in that county, has been forcibly resisted by bodies of men; that combinations to resist the execution of such processes by force, exist in that county, and that the power of the county has been exerted, and is not sufficient to enable the sheriff and his deputies, having such process, to execute the same; and have applied to me to exert the authority, with which I am clothed by the 19th section of the act, entitled 'An act to enforce the laws and preserve order,' passed April 15, 1845.

"The evidence presented to me, establishes satisfactorily, the following among other facts:

"That the execution of civil and criminal process, began to be resisted by bodies of men, in the county of Delaware, as early as March last.

"That combinations to resist the execution of such process, by force, under the denomination of anti-rent, or equal rights associations, commenced being formed in that county, more than one year ago.

"That these associations have engrafted upon the organization, a force of disguised, masked, and armed men, subject to the orders and directions of the officers of the associations, and by and through which force, under the protection of its disguises and masks, the resistance to the execution of legal process is to be made, and is made.

"That the members of this armed force are denominated Indians, or Natives; are organized in bands called tribes, and have their leaders and commanders, called chiefs, having names in imitation of Indian chiefs.

"That the officers of the associations, and all the members of the armed force, are sworn to observe and support the constitution of the association, and to keep secret all things communicated, or known, to them, which require to be kept secret, and in the case of the disguised and armed men, the further clause is added, that they will stand by each other as long as life shall last.

"That the avowed and declared object of the associations is to prevent by force, the collections of rent, and that the express duty of the armed force, is to resist the execution of process issued for that object; but that the cases of resistance by force against the execution of legal process, and the discharge of their duties by the officers of the law, have not been entirely confined to proceedings for the collection of rents, but have been extended, in some instances, to other legal process.

"That these associations, and organizations of a disguised, masked, and armed force, are not confined to the county of Delaware, but exist to a great, if not to an equal extent in several adjoining counties, and that the organizations, armed and unarmed, wherever they exist, have and avow a common object, make common cause, and act in entire concert and cooperation.

"That in all the prominent and flagrant cases of resistance to the process and officers of the law, in Delaware and other counties, the members of these armed bands of disguised and masked men, have been prominent actors; and that, in the county of Delaware, before the passage of the law above referred to, this resistance had been carried to such an extent, as to require the utmost exertion of the power of the county to preserve peace and order, and execute criminal process only.

"That early in the month of May, after the passage of the law of the 15th of April last, above referred to, the sheriff of the county of Delaware, applied to the Governor, under the 2nd section of that law, and received authority to organize an armed guard of 400 men, to aid him in the preservation of order, and the execution of civil and criminal process, within the county.

"That a strong feeling has existed in the county against that provision of the law which charges upon the county, the expense of such an organized and armed force, the citizens contending that it was unequal and unjust, to require of them to encounter, in their persons, the labor and peril of enforcing the law against these armed combinations, of their own and the adjoining counties, and thereby subject the property of Delaware county only, to the taxation necessary to meet the expenses thus incurred; and that the sheriff has been unable to organize a guard, under the second section of the act, of sufficient strength and permanency to enable him to execute the civil process placed in his hands, or calling for execution.

"That the consequence of this state of things has been a substantial suspension, in the county of Delaware, of all process for the collection of rents, from the close of the serious disturbances there, in March last, until a very recent and very signal instance, to be hereafter particularly noticed; the sheriff having undertaken, within that time, to execute and carry out such process in but one instance, and in that, a voluntary settlement between the parties relieved him before the point was reached, at which resistance has been usually met; and he having, in numerous other instances, declined to receive and attempt to execute such process.

"That some time during the last month, pursuant to proceedings by way of distress for rent, against a man by the name of Moses Earle, of the town of Andes, in the county of Delaware, the sheriff had appointed a day for the sale, upon the premises, of the property distrained, and upon the day of sale, attended at the place, and met a large collection of persons, whose appearance and conduct satisfied him that their object was to prevent his sale; not one of whom would make a bid upon any part of the property offered for sale, and from whom he learned that a disguised and armed force of some sixty men was secreted in the woods adjoining the field, where he was trying to sell the property; whereupon he adjourned the sale to the 7th day of the present month, at the same place.

"That on the 7th day of the present month, the sheriff attended at the place of sale, accompanied by his under sheriff Osman N. Steele, Erastus S. Edgerton, a constable of the county, and Peter P. Wright, the agent of the landlord, who attended to bid upon the property. The persons found upon the premises a force of disguised, masked and armed men, about 220 strong, by which they were surrounded as soon as movements were made indicating a preparation to enter upon the sale of the property, and by a portion of whom, in obedience to the order of one acting as their chief, the horses upon which Steele and Edgerton were mounted, were shot and killed, and Steele was mortally wounded, and survived but six hours, three balls taking effect in his person, and from twelve to twenty guns being fired. The execution of civil process was thus resisted, the enforcement of the law prevented, and the order and peace of society deeply and irreparably disturbed and broken, in this instance.

"That this cold and cruel murder of a most estimable and valuable citizen, and brave and faithful public officer, for no other cause or provocation, than the discharge of his official duty, as he had solemnly sworn to discharge it, has so aroused the energies of the patriotic and law-abiding citizens of the county of Delaware, as to enable the sheriff, for the purpose of the arrest and punishment of the murderers, their aiders and abettors, to organize a guard, or posse, under the 2nd section of the law referred to, in conformity to the authority obtained from the Governor, in Delaware for that purpose; but only for a very short period, which has already expired, or is just about expiring, and without the hope or expectation on the part of the sheriff, of being able to avail himself of the aid of that guard, or posse, for any other purpose than the execution of the criminal processes, to which this startling murder may give rise.

"That it has been subsequently ascertained that, in addition to the disguised and armed force of 220 men, which actually surrounded the sheriff and his assistants, and shot down the under sheriff, an additional similar force of forty picked riflemen was stationed in the bushes by the side of the road, and near to the place of sale, with directions to watch the posse, which it was apprehended would follow the sheriff, and come to his aid; to order it to halt, if it should attempt to pass; and to shoot down the men who composed it, if they should not obey the order to halt; thus making the whole disguised and armed force, assembled upon this occasion, to resist the execution of the law, and of civil process, 260 men, or more than that number.

"That considerable portions of this disguised and armed force were drawn from two of the adjoining counties, and were not citizens of the county of Delaware.

"That these organizations to resist the law and the execution of its process, have extended themselves to the magistracy of the county of Delaware, and that justices of the peace of some of the towns in that county are found enrolled as members and officers of the associations, if not under the Indian disguises, bearing arms to resist the law by force; forgetting the oath of office they have taken, and taking themselves, and administering to others, oaths to conceal violations of the law;—to the ministerial officers of the county, and that constables are also found members of one, or both, of these combinations;—to the officers of the towns, and that supervisors, the members of the local legislature of the county, are members of the anti-rent associations, swearing to support their constitution and pledge, if not Indians, swearing to bear arms against the law.

"That one of the obligations, which every person takes upon himself, on becoming a member of an anti-rent association, is to make fixed and regular contributions to the funds of the association; that a stipulated rent of two cents upon the acre of all the land held by the members of these associations is levied and paid to the treasurers, to meet the expenses of the organizations; that the moneys thus collected are paid out, under the direction of a committee, to purchase materials for dresses, masks, arms and ammunition for the Indians, and to pay the expenses of their subsistence and entertainment, when called out, as well as to meet the expenses of law suits, and litigations; and, where there is a surplus in the treasury, to pay the Indians for their time spent in the service to which they are devoted.

"That 1000 or more persons have enrolled themselves and taken the prescribed oath, as Indians, within the single county of Delaware, while a much larger number have become members of the anti-rent associations, and that the obligations assumed toward each other, certainly by the Indians, if not by the members of the associations also, strongly imply, if they do not expressly enjoin, efforts on the part of those at liberty, to rescue those under arrest, and in the custody of the law, for acts performed as Indians, or as members of an association, and in furtherance of the objects of those organizations.

"That, since the murder of the under sheriff Steele, in the manner before related, the proceedings of the authorities and citizens of the county of Delaware have been marked by a most praiseworthy vigilance and energy, to arrest and bring to justice these resisters of the law and disturbers of the peace of the county; that many arrests have been made, and fifty or more prisoners are now confined in the county jail, either awaiting examinations, or committed to answer to charges of crime, some twenty or more of whom are charged as principals or accessories in this murder.

"It may be added, too, that individuals, and assemblages of men, have, within the period mentioned, frequently appeared in the public highways; in the fields, woods, and other places in the county, and sometimes in the face of the sheriff and his officers, both disguised and armed, in open violation of the provisions of the act entitled 'An act to prevent persons appearing disguised and armed,' passed 28th January. 1845; and that such persons, so committing offences subjecting them to punishment in the State Prison, have not been arrested; thus affording evidence that the power of the county, as faithfully exerted as the sheriff and his officers could exert it, has been insufficient for the execution of criminal process and the preservation of the criminal law within the county, in cases where the violations of that law have not been attended with consequences calculated to shock the feelings of the citizens, by the imminent danger to, or the wanton destruction of, human life.

"The fact that the law makes no provision for mounting the men to be employed by the sheriff as a posse, or guard, or for the payment for the service, or for the subsistence of horses for their use, is stated by him as one prominent cause of his inability to enlist and organize an efficient body of men for the service required. The nature of that service palpably required that a large share, at least, of the sheriff's guard should be mounted, and it is scarcely possible that any moderate number of men could have made him an efficient posse, all serving on foot.

"In the face of these facts, I cannot entertain a doubt that the testimony presented brings the case fully within the provisions of the 19th section of the act of the 15th of April last; that the execution of civil or criminal process has been forcibly resisted in the county of Delaware: that combinations to resist the execution of such process by force do exist in that county; that the power of the county has been exerted within the true intent and meaning of the act, and that it is not sufficient to enable the officers of the county having such process to execute the same.

"I do therefore, hereby, in conformity with the provisions of the said 19th section of the said act, proclaim and declare the county of Delaware to be in a state of insurrection, according to the provisions, and true intent and meaning of the act of the legislature of this State, entitled 'An act to enforce the laws and preserve order,' passed 15th April, 1845.

"In making this declaration, it becomes my duty to draw the particular attention of all the citizens of the State, and especially the citizens of Delaware and the adjoining counties, to the provisions of the 20th section of the act referred to.

"'Any person who shall, after the publication of this proclamation, resist, or assist in resisting, the execution of legal process; or who shall aid, or attempt, the rescue or escape of any prisoner from lawful custody or confinement, or who shall resist, or aid or assist in resisting, any force ordered out by the Governor, in the county of Delaware, is, by this section of the law, upon conviction of either of these offences, to be adjudged guilty of a felony, and punished by imprisonment in the State Prison for a term not less than two years.'

"It becomes my further duty to invoke the especial and earnest attention of all civil and military officers of the State to this proclamation, to the provisions of the two acts of the legislature particularly referred to in it, and of the responsible duties it devolves upon them. They are the guardians of the law for the people of the State, whom they have been appointed to represent and serve. They have been selected to expound, administer and execute the law, and they have solemnly sworn that they will faithfully discharge the duties of their respective offices, according to the best of their abilities.

"To such officers within the county of Delaware, and the surrounding counties, this appeal comes with peculiar force. It is to enforce the law in their immediate neighborhoods that the aid of the State is invoked. Around and among them the spirit of insurrection, of combined and organized resistance to the law, prevails and shows itself. The discharge of their whole duties, and the faithful redemption of their official oaths, are demanded alike by patriotic feeling, moral duty, and a plain sense of personal justice; and especially, if any one among their number, holding a public trust, and resting under the obligations of that oath, shall become lost to a just sense of his duty to himself and his State, and shall yield to the insurrectionary influences around him, it is incumbent upon them, while they boldly detect and expose and bring to justice the delinquent, to show by their better conduct and example, that our free institutions are not to be surrendered for a state of disorder, and violence, and crime, and murder, even though some few of their constituted guardians should not be proof against such delusion.

"To the freeman of the State I can make no stronger appeal than is presented in the simple narration of facts I have set forth. These facts show the regular progress to its result in crime and blood of every attempt to set aside the regularly constituted tribunals of civil society, organized for the protection of personal rights and the redress of personal wrongs,—to make might the measure of right between citizen and citizen. Masks and disguises are never assumed to protect men in the performance of acts toward their neighbors, which the judgment and the conscience approve; and no other acts will promote the peace, order or prosperity of society, or the happiness, or true interest of him who performs the action. Secret oaths are only administered to add to the protection of the masks, when the conscience proclaims that he who is trusted to look behind the mask may be as dangerous as he who looks upon it; that the danger is in the truth, and is to be apprehended from all who can tell it. When the mind becomes so deluded as to rely upon protections like these, and to act from the promptings which a sense of security of this character, if indulged, will never fail to engender, high crimes are the certain fruit, and the charm of the protection vanishes only when the guilt is incurred. The intelligent freeman of our State will not seek to change their peaceful and happy and prosperous institutions, the fruit of the toil and blood of our Revolutionary fathers, for a government resting upon such a basis and producing such fruits. Justice is the emblem of their government, and her light is truth.

"To the tenants who disapprove of this disguised and armed force, and have refused to give their aid or countenance to its organization and action,—and they are believed to constitute a numerous and influential body of men,—the present presents a peculiarly appropriate occasion to mark more distinctly their separation from proceedings which cannot fail to be fatal to a good cause, and to prejudice good men. If they feel that the tenures by which they hold their farms are onerous; not in accordance with the genius of our institutions, or the spirit of our people; and that they ought to be changed to freeholds; let them see, and feel also, that the natural sympathies of the great body of our freeholders must be with them in these impressions, and that the sure way to avert these sympathies is to attempt to accomplish a worthy end by unworthy means. Let them remember that their present tenures have resulted from voluntary contracts, freely entered into between themselves, or their worthy ancestors, and the landlords from whom they hold; and that the readiest, if not the only way, to make the change they desire, is by a contract equally voluntary between themselves and those same landlords. Let them be assured that, if they fulfil their contracts hitherto, and offer terms of commutation of their titles, which are just, and which appear to be so to fair and impartial minds, an enlightened public opinion will bring about the acceptance of such terms by the landlords.

"To the proprietors of these leasehold estates, the landlords of these tenants, the present crisis should not be without its lessons of wisdom. Indefensible as have been the attempts to repudiate their solemn contracts, and to wrest from them by force the remedies secured to them by the constitution and the laws for breaches of those contracts, they should not fail to see, at the foundation of these lawless proceedings, a rapidly growing dissatisfaction at the perpetuation of tenures, not in accordance with those by which the great body of the lands of our country are held, and not consonant with the feelings of our people.—And, while the power of the State must and will be exerted to enforce the law, protect private rights, preserve the peace and order of society, give security to the life of the citizen, and prevent the prevalence of anarchy and violence, so far as it rests in their power they should be ready to remove the causes of like troubles for the future, by a prompt and liberal arrangement of arrears of rent, whenever an opportunity shall offer; and, by tendering generous terms to the tenants, upon which they will change the tenures to fee simple titles, put an end for ever to this perpetual relation of landlord and tenant,—a relation already so fruitful of anything but peace and prosperity to either of the parties. Even if it shall become necessary to employ the military power of the State to enforce the law, as connected with their peculiar interests, they should be prepared, upon all occasions and under all circumstances, to show to the public that it is no part of their object to be benefited in their pecuniary interests, by the misfortunes or the faults of their ill-advised and misguided tenants; but that they are ready to consider, generously, the ability and the means of each tenant to pay, and, even if a coerced sale of his property must be the only rule of settlement, that they are prepared to become liberal purchasers at such sales.

"To the disguised men themselves, and to those less worthy than they, who press them forward into the danger from which they themselves shrink, I have only to say that wrong acts never serve even a good cause; that persistence in crime cannot mitigate the heavy weight upon the mind and conscience of the first crime; and that no disguises are perfect enough to protect the heart from the eye of Him who sees its thoughts and intents.

"For the sake of the character of our State and of our people, as well as for the peace and prosperity and harmony of society, I earnestly hope the day may not be distant, when I may be called upon to discharge another and a far more pleasant duty, under a provision of the same law under which I now act, by revoking this proclamation.

"Yet the law must be enforced. Our institutions must be preserved. Anarchy and violence must be prevented. The lives of our citizens must be protected, and murder must be punished. And when that portion of our citizens who, now transported by passion and led away by singular delusions, are ready to strike down the law and its ministers, shall become convinced that a different course is alike the part of wisdom and of duty, and shall again submit themselves to the laws of the State, then, and not before, can I expect to be permitted to perform that more pleasing duty.

"In testimony whereof, I have hereunto affixed the Privy Seal of the State. Witness my hand, at the city of Albany, this twenty-seventh [L. S.] day of August, in the year of our Lord one thousand eight hundred and forty-five.

"SILAS WRIGHT."

The same day the proclamation of Gov. Wright, was received by mail in Delhi, Adjutant General Farrington, with instructions to superintend the organization of an armed force, also arrived from his residence in Oswego. The same evening two companies of volunteers were formed, elected their officers, reported themselves to the Adjutant General, and were formed into a separate battalion of light infantry. Benjamin T. Cook of Franklin, was elected captain of the first company, William Buckingham, of Harpersfield, lieutenant, and Angus Mc Donald, Jr., of Stamford, ensign.

The second company elected John R. Baldwin, of Stamford, captain, Thomas E. Marvine, of Walton, lieutenant, and Palmer L. Burrows, of Tompkins, ensign.

Thomas Marvine, of Walton, was unanimously elected major of the battalion, whose experience and judgement rendered him peculiarly fitted for the station. A correspondent writes as follows:

"The company of light infantry under the command of Captain Bolles, of the one hundred and fifty-first regiment, has been ordered to active service and report themselves to Major Marvine at this place.

"Col. Horton, of the sixty-ninth regiment, and Col. North, of the one hundred and fifty-first regiment, have been ordered to hold their respective commands in readiness to answer any call that may be made for additional force, should it be deemed necessary."

The next evening, the light infantry company, from Unadilla, under the command of Capt. Bolles, arrived and reported themselves to Major Marvine. The company was composed mostly of young men, who with a little drilling made excellent soldiers.

A correspondent of this date writes as follows:

"Major Marvine has now three hundred efficient and well-armed men; one hundred of whom are well mounted, ready to assist the sheriff in the execution of any process required, and to guard the jail and prisoners. This force, it is believed, will prove sufficient to answer the purpose intended, and we hope the necessity will not exist a great while for this or any other force. If those who have heretofore favored the anti-rent associations, will read the proclamation of Gov. Wright, with calmness and candor, they must be convinced of the utter impossibility—and the injustice—of standing out against the power of the State.

"After completing the organization, Adjt. Gen. Farrington left on Monday afternoon, on his return to Oswego."

Small companies were constantly kept out scouring the infected districts, in search of those who had either abetted or assisted in any of the outrages connected with the history of the disturbance for the past year. Almost every day additions were made to the number of prisoners, and in the course of a few weeks the county jail was completely filled, and it was found necessary and expedient to erect two temporary log buildings, to accommodate the increasing demand.

The following extract is from a letter dated September 2nd:

"A large number of troops have been out to-day, getting out logs to make two log- prisons. They are to be about twenty-five feet square, and very roughly constructed. Their erection becomes necessary, as the Common Pleas and General Session sits here next week, and the court-room is now occupied by some twenty-five prisoners, and the jury-rooms by some eight or ten more. The jail is full to overflowing."

The September term of the Court of Common Pleas and General Sessions of Delaware county, commenced on the 8th instant. The Court of General Sessions did not close until the 20th instant, up to which time the whole number indicted for violation of law, for being disguised, armed, &c., was two hundred and forty-two.

The Circuit Court and Court of Oyer and Terminer, commenced its session on the 22nd instant, his Honor, Judge Parker, presiding.

The following individuals were sworn, and composed the Grand Jury, to wit: Orrin Griffin, foreman; Fitch Ford, Gorsham H. Bradley, Platt Townsend, John Sextell, David M. Smith, James W. Knapp, Daniel S. Smith, Samuel S. Scudder, Warren Dimmick, Amasa Birch, John Hammond, Abraham Shell, Reuben S. Smith, Milton Bostwick, Edwin J. Smith, Aristarchus Blish, Gabriel S. Mead, Edmund Crooker, Novatus Blish.

After an able and lucid charge from Judge Parker, in which he dwelt at length upon the history and origin of the anti-rent troubles in the county—concluding by impressing upon them the imperative duty of prompt and fearless action as the only method of restoring peace and quiet, they retired to their room.

In the course of his charge he thus depicts the demoralizing effect upon the society and best interests of the county:

"I regret to say that in all the disorder and violence exhibited in this State, this county has occupied a prominence lamentable in the extreme; and I should suppose that the deplorable effects that are evident upon the state of things here amongst you, would restrain all from engaging hereafter in such transactions. But one year since I saw your county in a most flourishing condition—your green hills and beautiful valley bore upon their face evidence of prosperity hardly to be found elsewhere. It was a flourishing county, even under the leasehold system, and no county had gone forward more rapidly than this in the acquisition of wealth and enjoyment of social happiness. The contrast that is now presented is most deeply to be regretted. In portions of your county I am told that the crops have not been harvested. Although heaven has continued its blessings upon the labor of the husbandman, yet the husbandman—having in an evil hour been led to the commission of crime, having listened perhaps to foreign lectures, and having been thus induced to place himself in an attitude of hostility to the law—has fled, and left his crops to perish.

"And here the contrast is equally striking. In a community where but little crime was manifested, hundreds are now crowding your jail, awaiting trial—many of them, I regret to say, for a capital offence. It is surprising that in a government like ours, things of this kind should exist; that a portion of the people should be warring against their own government—for it is here a government strictly of the people. If errors in legislation have been committed, you have the power to correct them. You can give government a right direction. And yet, strange as it seems, you find a portion of the people placing themselves in open rebellion against that government, refusing to enjoy the rich blessings purchased by the blood of their fathers, and placing themselves in a position to destroy all the institutions that have thus far blessed them. This is indeed greatly to be regretted. There never can be in a free government, a government of the people, either necessity or excuse for treason. If there be anything wrong, the ballot-box is the place where redress is certain. The power is the peoples' own. But it must always be peacefully exerted—never by force."

Our space will hardly permit us to dwell in detail upon the trial of the different prisoners—suffice it to say that they resulted in two convictions for murder, four were sentenced to the State Prison for life, and thirteen for a term of years. The follow prefatory remarks and sentences of the two prisoners convicted of murder is from the Albany Argus:

"Long before the hour to which the court stood adjourned, persons began to flock in. Many little groups were collected around the court room, speculating upon the nature of the various sentences that were soon to be passed; and many with eager countenances were inquiring, whether those found guilty of murder would be hung. Sometime before the bell rang for the court to convene, the room was filled to overflowing; and many an anxious face and palpitating heart were there.

"At 10 o'clock Judge Parker took his seat on the bench and ordered the sheriff to bring up John Van Steenburgh. The prisoner being brought up, Judge Parker addressed the prisoner in substance as follows:—

"'John Van Steenburgh—You have been convicted of the murder of Osman N. Steele. Have you anything to say why sentence of death should not be passed upon you?'

"The prisoner, with some emotion, replied: 'all that I can say is I am not guilty.'

"*Judge Parker.*—'The court entertain no doubt of your legal guilt. You were one of more than two hundred men present, disguised and armed, when Steele was murdered. There is suspicion that you fired your gun. It is a painful duty that devolves upon us, but we discharge it without hesitation or fear. You have had a fair trial. You have forfeited your life. You have but a short time more to live—to prepare yourself for eternity. During that time your friends will be permitted to see you; they will see that you have religious instruction. Your fate is an awful one. The sentence of the law is, *that on the twenty-ninth day of November next, you be taken from your confinement to the place of execution,* and there hung *by the neck until you are dead.*'

"The prisoner said: 'will you allow me to say a few words?'

Judge Parker: 'It will be as well for you to confer with your counsel.'

"The prisoner was then remanded, and the sheriff brought up Edward O'Connor.

"Judge Parker then addressed the prisoner as follows:—

"'Edward O'Connor. You have been found guilty of the murder of Osman N. Steele—have you anything to say why sentence of death should not be passed upon you?'

"*Prisoner.*—'I am innocent.'

"*Judge Parker.*—'Upon that subject there is no doubt: you have had a fair and impartial trial. You were one of two hundred disguised and armed men present when Steele was murdered. You are clearly guilty of murder in law, if you did not fire. A most painful duty devolves upon the court. I have known you and your family for years. You are intelligent—you have had advantages—you should have better appreciated them. You were just entering upon the duties of life. We have a most painful duty to discharge; nevertheless we are ready to do it. You have but a few days to live. You should prepare for eternity. You will have time to reflect. It is not the murder of Steele only that you are guilty of, but the laws themselves have been violated. An awful fate awaits you. You will have an opportunity to see your friends, and will also have religious counsel if you desire it. The *sentence of the law is, that on Saturday, the twenty-ninth day of November next, you be taken from your confinement to the place of execution, and there be hung by the neck until you are dead.'*

"The prisoner remarked, as he turned to be conducted back to jail—'I die innocent; remember that, my friends.'"

The court finally adjourned, after a prolonged session of about three weeks, having accomplished a great amount of business. All agreed in awarding great credit to Judge Parker, for the uniform calmness and decision preserved throughout the trials of the prisoners. Indeed, his integrity and honor were so highly appreciated by all parties, that even the prisoners, many of them, preferred throwing themselves upon his mercy to risking the verdict of a jury.

During the trials, the court-house and jail were strictly guarded by an efficient force. A rumor was circulated during the trials, that a numerous body of disguised Indians, many of whom were from adjoining counties, were collecting in the vicinity of the village of Bloomville, preparing to make a descent upon the village and rescue the prisoners, as soon as their strength became sufficient. And these rumors were not altogether groundless, as facts afterward elicited went to show. A plan of attack had been concerted, but owing to the guarded condition of the village, it was not deemed expedient to risk an engagement. The following attempt upon the life of one of the picket guard, was published at the time: "Between eight and nine o'clock, on Tuesday evening of last week, considerable excitement was created in the village, by the report that one of the picket guard (Mr. Claghorn, of Masonville,) had been fired upon, a short distance this side of Mr. Wright's, on the opposite side of the river. The night was very dark and rainy, and hearing a slight noise, he stopped his horse, while his companion advanced a short distance, both listening to ascertain the cause; and while Mr. C. was in the act of pulling the skirts of his overcoat to cover his holsters, for the purpose of keeping them dry, he was fired upon; the ball passed through the skirts of his coat, so near to his hand as to cause a numbness, and the hand to swell.

"Mr. Claghorn remained on the ground to keep a look-out, while his companions made all haste and reported the case to Major Marvine, who promptly dispatched a posse of thirty or forty men, in hopes of being able to obtain some clue to the perpetrator of the foul deed; but the darkness of the night effectually prevented the detection of the assassin. The next morning Major Marvine himself went with others to examine; tracks were plainly seen, and followed through a ploughed field; the track was carefully measured and a pattern taken. It is ardently hoped that some clue may yet be obtained that will lead to the detection of the person guilty of so cowardly and base an attempt at murder.

"At the opening of the court, on Wednesday morning, Judge Parker requested the Grand Jury to come into court. The Judge stated that he had sent for them for the purpose of laying before them the transaction of the night previous, which he did in strong and decided language of condemnation, and exhorting the jury to be vigilant, and use every possible means within their power to ferret out the offender."

Having thus briefly reviewed the causes which led to the late anti-rent disturbance, and glanced at their immediate history, it now becomes our province to draw it to a close. It is but proper, however, to say, that the Governor commuted the sentences of O'Connor and Van Steenburgh to imprisonment for life. A leading journal thus comments:

"It is rare that the public sentiment of all parties is so unanimous in sustaining an executive in one of the most trying and important exercises of constitutional power, as in this instance. The opinion seems almost universal, that the commutation was not only wise, but right.

"We believe that this opinion is not confined to our State alone, but extends elsewhere. We have now before us a letter from a sound and able democratic member of Congress from the east, who writes from Washington: 'I rejoice to hear that your Governor has commuted the sentences of Van Steenburgh and O'Connor. It is both wise and right, and must receive the cordial approbation of the people.'"

In the month of December, the Governor was officially informed of the suppression of the insurrection, and the declaration "declaring the county in a state of insurrection," was revoked. The worst stages of anti-rentism had now passed, and those who had shrunk with fear before the dark clouds of political discord, and faltered in their confidence in the stability of a peoples' government, now saw in the dim distance of the future, the sure triumph of those principles.

So far as the principle of anti-rentism existed in its purity, as a question of right and wrong, so far as the validity of the manorial titles was brought in question, so far as legal and persuasive means would prove effectual, we have ever deemed it a privilege and a duty to raise our voice uniformly on the side of the oppressed against the oppressor. But when we behold an infatuated and infuriated mob, disguised as Indians, regardless of law, determined, by force, to make all things subservient to the consummation of their own ends, without truth, reason or justice on their side, shaming, by conscious guilt, to bare their features—the impress stamp of heaven, to the light of day—concealing them beneath the well-known covering of another species, to render them impregnable against the shafts of recognition; here our co-operation terminates, and we must henceforth regard them with pity for their errors, as the lamentable victims of the machinations of a diseased and erroneous imagination. We should review with careful candor their mistaken policy and notions, and learn from their practical example that, although error may flourish for a time, and even seem to overshadow the principles of justice, yet without any stable foundation, it falls at last by the weight of its own superstructure, and its retainers and supporters become the wanton victims of their own cupidity. The result which, in this instance, placed the finishing touch upon that sad picture, the final triumph of truth over error, can but strengthen our faith in the tenacity with which Americans still adhere to the principles of our free institutions—a fixed and nerving principle, graven deep in the heart, a stream deep and pure, which, although its surface may become ruffled by the breath of discord—although for a time its noble destiny may seem perverted and forgotten—yet it possesses a principle which, in the end, will work its signal triumph.

CHAPTER XIV

The following sketch of the services of the late Timothy Murphy in the border warfare of the Revolution, were kindly furnished the author, and although in some respects they deviate from what he conceives to be truth, in the main he has ascertained them to be correct.

LIFE AND ADVENTURES OF TIMOTHY MURPHY.

TIMOTHY MURPHY, the hero of this narrative, was born in the town of Minisink, in the county of Sussex and State of New Jersey, in the year 1751. His parents emigrated to this country from Ireland, and settled in New Jersey some years previous to the commencement of the French and Indian war; where they remained until the year 1757; they then removed to the State of Pennsylvania. Of his history previous to the commencement of the Revolution, we know but little, and have not been able to collect any thing that will in the least interest the reader. He had very little or no education, except such as was obtained from the pure study of nature.

In the year 1776, when at the age of twenty-four, he enlisted in the United States service under Col. Morgan, the well known 'old waggoner,' as the British used to term him. In the year 1778, he was engaged in the battle of Monmouth in New Jersey, and escaped unhurt. After the battle of Monmouth, two companies, detachments from Morgan's riflemen, were sent to the northward under the command of Captain Long, to which Murphy was attached. After the battle of Saratoga and capture of Burgoyne, they were ordered to old Schoharie, where the Indians and tories were murdering and carrying off in concert captives to Canada.

The first service on which Murphy was sent, was in connection with a small body of riflemen under command of Capt. Long, to take dead or alive a person strongly suspected of toryism, living on the Charlotte river, by the name of Service, who was not only torified in principle, but was an active agent of the British in aiding, victualling and secreting the enemies of the Revolution. When they arrived at his dwelling, they silently surrounded it, gathering closer and closer, till at length two or three made bold to enter the room in which he was, before they were discovered: Service instantly stepped out of the door with them, when he was informed that they had orders to take him to the forts at Schoharie. He appeared at first somewhat alarmed, and strenuously objected to the proposal, pleading innocence and rendering many other excuses, but in the meanwhile was evidently working his way along from the door to a heap of chips lying between Murphy and one Ellison, a companion of his. The reason of his approaching the chips so cautiously, now appeared obvious, for on coming to the spot, he seized instantly a broad-axe and made a most desperate stroke at Murphy, which, however, by his keen vigilance was eluded, and the fruitless attempt rolled back in vengeance upon its author:—Murphy stepped back, drew his faithful rifle to his face—a flash, a groan, and he lay weltering in his own blood, with the axe in his hand, a victim of that retributive justice which watched over the fortunes of the Revolution. They returned, not a little elated, with the scalp of the notorious Service, to the forts at Schoharie, where Murphy and his company remained during the winter, engaged at times in small parties of scouts, and at others stationed at the forts.

Murphy's skill in the desultory war which the Indians carried on, gave him so high a reputation, that though not nominally the commander, he usually directed all the movements of the scouts that were sent out, and on many important occasions, as the reader in the course of this work will perceive, the commanding officers found it dangerous to neglect his advice. His double barrelled rifle; his skill as a marksman, and his fleetness either in retreat or pursuit, made him an object both of dread and vengeance to the Indians. He fought them in their own way and with their own weapons. Sometimes habited in the dress of the Indian, with his face painted, he would pass among them, making important discoveries as to their strength and designs, without detection. He early learned to speak the Indian language, which of course was of great service to him.

During the succeeding winter, the Indians were continually on the alert. They generally formed themselves into small parties, and a particular portion of country was assigned to a party of Indians for their direct destruction. At that time the German flats, or that portion of country lying on either side of the Mohawk between Utica and Schenectady, was their more immediate sphere of action. Murphy, together with a small party of riflemen, were ordered to that part of the country to watch, and to prevent if possible, the destruction of human life, and devastation of property, then so rapidly being made by the inhuman savages.

It was on this occasion that Murphy and two other individuals had strayed from the main party to which they were attached, and were rambling about among the woods and brush, studying the plans and watching the movements of the Indians. They had not been long separated from the main party, when they discovered a number of Indians skulking about among the weeds and brush, apparently watching the movements of Murphy and his companions. They had proceeded but a short distance farther when they saw two Indians sitting upon the trunk of a masterly looking oak, with their backs toward them; they immediately fired, each brought his man, and then ran back to join the main party. The report of the guns, and the death of their fellows, roused the revengeful blood of the savages, and they were almost instantly surrounded by a large body of them. They fought like heroes, but were overpowered in numbers by the bloodthirsty demons, who as it seemed had at that moment risen from the very bowels of the earth. At length Murphy saw his associates fall one after another till there were but a few left; at this period Murphy made a rush to pass the Indians, and himself and six others succeeded. Murphy ran with all possible speed, but the weeds and brush through which he had to pass, prevented in a measure his progress; however, by jumping up and over the weeds, and being very expert in running, he easily outstripped all the Indians, except one, whom he turned to shoot several times, but believing his gun unloaded, he determined to reserve his fire for the last exigency. Murphy succeeded in eluding the vigilance of the Indian, and secreted himself in a very dense collection of weeds, and there lay until the Indians came up and stood some distance from him. The Indian that first pursued him, now bent forward, and pointing in the direction in which he lay, exclaimed to his companions "kong gwa," which in English, means, "that way." Murphy jumped up and ran as fast as his limbs would carry him: the Indians fired several times at him, but with no effect: he finally succeeded in getting entirely out of their view, and being, from fatigue, unable to proceed farther, he secreted himself behind a large log. The Indians came up to very near him, but supposing him to have passed on, they turned and went back. There was one circumstance that happened during the heat of the affray, at which, though surrounded by the dead and the dying, and with not much hope of a better fate, Murphy, as himself states, could not refrain from laughing. It appears that there were among the Indians a negro, and an Irishman on the other side:—the paddy was chasing the poor negro with a long butcher knife, and every now and then making a desperate thrust at the most sensitive part of the poor fellow's seat of honor. Murphy afterward inquired of the paddy, why he wished to kill the unarmed black; "because," he said, "the davlish naggar had no business to run afore me."

The next spring, Long's riflemen, to which Murphy was still attached, had orders to move under Colonel Butler, in connection with other troops, in all amounting to seven hundred, to Springfield, at the head of Otsego lake, where they were to await the arrival of Gen. George Clinton, and the troops expected with him, all of whom when there concentrated, were to pass down the Susquehanna, and form a junction with General Sullivan at Tioga Point. The object of this arrangement was the destruction of the Indian tribes on the Chemung and Genesee rivers; who had so often been employed in small parties by the policy of the British Government, to distress in a predatory manner the inhabitants of the frontiers; the leader of whom was Brant, so renowned for his warlike achievements in this part of our country, and who was alike notorious for his humane treatment to many of his prisoners, as well as his barbarity and savage discipline, in inflicting the most cruel tortures on them, in their expiring agonies. While encamped at some place unknown near the Chemung river, and previous to their joining the main army, Murphy obtained leave for himself and three others, by name Follok, Tufts, and Joe Evans, to go out on a scout to the Chemung. They started in the morning of a fine July day; they travelled until four in the afternoon, at which time they arrived upon the lofty banks that overlooked the Chemung river. Making no discoveries, and finding nothing to interest them during their travel, and being somewhat fatigued, they determined to encamp for the night, and accordingly preparations were made. The scene was passing fair. A little in advance and directly in front of them, rolled the Chemung river in all the pride and loveliness of nature; a little to the left and still beyond the river, was a vacant field, on which were scattered a number of cattle feeding upon the wild luxuriance of nature, which at some day had been the object of cultivation by beings equally as rude as Nature herself. They had not been long upon this proud eminence, ere they espied three Indians towing a canoe up the rapids; one standing in the canoe steering it, one on the shore tugging away at a rope, and the other using a pole to keep the boat off the shore. No sooner were they observed, than Murphy turned to his companions and said: "I've a notion to try the one standing in the canoe," and suiting the action to the word, he drew up and fired,—the distance being somewhat great, he had no expectation of doing effect, but to their utter astonishment he reeled and fell backward over into the river. The other two Indians let loose the rope, dropped the pole, and fled to the woods, not even looking behind to see from whence proceeded the bullet that proved so fatal to their companion.

In the morning they proceeded up the river for some miles, but finding slight traces of Indians and discovering none, they crossed over the river, wheeled about, and commenced their march for the encampment, then about thirty miles distant: they had proceeded on their backward course until they arrived opposite the place where the scene just related was enacted the day before, where they discovered at a distance a boy apparently fifteen or sixteen years of age, in pursuit of cattle. They hailed him, but he fled, Murphy at the same time pursuing; he very easily overtook, and secured him prisoner: they then proceeded several miles into the woods, lit a fire, and prepared for the night's repose:—the boy, whose hands were tied behind, was placed between Murphy and Tufts. Sometime in the night Murphy awoke, and on raising up, he discovered the boy, his rifle and moccasins among the missing. He instantly sprang upon his feet, and gave the Indian war-whoop, which, by the by, he mimicked to perfection, to arouse his companions. Murphy, not a little aggravated at the loss of his rifle, moccasins and prisoner, and feeling himself chagrined at being duped by a boy of but fifteen years of age, immediately proposed that they should proceed in search of him; but his companions, knowing the result if he persisted in so rash an undertaking, persuaded him to abandon it. What was to be done! Murphy was without shoes or moccasins wherewith to cover his already tender feet, made so by his continual travel—But that benign Providence who never fails to provide for emergencies, had upon this all important occasion, more than blessed Follok with a pair of leather breeches, which, as soon as discovered, were sacrificed to the unmerciful treatment of Murphy's jack-knife. His moccasins completed, they commenced in the morning their homeward course. When they arrived at the encampment, Murphy was thus accosted by an officer: "Murphy, where the devil is your rifle:" he made no reply—the rebuke was too much for his naturally proud spirit to withstand, and he again determined to solicit for himself and companions the privilege of going in search of the lost rifle; which being granted, they commenced pursuit. The next day, about the same hour, and upon nearly the same spot of ground, they saw the identical boy driving cattle as before: they followed on in the rear until they observed him to enter an obscure hut in a remote part of the wilderness—they immediately entered the hut, where were some old women, and more than all, the wished-for rifle. They took the boy once more and proceeded on their way back; when about five miles on their return, they met a man on horseback, whom after some close quizzing they likewise took prisoner. While crossing the river, he threw himself intentionally into it; but on Murphy's drawing his rifle to his face, and threatening to shoot him through, he was glad to make for the shore.

They finally arrived safe at the encampment with their prisoners and lost rifle, when in a few days they joined the main army of Sullivan, which numbered in all about five thousand, and then proceeded west, burning and laying waste all the Indian settlements in their reach. After an absence of six months, and enduring many hardships and privations, Murphy and his company returned to the forts at Schoharie.

There is one circumstance that transpired during his campaign to the west, which we cannot omit to mention. When near what is now called Canandaigua lake, Murphy, with a company of some twenty other robust fellows, was dispatched round the upper end of the lake to destroy a small Indian village which was rapidly increasing. After destroying the village, and on their return to the main army, they found themselves almost instantaneously surrounded by a body of Indians more than double their number, and led by the celebrated Brant. What was to be done? Murphy, knowing Brant, and judging what must be their inevitable fate if they fell into his hands, said to his companions, "we must fight or die." The war whoop was given, and the savages rushed forward, making the woods ring with their yells, as if the very lightnings from heaven had burst their bounds, and were spreading their deathlike gleams upon our little band. They returned every attack with spirit and coolness, and with as much effect as their situation would admit. Murphy saw his companions fall one after the other until there were but five left; the contest not diminishing in the least in fury. At one moment all hopes of escape seemed shut out, at the next prospects would brighten for an instant. Their courage never for a moment forsook them; they struggled with desperation; death and the diabolical infliction of savage torture stared them in the face, and they determined to sell their lives as dearly as possible. At this juncture, four of the party made a rush to pass the Indians; the savages immediately ran before them to prevent their escape, which left a vacancy behind, in which direction Murphy ran with the fleetness of a deer: he gained rapidly on them until nearly exhausted, when coming to a brush fence, that stood at the top of a bank which descended to a fosse, he jumped over and secreted himself directly under the fence; the Indians came up, and one of them stood upon the fence directly above him gazing around (Murphy watching his eyes through the brush of which the fence was composed,) for some minutes, when the Indian went back. As soon as sufficiently rested he proceeded on his course to the army, which he reached after encamping one night without fire or a particle of food. His companions doubtless were all sacrificed to the bloody tomahawk, as Murphy never heard any thing of them to the day of his death.

Soon after, he returned to Schoharie, where he was greeted with joy and exultation by every patriot of his country. The women felt themselves secure under his protection. The men, knowing his superiority and skill in tracing and ferreting out the Indians on all occasions, submitted to his judgment and command; and finally, where there seemed to be a general panic previous to his return, there was a sudden change as if by magic at beholding the noble and fearless countenance of Tim Murphy. Nor were the Indians less surprised at finding their daring opposer crossing their trails, and frustrating their plans. They fled at his approach, trembled lest his bullet should find from a secret covert a hiding place in their breast, and feared, perhaps, that his spirit would haunt them in an evil hour.

Soon after our hero came to Schoharie with the detachment of Morgan's riflemen, he obtained permission to go on a scout through the delightful vale of Fulton. It was in the spring, and all nature was waking from the icy lethargy of winter. The Oneistagrawa was shaded with various hues as the sun was dancing on its brow. The snow had melted on the plain below, yet small banks might be seen at intervals, which he eyed with apparent suspicion. Now he gazed on the adjacent mountain, now on the vale around, as he passed leisurely along. He advanced until he arrived where his sons Jacob and Peter now reside, when his attention was arrested by

—"A rose complexioned lass,
Nimbly tripping through the grass,"

with a milk-pail on her arm. He stood perfectly still and saw her pass towards a barn where cattle were feeding. She stepped off with all the poetry of motion imaginable. How unlike the mincing step of coquetry! Like Milton's Eve,

"Grace was in all her steps, heaven in her eye,
In every motion, dignity and love."

Her dress was exceedingly plain, and which was admirably calculated for the exhibition of her exquisitely chiselled form to the best advantage. A handkerchief white as her lily hand was tied loosely over her head. Her hair did not hang in ringlets—by no means—but was carefully and neatly done up. Neither was her waist girted small as a city belle's, but was of a proper size, or to be more specific, an armful! Her eyes were not diamonds, nor were her teeth pearl; yet we defy all christendom to produce a brighter pair of eyes or a finer set of teeth than were possessed by Miss Peggy Feeck. In short, she was not such a girl as would make fifty lovers commit suicide and after all die an old maid, but was one whom you would love for her artless innocence and real beauty. As Walcott justly observes:

"The dullest eye can beauty see,
'Tis lightning on the sight;
Indeed it is a general bait,
And man, the fish, will bite."

As Murphy approached he thought almost audibly, "J—s, what a swate creature!" and slowly advancing, he bade her "Gude morning," and they were soon in familiar talk. Reader, what do you think they talked about? Not about the weather—nor about Such-a-one's courting such-another—nor about each other's appearance—nor about love—or any such trash. But they conversed like persons of common sense, on subjects of some importance. Her conversation pleased him extremely, and time passed with unusual velocity, until she arose to return, when she very politely invited him to walk along and take breakfast, which request he as politely accepted. A hearty breakfast was prepared in the true Dutch style, and after indulging some chat with the "old folks" (which was somewhat difficult, as they had but a partial knowledge of English, and he less of Dutch), he departed, not, however, without a request to "call again."

Here an old lady remarked, with a knowing twist of the head, that Murphy frequently passed in that direction as he went on a scout. Whether he went to see the romantic scenery in that region, or in pursuit of Indians, or to see

> "That lovely being, gently formed and moulded,
> A rose with all its sweetness just unfolded,"

we leave for the prolific imagination of the reader to determine. At length her parents, considering his visits rather too frequent, directed her to inform him peremptorily that they were not acceptable. But little were they aware of the moral courage and determination of a girl in the vigor of youth, who has fixed her love. Byron told the truth when he says:

> "The tree
> Rent from its forest root of years, the river
> Dammed from its fountain; the child from the knee
> And breast maternal, weaned at once forever,
> Would wither less than these two torn apart—
> Alas, there is no instinct like the heart."

What could she do? Should he be sacrificed to the avarice and cupidity of parents? No!

> "Sooner let earth, sea, air, to chaos fall;
> Men, monkeys, lap-dogs, parrots, perish all."

She informed him, with alternate sobs and tears, of her parents' resolution. Murphy was thunderstruck; not a word was spoken for some moments, when, after making a single request that they should meet again at a time and place specified, he hastily departed. As he was returning toward the fort, he reflected; why this unkind prohibition? At length the thought struck him—it was because he was poor!

Time passed with a heavy step. Murphy endeavored to calm his feelings by continued action, and engaged in numerous skirmishes with invariable success; yet his downcast eyes in the midst of triumph, indicated that something was wrong. Alas, how true the exclamation of the poet:

> "For mighty hearts are held in slender chains."

At last the night of their meeting arrived, and seating himself beneath a spacious oak, he patiently waited to perceive the object of his pursuit. A faint light was glimmering through a window. At length that was extinguished; moments then seemed hours, as he sat reclining against the oak. He waited half an hour longer, when the window was softly raised, and his "lady love" peeped through, and on recognizing him, beckoned for him to approach. After a serious consultation, they came to the determination of being united by

> "That silken tie that binds two willing hearts."

They agreed to meet at the same place a few days afterward. Murphy returned to the fort with a weight of lead from his heart. He consulted confidentially with one of the officers, who applauded his *gal*-lantry, and afterward gave permission to go "any distance" in pursuit of a Domine. He accordingly went on the appointed evening in pursuit of his bride, and after a short time, she escaped through the window in her best petticoat and short-gown; and after she was seated behind him, they departed as rapidly as convenient for the fort, where they arrived about day-break. They were received by the garrison with three cheers which made the welkin ring. Murphy walked into the fort, escorting his prize, with as much pride as he would half a dozen captive Indians. The girls all kissed sweet Peggy, the women admired her courage, and the men all declared she would make a good soldier! But time was not to be lost; for already they might be pursued by the avaricious father. They soon departed, in company with a William Bouck and a lady, in pursuit of a minister. They arrived at Duanesburgh in the afternoon, where Domine Johnson finished

> "That consummation devoutly to be wished."

They then returned to the fort, when they were again cheered by the soldiers.

The next day her father came to the fort, and with a long face inquired for his daughter; but finding he was "a day *after* the *fair*," he adopted, like a man of sense, the motto that "discretion is the better part of valor," and surrendered this *best* prize ever captured by man! Making true what Virgil sang two thousand years ago: *Omnia vincit amor; et nos cedamus amori*. Or as Dryden freely translates it:

> "In hell, and earth, and sea, and heaven above,
> Love conquers all, and all must yield to love."

In the fall of 1780, the enemy, about 800 strong, under Sir John Johnston, made preparations for destroying the valleys of Schoharie and the Mohawk. The forces, consisting of British regulars, loyalists, tories and Indians, assembled on the Tioga, and marched thence up along the eastern branch of the Susquehanna, and crossed thence to Schoharie. On the 16th of October they encamped about four miles above the upper fort. It was their intention to pass the upper fort in the night, and to attack the middle fort* at day-break ; as it was expected that the upper fort would be the first object of attack, they hoped to surprise the middle fort by this unexpected movement. Sir John had ordered his troops to be put in motion at four in the morning; but from some mistake it was five before they began their march; consequently, the rear guard was discovered by the sentinels of the upper fort, and the alarm-gun was fired, which was quickly answered from the other forts, and twenty riflemen, under the supervision of Murphy, were sent out from the middle fort to watch the motions of the enemy; they soon fell in with an advanced party, and retreated back. At the firing of the settlement, houses, barns, and stacks of hay were burned, and cattle, sheep, and horses, were killed or driven away.

The Indians, being in advance of the regular forces, were the first to approach the fort. Murphy, whose eye was ever watching the enemy, had stationed himself in a ditch a few rods south of the fort, that he might, unperceived, the better view the movements of the enemy. The Indians approached to within about eighty yards of the fort, when Murphy fired upon them; and as he arose the second time to fire, a bullet struck within two inches of his face, and glanced over his head, throwing dirt in his eyes. He then ran into the fort, not, however, without bringing to the ground another Indian.

About 8 o'clock the enemy commenced a regular attack on the fort, which was returned with effect from the garrison. The regular troops fired a few cannon shot, and threw a number of shells, one of which burst in the air above the fort, doing no injury; another entered, and burst in the upper loft of the fort, doing no other mischief than destroying a quantity of bedding and nearly frightening to death a little Frenchman who had fled to the chamber for protection, and came running down stairs, at the same time exclaiming, "de diable pe among de fedders." The interior of the fort was several times on fire, but was as often extinguished by the exertions of the women. The Indians retreated behind a row of willow trees, and kept up a constant fire, but at too great a distance to do effect. In the fort, all was gloom and despondency; the garrison only amounted to 150 regular troops, and about 100 militia. Their ammunition was nearly exhausted—to attempt to defend the fort, appeared to be madness; to surrender, was to deliver up themselves, their wives and children, to immediate death, or at least to a long captivity. Major Wolsey, who commanded the fort, was inclined to surrender on the first appearance of the enemy, but was prevented by the officers of the militia, who resolved to defend the fort or to die in the contest. Wolsey's presence of mind forsook him in the hour

---

* The remains of this fort are still to be seen, standing on the farm of Ralph Manning, in the town of Middleburgh. The Upper Fort was about five miles above, and the Lower Fort five miles below. The Lower Fort was built for a church, and is at present unoccupied. It stands about a mile north of the court-house.

of danger; he concealed himself at first with the women and children in the house, and when driven out by the ridicule of his new associates, he crawled round the intrenchments on his hands and knees, amid the jeers and bravos of the militia, who felt their courage revive as their laughter was excited by the cowardice of the Major. In the times of extreme danger, every thing which has a tendency to destroy reflection by exciting risibility has a good effect.

The enemy, perceiving that their shot and shells did little or no execution, formed under shelter of a small building near the fort, and prepared to carry the works by assault. While the preparations were making, a flag was seen to approach the fort; all seemed inclined to admit it, when Murphy and Bartholomew Vrooman, who suspected that it was only an artifice to learn the actual strength of the garrison, and aware that for them at least there was no safety in capitulation, fired upon the flag. The flag retired and some soldiers were ordered to arrest Murphy; but so great was his popularity among the soldiers, that no one dared to obey. The flag approached a second time, and was a second time driven back by Murphy and his adherents. A white flag was then ordered to be raised in the fort, but Murphy threatened with instant death any one who should obey. The enemy sent a flag a third time, and on Murphy's turning to fire upon it, Wolsey presented his pistol and threatened to shoot him if he did; but not in the least intimidated by the major's threat, Murphy very deliberately raised his rifle, and pointing it towards him firmly replied, "I will die before they shall have me prisoner." Maj. Wolsey then retired to his room, where he remained until Col. Vrooman was dispatched in search of him. He was found covered up in bed, trembling like a leaf. Col. Vrooman accosted him: "Was you sent here to sneak away so, when we are attacked by the Tories and Indians? and do you mean to give up the fort to these bloody rascals?" To which Maj. Wolsey made no reply, but consented to yield up the command to Col. Vrooman. At this change of officers, unanimous joy pervaded the whole fort. And even the women smiled to behold the portly figure of Col. Vrooman stalking about the fort—directing and encouraging the soldiers in his melodious Low Dutch tones.

The British officers now held a council of war, and after a short consultation withdrew; and then proceeded down the Schoharie creek, burning and destroying every thing that lay in their way.

Soon after Gen. Johnston departed towards the Lower Fort, Murphy followed in his rear and secured prisoner a man by the name of Benjamin Buttons.

The loss of the garrison in this affair was only one killed and two wounded, one mortally. It is not known what loss the enemy sustained, or why they retreated so hastily. The true, and most probable cause was the determined spirit of resistance manifested in firing upon the flag, leading them to suppose the defense could be obstinate. The tory leaders, satiated with blood, may have been unwilling to act over the tragedies of Wyoming and Cherry Valley.

A small body of men then left the Middle Fort under Col. Vrooman, and by a circuitous route reached the Lower Fort, just as the tories and Indians were passing where the village of Schoharie now stands. Several buildings which were there erected, were burned to the ground. When they arrived at the Lower Fort, they showed little disposition to attack it, although its garrison did not amount to 100. They separated into two divisions, the regular troops marching along the bank of the creek, and the Indians filing off a quarter of a mile to the east of the fort. The regulars fired a few cannon shot without effect, one only lodging in the corner of the church.—The Indians and tories, in preparing a small brass cannon, received a brisk and deadly fire from the fort, which so frightened them that they sunk their cannon in a morass, and marched to where the road now runs, where they were joined by the regulars. They then fired a few shots with small arms, and the Indians approached near enough to throw their bullets into the tower of the church, where some marksmen had been stationed. A discharge of grape drove them back, and passing over the Fox creek, they set fire to a house and grist-mill, after which they proceeded to Fort Hunter.

The beautiful valley of the Schoharie creek presented a scene of devastation, on the night of the 17th October, not easily described. Houses, barns, and numerous stacks of hay and grain were consumed; domestic animals lay dead every where over the fields; a few buildings belonging to the tories had been spared, but Murphy, among others, sallying out, set fire to them in revenge. After the burning of Schoharie, this settlement ceased to be so much an object of tory vengeance, and during the years 1781 and 1782, though there were frequent alarms, little damage was done by the enemy.

The savages appeared once in Cobleskill, burned a few buildings, killed one man and carried off five prisoners; but the body of the inhabitants had taken refuge in a fort which they had built on their return from Schoharie, in 1781, and were safe.

Soon after Sir John Johnston passed through Schoharie, Murphy and his three friends, Follok, Tufts and Evans, went over the hills of Summit. Murphy, by some mishap, strayed from the rest and wandering in the woods, he at length saw an Indian skinning a deer, which he had recently killed. Murphy being unperceived, took aim and shot the Indian through the head, who reeling fell beside the deer. He then ran up, took off the Indian's scalp, and laying him over a log, placed the deer's skin over him in such a manner as to make it appear at a short distance like a large deer. This was scarcely done before he heard a rustling in the leaves a few rods off; as quick as thought, he crawled among the bushes and thick weeds near, where he could see distinctly three Indians moving their heads about, as if doubtful of what had the appearance of a deer. Finally, one of them fired at the supposed deer, and rushing up, what was their chagrin at discovering they had shot one of their own fellows! They gave several doleful yells to call others, and stood grinding their teeth and gesticulating wildly. Murphy, fearing that they might discover him soon, or that others might arrive, concluded it best to shoot one, and hazard a running fight with the other two. He accordingly fired, brought down his man—and rushed behind a very large tree. Before they had recovered from their panic, he discharged his other rifle barrel and mortally wounded a second. The only remaining Indian fired; the ball passed through the bark of one side of the tree, within a few inches of Murphy's face. The Indian then seized a rifle from one who was rolling and howling over the ground. By this time Murphy had reloaded his rifle, and both of them sprang behind trees some fifty yards apart. The moment one looked out, the rifle of the other was raised, and the head immediately drawn back. At last Murphy put his hat on the end of his ramrod, and pushed it slowly to the side of the tree. The Indian immediately fired—his ball passed through the centre of the hat. The hat was then dropped, when the Indian rushed up with hatchet and scalping knife. Murphy fired—he staggered a few paces forward, and fell down dead. The Indian was very large and powerful, and Murphy being exceedingly angry, skinned his legs, and drew the skin over his stockings. He then went in pursuit of his companions. He was unable to find them, and about 10 o'clock at night he stopped, and kindled a fire on the side of a little rivulet, where he roasted a small piece of the deer, which he had carried in his pocket. He had also a small biscuit, which he ate with his meat. After his repast, he procured water from the brook, with which he extinguished the fire. He proceeded on a quarter of a mile farther; he crept in among the limbs of a tree, that apparently had fallen a few days before. In the morning, he advanced several miles, when he was unexpectedly surrounded by a large body of Indians, who had followed in his trail. He shot down two, who were on the side in which he wished to fly. Several of the Indians fired, and as he afterwards often remarked, the balls whistled by him. He ran with the utmost velocity, and after leaving them far behind, he managed to reload his rifle as he ran. But the skin of the Indian having shrunk, began to gall his legs, whereupon, he took his hunting knife and ripped it off. Yet his legs were so galled that his speed was greatly retarded, and he had not advanced more than two miles more, before a dozen Indians were in view. 'Twas then that his courage began to forsake him; faint and tired, he was ready to sink upon the ground. *"We've got you at last!"* exclaimed one, and coming up, struck him a blow over the shoulders with the end of his musket. It was then that Murphy,

> "Stood a foe with all the zeal,
> That young and fiery converts feel,
> Within whose burning bosom throngs
> The memory of a thousand wrongs;"

and turning indignantly around, he dashed his brains out at a blow. The others came up yelling like wolves sure of their prey. Murphy again plunged with his gun and the Indian's, into the woods; but finding himself unable to run, he stopped abruptly behind a tree and discharged his own, and the Indian's gun. On his firing the second time, their superstitious fears began to rise, but when he fired the third time, they were confirmed in their suspicions of his being leagued with the *Wicked Spirit*, to destroy them, and believing that he could shoot all day, they immediately decamped with all speed. He did not stop for a scalp, but slowly wended his way toward the fort, where he arrived in safety.

ANECDOTES, ETC.

At one time Murphy, and a small body of riflemen were dispatched to destroy an Indian and tory village near Unadilla. After a laborious march through marshes, and over mountains, in which they endured innumerable privations, they arrived in sight of the village, which lay in a beautiful valley. They remained on the mountain until midnight, when they advanced slowly and cautiously. Luckily most of the Indians were absent, and after a warm contest, in which clubs, fists, feet and tomahawks, were used by the old Indians, squaws, and papooses, and were resented by the riflemen, with fists, feet, and the ends of their guns, the village was reduced to ashes. They had not returned far, before they were attacked by the Indians, and most of them destroyed. Murphy, who was in advance of the rest, ran some distance and crawled into a large hollow log, that lay near a small stream. He had not remained there long before he heard the voices of Indians, and as they came nearer, found to his amazement, they were going to encamp there. They came up, and one of them, perceiving the cavity of the log, stooped down, but seeing a spider's web hanging over the aperture, (which luckily Murphy had not displaced,) he took no pains to examine further. They then built a fire beside the log, in which he was; after which they lay down to sleep, with their feet toward the fire. Murphy lay quietly until they began to snore, when he crawled softly to a split in the log, and looking through, observed eight Indians, laying with their rifles beside them: while one sat with his tomahawk and scalping knife, in his belt, to keep watch. Murphy drew himself back to his former position, concluding it most expedient to remain where he was for the time being. His position was by no means an enviable one, as ever and anon his olfactories were saluted with a discharge of light artillery, and the log was so burned, that he could see the Indians through the holes made by the fire. Early in the morning, one of the Indians, (who was dressed in English style,) went down to the stream, and bent over to drink, until his coat flaps fell over his back. Murphy saw him through the end of the log, and being irritated by the heat, and having the end of his rifle in that direction, he fired: the Indian fell headlong into the water. The other Indians fled precipitately, when Murphy backed out of the log, scalped the Indian, and running as fast as his feet would carry him, escaped.

Just before the battle of Saratoga, he went out of the American camp, and having ascertained the British countersign, he went into one of their camps, and seeing an officer writing, alone, he whispered to him, (pointing to his hunting- knife,) that if he spoke a word he would make daylight shine through him. The officer, not having sword or pistols near, reluctantly marched before him to the American camp.

At the last battle at Saratoga, in which both armies were engaged, Murphy was, as he states, within five feet of Arnold, when he passed over the fortification, sword in hand. Murphy ascribed, to the day of his death, the chief honor of Burgoyne's defeat to General Arnold, and believed Arnold would never have betrayed his country, had he received the honors which he so richly merited.

At Unadilla, he also went into a fort, several years afterward, where he made important discoveries of the strength of the enemy.

As Murphy was passing toward Summit, in company with Follok, (a half-blood,) who generally acted as his pilot, he saw four Indians, headed by a tory, with scalps hanging on their bayonets. They crawled through a swail; and as they came within plain view, they saw on the bayonet of the tory, what appeared to be the scalp of a woman. They moved carefully, but at last one of them, stepping on a limb of a tree, which made a creaking, three of the Indians fired before them. They both aimed at the tory, who fell, when they escaped by running.

On another occasion, as himself, Follok, Tufts and Evans, were passing through the woods, they saw ten or twelve Canadians, marching toward them, in Indian file, with what appeared to be muskets on their shoulders. The four secreted themselves until the Canadians got between them, when what appeared to be guns, were mere clubs of black birch. They all arose simultaneously, and presenting, ordered them to surrender. Being unarmed, (except with hunting-knives,) they complied, and very demurely walked to the American camp.

Soon after Murphy came to Schoharie, he went on a hunting and scouting excursion, and as he was returning, late in the evening, he saw several men setting fire to an out-house of a building near the Schoharie river. When he arrived within half a mile of the place, he saw several tories standing at the corner of the house, and one peeping in the window.

After a short time the inmates were aroused, and a man, a negro and two boys, came rushing out of doors to extinguish the fire. The tories then hid behind the fence, excepting one, more resolute than the rest, who fired, most probably at the man, but hit one of the boys, who fell, and was carried into the house by the mother who had been alarmed by his cries. This aroused the vengeance of Murphy, who stood on his knees behind a stump, and laying his rifle over the stump, he shot the tory to the very heart. The others, on seeing him fall, and hearing the report in an unexpected direction, scampered away. Murphy then walked up, and was hailed by the inhabitants with tears of joy. No sleep was enjoyed by them that night. In the morning, the tory killed was found to be no less a person than _____, who had pretended to be a whig. Verily, he received the reward of his treachery! The next day the family removed to the fort, where the boy recovered in a short time from his wounds.

Shortly after the war, a Fourth of July was celebrated, at a tavern near Gallupville, which Murphy attended. In the evening they commenced drinking healths, and after several patriotic toasts were offered, a tory gave, in ridicule, "A health *to George III.*" This Murphy determined not to suffer with impunity, and rising, as the tory walked toward the door, he pitched him headlong from the stoop. The tory picked himself up, and left for Canada, or some other country, as he was never heard of afterwards.

Just before the conclusion of the war, as Murphy was at labor in clearing a piece of woodland, he saw a tall Indian approaching him from the woods, with a rifle on his shoulder. As he came nearer, a belt might be seen around his waist, in which were a tomahawk and scalping-knife, that were partially concealed by a large blanket thrown over his shoulders.

"Which way are you travelling?" asked Murphy.

"Don't know," said the Indian.

"Where do you live?" inquired Murphy.

"There," returned the Indian, (pointing toward Canada,) "and where do *you* live?"

"Down here."

"Do you know old Murphy?" was the next question.

"Well—well—yes!" was the response.

"Where does he live?"

"Away off—yonder," (pointing in a wrong direction,) "but what do you want of him?"

"Oh, nothing," said the Indian, apparently embarrassed.

"Murphy was a wicked old devil."

"Yes," said the Indian; "he kill my brother—he kill Indian—he scalp Indian. They say he witch—he shoot without loading—Indian no hit him—he kill good many Indian—but he no kill me—I kill him." Murphy's blood began to boil, but he concealed his excitement as much as possible, and remarked:

"You've a very good rifle there."

"Yes."

"Did you ever shoot at a mark?"

"Oh, yes—do you shoot at mark?"

"Well, suppose we try," said Murphy.

The Indian then ran off some distance, and putting up a mark against a stump, returned.

"You shoot first," said the Indian.

"No, no," said Murphy, "you shoot first."

The Indian then shot, and to the astonishment of Murphy, pierced the centre of the mark. The rifle was then reloaded, and on Murphy's receiving it, he bounded back, exclaiming, *"I am Murphy!"* The savage gave a yell that reverberated through the hills, and drawing his hunting-knife, sprang toward Murphy; but ere he reached him a ball from the rifle entered his breast.

In stature, Murphy was about five feet six inches, with an eye that would kindle and flash like the very lightning, when excited. He was exceedingly quick in all his motions, and possessed an iron frame that nothing, apparently, could affect. And what is very remarkable, his body was never wounded or scarred during the whole war.

He had nine children by his first wife, and was married again in 1812 or 1813, to Miss Mary Robertson, by whom he had four children. Soon after this marriage, he removed to Charlotteville, in Schoharie county, where he remained until a short time before his death, when he moved back to Fulton. He had suffered many years from an obstinate cancer on his neck, which finally terminated his existence in 1818, in the 67th year of his age. He was a good and charitable neighbor, but inveterate to his enemies. He detested the very name of tory, and if possible, with more acrimony than that of Indian; and took the greatest delight in relating the feats and adventures in which he participated; saying that he was resolved to kill himself rather than be taken a prisoner, knowing that they would inflict on him the most inhuman tortures. He repeatedly declined holding civil office, considering it would infringe on his natural independence; he always refused promotion during the war, on the ground that it would confine him to one fort, and frequently prevent his joining scouting parties. In his pecuniary transactions he was perfectly honest, and liberal to the indigent. That he had faults, we are not disposed to deny; but his greatest errors were in furtherance of what he conceived to be the best interests of his country, rather than from any selfish or sinister designs. Those who knew him, speak most in his praise. And it is to be hoped, that it will be long ere the citizens of Schoharie and Delaware, will forget the name of Murphy.

"He was a man, take him all in all,
We shall not look upon his like again."

Among the veterans of the American Revolution, were two noble and brave spirits, whose thrilling stories were deeply impressed on my mind when a boy. Unconnected with the army called to protect the settlements in a confined interior; their names were not entered upon the public roll, and have not appeared upon the historic page. Their services and fame were known, and highly appreciated by those around them, and their memories are still held in high veneration in my native neighborhood, where their bones lie beneath the clods of the valley. Their names were Harper and Murphy, the latter an Irishman. They were among the pioneers who settled at the head of the Delaware river, which rises from a fountain of pure water; called by the Indians Utstayantho. Around this lake is a small valley, then central rendezvous of the savage tribes, whose walks extended from the Mohawk in the north, far down the Delaware, Lackawaxen, Lackawana and the Susquehanna in the south. It was an isolated spot surrounded by mountains and hills, covered with lofty pines, and a variety of evergreens. Its scenery was romantic and beautiful; formed by nature for a retreat such as the rude children of the forest suppose the Great Spirit delights to dwell in. For a long time the lords of the forest built their council fires in the amphitheatre of Utstayantho. There they manufactured their stone pots, their flint arrow-points and their bows. There they smoked the pipe of peace, performed the terrific war dance, and tortured their unfortunate prisoners. There, too, many of their bravest warriors fell, beneath the avenging hand of the enraged inhabitants. There (says the author,) I first drew my vital breath, there I grew up to manhood, there I have ploughed up the bones of those who were slightly buried, and there I have often listened to the following narratives:

At the commencement of the American Revolution the Indian tribes in that section of country, were influenced by two tories, Brant and McDonald, to enlist in favor of the British. Their tomahawks and scalping-knives were soon bathed in the blood of mothers and infants, as well as in that of husbands and fathers. In the spring of 1777 they murdered several families and took a number of prisoners. Among them were Harper and Murphy. As these were the leading men of the settlement, it was decided to take them down the Delaware about 60 miles to an Indian station called Oquago, now Deposit. They were put in charge of eleven warriors, who started with their victims pinioned and bound. The second night, fatigued with their march, they all lay down before a fire, and the savages were soon soundly asleep. A supply of rum during the day and a hearty drink as they stretched themselves out to sleep, rendered their stupor more complete than it otherwise would have been. This opportunity could not pass unimproved by such men as Harper and Murphy. Although closely wedged between the Indians, they arose with such caution as not to awake them. They soon released each other from the bark thongs, with which their arms were bound, and hesitated for a moment, whether to flee or attempt to dispatch the cruel foe. They soon decided upon the latter, removed the arms to some distance, and with tomahawk in hand, commenced the work of death. Each blow was sure and deep—a messenger of death. So profound was their sleep, and so rapid the work of death, that eight of the eleven were dispatched before the other three awoke. While attempting to rise upon their feet, two of them met the deadly blow of two champions, and fell dead beneath their own weapons. One alone escaped and fled to Oquago to relate the doleful tidings. The two heroes each took a gun and all the ammunition, secreted the other guns, and with some parched corn and dried venison, guided by the polar star, commenced their journey back, keeping near the river until daylight, when they took the ridge to avoid meeting Indians, and in the evening reached a small settlement within ten miles of home. They were there met with joy unspeakable, as the news of their capture had already reached that place, and with most as much surprise as if they had arisen from the dead.

When taken by the Indians, Murphy and Harper were in the woods, making maple sugar, and knew not that their families had just been murdered by the brutal savages. Imagine, you who are husbands and fathers, the bitter anguish of their souls, when informed that their wives and children had been butchered by a party of Indians, led on by the tory Brant. The day following, most of the men left the block-house, and escorted them home, there to behold a scene, too awful for reflection, too horrible for description, too painful for humanity. Murphy had two children, one two years old; the other three months. The eldest had fled under the bed, and been pulled out far enough to be tomahawked and scalped, and then left. The mother, a beautiful woman of about twenty-two, seemed not to have attempted an escape, as her hands and arms were much cut, and she lay in the back part of the room. She had received three blows on the head with a tomahawk, one of which penetrated the brain. Her cranium was literally bare. Across her lifeless body, lay her lovely babe, smiling in death. It had been finished by a single blow, and was not mutilated. The tears of sympathy flowed from all but Murphy; he stood silent, with dry and glaring eyes, immovably fixed upon the companion of his youth, and the pledges of their love. Dark and awful was the storm that gathered in the bosom of Murphy. At length he took his murdered infant in his arms, and with a firm and desperate resolve, swore to be avenged or die, and sealed that vow by a kiss upon the cold cheek of the lifeless infant. How well that vow was kept, the history of his after life tells. A rude grave was then prepared, lined with bark, in place of a coffin, and the mournful duties of sepulchre closed the bloody scene. The children were placed in the arms of the mother, upon that bosom that had so often nourished them.

They then proceeded to the dwelling of Mr. Harper, and found it empty. His wife was an amiable young lady, only nineteen years of age, with an infant at her breast. She had attempted to escape to the woods, and was overtaken a few rods from the house, where she and her babe had been murdered, and their bodies had been subsequently torn to pieces by wolves or some other wild animals. This scene was more heart-rending than the other. The husband wrung his hands in anguish, as his friends deposited the scattered fragments beneath the clods of the valley. Harper also resolved to subdue the foe; but his was not that maniac revenge of Murphy. His resolution was equally firm as the other, but his designs more expansive. A block-house was immediately erected, to which the surviving settlers all removed. This done, immediate measures were taken to meet the attack which they expected from the Indians, to avenge the death of those Indians who had been killed by Harper and Murphy. Murphy returned to Schoharie to obtain assistance from the fort, and Harper went to Albany and obtained a captain's commission, authorizing him to organize a company from the contiguous settlement. Col. Hager, who commanded the fort at Schoharie, immediately accompanied Murphy, with ninety men, to Ustayantho: when in the narrows, about two miles east of that place, the advance guard returned hastily, having met a large body of warriors, fresh painted, advancing furiously.

One of the guard, a brother of the Colonel, had been so closely pursued as to receive a wound in the shoulder from a tomahawk, when suddenly turning around, he plunged his bayonet through the body of the Indian. Mr. Hager afterward pointed out to me the precise spot, (says the historian,) where it occurred, being at the junction of two small streams that empty into the lake. The Colonel immediately formed his men in order of battle. Pausing a while for the approach of the enemy, and hearing nothing from them, Murphy was dispatched with five men to reconnoitre their position, followed with the main body about forty rods in the rear. When passing out of the narrows, within half a mile of the lake, three of the enemy were seen retreating, one of whom fell beneath the unerring aim of the enraged Irishman. This was the signal for the Colonel to rush on, and in a few minutes he was engaged with the whole savage force. Murphy took his station behind a large pine tree, within twelve rods of the Indians, who lay in a ravine directly before him. For a moment they directed their whole fire to that point, and pierced the tree with more than fifty balls, many of which I cut out after I was old enough to use an axe. In front, Murphy discovered the very savage who escaped from him and Harper to Oquago. He drew up his rifle, and called the savage by name, who gave a terrific whoop, and fell lifeless to the ground, another victim to the unerring aim of the *Indian Killer*. At that moment, a charge was ordered. With the force of an avalanche the men rushed on, and in less than three minutes the Indians took to flight. A part of them, with Bennett, fled down the Delaware, and a part down the Charlotte, a stream that empties into the Susquehanna. Four of Colonel

Hager's men were killed, and about thirty of Brant's allies. Harper left the fort in charge of a small force; the Colonel proposed to return, and buried his dead in one common grave, (on the peak of a round bluff near the lake,) whose bones I assisted in removing to a more proper place of repose, about forty years ago. The account of this battle, I had from Col. Hager, as well as from several of his men.

In the mean time Captain Harper was returning by the way of Cherry Valley, deeming that the safest route. As he was crossing the hills west of the white settlements on the Delaware, he came suddenly in contact with a party of fifteen Indians, who had been at the recent battle. To flee he knew would be certain death; he therefore advanced boldly, gave them his hand, and succeeded in making them believe that he was their friend. Their leader he knew well, but, fortunately, he was not recognized in turn. He learned from them, their disasters at the lake, and learned that they were on their way to a white settlement on the Susquehanna, probably for the purpose of murder. He then shook hands with them, and hastened to a settlement a few miles distant, where a number of armed men were making maple sugar. Supposing that the savages would encamp at the foot of the hill, on the bank of Schenevus creek, the Captain had no trouble in persuading them to accompanying him in pursuit of the savages he had met. With two days' provision, they immediately started in pursuit, and just before day the next morning gained the top of the hill above the Indian encampment. Capt. H. and his men descended, forded the creek, succeeded in taking away the guns of the enemy without awaking them, and took the whole of them prisoners, and safely lodged them in a fort, a few miles distant. Learning from them that they had left a party of nineteen in the Charlotte valley, Capt. Harper and his men determined to pursue them. They replenished their provisions, commenced their march, and on the second day struck on a fresh Indian trail. They advanced rapidly, and toward evening heard the report of a gun at some distance in the forest. They then halted to refresh them and wait until the savage foes should encamp for the night. Soon after dark the Captain and his men advanced with the utmost caution, and in about an hour discovered their encampment. Hours glided slowly away, and yet several of the red men did not lie down. At length all but one appeared to be asleep. A slow and cautious advance was soon commenced. Every man was instructed in case the Indians aroused, to take his station behind a tree, and not to fire until the enemy came near enough to reach them with the muzzle of his gun. They all examined the priming of their guns and fixed their bayonets securely. A deep silence pervaded the dense forest of hemlock and pine. Not a breeze was perceptible, not a leaf was moving on the trees. The moments were full of suspense and deep anxiety. The recent murder of his wife and babe nerved the Captain for the combat. Courage, fearless and strong, nerved every man to death or victory. They drew nearer and nearer. The quick ear of the wakeful savage soon caught the sound of their foot-steps on the dry leaves. A piercing war whoop startled all upon their feet.

They seized the arms and stood ready for action; for a moment no motion agitated the parties, but the beating heart, and the purple current rushing through their veins, with a tenfold velocity. At length the savages commenced a slow and cautious movement towards the Captain and his men. They were between the fire and the avengers of blood, each of whom marked his victim. Sure and deadly was the aim. Twelve of the warriors fell at the first fire, and three were mortally wounded. The whites advanced and surrounded the survivors. A short and desperate conflict ensued; the nineteen savages were all in a few moments locked in the embrace of death.

The Captain and four of his men were wounded, but not dangerously. This tragedy was ended about 1 o'clock in the morning. Exasperated by these misfortunes, the fiendish Brant collected about 300 savage warriors, and made a descent on the fort in Schoharie. It was too strongly fortified to be taken by this force; but there were not men enough to make a sally. Learning their situation, Captain Harper disguised himself, mounted a horse, and started for Albany to obtain aid. He passed through the midst of the enemy as a tory by the name of Rose. In the evening he stopped at a public house for refreshment, where were several men whose appearance was suspicious. He went into another room and locked the door. Shortly after, four tories, one of whom had recognized him, demanded entrance. He cocked his pistols, drew his sword, opened the door, and inquired their business. When informed they wished *him,* he coolly remarked: "Pass that door, and you are dead men." He received no further molestation at the house, but was fired at soon after he resumed his journey, but was not injured. On his arrival at head-quarters, the commander dispatched a squadron of mounted men, who rode all night. The first intimation received in the fort of any assistance, was a furious attack on the enemy by the cavalry, just as the day dawned.—The troops in the garrison immediately made a sally; the rout was complete, the slaughter of the Indians dreadful, many of them plunging into the stream, reddening its waters with blood. Harpersfield was named in honor of this said Harper, who resided in this town during the Revolution, and enjoyed the esteem and respect of all, for his valuable services in the Revolution. Harpersfield in Ohio was settled by his descendants, and named after him.

We will now return to Murphy. From the time of the battle of Utsayantho, (Harpersfield,) he commenced fighting on his own hook. His thirst for revenge knew no bounds. He was a man of great muscular power, near six feet in height, of an iron constitution, and swifter on foot than any one that ever pursued him. He obtained a double-barrelled rifle of the best kind. He carried the tomahawk and scalping-knife he took on the night he and Captain Harper killed the ten Indians, and could use them all as skilfully as any Mohawk. He soon became a terror to the red men. His many miraculous escapes and bold exploits led them to believe that he was protected by the Great Spirit. He hovered around them like a vulture; many of their braves fell beneath his brawny arm. He spent most of his time in the woods alone, seeking his hated foe. He never hesitated to attack a party of three Indians, and not unfrequently dispatched the whole. His courage was as cool as his revenge was direful. Such was Murphy, a revenging foe of the red man—with a warm heart for his friends.

The next day after the battle at the lake, he prepared himself, and pursued a party of Indians that retreated down the Delaware. On the 2d night, he came in sight of their encampment, and by the light of the fire, counted twenty-seven warriors, some of whom were evidently wounded. He determined to wait until all was quiet, and make their number *less by one.* This he effected about midnight, and retreated without being pursued, as the night was quite dark. He followed this party until he dispatched six of their number, when he returned to his friends, who received him with joyful hearts, fearing he had fallen into the hands of his butchering foe. They entreated him to desist from such exposure to danger, but all in vain. He rested under an oath, and most fearfully did he perform it. He desired no angel's tear to blot it from the record; he held his life in his hands, but put upon it a high prize.

He then replenished his knapsack and started for the hills bordering on the Mohawk river. On the 2nd day he arrived at a settlement of whites, who were much distressed for the loss of one of their number a few hours before. Early in the morning, a young lady had ventured outside the block-house to milk a cow, when four savages suddenly sprang upon her, and dragged her to the woods. Her cries were heard, her frantic friends could see her struggles, but dared not venture out, as all the men who were able, had left a few days previous for the northern army, among whom were her father, two brothers, and a young officer, to whom she was engaged to be married in a short time. Her mother was overwhelmed with grief, and gave up her child as lost. She fancied her expiring beneath the ruthless hand of the barbarians, perhaps writhing under the agonies of a slow fire, surrounded by demons in human shape, drowning her cries with their savage yells. No other heart beat higher or warmer for woman, than did that of Murphy. Like a knight of chivalry he darted off in pursuit. It was then ten o'clock; four hours had elapsed since the capture. He soon found the trail, and advanced rapidly. About five o'clock, when on the top of a bold hill, he discovered the party in the valley below. The fair captive was still alive, but expected that night would close her career forever. Her anticipated happiness had faded away; she thought an awful fate was about to seal her doom. She said in her heart, *farewell* father, mother, brother, lover, friends, resigned herself to God, and became abstracted from the world. The images of her fond parents, her dear brothers, and of him, with whose soul hers had sweetly mingled, all passed in review before her imagination. She could only hope to meet them in heaven.

The encampment for the night was soon arranged by the red men, during which, Murphy approached as near as prudence would admit, before the mantle of night should cover him, determined that if they attempted any violence to the young lady, he would immediately rush upon them. With an eagle eye he watched every motion. They built a large fire, prepared their last supper, and about ten o'clock tied the hands and feet of their prisoner to two poles, and were soon in a profound sleep. For a few minutes she struggled, but soon found she was unable to extricate herself. Her bosom heaved with sighs, her eyes rolled wildly in their sockets; she seemed already on the torturing rack. Our knight was so near, he could see all this by the light of the fire. It was too much for him to endure. He drew his knife from its scabbard, and advanced with slow and cautious steps. He was soon discovered by the young lady, and motioned her to keep silence. He unbound and removed her and the guns to some distance, and enjoined her to keep silent, and if he became overpowered, to flee for her life; for he had determined to kill his hated foes, or perish in the attempt. With his tomahawk in one hand, and his knife in the other, he returned. Waiting a few moments for their sleep to become more sound, he approached their muscular frames. He plunged his knife into the hearts of three,—the fourth awoke, aimed a blow at Murphy with his tomahawk, which he parried, and cleft the head of the savage to the brain. As the Indian arose, the heroic girl, instead of making her escape, seized a gun and rushed to the aid of her deliverer. But the work was done, and the heroic knight stood contemplating with a species of maniac delight, the quivering bodies, expiring in the agonies of death. The liberated captive now gazed on the stranger. To her, all was inexplicable mystery. In a few words he explained the whole matter, and assured her of his protection back to her habitation. She lifted her hands and eyes to heaven and exclaimed, "May God reward my benefactor!" A flood of tears choked further utterance, she clasped his hands in gratitude, and invoked her God to command the richest blessings of heaven to rest upon him. That was the happiest moment of Murphy's life. His pleasure was purer and nobler, than if he had gained a crown or conquered a world.

The Rubicon passed, he took the blankets, which had not been unpacked, and persuaded his fair charge to take a little rest, which she much needed, after the trying scenes she had passed through on that gloomy day. Although sleep came not to her on that memorable night, she felt refreshed when the day dawned. The sun arose in all the beauty of a June morning; not a cloud obscured the sky. They started for the block-house, following the track, where they arrived about three in the afternoon. No one knew that the gallant Murphy had gone in pursuit of the captured girl. He had listened to their story the morning previous, with apparent indifference, without making any reply; concealing his design, fearing it might prove an entire failure. He was half suspected of being a tory, and in league with the savages, who had abducted the young girl. He was a stranger, of whose business and distinction they knew nothing. Under such peculiar circumstances, their feelings can be but faintly conceived, much less described. It was a scene of thrilling interest, calculated to awaken the finest feelings of the human heart, the loftiest tones of unalloyed gratitude. The next morning he left them, under a shower of invoked blessings and benedictions, and proceeded to his place of destination.

He arrived safely in the neighborhood of the Mohawk river, where he killed several of the red men, and narrowly escaped being killed himself. As he was lying in ambush he discovered an Indian, who from his actions he believed to be alone, and at once shot him. Instantly two brawny warriors rushed upon him with uplifted tomahawks. One he brought to the ground, from the contents of the barrel of his rifle; the other advanced and aimed a blow at his head, which he warded off, and plunged his knife to the heart of the savage.

He at once retreated to the fort at Schoharie, for fear he might in turn be ambushed. From thence he again returned to his friends at the block-house, and found them in great distress. About two hours previous to his arrival two men, who were at work in the corn-field, had been taken by a party of Indians. The number of savages was not known; there were but five remaining at the place with them. Murphy commenced an immediate but cautious pursuit. Early in the evening they discovered the fire of their encampment, and discovered eight warriors who were preparing a war dance, and to wreak their vengeance upon their unhappy captives. As their preparations increased, Murphy and his comrades drew nearer. The prisoners were bound to a tree, around them faggots were placed, for the fire was to cap the climax of the festivity of the savages. Dreadful must have been the sufferings of the victims, now beyond the reach of hope, and about to be tortured by a slow fire. The firing of the faggots was made the signal of attack. At length the blazing torch was raised, the heroic party rushed upon the Indians, placed the muzzles of their guns to their heads, and blew them into fragments. Six of them were instantly killed, and the next moment the spirits of the other two joined their companions, in their journey through the air. The deliverance of the captives was unexpected, as it was joyful and soul-cheering. Of such thrilling scenes, nothing but experience can convey a correct idea, or draw a faithful picture. On the next day the party reached the blockhouse, where high-beating hearts and convulsed bosoms were awaiting the result of the bold expedition. With open arms and joyful hearts the wives embraced their husbands, a flood of tears spake the feelings of their enraptured souls, with an eloquence unknown to words. Murphy was the hero, who richly merited and warmly received the gratitude of all. In the same manner this enraged Irishman, who was known by the cognomen of *Indian-killer,* continued to harass and murder the Indians, until they were driven from their ancient haunts. To relate all his wonderful exploits would require a volume. He had many hair-breadth escapes, was never taken prisoner, but once with Harper, nor dangerously wounded. He was much dreaded and feared by the Indians. He had a great desire to wreak his vengeance on Brant. But that murderous tory always remained with the main force, and cautiously avoided danger. For the Indian warrior, Murphy had no sympathy. The squaws and papooses he never molested, nor would he stoop to sacrifice any but their fighting men. To the day of his death, he indulged in feelings of the most direful revenge toward the natives of the forest.

At the restoration of peace, Murphy married and settled in Schoharie, but, in a few years after that period, he lived on the Charlotte, bordering on Harpersfield, and remained there until his death, which is about twelve miles, as Judson says, from Utsayantho, or Harpersfield, where the battle was fought, which place he often revisited, until prevented by old age. It was there, that I often listened to his stories. That ground had been enriched by the blood and moistened by the tears of hundreds. During the Revolution three pitched battles were fought there between the whites and Indians, the last of which was so disastrous to the red men, that they abandoned that ground to their enemy, the whites. In that beautiful valley, now improved by cultivation, Murphy always appeared animated, and would "fight his battles over again." The scenes of past life, with all their dreadful and thrilling interest, would rush upon his memory, and often have I seen the big tears chasing each other rapidly down the furrows of his war-worn cheeks. He lived to the age of about seventy-five, beloved and esteemed by all, when his brave spirit took its final leave of this world of vicissitudes and changes. His bones moulder in Schoharie, near where the old fort stood, and not a stone is reared to tell the inquisitive stranger where they lie.

CHAPTER XV

The following interesting production, from the pen of a daughter of E. B. Fenn, Esq., is inserted, at the request of numerous friends.

THE ADVENTURES OF A YANKEE WOMAN,

BY MAUD SUTHERLAND, JR.

I.

> "*Honor* and *fame* from no *condition* rise;
> Act well *your* part—there all the honor lies."

MAN was created for the stern realities of life; to wield with a giant's hands the destinies of nations; to dive into the hidden mysteries of this beautiful world; to perfect the arts and sciences, and to perform deeds of noble daring; while woman's sphere is to dispense *benevolence, love* and *charity,* to those around her. To *this* rule there are exceptions. There are females, whose minds are so constituted, that no task is too arduous, no danger too great, for them to grapple with and overcome.

Of such was Harriet Lovejoy. Endowed by nature with a mind far above the common level, and rendered more brilliant by cultivation, she pursued a course that many of the sterner sex would have avoided gladly. She became acquainted with a man, whose sphere of action was the battle-field. Acquaintance strengthened into friendship, and friendship ripened into love. During the winter previous to the close of the last war, they were married. No pomp or splendor reigned during those nuptial services, but there were hearts present that beat high with fond hopes and anticipations. Colonel Leavenworth was to leave immediately for Chippewa, Bridgewater, and Lundy's Lane, and thither Mrs. L., alias Harriet Lovejoy, was to accompany him; and she shrank not from the trials and difficulties attending this undertaking. Early on the morning following their marriage, was the time appointed for their departure. Parents and friends breathed many a prayer for their safe return. Good wishes for their success and prosperity, were tendered them, and the pangs of parting were rendered less acute in the hope of soon returning to their loved home; yet, ere their departure, they were joined by four hundred and thirty brave men, the flower of Delaware county militia, who were to repair with Colonel Leavenworth, to the battle-field, to maintain the peace, rights, honor, prosperity and happiness of their own country; to dispel the dark cloud that hung over a nation's destiny, and to perpetuate to future generations, the rich inheritance bequeathed them by their Revolutionary fathers,—thus proving by their heroic deeds, that they were not degenerate scions of a noble stock. Many hardships and difficulties stared them in the face, sufficient to appal the stoutest heart; but *their* courage failed not, although exposed to the rigors of intense cold, and with barely provisions sufficient to sustain life. At length their journey is accomplished. They have reached the battle-ground—their feet are treading foreign land.

II.

"There are swift hours in life—strong rushing hours,
That do the work of tempests in their might."

Let us draw aside the curtain. The battle has commenced. The veteran troops of Old England, and the hardy sons of America, are in close contact. Onward they rush to the charge, with hearts burning for victory. Several times the American forces are driven back, and again they rally and rush upon the enemy, eager to obtain *that* which is dearer to them than life—their altars and their homes. Two horses are killed, on which Col. L. rode, and still he escapes uninjured. Fortune seems to smile on the efforts of the British troops; but *this* is not a damper on the spirits of the Americans. *They know* that their cause is a *just one,* and *they feel* that the smiles of a righteous Providence will yet be theirs. They are seeking to retrieve their country's safety, that lay bleeding at every pore.

Naught is heard but the clashing of arms, the roar of artillery, and the groans of the wounded and dying. The fate of the day is decided—the British troops are routed—the American flag floats in triumph over the battle-field. Dearly was this victory purchased, for the bravest troops are slain, and only a handful of men are left, to relate the horrors of the day. Among the number of wounded, is Colonel Leavenworth.

Now the assistance of a wife is requisite; and faithfully Mrs. Leavenworth performed her task: tenderly she watched over her husband, administering everything necessary for his comfort, through those long days and nights of pain and anguish; yet her attention was not confined to her husband alone. Like an angel of mercy sent to bless mankind, she visited the sick and dying soldiers, performing all those acts of kindness—springing from a heart formed of benevolence and love—that were necessary to alleviate their distress, to comfort them in their afflictions, and pour the balm of consolation on their stricken hearts.

O woman, kind and tender-hearted! *Thou* hast a heart to feel for others' woes and sorrows. *Thou* canst dispense blessings and happiness, that will cause the faint and weary heart to revive, like the parched and withered plant after the gentle rain. Under the kind care and attention of Mrs. L., her husband and his soldiers recovered speedily. Here let me remark, that the soldiers loved Mrs. L. as their own life, and to use the words of one: "I never loved my mother with a greater intensity than I do this woman." There was not one of the army but would have sacrificed his own life to preserve hers.

Delaware county was clothed in mourning for the loss of the slain. Of four hundred and thirty soldiers, who left their happy homes to sustain their country's honor, only twenty-eight survived to accompany their brave Colonel and Lady on their return home.

III.

"Leave me not, leave me not,
 Say not adieu;
Have I not been to thee
 Tender and true?"

Two years passed away,—the clarion of war is no more heard—peace and plenty is smiling on happy America. Instead of the soldier in uniform, we behold the busy multitude at work in their shops and fields.

They are enjoying the liberty for which they fought so bravely. At this time Colonel L. received an appointment as Indian Agent, to the Northwest Territory. He must now leave his wife and child for the first time, and struggle on in the wilds of the distant West, with no one to cheer him in his hours of loneliness. Vainly Mrs. L. urged her husband to allow her to accompany him, but there were hardships to encounter, that he wished his wife not to meet. The hour of separation draws near, and tender was the scene of parting. A tear stole down the manly face of the husband, as he repressed the heaving sigh that was swelling his heart with deep emotion, for he wished not to break up the fountains of a heart, dearer to him than his own life, already heaving with anguish.

"Harriet, Harriet, I must leave you. To the tender care of the 'widow's God,' I now commend you. In *His* hands you are safe, and may *He* protect and watch over you and our child, until in His own good time we meet again. Farewell:" and the next moment Colonel L. sprang into his carriage, and was fast receding from those who loved him devotedly, sincerely.

Amid the ever-changing scenes he was called to realize, the image of his lovely wife and child was ever with him, serving as a beacon-light to cheer and guide the husband and father, during his lonely pilgrimage.

Could Mrs. L. be forgetful? No. Sweet thoughts of her husband would steal over her mind, ravishing her senses with love and beauty, and causing her heart to grow fonder and fonder, and long more and more for the companionship of an absent dear one.

Soon after Colonel L.'s departure, Mrs. L. occupied her time in teaching a select school, that afterwards laid the foundation for the Delaware Academy. *This* served in a great measure to dispel her loneliness. Great was her joy whenever she received messages from her husband, filled as they were, with fond regrets and tender recollections. He revealed his heart fully to his wife, and she read therein naught but constancy and affection. Her letters in turn, were such as would inspire his magnanimous soul with confidence, and so deeply was his mind absorbed in their contents, that he seemed to forget his cares and perplexities—I had almost said, their very existence.

IV.

"The scene is changed. Once more
I feel the pressure of thy hand, and
Thy warm kiss on my cheek."

A few years passed, and Mrs. L. received a letter from her husband, wishing her to join him at Prairie Du Chien, and bring their daughter with her. Hasty were the preparations for their departure. Minutes appeared like hours, and hours like days to her. A person unlike Mrs. L. would have shuddered at the idea of undertaking so long and tedious a journey, alone and unprotected, but with her usual courage and fortitude, she only said: "I will try," and half of the task was accomplished.

We now behold her wending her way to the "Far West." Her course is south on the Atlantic, across the Gulf of Mexico, and north on the Mississippi river, to St. Louis. These were lonely hours to her; yet, as she was a great admirer of Nature and its works, she enjoyed many pleasant hours in beholding the sun as it seemed to rise out of the bosom of the sea, decking the eastern sky with all possible loveliness, or watch its decline as it sunk gradually in the ocean, burnishing the waters with a golden light, or watch the foam of the ocean's billow as the noble ship sails swiftly o'er its bosom.

Arriving at St. Louis, she repaired to the hotel her husband had directed her to. Reaching the inn, she inquired of the landlord, "If any person was waiting at his house for Mrs. L." He replied, "there was," and left the room. A few moments elapsed, and Mrs. L. heard a gentle rap at her door. She obeyed the summons. Before her stood the tall and athletic form of an Indian chief. The feathers that adorned his head were beautiful, and waved gracefully to-and-fro. His face was painted after the customs of the chiefs, and this gave a frightful aspect to his countenance. In his belt was a scalping knife, and by his side hung a tomahawk. For the first time

Mrs. L.'s heart sank within her, and she thought: "Is this the person who will accompany me during the remainder of my journey?"

Summoning all her courage, she invited him "to be seated." He declined the invitation politely, and handed her a package. She recognized the handwriting. It was her husband's, and this inspired her with new confidence.

"Mrs. Leavenworth, I am sent by your husband to conduct you to him. When will you be ready to commence the journey?"

"To-morrow at sunrise," she replied.

"I will call for you at that time," he replied; and bowing with the native hauteur of an Indian chief, he left the room.

With pleasure and interest, she perused her husband's letters, assuring her of her safety while on her journey through the wilderness. The Indians were friendly, and would protect her from all harm. The distance yet to travel was 700 miles, and a great part of the distance was through a dense forest where the foot of the white man had never trod. At her usual hour for retiring she laid her daughter by her side, and sweet were her dreams. She dreamed of happy hours whose existence seemed the present; while the reality was yet in the future.

Morning dawned. The sun rose in splendor and shed its rays over the earth, giving light and beauty to all around: joy and gladness beamed on the face of nature, cheering her sad and lonely heart. Precisely at the appointed hour the chief called for Mrs. Leavenworth. She made her appearance, and the chief taking the little daughter in his arms—led the way to the door. Here were fourteen Indians dressed in full costume and ready equipped for the journey. They were formally introduced by the chief to Mrs. Leavenworth.

The carriage that was to convey the wife and daughter, was a palanquin, so constructed that the occupants could sit or recline at their pleasure, and this was to be their home for 700 long miles. We now behold them seated in their carriage. The baggage is in order and firmly secured. Everything is ready. Four stout Indians step forward from their fellows, raise the palanquin on their shoulders, and commence their march. Five of the remainder walk before in Indian file—headed by their chief, and the remainder follow the palanquin in the same order. The curtain of the carriage is raised. Mrs. Leavenworth gazes on the scene with mingled feelings of hope and fear. She casts one long and lingering look on all around, as the last abode of civilization fades from her view. Before her lies the pathless forest and the wide prairie, behind her the cultivated fields of the white man. Before her stands the rude wigwam of the savage, behind her the princely dwellings of her own countrymen. Before her roam the savages and ferocious beasts, behind her are the peaceful walks and shady retreats of America's enlightened sons. Before her is *Nature* in its wildest and most picturesque beauty, while behind her *Art* gives finish to the painting, and renders it more attractive and beautiful.

The day has nearly passed; night draws her sable curtain over all the earth; The last rays of the setting sun gild the mountains, burnishing the western sky with a gold and purple light, as the Indians encamp for the night. A fire is kindled, and the evening repast neatly and comfortably prepared. The wild flowers and green grass serve as a carpet, a board forms the table, and the blue arch of heaven is spread over them as a canopy. The studied formalities of the white man enter not their circle. Order and neatness reign here. The frugal repast is finished. The hour of rest draws near. Weariness and sleep steal over them, and they seek refreshment in repose. Mrs. L. and child lie down to rest, for the first time, among savages and in a wilderness, in their palanquin. The Indians, except two, who are stationed as guards—spread their blankets on the ground, lie down, and are soon "locked in the arms of Morpheus." Not so with Mrs. L.; the screeching of the owl, and the howling of the wild beasts, disturb her slumbers. *This* was noticed by the guards, and they told her "to sleep as fearless as though in her own home, nothing should harm her." At last the god of sleep woos her to his own home, and her thoughts are wandering over the regions of dreamland.

Morning dawns, and sleep forsakes the eyelids of the sleepers. The morning meal is prepared and finished, and again they proceed on their way. Myriads of flowers strow their pathway, and throw their odors on the passing breeze. Birds of beautiful plumage sing their sweetest notes, cheering the hearts of Mrs. L. and daughter.

The chief and his escort are very kind, showing them every attention necessary for their comfort and happiness. Sometimes they cull the choicest flowers, and weave them into bouquets and garlands, or pick the finest fruits, or bring the sparkling water as it gushes from the mountain side.

The Indians often quarrelled among themselves, fearful that one would confer a greater favor on their charge than the other. No insult of any kind was offered the lady and daughter, and the Indians set an example worthy the imitation of the white man.

Thus passed the several days of their pilgrimage. On the 34th day after their departure from St. Louis, the chief stepped to the window of the palanquin, and said: "Do you see those white tents yonder? That one—pointing—is Colonel L.'s."

What must have been Mrs. L.'s feelings, as she drew near her husband's tent? Pen cannot describe; language is inadequate to the task. In a few moments she was locked in her husband's arms. "Harriet, you have come at last;" was all that Colonel L. could utter; and taking his child, he pressed it to his bosom, while tears of heartfelt joy coursed down his manly cheeks, that were never moistened in the din of battle. Here it would be well to remark, that Mrs. L. was the first white woman who had crossed this trackless forest, or these extended and delightful prairies; emphatically termed Nature's flower garden.

The trio were happy, for after many lonely and wearisome days, they were permitted to meet again. The savages gazed on the scene in mute astonishment. Day after day sped rapidly by, and still there was happiness. A few years passed, and Colonel L. was sent by government, 1100 miles father south. Thither his wife and children accompanied him, where they arrived in safety.

V.

"I miss the warm clasp of thy hand,
And thy warm breath on my cheek,
And I still keep listening for the words
That you never more may speak."

A few months passed after their arrival at Cross Timbers, and Colonel L. was taken sick with a fever incident to the climate. With all the care and solicitude of a kind and tender wife, she watched over him day and night with untiring zeal, barely allowing herself time for a moment's repose, and ministering to all his wants; yea, anticipating them, and consoling him with the reflection that "he would once more return to his far distant home." Alas! Death loves a shining prize, and marked him for his victim. The truth became manifest to himself, and those around, that he must die. But how agonizing the thought, that he must leave his wife and children, alone and unprotected, in a strange land. The thought was like the sundering of soul and body. His soul was unnerved for the conflict. Long and earnestly he prayed for strength to support him in his dying hour. By degrees his soul became more calm, until he was fully resigned to the will of God. Once more he commended his wife and children to Him, who has promised "to temper the winds to the shorn lamb." He gave them his parting blessing, and sank to rest in the arms of his Redeemer.

This was the severest trial that Mrs. L. had ever been called to meet. Her spirit was crushed to the earth. The hopes and bright anticipations, she had nurtured so long and fondly, were prostrated in the dust. But for her children, she could have calmly laid herself beside her husband, and "breathed her life out sweetly there." She looked to her Heavenly Father for aid, and he granted it. Heavenly messengers were sent to comfort her, and she was prepared for the worst.

Mrs. L. had the body of her husband wrapped in spices, and placed in a vault; she immediately settled her deceased husband's pecuniary affairs, and prepared to return to New York State with her four children.

Did she leave the body of her husband in a strange land? No, no. The feelings of the widowed wife were still strong in death. She takes his mortal remains, and carries them with her to her home, in Delaware county. The same Indians that once escorted Mrs. L. and her daughter through the wilderness, are now the escort of herself, four children, and the body of her husband, from Cross Timbers to St. Louis. Their passage on the ocean was very stormy, but they reached New York in safety. At Catskill, the dragoons of Delaware met the remains of their honored friend, and conveyed them to Delhi, where the Rev. Mr. Fenn pronounced the eulogy, and the few remaining soldiers that accompanied Colonel L. to the battle-field, now followed his remains to their last resting place. "Truly a great man hath fallen in Israel." The Freemasons and Military erected a monument to the memory of the departed. No marble monument was necessary to perpetuate *his* fame, for his memory was graven on every heart, and his heroic deeds were written in his country's history.

Delhi became the home of Mrs. L. and her four children, for a short time. From thence they removed to Newburgh, where another severe trial awaited them: the eldest daughter was removed by death.

It was my good fortune, a few years since, to see Mrs. L. Her countenance bore the deep traces of sorrow, but grief had not robbed her of her beauty and commanding appearance. Courage and ambition, those predominating faculties of her mind, were unimpaired, and like the sun after the cloud passes away, they show with a brighter and steadier lustre.

Florida is now the home of Mrs. L. and her three children. Thus passes the life of one who is fitted to adorn and shine as one of the brightest gems in the higher walks of life.

Davenport, Feb. 26th, 1849.

The following obituary announces the death of this lady:

DIED—On the 7th September, 1854, at Barrytown, Dutchess county, Mrs. HARRIET LEAVENWORTH, widow of the late Gen. Henry Leavenworth, U. S. Army. Mrs. Leavenworth, during the first few years of her married life, was a resident of this village; and although many years have passed, she is still remembered with pleasure by the few remaining of those who had her acquaintance and friendship. Her early life was diversified with many incidents of interest. When her gallant husband was ordered to the frontier, hundreds of miles in the wilderness, to protect the inhabitants from the invasions of the savages, she, like a faithful wife, was at his side, regardless of the many dangers, hardships and privations she had to endure. After the death of Gen. L. she returned to this State, and has resided most of the time at Newburgh, occasionally visiting this, the place of her early joys, and where the remains of her lamented husband rest.—[*Delaware Gazette.*]

CHAPTER XVI

Obituary Notices—Captain Abraham Gould—Aaron Hull—Gabriel North—Rev. Stephen Fenn—Hon. Roswell Hotchkiss—Rev. Daniel Shepard—James Hughston—Hon. Samuel A. Law—Daniel Gould—Col. Adam Shaver—T.H. Rathbun—Simeon McIntosh—Richard Peters—Thomas Hamilton—Major Joseph Duren—William C. Christiani—Abel Gallup—Jacob Every—Pierce Mitchel—Margery Walcott—Edmund Kelly—Abram Thomas—Gen. Orrin Griffin—Claudius Flansburgh—Levi Hanford—Abigail Marvine—Hon. Selah R. Hobbie—Frederick L. Hanford—George B. Foote—Peter Penet—William Holliday—Col. Amasa Parker—Joel T. Headley

THE following are a few of the many obituaries we should have been happy to have noticed, had we the limits in the volume, and the material for their preparation. We had delayed some time for a promised notice of the Hon. Noadiah Johnston. A tribute to his memory certainly deserves a conspicuous place among the reminiscences of his native county. He spent the prime of his life in the county of Delaware, and was for many years, a distinguished member of our State and National Legislature. A sound and practical lawyer, his strong genius first exhibited itself through his eloquence at the bar. We have compiled most of these notices from files of the various county papers, and in many instances, have adopted the language of the communications.

DIED—January, 1824, CAPTAIN ABRAHAM GOULD, in the 28th year of his age, after a lingering illness. He was the only survivor of four hardy young men, who emigrated at an early day into this county, (1790) and were the first settlers in the town of Roxbury.

DIED—AARON HULL, ESQ., in the 74th year of his age. He was engaged in the sanguinary struggle of Independence, and was one of the first to encounter the hardships and privations of the wilderness.

DIED—January 2nd, 1827, GABRIEL NORTH, of Walton. A correspondent writes: "It is but due to the memory of the deceased, to say, inasmuch as it evinces the merit and estimation of his fellow citizens, that he occupied for some time, a seat on the Bench of the Common Pleas of this county,—twice elected to the assembly—was a member of the electoral college in 1816, and gave the vote of the State for President and Vice-President. But Judge North deserves a more lasting and careful remembrance, for having been one of the pioneers in the settlement of Delaware county. He, with two or three of his associates, were the first settlers of Walton, to which place they emigrated from Connecticut, upwards of forty years ago. (1784.) That region of country, then, was almost an unexplored wilderness, remote, by a great distance, even from the frontiers of civilized habitations. There they literally pitched their tents, for these were their first dwellings, and with the unshrinking courage, patience and confidence in Divine protection, so characteristic of the adventurous spirit transmitted by the New England pilgrims to their descendants, they, with their wives and children, sustained hardships, privations, and perils, alike interesting in their details, and propitious in their results."

GIDEON FRISBEE, died in 1828, aged 71. He came to this county forty years ago, (1788,) and settled upon the same farm where he resided until his death. It was the county of Montgomery, afterward the county of Otsego, and in 1797, the county of Delaware. Judge Frisbee, in the early settlement of the county, was distinguished among his fellow citizens as captain of the militia, justice of peace, and the highest offices in the gift of the town. Not many years after the formation of the county, he was elected county treasurer, and about the same time, judge of the Common Pleas. Both of these offices he held with fidelity, until within a few years of his death he resigned them.

IN Harpersfield, September 26, 1833, REV. STEPHEN FENN, aged sixty-four years. Mr. Fenn, was born in 1769, in Watertown, in Connecticut. Possessing strong natural powers of mind, and a love of study, he prepared himself for college at an early age, and graduated at Yale in 1790, and soon after commenced the preaching of the gospel. After laboring about one year in the State of New Hampshire, he came to Harpersfield in 1793. At this time the town was in its infancy, the inhabitants were few, and almost as a matter of course poor, or in limited circumstances. He was regularly ordained in January, 1794, and took pastoral charge of the church in Harpersfield. He continued in this situation until 1829, a period of thirty-six years, or about the time of his death.

At the time he emigrated into the county, there were few, if any regular ministers, (indeed, he is said to have been the first liberally educated minister that ever preached within the limits of the county,) and his services were frequently in requisition, in not only neighboring towns, but counties, and he is said to have officiated at more weddings, than any other person in the county since. He is described by those who knew him, as mild in his deportment, affable in his manners, attractive and witty, as well as grave in conversation, with a mind stored with an inexhaustible fund of humorous anecdotes, many of which were gathered from his own personal experience.

AT Harpersfield, on the 28th of December, 1845, Hon. ROSWELL HOTCHKISS, in the 84th year of his age. The following article is from the columns of "The Express."

"In our obituary department to-day, is announced the decease of one of Delaware's oldest and most respected citizens, Hon. Roswell Hotchkiss.

"Judge Hotchkiss, died at Harpersfield, on the 28th ult., at the advanced age of 84 years. He was one of the earliest settlers of that town, having removed there, from Connecticut, the year after the close of the Revolutionary war. During all this time, a period of more than sixty years, he has sustained an important place in the community where he has lived. In the county he has held in succession, the offices of justice of the peace, sheriff and judge of the county courts; he was also a member of the convention which framed the present Constitution of this State. In his early youth Judge Hotchkiss entered the Revolutionary army, in which he served several years, and remained till the close of the war. Under the Federal government, soon after its establishment, he received the appointment of post-master, which office he held without interruption till the day of his death.

"During the greater part of his protracted life, he was an exemplary member of the Presbyterian church. Though by reason of the peculiar infirmities, he has been for some years deprived of the privilege of frequent attendance on the worship of the sanctuary, he did not lose his interest in those services, nor a disposition to contribute of his substance for their support. Nor did he wholly forget the cause of missions.

"Judge H.'s ability to use his pen and to transact business, was rather uncommon for a man of his age. Though it was perceptible that his ability for active service was gradually diminishing, yet his removal from amongst his friends leaves a sensible chasm, not only in his own family, where he was highly respected and beloved, but in the community at large."*

DEATH OF REV. DANIEL SHEPARD.—This community has been called upon to mourn the loss of one of its brightest ornaments, Rev. Daniel Shepard, A.M., Principal of the Delaware Academy. Mr. Shepard, at the close of the summer term, took a tour west, where he contracted the disease peculiar to that section of country, congestive fever. He did not suppose his sickness was of sufficient virulence to render it necessary to stay his journey, and he proceeded on, and finally reached home some two weeks since. The disease had taken a firm hold of his system, so much so as to baffle the efforts of his physicians to conquer it, and on Saturday

---

* "*Errata.*—In our obituary notice of the death of Judge Hotchkiss, last week, we were in error in saying Judge Hotchkiss was a member of the Convention of 1821. Gen Root, and Dr. Robert Clark, then of Stamford, were the members from Delaware, in the convention which framed the present Constitution. Judge Hotchkiss, and Elias Osborn, then of Franklin, were members of the convention of 1801, which amended the Constitution in respect to the relative power of the president and members of the Council of Appointment, and in limiting the number of senators and members of Assembly."

night last, November 29th, 1846, his spirit departed to dwell with HIM whom he had so delighted to honor and worship. He was 31 years of age.

Mr. Shepard has been at the head of the Delaware Academy for some ten years; and it is only necessary to point to the manner in which that institution has flourished, now having a stand among the first in the State, to show his fitness for the responsible station. It was not with him a mere matter of gain; he loved his school; he loved his pupils; he sought their welfare with untiring zeal and assiduity, not only their welfare in this world, but he aimed, while preparing them for the duties of life, to instil into their minds those great principles of religion, which would render them useful here, and prepare them for a brighter world. He took pride and satisfaction in seeing those under his care pass an honorable and creditable examination in the several pursuits of knowledge; but his interest in them did not cease there: he besought them frequently and fervently, to be preparing for the great and final Commencement-day, that there too, they might pass an examination, that would be a happy one to them, an examination, which was to decide their fate, not for a few years, but for eternity. He always, before entering upon the academical duties of the day, assembled his pupils around him, implored a Divine blessing upon them, and together, worshipped around the throne of Grace; and we learn, that from the time he established morning service in the Academy, some eight years since, he has been absent from those services but on *one* occasion, and that was the death of his child. He was truly a pattern to follow; what he taught, he himself practised; and his teachings and practice were those of the devoted, exemplary Christian. To do good, seemed to be the paramount object of his life; and the only desire he manifested when on his death-bed to live, was, that he might do more good. We can call to mind nothing that has been started since our residence here, to advance the morals of the place, or to benefit our fellow-creatures in any way, that did not find in our departed friend a hearty, assiduous and successful advocate. Devotedly attached to the communion of the Episcopal Church, in which he had taken orders, he knew no sectarianism, but looked upon all who bore the impress of Christ, of whatever name, as co-laborers in the same field; a characteristic which much enhanced his usefulness.

His funeral was attended at the Episcopal church, on Monday, by a large concourse of his friends and fellow-citizens, and by a large number of his former pupils, all of whom were dressed in the habiliments of mourning. The sermon was preached by the Rev. Mr. Waters, rector of the church, from Job xiv., 14: *"If a man die, shall he live again?"* As he eloquently portrayed the moral worth and the character of the deceased, and gave to the youth the last dying message of their late friend and preceptor, the scene was indeed a sad and affecting one. In that large assemblage, we doubt whether there was a dry eye; for all loved, and felt keenly the loss of him, whose cold remains lay before them.

His remains were temporarily placed in the family vault of Gen. Root, from whence they will be removed to the new cemetery, when completed.

DIED—At his residence in the town of Sidney, on the 27th December, 1846, JAMES HUGHSTON, Esq., in the 74th year of his age.

Mr. Hughston was one of the first settlers of the Susquehanna Valley, and has held many stations of public trust. He died lamented by a large circle of relatives and friends.

DIED—on Tuesday, the 28th ult., 1845, at 7½ o'clock P.M., at Meredith, HON. SAMUEL A. LAW, in the 74th year of his age.

He was born in November, 1771, at Cheshire, Conn., and in 1788 entered Yale College, at which institution he graduated in 1792, with distinguished reputation as a scholar. The class of which he was a member, although small in numbers, furnished many distinguished men; among whom may be mentioned, Hon. Roger M. Sherman, Judge Chapman, and Eli Whitney, of Conn., Hon. Samuel Lathrop, and Rev. Dr. T. M. Cooley, of Mass., Hon. Charles Chauncey, of Penn., Hon. James Christie Estin, for many years Chief Justice of the Island of Bermuda,—and others. After pursuing a regular course of professional study in the Law School at Litchfield, Conn., he was admitted to the bar in 1795; and about the same time received honorary degrees from the Colleges of Columbia and Harvard. In 1798 he came into this county as agent for the owners of the Franklin Patent, and commenced the settlement at the place of his late residence. Some years subsequently he received the appointment of Judge of the Common Pleas, the duties of which office he continued to perform, as the writer believes, for several years. He was a member of the Congregational church, and had the consolation derived from the Christian's hope, through a long and distressing illness.—[Com.

DIED—at his residence, at Kendall Green, near the city of Washington on the 3rd of January, 1848, of pulmonary disease, DANIEL GOLD, Esq., a native of Roxbury, in this county, and formerly a resident of this village.

Mr. Gold was for several years deputy clerk of the House of Assembly of this State, and for some years past and up to the time of his death, deputy clerk of the United States House of Representatives. He had also held several minor offices in this county, the duties of which he fulfilled with ability and integrity. Mr. Gold leaves an amiable wife, daughter of Hon. Amos Kendall, with two children, also an aged mother, and other relatives and friends in this county to mourn his loss.

On the announcement of the death of Mr. Gold in the House of Representatives, that body resolved to adjourn, out of respect to the deceased.

DIED.—At Andes, in this county, on the 8th of June, 1852, after a brief illness, Col. ADAM SHEARER, Jr., in the 70th year of his age.

Col. Shearer was a native of Claverac, Columbia county, in this State, and came with his father's family into the town of Andes, at the age of twelve years. That town was then a comparative wilderness. As a citizen, and neighbor and friend, he lived respected and esteemed, and "his death," says our informer, "was sincerely regretted by all who enjoyed his friendship or acquaintance."

The following obituary is from the "Bloomville Mirror."

DIED—In Davenport, on the 21st ult., 1852, (at the residence of his son-in-law, T. H. Rathbun,) SIMEON DURHAM, aged 88 years and 10 months, a soldier of the Revolution.

It is due to the memory of the deceased aged patriot to say, that through the many years allotted him, on earth, his deportment has ever been characterized by a consistency which the present and the future generations of our country may do well to emulate. At the age of sixteen years, near the close of the Revolution, he was in the field with the Connecticut troops three months, for which service he drew a small pension for the last few years of his life. He ever made the Bible the book of his choice, which he read with great assiduity, believing in its gospel truths and in the Abrahamic promise, "that in his seed all the families of the earth shall be blessed." He has left a numerous family of children, grandchildren and great-grandchildren, to mourn his departure.

Another: In Bloomville, on the 29th of January, 1853, Mr. SIMEON MCINTOSH, in the 92nd year of his age. He was one of the earliest settlers in this town.

DIED—at Harpersfield, on the 12th of February, 1853, suddenly in his chair, from an apoplectic fit, THOMAS HENDRY, aged seventy six years. In life respected, in death lamented. He was a kind neighbor, and has gone down to the grave like a "shock of corn fully ripe." His parents emigrated into this county prior to the Revolution, and he was one of the party captured in Harpersfield in the spring of 1780, the particulars of which are narrated in a previous chapter. An informant says, "He was a true patriot, and devoted his leisure hours to reading ancient and modern history, in which he was well versed."

The "Bloomville Mirror" of March 8th, 1853, contains the following obituary:—

DIED—In this village, on the 6th inst., after an illness of two days, Mr. RICHARD PETERS, father of Mr. John Peters, in the 80th year of his age. He was one of the first settlers of Stamford, where he resided for some forty years. About twenty years since he removed to Onondaga county, where he remained eighteen years. About two years since he changed his residence to Preble, Cortlandt county. Last fall he came to this village, and arranged his affairs to make Bloomville his permanent residence, but death has taken him to the spirit land. While a resident of Stamford he was a member of the Methodist church of this place. He was prepared and resigned to die, and assured his friends that it would be well with him. It is only seven weeks since we recorded the death of his wife.

His funeral will take place to day at 1 o'clock P.M., at the church in this village. Sermon by Rev. D. Gibson.

From the same paper of May 17, 1853.

DIED—In Bovina, on the 7th inst., Mr. THOMAS HAMILTON, aged seventy-nine years. He has been a resident of Bovina some fifty-two years.

DIED—In Middlebury, Vt., on the 8th of June, 1853, Major JOSEPH DUREN, (father of Charles W. Duren, of Bloomville, N. Y.) in his 70th year. He was a major in the war of 1812, and participated in a number of engagements, particularly at Plattsburg and others, when the passage of the lake was so sharply contested in that remarkable war. He died universally respected, and a large circle of friends mourn his loss.— [*Rutland Herald.*

In Delhi, on the 3rd of October, 1853, WILLIAM CHARLES CHRISTIANI, aged forty-six years.

Mr. Christiani, at the time of his death, was a copyist in the county clerk's office. We examined a book of six hundred pages, executed by him, the other day, and think it the neatest and best copied book in the office. Mr. Christiani, was a German, and soon after his arrival to this country was employed in painting window-shades in this village. He was respected by all who knew him.—[*Ed.*

DIED—in Meredith, Delaware county, on the 17th December, 1853, ABEL GALLUP, brother of Ezra Gallup, Esq., of Gallupville, aged sixty-two years.

He was one of the first settlers in the town of Meredith, and had by industry and perseverance acquired a handsome property. He was much esteemed by all who knew him, for his many amiable qualities.— [*Schoharie Rep.*

DIED—In this village, on the 12th inst., Mr. JACOB EVERY, aged eighty-four years. At the time of his death, Mr. Every was the oldest resident of this place. He came here some sixty-three years ago, and built a log-house, on nearly the same spot now occupied by our printing-office. There was but one other building, (Mr. N. Gregory's) in the place. He was a stirring, enterprising business man, and his presence soon made the wilderness echo with the notes of improvement. He built dams, grist-mills, saw-mills, clothing establishments, and dwellings, and everything prospered before him. But the tide was changed as the sun of life began to recede. His grist-mill was destroyed by fire, and other reverses took from him the motive power of business. He has always resided in the village since he first moved here from Connecticut on horseback, and was respected and esteemed for his many good qualities. Peace to the ashes of this once faithful and enterprising pioneer of our village.—[*C.*

DIED—In this village, on the morning of the 14th inst., Mr. GEORGE BUNNELL, (merchant) aged thirty-six years, of typhoid fever. In the death of Mr. Bunnell his parents and relatives have lost a true and tried friend, and the public a valuable, capable and worthy business man. He has resided in our village about seven years, and had become endeared to our citizens for many virtues and benevolent deeds. His death has thrown around us a badge of mourning that time alone can obliterate. For the past two years he has held the office of supervisor of this town.—[*Mirror*, Jan. 17*th*, 1854.

DIED—In Meredith, on the 9th January, 1854, after a long and painful disease, Mr. PIERCE MITCHELL, age seventy-two years. Mr. Mitchell was one of the oldest settlers of the town. He was a native of Connecticut, but nearly, or quite fifty years ago came to this town, where he has since resided, respected and esteemed as an honest man and valuable citizen, encouraging others by his example of temperance, industry, and frugality, to persevere in the task before them. Mr. Mitchell has left numerous descendants, and a multitude of friends and acquaintances, who will long cherish and revere his memory.

DIED—At Croton, N. Y., June 16th, 1854, Mrs. MARGERY WOLCOTT, relict of Deacon Thos. Wolcott, aged 71.

Deceased was one of the earliest settlers of the place, and of her disinterested benevolence, particularly in sickness, a survivor has aptly remarked, "she had always been a mother to the neighborhood." She leaves a large circle of relatives, who, with the community, will deeply mourn her loss. For the last thirty years of her life, she was united with the church of Christ, and died as she had lived, an exemplary christian.—*Com.*

DIED—In the town of Roxbury, Delaware county, at the residence of his son, Martin Kelly, EDMUND KELLY, Sen., aged eighty-seven years, five months and fifteen days.

He was born in Frederickstown, Dutchess county, on the 25th of February, 1767; he enlisted at the age of fourteen under Washington, and served under him until the close of the Revolutionary war, doing justice to his country and honor to himself.

He was married to Lovina Liscom, in July, 1787. He leaves to mourn his departure the aged partner of his bosom, nine children, eighty-four grandchildren, one hundred and two great-grandchildren, together with a large circle of friends.

Among the obituary records of 1854, perhaps none were announced with greater regret than that of ADAM THOMAS, Jr., Esq. A correspondent says:

"The sudden death of this gentleman, which occurred on Tuesday of last week, from congestion occasioned by the too free use of cold water, while heated by labor under a burning sun, is deeply lamented by his numerous friends, and his loss is felt by all as a public calamity; cut down in the prime of vigorous manhood, in the midst of an energetic, useful, and upright life, the remembrance of his amiable qualities and many virtues will long continue. To his bereaved family his loss is irreparable."

One of the most prominent traits of Mr. Thomas was his enterprise and public spirit. A few weeks before his death he accompanied the author in making the preliminary surveys of a railroad route, known as the "Rosebrook and Bloomville route," to ascertain the feasibility of constructing the Syracuse and Newburgh *proposed railroad,* through the places mentioned. And it is due to him to state, that it was mainly owing to his efforts that this survey was finally made.

DIED—In Hobart, August 31st, 1854, Gen. ORRIN GRIFFIN, aged about 50 years.

A correspondent says: "The village of Hobart has again been called to mourn the loss of one of its most active, estimable business men. Gen. Orrin Griffin died on Monday evening, the 31st ult., aged fifty years. The funeral solemnities were celebrated on Wednesday, at the Episcopal church, where an appropriate and impressive discourse was delivered by Rev. Wm. A Curtis, to an unusually large congregation. The occasion called together many persons from adjoining villages and towns; from Bloomville, Bovina, Roxbury, Kortright and Harpersfield. The decease of General Griffin, will be irreparable to his surviving widow, greatly lamented by his numerous relatives, and deeply felt by the community at large. Taken from his ordinary business, apparently in usual health, he was confined to his house only a week. His illness, a disease of the heart, was short, to be sure, but stern, unrelenting, and painfully severe. Though desirous of living, it would seem as much for the sake of others as himself, yet he met his end with a calm and decent fortitude and tranquil resignation, fervently expressing his belief in the articles of the Christian Faith, and uniting in the devotional services of the church. He had sustained, for many years, the reputation of a correct and honorable merchant, and was distinguished for his public spirit, benevolence and charity."

DIED—At San Francisco, on the 9th of October, 1854, Mr. CLAUDIUS FLANSBURGH, aged 18 years and 8 months, of the Panama fever.

Mr. Flansburgh was a young man of high talent, and a noble scholar. He was born in Harpersfield, in this county, where his parents now reside. He started for the land of gold on the 5th of Sept., full of hope and expectation; but alas! how frail is life! He was cut down in the bloom of manhood. He leaves a large circle of friends and acquaintances to mourn his early death.

In Walton, October 19th, 1854, LEVI HANFORD, a Revolutionary soldier, and it is believed the last one of the Old Sugar House prisoners, in the 95th year of his age.

He was born in Norwalk, Conn., in 1759. In 1775, at the age of 16, he was enrolled in the militia, and called out for short periods of time. In the spring of 1776, he volunteered to go to New York, and while there, was sent with a detachment of men to Governor's Island in the night, and commenced the first fortification that was ever made on that now strongly fortified place. In March, 1777, he was taken prisoner by the British and Tories at Norwalk, Conn., and taken to New York and confined in the Old Sugar House prison, in the different hospitals, and on board of the prison ships, for fourteen months, suffering every thing but death, and when exchanged, himself and one other, were all that remained of the guard of thirteen taken with him. After he left the prison, he continued in active service at different times and places, to the close of the war. In 1782, he married Mary Mead, daughter of Gen. John Mead, well known in Revolutionary times as the commander of the American lines at Horse Neck. She too, saw much of the cruelty, hardships and sufferings of our Revolutionary struggle. At one time, she was unexpectedly surrounded by British light-horse, and with a sword presented to her breast, was, with horrid oaths and imprecations, threatened with instant death, unless she revealed where her brother was secreted, who had fled, and was at the time but partially concealed, in sight, and almost within the sound of her own voice; but by her resolute firmness and intrepidity, she caused them to believe that, from the circumstances, she could not know the place of his concealment, thereby saving herself and her brother. At another time the house was surrounded, and a British light-horseman struck at her twin sister, and missing her head, the sword struck the casing of the door, (an inch board,) cutting it quite in two. She was repeatedly plundered of her clothing and valuable effects. In 1808, they removed from Connecticut, into this county, with a family of nine children, all of whom are now living, and after living together for more than sixty-five years, her death, which occurred seven years since, at the age of 87, was the first death in their family. In 1809, they united with the Baptist church in Franklin, then under the pastoral care of Rev. Daniel Robertson, and to the close of their lives, lived in christian fellowship with the church, and by their daily deportment, evinced to themselves and the world, the genuineness of their love for the religion they professed. A large circle of relatives and friends will cherish their memory, and now sympathize with the afflicted family, in that dispensation of Divine Providence, that has bereft them of an honored parent, and borne another of our Revolutionary fathers to the tomb.

At Davenport Centre, on the 28th October, ABIJAH PAINE, Esq., aged about eighty years, formerly of Meredith.

In New York City, on the 12th ult., at his residence, after a short illness, SAMUEL SHERWOOD DAVENPORT, in the 43rd year of his age. His wife, Martha Davenport, survived him only five days. Their remains were interred in the Masonic grounds, at Cypress Hill Cemetery. The deceased formerly resided in Delhi, and will still be remembered by numerous acquaintances.

In Hobart, on the 28th February, 1854, Mrs. ABIGAIL MARVINE, relict of Anthony Marvine, Esq., in the 80th year of her age.

Though not the oldest inhabitant of Hobart, yet it is not known, that any person has resided in this region so many years, or that any one came earlier, she having removed hither in 1784, with her father's family, then a child of ten years. For many years, there was neither school-house nor place of public worship. The early settlers were subject to many privations and hardships, but they were gradually surmounted, and a number of Episcopal families having removed hither from Connecticut, they were enabled to erect the church edifice now standing in Hobart, on the 4th of July, 1801. Mrs. Marvine was then 27 years old. It was the only place of public worship in the town of Stamford for some time, and is believed to be the oldest Episcopal church within a circuit of fifty miles. In 1810, Mrs. Marvine lost her husband, a lawyer of large practice for those times, and living as he died, among a rural and scattered population, leaving his widow with eight children, the eldest being only seventeen years, and the youngest about four months old. The care of providing for, and educating so large a family, together with the responsibility of closing up her husband's estate, which by his sudden death, was left in a very unsettled condition, would have been enough to discourage a female of ordinary mind; but she survived to see all her children become heads of families, and some of them grandparents. Though of Presbyterian parentage, she became afterwards a communicant in St. Peter's church, and her six sons and two daughters were baptized, and brought up in attendance on its services, so far as circumstances permitted. They are now mostly connected with the Episcopal communion, though widely scattered in different countries, and different States. But two are now remaining in Hobart; these, with Mr. C. Marvine, of Delhi, are the only children now residing in the county of Delaware. The death of Mrs. Marvine was calm and peaceful, full of christian faith and hope.—*Com.*

THE HON. SELAH R. HOBBIE, First-Assistant Post-master General, died at the city of Washington, on the 23d March, 1854, of an affection of the lungs, with which he had been for a long time afflicted. He was born at Newburgh, New York, on the 10th of March, 1797, and died at the age of 57. While a boy, he removed with his father to Walton, in this county, and soon after, while yet quite young, was deputy clerk of the Assembly at Albany, where he became acquainted with Gen. Root, then a member of the Assembly, in the meridian of his great power and influence. At an early day, he established himself at this place, in the practice of the law, where he married Julianne, eldest daughter of Gen. Root, with whom he was connected in business. He ranked among the first lawyers of the Delaware bar, having an extensive and lucrative practice. As an evidence of the public appreciation of his talents and standing, he was commissioned District Attorney and Brigade Major and Inspector, the duties of which he discharged with distinguished ability and success. He held these appointments till 1826, in the fall of which year, he was elected to Congress from the counties of Delaware and Greene. At the close of his term in Congress, his numerous friends from all parts of the country, were bringing him forward as a candidate for clerk of the House of Representatives, which was superseded by his being appointed Assistant Post-master General, on the accession of Gen. Jackson to the Presidency, in 1829.

To his skill, judgment and perseverance, the Post Office Department owes much of its success for the past twenty-five years. It will long continue to feel the beneficial effects of his services. His severe and unremitting labors impaired his health; and in 1850, after the accession of Gen. Taylor, he voluntarily resigned, and retired from the office which he had held from his appointment, in 1829. Relaxation from the arduous duties of the office, and his visit to Panama, as agent of the Mail Steamship Company, to regulate and improve our postal system in that quarter, somewhat restored him; and on President Pierce coming into office, he yielded to the request of friends, and consented to resume his duties of First Assistant Post-master General. His strength however, impaired by pulmonary disease, was unequal to the labors of the position, and he soon sunk under them. He was prompt in the dispatch of business, easy, frank, and candid in his intercourse, and these qualities, added to his extensive knowledge, made him a most popular public officer. He was universally esteemed. As a husband and father he was devoted, kind and affectionate. He was beloved, and exemplary in all the relations of life. In his death the national service has sustained a great loss, society an ornament, and mankind a friend.

At Alexandria, (Va.,) on the 21st of November, 1854, Mr. FREDERICK D. HANFORD, of Hobart, (N.Y.) aged thirty-two years. For several years he was principal of the Hobart Seminary. His remains have been deposited in the burial ground of the Episcopal church in Hobart.

Mr. Hanford was one of the earliest graduates of the State Normal School, from Delaware county. Returning to the town of Stamford, he established the Hobart Seminary, and during his connection with that institution it maintained a high reputation for thoroughness of instruction among the neighboring seminaries. His close attention to the interests of his students and the school, was doubtless one of the principal causes of the early termination of his useful life by consumption.

DIED—In Stamford, on the 21st of August, 1854, of consumption, BAILEY FOOTE, son of George B. Foote, in the twentieth year of his age.

He was a young man of stern integrity, and promised to make a man of worth in the town where he lived, and was distinguished for the many virtues he possessed. He was always found casting his influence on the side of virtue. During an illness of four months, he suffered severely from weakness; he was never heard to complain, but exhibited that cheerfulness of character which so naturally belonged to him. When told by the writer of this communication that, in all probability, they soon must part, tears rolled from his eyes for a few moments, and then, with the spirit of a man, he said it was all right, or it would not be so. The day of his death will long be remembered. He said he felt his time was short, and conversed about his final departure with as much composure as if he was preparing for an earthly journey.

He wished to see the pastor that had visited him during his illness, and requested him to speak from these words: "Remember now thy Creator in the days of thy youth." There is a power in religion that sheds a brightness over the hour of death.—[*Delaware Gazette.*

DIED—In Andes, March 1st, 1855, PETER PENET, aged sixty years. Mr. Penet, was one of the oldest settlers of the town of Andes, and was a quiet and industrious citizen. The confidence and esteem of his townsmen is shown, in the fact that he has been annually elected town-clerk of that town for the last twenty-five years.

WILLIAM HOLLIDAY, aged one hundred and four years, one month and twenty days, died at Colchester, in this county, on the 21st of February last. Mr. Holliday was born in the town of Rye, Westchester county, in this State, on the 26th of December, 1750. He removed to the town of Harpersfield, in this county, in 1791, where he remained until 1795. He then removed to Colchester, where he has since resided. At the time he came to this county, he had to place his movables on the backs of horses, there being no carriage-roads. He assisted in making the first ten miles of road ever made in this county, which was at the head of the West Branch of the Delaware river. Where the village of Delhi now stands, there was but one log hut. Mr. Holliday was a professor of religion, and was a member of the Baptist church for seventy-six years, and for fifty-six years a deacon. He had thirteen children, eighty grandchildren, one hundred and fifty-one great-grandchildren, and seventeen great-great-grandchildren—total 261.

There are very few, if any persons now alive, who were in the county at the time Mr. Holliday came into it, and he has, after outliving the generations that came on the stage with him, been gathered to those that went before him.

The sudden decease of Col. AMASA PARKER, at his residence in this village, on the 1st of March, 1855, in full health and vigor of mind, though at an advanced age, has cast a gloom over this community, and left a void that will not soon be filled.

He was born at Washington, Litchfield county, Connecticut, October 28th, 1784, and was a graduate of Yale College. He attended the law school at Litchfield, and finished his studies with Peter Van Schaick, of Kinderhook. He came to Delhi in 1812, where he practised in his profession till his death. He was a partner of Hon. Samuel Sherwood from 1812 to 1827, when the latter removed to New York. He then entered into copartnership with his nephew, Amasa J. Parker, Esq., now one of the Justices of the Supreme Court of this State. After the promotion of Judge Parker to the bench, he connected himself in business with his son, Robert Parker, with whom he continued through life. He was Surrogate of this county about nine years, and for a long time Master in Chancery. He devoted his whole time to his profession, made that his principal business, and closed a professional career of uncommon success, at the mature age of seventy.

Though his death was sudden, he was not unprepared. He had set his house in order. Those who knew him, will remember him as he looked in robust health. Few men who have died at his age, have exhibited so little of decay in body or mind.

He was proverbially faithful to his clients, courteous to his adversaries, vigilant in the preparation, and able in the trial of causes. He belonged to the old school of lawyers, and though averse to radical changes in the practice made by the "The Revised Statutes" and "The Code of Procedure," he profoundly studied and mastered them.

As a citizen, he was just, without reproach, and highly esteemed as a neighbor. Indeed, in all the relations of life, he faithfully discharged his duties to all men, kindred and strangers. For many years he had been a prominent member of the Episcopal church.

Such men are not only ornaments, but pillars of society. Their like is not often found—their loss is irreparable.

AMASA JUNIUS PARKER, L.L.D.,
LATE JUSTICE OF THE SUPREME COURT.

It is both interesting and instructive to read the biographies of those who have, by their own energies, achieved success in this world; appealing as they do, to the hopes and aspirations of the human heart, and teaching the way and manner through which that success has been secured. How many struggling along an adverse path, have been aroused and cheered to renewed efforts by the examples set before them in such lives, and who have themselves in the end attained eminence in learning from the healthy influence which such examples inspire! The incidents may be few or crowded, vivid or otherwise; still, if they record the triumph of talent and virtue, they are of great value, and should be sought after and studied.

Few memoirs will, we apprehend, afford more interest and instruction, than that of the eminent jurist whose name heads this article.

Although as citizens of Delaware county, we claim him with pride as our fellow citizen, yet he was born in Connecticut, at Sharon, in the parish of Ellsworth, and county of Litchfield. The region of his birth-place is secluded from the busy world,—a spot of sterile hillsides and stony valleys, but nourishing a race of men, trained in habits of industry, and full of the energy and perseverance which never fail to make way through the difficulties of life. Many are the distinguished men which Litchfield county has produced, men who have trod the path of eminence with a firm step and courageous heart.

The ancestors of Judge Parker were of the old Puritan blood of New England, and residents of the western part of Connecticut for successive generations. Amasa Parker, and Thomas Fenn, his paternal and maternal grandfathers, were soldiers of the Revolution, and widely respected for the sterling virtues of their character; the latter filling various offices of public trust. He was for thirty-eight successive sessions a member of the State legislature. Both were residents throughout their lives of the county of Litchfield, of the above State.

The subject of our memoir was the eldest son of the Rev. Daniel Parker, who was pastor for almost twenty years of the Congregational church of Ellsworth, Connecticut. He was a graduate of Yale College; married Anna, the daughter of the above-mentioned Thomas Fenn; and during the time he lived at Ellsworth, established and took charge of an academy which enjoyed a high reputation, and where many men who subsequently became distinguished, were educated. In 1816, he removed to Greenville, Greene county, New York, and the academy there was placed in his charge. It was under him that the subject of our sketch, then only nine years of age, commenced the study of Latin, continuing in the academy two years. He then went to the Hudson Academy for the same period, and afterwards for three years in the city of New York.

Eager for information, the son received from the father the most devoted educational information. He obtained for him the best instructors in the country; and it was thus that the first foundations of that fine classical learning and taste for *belles-lettres,* that, independently of his professional attainments, distinguish Judge Parker, were laid. Such was his diligence, that at the age of sixteen he had completed the usual course of collegiate study. At the same immature age, May, 1823, he was made the principal of the Hudson Academy, and continued in that capacity for four years.

Under his supervision, the academy was placed in a most prosperous condition, and attained a wide reputation; and such was his youth, that many of his pupils, since distinguished, were older than himself. He was not, up to that time a college graduate; but in consequence of a rival academy adducing this as an objection to the young principal, he in July, 1825, caused himself to be examined at Union College for the entire collegiate course. He passed the ordeal triumphantly, graduated with the senior class, and obtained his degree of Bachelor of Arts; and afterwards in due course received the degree of Master of Arts.

After graduating, he resumed his duty at the academy; and during the latter portion of his career here, he entered the office of the present Judge John W. Edmonds, then of Hudson, to prosecute the study of the law.

In the spring of 1827 he resigned his trust as principal of the Hudson Academy, and at the age of twenty, removed to Delhi, where his uncle Col. Amasa Parker, a lawyer of distinction, was practising his profession. He entered the office of his uncle, finished his studies, and in 1828, at the age of twenty-one, was admitted to the bar. He then became a partner of his uncle, and for fifteen years a very large practice engaged the attention of the firm.

The professional business of these two gentlemen is said to have been the most extensive country practice in the State, and the most systematically conducted. Col. Amasa Parker was a lawyer of thorough reading, long experience, and proverbial integrity. He preferred however, to leave his partner to discharge the duty of trying and arguing causes. This division of labor could not fail to give to the subject of this memoir great experience in the various courts. It is said that he had tried more causes at the circuits than any young man of his age in the State at the time of his elevation to the bench.

We recollect seeing him in attendance at one of the Ulster circuits, where he was engaged as counsel in every cause tried, the court lasting two weeks. His opponent throughout, was that veteran of the bar from Poughkeepsie, General Swift. The circuits in Ulster were then held by Judge Ruggles, late a member of the Court of Appeals: and for years it seemed a matter of course, if one of the parties employed as counsel at that circuit either Mr. Parker or General Swift, the other of the two was immediately engaged on the opposite side.

Judge Parker was always distinguished for the energy of his character, and the promptitude of his business habits. It was a rule of his office that no business letter should remain on the table unanswered over a single return of mail. He had great facility in the dispatch of business, and with his untiring industry and application, and the admirable system adopted and enforced in his law-office, the amount of business was as large as it was various and diversified in character.

It was not only as a lawyer, however, that Judge Parker became known to the public. He was called into the political arena. In the fall of 1833, he was elected a democratic member of the State legislature, and was placed on the committee on ways and means, and in other prominent situations, during the ensuing session. In the subsequent year, being then twenty-seven years old, he was elected by the legislature a Regent of the

University; younger than any one ever before, or since that time, made a member of that distinguished body.

At twenty-nine, he was elected without opposition to Congress, from the counties of Broome and Delaware, then forming a congressional district. During his term he acted upon important committees, and addressed the House upon many important subjects, amongst which were the Mississippi election case, the Public Lands, and the Cilley Duel, preserved in the columns of the "Congressional Globe." All his speeches were of a high order, and upon the former subject, which was of a very intricate kind, his effort called out the praises of both parties, as most masterly, and shedding the clearest light upon it.

In 1839, he was nominated as senator in the Third Senatorial District of this State. Great excitement prevailed; as a successor to Nathaniel P. Tallmadge, in the Senate of the United States, was to be chosen by the ensuing legislature. About fifty thousand votes were cast. In consequence of the unwonted exertions used, the whig candidate, Gen. Root, prevailed, although by a majority of only a few votes.

The five years that followed, were employed by Mr. Parker in the energetic and laborious practice of his profession. At the end of that time, in 1844, he was appointed Circuit Judge of the third Circuit, when he removed to Albany, where he has continued to reside until the present time.

The duties of this distinguished post were most arduous, combining, as they did, those of a judge of the Circuit, and vice-chancellor of the Court of Equity. To them he devoted, untiringly, the best energies of his mind, and met in an unfaltering manner his great responsibilities.

The same promptness and system which distinguished him as a lawyer, characterized him as a judge, and enabled him to dispose of an almost incredible amount of business.

In 1845, he held the Delaware Circuit, and no greater responsibility was ever cast upon a judge, than fell to the lot of Judge Parker, in holding that court. The county had been declared in a state of insurrection, (see chapter XI.) by the governor, in consequence of the violent resistance made to the laws. Assemblages numbering two or three hundred persons, armed and disguised as Indians, had appeared in different parts of the county, and set the law and its officers at defiance. Under-sheriff Steele had been shot down while engaged in the discharge of an official duty, under the painful circumstances already fully narrated. The governor had therefore found it necessary to call into service a military force, which had been maintained at the county seat for several weeks, by whose aid arrests had been made, and public order maintained.

The jail of the county, and two temporary jails, had been filled with prisoners, charged with every grade of crime, from murder down to misdemeanor. It was under such a state of things, and in the midst of an excited community, divided in opinion as to the causes which had led to the commission of such crimes, that Judge Parker opened the Court of Oyer and Terminer. He found over one hundred prisoners confined. He announced, that he should continue court until every indictment was tried, and the jails all cleared. The Attorney General, aided by Samuel Sherwood, Esq., assisted the District Attorney on the part of the people, and the prisoners were defended by other distinguished counsel. The trials progressed one by one, with untiring perseverance; and at the end of the third week, the jails were cleared, every case having been disposed of, by conviction or otherwise. Two were sentenced to death, thirteen to imprisonment in the State prison,* some for life, and others for a less period; and for the lighter offences, fines were in many cases imposed. The course pursued by Judge Parker, met with general approbation. While the anti-renters who had openly violated the laws, felt that the hand of justice had fallen heavily upon them, and were satisfied that the law could no longer be resisted with impunity, the more intelligent among them, were also ready frankly to acknowledge, that justice had been tempered with mercy.

After the adjournment of the court, the military force was discharged, peace was restored, and in no instance, has resistance to process since occurred in that county.

In the summer of 1846, Geneva College conferred the degree of L.L.D. upon him, a distinction eminently due to his well known attainments as a scholar and jurist.

In the same year, his term of office ended with the constitution then existing and under the present one, adopted at that time, he was elected a justice of the Supreme Court of the State of New York, the duties of which office he continued to discharge until the expiration of the term, with distinguished ability. It was conferred upon him by the votes of not only his only party, but of a large number upon the opposite side, the suffrages being given as a token of the confidence and respect entertained for him in the Third Judicial District, from which he was elected.

It has been frequently remarked of him, that he has never since his accession to the bench, either as Circuit or Supreme Court Judge, failed to be present to open court at the precise minute appointed. Not a moment of time was thus lost; the members of the bar, and all others attending court, being expected, and thus by example, soon learned to practise similar promptness. A writer in describing one of his circuits, says, "he accomplishes an infinity of business with the precision of machinery."

At the organization of the Law Department of the University of Albany, in 1851, Judge Parker was appointed one of its professors, and since that

---

* See note, 1 Parker's Criminal Reports, published in 1845.

time, has devoted every year a portion of time to lecturing before that department. Coöperating with the other able professors associated with him, Judge Harris, and Professor Dean, the law school has been constantly increasing in numbers, and has now become one of the most flourishing institutions in the country. The thoroughness of its instruction, and the high standard of excellence demanded for its graduates, have already given to this department of the University a distinguished reputation, and made its impress upon the character of the profession. Its students are found settling in all the northern, western, and most of the southern States.

Judge Parker has recently commenced the publication of a series of Criminal Reports, of which the first volume only, has yet been published. It is said the second volume is now in press.

Such is the career of one who received no patrimony but his education, and had no aids but his own energies and talents. How he has succeeded, this "plain unvarnished" memoir relates. It furnishes the loftiest evidence of the mighty force of industry, perseverance and integrity, in elevating those who practise these severe but benign virtues.

As a public speaker, Judge Parker is of superior excellence. His voice is melodious and well cultivated, his bearing is dignified, his language is fluent and well chosen, and his ideas are clear and abundant. In extemporaneous speaking, he has few equals in the State. Always ready to meet an occasion, his off-hand powers of addressing an assemblage are remarkable. In circumstances where he might well have been at fault, surrounded with the loftiest and most dignified in the land, with celebrated statesmen and orators, we have known him called out without a moment's notice to address the company, and have witnessed the triumph of his eloquence.

His speech at Dunkirk, at the celebration of the New York and Erie Railroad completion, with President Fillmore, Mr. Webster, Mr. Crittenden, and others of the Cabinet, a host of dignitaries and gentlemen from all parts of the State, around him, and his remarks at the Webster dinner, in Albany, in June last, and at the Litchfield celebration, exhibited conclusively his powers in this respect.

In 1853, Judge Parker availed himself of an opportunity afforded him by a summer vacation, to make a hasty visit to Europe, in pursuit of the advantages to be derived from observation, and the benefits of relaxation from mental labor. In a hurried term of a little over two months, he was enabled, by the modern facilities of travelling, to visit different parts of Great Britain and Ireland, and a large portion of Continental Europe. Judge Parker was well received by the members of his profession, and as the guest of the Law Reform Association of England, at their annual dinner, Lord Brougham presiding, was called upon to explain the results of the recent law reforms made in this State, and particularly of the uniting of law and equity powers in the same tribunal. The favorable impression made by Judge Parker, secured to him many tokens of respect, and the kindest civilities from the bench and the bar.

The term of Judge Parker as Justice of the Supreme Court being about to expire, he was again, in September, 1855, unanimously put in nomination for reëlection, by the democratic convention of his district, at which both sections of that party were fully represented. In the unsettled state of political affairs, two other candidates were also nominated by other parties for the same office. The result of the canvass showed the election of Judge Gould, the worthy candidate of the American (K. N.) party, by a little over one thousand majority. The result was equally a surprise to all parties: but on learning the comparative strength of political parties in the district, it was plain that no different result could reasonably have been anticipated. Judge Parker received at the election the undivided and cordial support of both sections of his own party, the almost undivided support of the members of the bar of the district, and of the leading and intelligent men of all parties. The result showed he was largely in advance of his ticket in every county in his district. He received four or five thousand more votes than any other candidate running on the same ticket. If he had been beaten by a party vote, the majority of his successful competitor would have been about six thousand. It is complimentary to the personal character of Judge Parker, that in Albany, the city of his residence, he was so generally voted for, without distinction of party, that he received a majority of nearly fifteen hundred.

In the peculiar state of parties, and with reference to the overwhelming strength in his district of the successful party, the result of the election is a proud personal triumph to Judge Parker. The expressions of the public press of different parties, in every portion of the State, are full of regret for the result, and have led to the rediscussion of the question, how far the system of electing the judiciary can be safely relied upon, in times of great political excitement.

To Judge Parker, personally, a release from the cares and labors of the Bench, and an opportunity of resuming for a time, his professional pursuits, can bring no regrets. He will gladly avail himself of the repose it affords him, after so many years of severe intellectual and physical toil,—a repose that will only give additional energy to the strength and vigor of middle age.

On his retirement from the bench, the following correspondence took place between the subject of this memoir and the Albany bar.

As a man and a citizen, Judge Parker has won the esteem and respect of all who know him. His temper is singularly equable and amiable, his heart kind and capacious, his disposition frank, manly and generous. His person is dignified, his countenance beaming with a smile, and his manners, polished in the best society, are easy, bland and courteous.

Shortly after Judge Parker had retired from the bench, he received a communication from a large number of the most distinguished members of the bar, of the city of Albany, who, to use their own expression, "entertaining a high regard for the ability, courtesy, and impartiality evinced by you, in the discharge of your late judicial duties, are desirous of offering you, on your retirement from the bench, some expression of their respect and appreciation.

"They therefore earnestly request, that you permit your bust to be sculptured, and when completed, deposited in the law department of the State Library."

In his reply, acceding to so flattering an expression of esteem, Judge Parker says: "The term of my judicial service, has been one of great interest in the jurisprudence of the State. It has covered the period of transition from an old to a new system of practice, a new organization of the courts, and the uniting of both law and equity powers in the same tribunal. It might well be supposed such radical changes would greatly increase the labors of the judiciary, and embarrass, for a time at least, the practitioners at the bar. It was only by mutual effort, that the difficulties could be overcome, and the progress of the public business facilitated. In earnestly endeavoring, without stint of toil, to give the utmost efficiency to our present system, and to dispatch promptly the business of the courts, I have never ceased to be sensible how much my labors were lightened by the assiduity and learning of the bar, and rendered agreeable by the kindness and courtesy, which have uniformly characterized your whole intercourse with me.

"I shall resume my place among you, justly proud of my professional associations, and enjoying, though with different relations, the unchanged sentiments of personal respect and regard with which, I am,

"Very truly, your friend,
"AMASA J. PARKER.

"To Messrs. P. GANSEVOORT,
JOHN H. REYNOLDS,
C.M. JENKINS,
JOHN K. PORTERS, and others of the Albany bar."

HON. JOEL T. HEADLEY. This distinguished writer, and the present Secretary of State, was born at Walton, Delaware county, December 30, 1814. His father, the Rev. Mr. Headley, was one of the first Presbyterian ministers in the county, and for some years preached at Walton. He had seven children, of which the subject of the present sketch was the fourth; three of them were girls, and four boys. The two eldest daughters are now dead. The oldest, Eliza, married a Rev. Mr. Brown, a descendant of President Edwards, the second, Catharine, married Rev. Alvah Selly, and died some years since in Gorham, Ontario county, in this State.

The eldest son died about a year since, at St. Thomas, in the West Indies, whither he had gone for his health. The next daughter, Irene, who was younger than the subject of the present sketch, married Wm. Burr, of New York city, and is now living in Pontiac, Michigan. The next brother, younger, Phineas C., is a clergyman, and is now settled in Sandwich, Mass. The youngest son, Wm. S., is a physician, now practising his profession in Owego, Tioga county.

Joel entered Union College, and graduated in 1839, and having fixed upon theology as his future sphere, studied at Auburn, where he prepared himself for the important duties of the ministry. Having perfected himself in the theoretical part, and by dint of application, stored his mind with those important truths which were to prove the foundation of his future course, he entered the ministry, and preached for a short time at Stockbridge, Berkshire county, Mass. Possessing naturally a weak constitution, it is not strange, that it should have proved unable to sustain and bear up under the labors of so vigorous and active a mind, and consequently, when he entered the practical field of his profession, he found his constitution and health rapidly giving way, warning him of the danger of yielding himself up to a sedentary employment.

He now resolved to travel, and marked out in his mind a plan of travel in foreign countries, that would occupy a term of years. His health, however, becoming worse rather than better, he did not carry out his original intentions, but hastened his return to America. Arriving in Italy, he spent several months on that classic soil, his mind drinking in the luxuriant beauties of that far-famed clime, while his vivid imagination was permitted to expand, beneath those ideal beauties, which afterwards so conspicuously distinguished his writings.

Passing out of Italy, he travelled through Switzerland, Germany, Netherlands, Belgium and France, thence passed over into England, and Wales, and finally returned home before the end of the second year.

The first publication of Mr. Headley, was a translation from the German, which appeared anonymously in 1844. The succeeding year, 1845, he published letters from Italy, Holland, "Alps and the Rhine." In 1846, "Napoleon and his Marshals," and "The Sacred Mountains." These books at once attained a wide circulation, and acquired a popularity for their author seldom equalled. A distinguished reviewer thus comments:

"The advent of a popular book, is about as evident, from certain attending signs, as the appearance of a comet among the steady and familiar bodies of the solar system. On the occurrence of the heavenly phenomenon, astronomers are busy in the investigation of its appearance and laws; the learned professor wheels out his long telescope, and gazes the livelong night at the misty thing he has espied in one of the constellations.

His accurate pupil turns to his books, to determine the element of its orbit, and whether it is Enckle's or Halley's; men stand in crowds watching its flight from star to star—journals of science, and heralds of news, spread authentic information of its progress, rate of velocity, and time of disappearance; and he who had not seen the celestial wonder, would know that it had actually appeared. It was somewhat so with the terrestrial phenomenon. As soon as it is fairly 'out' in the shape of letters from abroad, a romance, tragedy, a volume of poetry, or biography of warriors, literary circles are busy in the discussion of its merits, according to the established rules of criticism. Reviews, journals, magazines, quarterlies, and penny papers, are filled with extracts and comments. Circulating libraries of 'choice reading,' circulate with new velocity—there is a buzz in the saloons of Washington or Saratoga at the issue of 'Napoleon and his Marshals.' The bookseller, reduced to his 'last copy,' 'assures his eager customers 'that a new edition is forthcoming,' and a man a thousand miles from New York or Boston, is aware that a new star is blazing in the literary world. It would be impossible in the limits of a volume to sum up the entire comments of the press."

One editor calls this work "the most deeply interesting and widely popular book of the season;" another calls it "a philosophical estimate of the French Revolution." One praises the "august title," and the "portraits of the marshals," and says, "if there is such a thing as being born for a particular profession, Mr. Headley was born for a military commander." One discourses in this style: "He is an ardent admirer of Napoleon, worshipping him with almost poetical fervor, and had he been a follower of the great soldier in the days of his glory, he would have loved him with adoration." And yet another says: "If now and then a voice has been raised in another strain, it has been lost in the din of general approbation."

But the popular pen of Headley could not remain listless amidst such general admiration and applause; and "Washington and his Generals," "Sacred Scenes and Characters of Life," "Life of Cromwell," "Adirondack, or Life in the Woods," "Old Guard," "Scott and Jackson," and "Last war with England," appeared at intervals. He also published a volume of "Miscellanies," and one of "Sketches," to prevent the circulation of two books with these titles, which a printer in New York had published under his name. Nor ought we to omit to mention that Mr. Headley has now the "Life of Washington," in press.

At the election of 1855, Mr. Headley was put in nomination by the American party for Secretary of State, and his universal popularity demonstrated, by an overwhelming majority. He purchased a country seat some years since on the banks of the Hudson, a short distance above the Highlands, known as "Cedar Lawn," where he spends a portion of the season in his congenial occupation.

Mr. Headley is rather tall and slim in stature, while his manners are attractive and agreeable, exceedingly obliging, and his conversation fascinating and refined, while it is unpretending. We esteem him as a sincere friend, while we would do honor to his merit.

APPENDIX

DELAWARE GAZETTE

THE following extract, is from the first number of the "Autobiography of the Delaware Gazette:"

"At this period of my existence—a period in the age of newspapers when a prescriptive right to be garrulous has been fairly earned, I am disposed to sit down and have a little gossip of the 'good old times,' with my readers. I have attained to a greater age than is usually granted to *newspapers*,—in fact I am a kind of a *paper* Methuselah; and no candid person will deny that my gray hairs entitle me to a respectful hearing. Delaware county and its villages have changed vastly for the better, since my birth; so have I changed vastly for the better in my size and personal appearance, during the same period. I am to-day, (1854,) just twice as large as when I was first wrapped in swaddling clothes; and the miserable whity-brown complexion, and uncouth toggery I wore when I made my first weekly call at your doors, have given place to a clear, healthy-looking face, and a dress really genteel,—in fact, I am a kind of Beau Brummel among the hebdomadals of this region.

"It brings sadness to my heart to sit down with you and conjure up the memories of the past, from 1819, when I made my first appearance, down to the present time! Most of the friends whose kind hands were extended to guide my first faltering steps, went to sleep long ago in the quiet country church-yards; the few left are *old* folks, going about with frosty locks, in place of the rich brown curls they wore in my boyhood, or sitting by their fireside, clothed with flannel, and waiting that summons which has already called away their loved ones. My early and kind patrons, the Gazette sends a hearty 'God bless you' to you all.

"'So live, that when thy summons comes to join
The innumerable caravan that moves
To that mysterious realm, where each shall take
His chamber in the silent halls of death,
Thou go not like the weary slave at night,
Scourged to his dungeon; but, sustained and soothed
By an unfaltering trust, approach thy grave,
Like one who wraps the drapery of his couch
About him, and lies down to pleasant dreams.'

"In November, 1819, my then editor, John J. Sappan, issued the first number of the Gazette. It was the first newspaper ever issued in the county. This locality was thinly populated, and the people, then, as now, worshipped many political gods. Mr. Sappan wisely resolved, therefore, that he would not erect a shrine for the deities of any party, and sent me out a *neutral* in politics. I have not a copy of my initial number to show you, but I can call your attention to some of my numbers of that first year. Referring to them, I find that Isaac Ogden was then Judge of the Common Pleas; Robert North, of Walton, was Surrogate; Isaac Burr, still living, an aged and esteemed citizen of Meredith, was sheriff; Samuel Sherwood, Amasa Parker, Root, and Hobbie, Serinus Monson, Amasa Douglass, Phelps, and Romeyn, John B. Spencer, Henry Ogden, Foote, and Decker, and others, were attorneys; Gideon Frisbie, and Robert North, were Loan Commissioners; and from the post-office advertisement, I learn that Noadiah Johnson, afterwards the popular representative of the district in Congress, was assistant post-master."

The first number of the Gazette was issued, Thursday, November 18th, 1819. Mr. Sappan, its editor and publisher, who had been for some years associate editor of a paper in Otsego county, it is believed came to Delhi, then but a small village, and without any previous warning, commenced the publication of his paper.

In 1822, April 1st, Mr. Sappan sold out his interest to David Johnson, an apprentice in the office. Without any pecuniary resources, or capital of any kind, except the product of his own hard labor and industry, his successor was compelled to incur expenses and shoulder responsibilities, from which the profits of his paper proved hardly sufficient to release him. He was compelled by stern necessity to mortgage his office, and even type, to a heavy amount, to enable him to continue the publication of his paper, and to support his family.

In 1833, March 20th, Mr. Johnson left for New York, as was supposed with the intention of purchasing a fresh supply of material for his paper, leaving the office in charge of his assistant, J. D. Clark, a native of Hudson, N. Y., a practical and accomplished printer, who had spent the two preceding years in Sappan's employ, but not returning at the appointed time, the fact became publicly known that he had *absented* himself, and the creditors of the establishment came forward, and succeeded in effecting a sale of the entire establishment to A. M. Paine, the present editor, who associated with him in the management of the paper J. D. Clarke, referred to above, whose experience in the office, as well as his practical knowledge of the art of printing, rendered his services a necessary guarantee to the future success of the enterprise. Mr. Clark remained a copartner until May, 1839, when he closed his connection with the Gazette, disposing of his interest to his associate, Mr. Paine, who has since remained its sole proprietor.

The Gazette, as inferred from the extract we copied above from its "Autobiography," was established from considerations of policy, a *"neutral"* in politics; yet its editors, from the first, had been democrats of the old school, and whether the Gazette even under Mr. Sappan's supervision, did not frequently excite the watchful jealousy of leading whigs, we have not the data before us to infer, but it is certain that his successor, Mr. Johnson, could not long remain on neutral grounds, and the truth soon became obvious that the Gazette had become a decided organ of the interests of the democratic party.

The first opponent to the Gazette was the Delaware Republican, as appears from the following communication:

"Delhi, February 5th, 1855.

"J. Gould, Esq:—In our conversation yesterday I omitted, what I had previously mentioned, that the Delaware Journal was not the first paper started in opposition to the Gazette. The Delaware Republican was started, I should think, within the first two, or possibly three years of the Gazette. It seems to have been in existence during the election of 1822. The first mention of it in the Gazette is on the 11th of December, 1822, when it speaks as having been assailed for some weeks by the Republican. I find no notice in any file of the Gazette of its discontinuance. The Republican was first started by E. J. Roberts, but at the time I speak of, Wm. G. Hull sustained the relation of editor. The last mention of the Republican, in the columns of the Gazette, was on the 19th of March, 1823, and I think it closed its existence a short time after.

"Yours &c.,   A. M. PAINE."

The existence of the "Delaware Republican" is thus pertinently alluded to in the "Autobiography of the Gazette."

"On the 4th of July, 1821, a new candidate for popular favor, called 'The Delaware Republican,' made its appearance in this village, under the editorial care and supervision of Elijah J. Roberts. Mr. Roberts, I think, in after years, acquired some distinction as editor of the Craftsman, published at Rochester, and devoted to Trades' Unions. The Republican came into existence as a Bucktail Republican newspaper; and among other duties assumed by the editor in his opening leader, is that of 'watching the movements of the Clintonian remnant through the stages of their present decline, till the memorable epoch shall arrive, when the political recreant who now fills the Executive chair, shall descend from his high elevation, and the places which now know his party, shall know them no more.' The severe charges made against his political opponents, and the harsh epithets applied to them, would neither be made against nor applied to the same persons, now that they and their acts have become historical; and we may properly learn from such retrospect, the propriety of moderating the intensity of our party feuds, and of skipping over the hard words we are accustomed to apply to those whose politics are of a different school from ours. Our political opponents, it is fair to presume, maintain their 'confession of faith' with as much sincerity and honesty of purpose, as we do ours; and he who reads thirty years from now, the political articles of *our* time, will probably take note of our injustice, and illiberality to our political opponents. Mr. Roberts wishes "to impress upon the public mind the maxim, that abandonment of principles for temporary purposes, leads to ultimate defeat,'—a maxim carrying an important truth to the public mind; and worthy of a place in a sermon as well as in a political article." The Republican was discontinued for want of adequate support. The party of which it was the advocate were in a decided minority in the county. The discontinuance of the Delaware Republican, was a marked epoch in the history of the Gazette. That paper was immediately enlarged, and its columns declared free to the use of both parties. The editor says, "we shall hold our columns open to communications of all who may be disposed to engage in a liberal, dispassionate and manly discussion of such topics as may be deemed sufficiently interesting to engage the public attention, and shall afford every facility in our power to a free investigation of subjects of political importance."

The second opponent of the Gazette was the "Delaware Journal," established and conducted under the supervision of the president and directors of the anti-masonic society. George Mason was employed to conduct and publish it.

The excitement attendant upon the disappearance of Morgan, gradually died away, the anti-masonic society was disbanded, and at the expiration of one year, the Delaware Journal closed its existence. This paper was afterwards revived by Bowne and McDonald, and after a brief existence, was again discontinued.

There are at present, six weekly papers published in the county, viz. Weekly Visitor, Delaware Gazette, Delaware Express, Bloomville Mirror, Deposit Union Democrat, and the Hobart Free Press, to each of which, we design giving a brief notice.

For the following information, the author is indebted to S. D. Hulce, Esq., the able editor of the Deposit Union Democrat.

THE CENTRAL SUN.

The first attempt to establish a newspaper in Deposit, was in 1847, about the time, or soon after the announcement of the supposed discovery of the "Central Sun," from which circumstance, the paper took its name.

A Mr. C. D. Curtis, a printer by trade, and Mr. A. T. Borroughs, then a merchant at Deposit, originated a subscription for the organization of a joint stock company, for the permanent establishment of the paper.

The necessary amount of stock was readily subscribed, and about three hundred and fifty dollars, paid in, with which amount, Mr. Curtis was sent to New York, to purchase the establishment. A few days after the departure of the associate proprietor, a letter was received from him, stating that the money had been stolen out of his pocket. "Thus," says our correspondent, the "Central Sun went down in darkness ere it rose."

THE DEPOSIT COURIER.

In 1848, C. E. Wright, Esq., induced Marshal R. Hulce, Esq., brother of the present editor of the Democrat, to enter into an association with himself, and advance the necessary funds for the establishment and support of a paper. A purchase was made of a printing establishment at Montrose, Pennsylvania, where a paper had been published for about six months, and discontinued for want of adequate patronage.

Mr. Wright commenced the publication of the Courier, in March 1848, as editor and publisher. The politics of the editor being of the Hunker democratic, the paper took that stamp also. The publication of the Courier was continued until May, 1853, at a loss to all concerned of upwards of two thousand dollars, at which time a sale was effected to the present proprietor, who commenced the republication of the journal in September of the same year, under the cognomen of

THE DEPOSIT UNION DEMOCRAT.

As we stated above, the politics of Mr. Wright, were Hard Democratic, in opposition to the line of the administration, and some differences arising between him and the department, in relation to post-office matter, the ex-editor was removed from the office of post-master, and the present editor appointed in his place.

The removal of Mr. Wright, and the appointment of his successor, excited the indignation of his personal and political friends, and a fund was raised for the establishment of another paper, with Mr. Wright as editor. The sum of four hundred and seventy-five dollars was raised, and the future editor was commissioned to New York, to purchase the requisite material.

The first number of the

DELAWARE COUNTY COURIER

Was issued on the 15th of February, 1855, and continued until the following May, issuing in all twelve numbers, when it was discontinued. The establishment was afterwards purchased by Mr. Hulce, and is now used in the publication of the Democrat. The politics of the Deposit Union Democrat are Administration, Democratic. The editor says;

"I have published this paper just two and a half years, it just about paying expenses, and the business improving. The last six months has been much better than before."

BLOOMVILLE MIRROR.

It is a verified part of past history, that from little and apparently trivial causes, flow frequently the greatest results. It is a wise and a beautiful process of nature, that the apparently inanimate acorn causes the majestic oak to spring forth, take deep root, and spread wide its overhanging branches to the breeze. Nor is it any more a law of the vegetable kingdom, than it is in the social and the intellectual intercourse of human beings. The proud statesman, whose voice exercises a controlling influence upon a nation's destiny, forgets not the rude school-room where he imbibed the first pure draughts, from that fountain, from which he has since drunk so deeply.

It is with such reflections as these, that we come to congratulate our friend S. B. Champion, upon the success of his novel enterprise.

The first number of the "Bloomville Mirror" was issued May 28th, 1851. It contained but one hundred and one words, printed on a sheet five by seven inches. Some six numbers were issued at intervals of two weeks. Up to July, '51, no price of subscription had been fixed. The copies which had been previously printed, had been gratuitously distributed, and everywhere met with favor. The new postage law, which provided for the free circulation of newspapers in the county in which they were published, induced him to fix the price of the Mirror at twenty-five cents a year, and to publish it as often as sufficient local news accumulated, to make it interesting. Up to July 1st, about sixty names had been handed in, with a request to be furnished with the "Mirror," and they would pay for the same when the price should be fixed. The publisher declined taking pay, stating "that he only printed them to while away his leisure moments."

The capital invested in the paper, at this point in its history, was extremely limited. He had only ten pounds of old cast-off type, that had been given to him by a brother printer in Schoharie. He had no printing press, and performed his press-work with a square block covered with cloth, upon which he struck with a mallet, as printers in some offices frequently obtain their proof sheets.

After the issue of the paper containing the announcement that it would be sent to subscribers for twenty-five cents per year, each mail brought in new names, and the list soon reached one hundred copies. On the 1st of September, the publisher visited Prattsville, and obtained a box of old type, made some cases himself, and proceeded to increase the size of the Mirror. He also rigged up a sort of Franklin printing press, and on the

8th of September, the size of the Mirror was about eight by ten inches, and was printed on both sides. It was printed in this shape until the 3d of November, when its size was doubled, and printed in imitation of a large newspaper, the sheet being about the size of a sheet of commercial note paper, or two pages of this book. It was printed in this shape until the 5th of April, 1852, when it was again enlarged by the addition of another column to each page, and the price increased to fifty cents per year. By publishing the paper regularly every week, and inserting more local intelligence than either of the other papers in the county, the paper became a favorite with the people, and in the Mirror for February 15, 1853, the announcement was made, that the subscription list had reached *one thousand*.

Business thus increasing, the editor gradually became compelled to devote nearly his whole time to the management of his paper, his only office being a room rudely made in one corner of his grist-mill. After a time he procured a small building ten by twelve feet square, and his office soon began to assume more the air of a regular newspaper establishment.

Additions of new type, a new press, job type, &c., were obtained, as the publisher obtained means, and on the 4th of September, 1855, the Mirror was again enlarged, by the addition of another column. With a new plain and neat head, new type, and being a sheet sixteen by twenty-two inches, and four columns to the page, its appearance at once gave it a favorable reception among strangers, while its independent and fearless career, procured for it a large number of readers, and at this time (Jan. 1, 1856,) it has a circulation of *two thousand* copies per week, and has, at a fair estimate, twelve thousand weekly readers.

I copy the following appropriate remarks from the speech of the Hon. D. S. Dickinson, at Delhi, to the National Democrats, February 29th, 1854:

"It is said you have no press: remember this is not without a remedy. When the arid plains of Israel had become parched and heated by a long continued drought, so that all nature was burned and withered under the scorching rays of an eastern sun, at the invocation of the prophet there appeared upon the distant horizon, a little cloud no bigger than a man's hand, which gave out signs of abundance of rain, and its refreshing influences fertilized the earth, and gladdened the hearts of the people. And when the hot breath of sectional discord has withered and blasted the beauty of old Delaware's political verdure, when her sons have become thirsty for a return of the refreshing showers which formerly blessed them, they may descry in the distance a little cloud to cheer old Delaware, a little cloud (Bloomville Mirror,) which, though scarcely bigger than a man's hand, gives promise of copious streams of healing waters, which will cure all political diseases, and preserve the healthy from contagion."

WEEKLY VISITOR

The "Weekly Visitor" was established by George W. Reynolds, at Franklin, Delaware county, N. Y. The editor published his prospectus, March 28th, 1855. He says:

"The 'Visitor' will be printed on a sheet twenty-four by thirty-six inches, containing twenty-eight columns of matter, and in point of type and workmanship will be equal to any news-journal in this region.

"As a sheet of useful, entertaining, and instructive household reading, the 'Visitor' will endeavor to attain and hold a high rank, and make itself a favorite with old and young, and especially with all who seek for their families a literature wholly free from *everything that can deprave the sentiments or vitiate the taste.*

"In the columns of the 'Visitor' will be found the Latest News on all matters of Public interest—Local Items—Sketches from Real and Ideal Life—Original and Selected Tales—Biographies of Eminent Men—Choice Poetry, new and old—Travelling Sketches—Leaves from History—Instructive Anecdotes—Notices of New Books, with brief Reviews and Extracts—New Facts in Science and Art—a Careful Collation from the best Agricultural Journals—a Department for the Boys and Girls that love good reading—a Department of Religious Reading, and Local Religious Notices and Items. Besides all these matters there will always be room and welcome for good thoughts, in prose or poetry, that may aid the great movements of the present times—to educate, civilize, and make more *human* our own and other lands; to redeem the drunkard, and set free the slave.

"In regard to all the worthy reformatory efforts of the day, the great thing needed is full and free and *fair* discussion, and the same is true in regard to matters purely political. People will *act* rightly only as they think rightly, and that the people do more of their own thinking than formerly is apparent in the recent turn of affairs in our nation, as regards party arrangements, and the late elections. This paper will favor all such movements as may develop the true relation between parties and the people; and such as tend to bring out of the present chaos a coöperative policy in all that is really good.

"It is the purpose of the editor to pursue, as heretofore, an earnest warfare against all that wrongs or crushes any portion of the human race, yet he would always war with the weapons of truth and reason, and give to opposing views a candid hearing. The engineer on the car of progress must be heard, but so also must the brakeman. There will be room, then, in the 'Visitor' for the progressive, for the conservative, and for that better man than either, the progressive-conservative.

"Much attention will be given to the early history of Delaware and adjacent counties, and to the lives of those hardy pioneers who have made this 'Region of Hills' so full of beauty and fruitfulness, and who though dead or soon to die, have a right to be remembered. Facts for this department are earnestly solicited.

"To make the paper full of interest, the editor invites the correspondence of old friends everywhere; of all those whose student-life has been wholly or in part at Franklin; of old residents of this region, now scattered abroad; of the clergy, the mechanics, the farmers, the doctors, the teachers, the Lawyers, and of *all* who have something good and interesting to say for their respective localities, or for the general good.

"The 'Visitor' will be published on Saturdays, at one dollar fifty cents per annum, *in advance*. Any subscription unpaid for three months will be invariably charged two dollars. Advertisements for insertion, at the usual rates, are respectfully solicited."

DELAWARE BANK.

After several unsuccessful attempts to organize a banking institution, for the convenience and accommodation of the inhabitants of the county, the Delaware Bank was finally organized, in conformity with the general banking law, passed the year preceding, and went into operation January 1st, 1839.

The original capital stock of the association was $100,000, or one thousand shares, with power at the discretion of the directors, of increasing the same to $500,000.

The pioneer directors of the institution were Herman D. Gould, Gordon H. Edgerton, Amasa J. Parker, Samuel Gordon, Nelson K. Wheeler, Charles Hathaway, Dubois Burhans, Charles Marvine, John H. Gregory, Darius Maples, Jonas More, Martin Keeler, Jr., and Orrin Griffin.

The power and rights of stockholders were vested exclusively in a bond of thirteen directors. Every director must be a stockholder in the bank to the amount of $1000, or ten shares, to render him eligible to the office. The election of officers occurs on the first Tuesday in October of each year, in the village of Delhi. The board of directors appoint one of their number president, also elect a cashier and such other officers as shall be deemed necessary from time to time.

Herman D. Gould was elected the first president, and continued to discharge its duties until his death, in 1849, when Charles Marvine, Esq., one of the original directors, was elected to fill the vacancy, and has since been continued in office.

Giles M. Shaw, was elected first cashier, and was succeeded by Dubois Burhaus, Esq., who was obliged to resign on account of ill health. Walter H. Griswold, Esq. is the present cashier.

The location of the bank is at Delhi, the county seat of Delaware county. The Metropolitan Bank in the city of New York, is the established agency where its bills are redeemed at a discount of three eighths per cent.

DEPOSIT BANK.

The DEPOSIT BANK owes its origin to the enterprise of a private citizen, Charles Knapp, Esq. The inhabitants of the western portion of Delaware, and the adjoining sections of Broom Co., and Pennsylvania, had long felt the increasing necessity of an institution of this kind, to obviate the necessity of a journey to Binghampton, Delhi, or Unadilla, to transact their banking business. Deposit, since the opening of the New York and Erie Railroad, had grown to become one of the first villages in the county. The lumbering interests of that section of country, were important and extensive—a species of industry, which above all others, is peculiarly calculated to create a requisition for a large surplus capital.

The question of establishing a bank, had, at various times been agitated, and as often unsuccessfully, until Mr. Knapp came forward, and boldly embarked his capital in the establishment of an individual bank.

We are indebted to the politeness of Mr. Knapp, for the following particulars: "This is an individual bank, for which no particular amount of capital is required. At least $50,000 must be deposited as securities in the Bank Department, for the redemption of its individual notes, before the individual can receive any such notes. At first, in our book reports, we reported as capital, the stock, bonds, and mortgages in the Bank Department, amounting to $54,084. But lately, a special account has been opened in the books of the bank, for the bonds and mortgages, and the stocks only have since been counted as capital. The bank, was organized and commenced business, on the 20th, of February, 1854. The sureties now held by the Bank Department are:

New York State, 6 pr. ct. stock, redeemable in 1873,	$23,000
New York State, 5 pr. ct. stock, redeemable in 1856,	7,000
Bonds and Mortgages,	30,049
	$60,049

Enclosed I send a copy of our last quarterly report.

QUARTERLY REPORT.

Statement showing the true condition of the Deposit Bank of Deposit, an individual bank, on the morning of Saturday, the 2d day of June, 1855.

RESOURCES.

Loans and discounts, except to Directors and Brokers,	$78,562 68
All sums due from brokers,	183 28
Bonds and mortgages,	30,000 49
Stocks,	30,000 00
Loss and expense account,	567 14

Specie,	- - - - - - - -	4,146 54
Cash items, viz.: Checks,-	- - - - - -	209 50
Bills of solvent banks on hand,-	- - - - -	9,525 00
Due from banks, viz.: From solvent banks on demand, - - -		9,013 15
		$162,261 29

LIABILITIES.

Capital,	- - - - - - - -	$30,000	00
Profits,	- - - - - - - -	2,163	36
Registered bank notes received and not returned,		$59,700	
Less registered bank notes on hand, -	- -	2,911	
Leaves registered bank notes in circulation,-	- - -	56,789	00
Due depositors on demand	- - - - - -	42,783	33
Due individuals and corporations other than banks and depositors,		14	70
Due banks on demand, -	- - - - - -	461	90
Due to others not included under either of the above heads, -		30,049	00
		$162,261	29

County of Delaware, ss: Charles Knapp and Bolivar Radeker, being duly sworn, depose and say that the foregoing is, in all respects, a true statement of the condition of the said bank before the transaction of any business, on the morning of the 2d day of June, 1855, (being the day specified in the notice of the Superintendent of the Bank Department, next preceding the date of this report, and requiring the same,) according to the best of their knowledge and belief; that the said bank is an individual bank, and is located in the village of Deposit, in the county of Delaware, where it has a banking house for the transaction of its business; and that from the 20th of February, 1854, up to the day of making this report, the business thereof was transacted at such location, and that no person or persons are interested with the said Charles Knapp, directly or indirectly, in the securities deposited with the said Superintendent, for the circulating notes obtained by him, or in the business of circulating said notes, or in the benefits and advantages thereof.

CHARLES KNAPP, President,
BOLIVAR RADEKER, Cashier.

Subscribed and sworn this 7th day of July, 1855, before me,
S. D. HULCE,
Justice of the Peace.

SECRET ORGANIZATIONS.

FREEMASONRY.

WE scarcely deem it the province of the historian to enter the arena of discussion as to the merits or demerits of secret organizations, whether political or benevolent. The fact that they do exist, and have existed, is indisputable, and it belongs to us to glance at their origin, and delineate their history leaving the field of logical discussion for the eloquence of the statesman or the pen of the reviewer.

Freemasonry may be appropriately classed among the matters of interest connected with the early history of the county. This institution claims to trace its origin back to time immemorial. It is even asserted by some writers on the subject, that Adam was the originator of the institution, and was himself, the first free and accepted mason. Others give the date of its origin, at the erection of Solomon's temple, and accord to the inspired wisdom of that great lawgiver, the credit of its existence. But notwithstanding these vague suppositions, which it can hardly be necessary here to state, are as groundless as fiction, it is definitely established as having existed in a modified form at the Christian era.

Masonry was first regularly established in the United States by Lord Weymouth, who emigrated to the Southern States, and instituted a lodge in the State of Georgia, as early as 1730. In 1781, the Grand Lodge of the State of New York, was instituted, in consequence of a warrant from the Grand Lodge of England. It was from the Grand Lodge of the State, that all the sub-lodges derived their charters and vested powers.

The total number of lodges in the United States in 1816, as near as could be ascertained, was eight hundred and fifty eight. The number of lodges in the State of New York alone was three hundred and one, or more than one third of the total number.

The following is a list of the lodges organized in Delaware county, the town in which located, with the corresponding number by which each was recognized by the Grand Lodge, together with the date of the erection of each.

No.	Name of Lodge.	Town in which located.	Instituted.
91,	Morton,	Walton,	Feb. 12th, 1802.
168,	Delaware and Ulster,	Middletown,	June 1st, 1808.
170,	Charity,	Tompkins,	Sept. 7th, 1808.
180,	Cassia,	Delhi,	March 1st, 1809.
224,	Charity,	Harpersfield,	Sept. 27th, 1813.
227,	Aurora,	Meredith,	Nov. 25th, 1813.
251,	Franklin,	Franklin,	Oct. 13th, 1815.
296,	Colden,	Middletown,	Sept. 13th, 1817.
408,	Eagle,	Roxbury,	1820.

The number of degrees conferred upon accepted masons are in succession seven, viz., 1. Entered Apprentice, 2. Fellow Craft, 3. Master Mason, 4. Mark Master, 5. Past Master, 6. Most Excellent Master, 7. Royal Arch.

The principal symbols of the masonic order, are, the square, the plumb-line, the level, and the compass, as emblematic of the craft whose name they bear. The ornamental decorations of the lodge room are, the Mosaic Pavement, Indented Tassel, and the Blazing Star. The Mosaic Pavement represents the ground floor of Solomon's Temple, the Indented Tassel, that beautiful border which surrounded it, and the blazing star in the centre, is in commemoration of the star by which the magi, or wise men of the East, were conducted to the place of our Saviour's nativity.

The rigid oaths administered to each member, as well as the horrid penalties affixed thereto, had effectually barred for ages the world without from a cognizance of the secrets of masonry. Some vague reports of certain rites and ceremonies too ridiculous to be believed, except by the ignorant and credulous, and which subsequent demonstration proved to be far from truth, were the only items of the *modus operandi* of its internal machinery, which it had seen fit to give the world, until 1828 when Morgan published his world-renowned "Revelations of Masonry," which cost that author his life, and gave to the world the mysteries of masonic order.

The mysterious disappearance of Morgan, at or about the time of the publication of his work, together with the painful associations connected with his untimely death, struck like a magic chord upon the public ear. It was published in every newspaper, the theme of every writer, the subject of dreamers dreams, and the absorbing topic of conversation everywhere. The slumbering indignation of the masses of the people was aroused, and it was evident that public condemnation had passed a sentence upon Masonry, from which it could never recover.

The decline of Masonry was a marked epoch in the history of secret organizations—the supposed murder of Morgan, and the startling developments which the publication of his supposed work gave to the world, confirmed in truth as they were by the affirmation of members who seceded from the order, created in the public mind powerful prejudices, not only against masonry, but all organizations of a secret character, as conflicting with the spirit of our free institutions.

ODD FELLOWSHIP.

The decline and prostration of Masonry, and the universal antipathy lavished upon the order, affected to a greater or less extent all similar organizations. Foremost amongst these ranked the Independent Order of Odd Fellows, which had existed in a crude and detached state in various portions of the United States, prior to 1819, when it was formally and systematically established, through the energy and perseverance of Thomas Hildey, a gentleman residing in Baltimore.

The association of Odd Fellows in this country, is wisely affiliated and compacted in a fashion bearing some resemblance to the form of our civil constitution. Its genius, however, unlike that of our civil government, is the genius, not of state rights, but of consolidated sovereignty. The minor lodges, in the several States and territories, are subject to the supervision of the grand lodges; and these again are subordinate to the Grand Lodge of the United States. The primary source of power and legislation resides in this latter body. This superior grand lodge is composed of representatives from the inferior grand lodges, together with the following officers (who constitute the executive department of the order,) viz., the grandsire, deputy grandsire, grand recording secretary, grand corresponding secretary, grand treasurer, grand marshal, grand guardian, and grand chaplain. According to the first article of the constitution, this superior grand lodge "is the source of all true and legitimate authority in Odd Fellowship, within the United States of America—All State, district, and territorial grand lodges and encampments, assemble under its warrant, and derive their authority from it. It is the ultimate tribunal, to which all matters of general importance are to be referred, and its decisions thereon shall be final and conclusive. To it belongs the power to regulate and control the work of the order, and the several degrees belonging thereto; to fix and determine the customs and usages in regard to all things which concern Odd Fellowship. This grand lodge has inherent power to establish lodges and encampments in foreign countries. Such lodges and encampments shall work by virtue of a warrant granted by this grand lodge."*

Every minor lodge is required to make quarterly returns of all business done, to the grand lodge of the State or territory, and this again to the Grand Lodge of the United States, so that the executive department is correctly and constantly informed in respect to all the proceedings of the inferior lodges, spread over the face of the country and extending into foreign lands.

The principal business and objects of this association, so far as they are made public, are to provide a weekly allowance, for a brother when sick—the amount usually appropriated being $4 per week, except in the case of those holding certain offices, who are allowed $8 per week—an appropriation of $30, to cover funeral expenses of a brother, or half this amount if a brother is called to bury a wife. There is also some small provision made for the education of the orphan children of Odd Fellows. Inasmuch as this is not a matter regulated by law and statute, we know not how much such unfortunate children may or may not receive. It is also contemplated by means of these lodges to promote among the members a high degree of friendship, of which every member may avail himself at home and abroad. To accumulate a fund adequate to cover the expenses constantly accruing, the association demands of every member a proposition fee of one dollar, initiation fee of five dollars, one dollar for each of four different degrees, and two dollars for another. There are also

---

* Article first, Const. G. L. of United States.

small weekly or monthly taxes or dues, which every member is required to pay, besides two "intermediate degrees," as they are called, for which a given sum is no doubt required, though the amount is unknown to us, and we think not specified in any of their printed constitutions. The superior grand lodge, receives its funds chiefly by a tax of $30 for charters given to minor lodges and encampments; also from what is charged as "expenses" and "per centage on reports," from tax on representations, profits on the sale of books, cards, &c.

To prevent too great and sudden drafts upon the treasury of the order, it is directed in the several constitutions, that the association be composed exclusively of male members, of a sound bodily constitution, and under forty-five years of age; and if one is admitted beyond this age, an additional fee is charged of one dollar for each supernumerary year, so that if the applicant is seventy years old, his initiation fee will be $30.

The following list of the lodges in the county, the date of their organization, and the number of members, was furnished me by C. A. Foote, Esq., county secretary.

Delaware lodge was organized March 7th, 1847, in Delhi the number of members, as reported in August, 1855, was sixty-six.

Hobart lodge, at the same date, contained sixty members; Oleout Valley, contained thirty-eight members; Chehocton lodge, fifty-one members; Pakatakin lodge, at Margaretville, contained forty-one members; Tremperskill lodge, organized in 1854, in Andes Village, contained about thirty members; and Deposit lodge, at Deposit Village, contained about sixty members.

IODINE SPRING.

This spring is situated on Elk creek, about four miles from the village of Delhi. It is the property of Mrs. H. D. Gould. The analysis of the spring is contained in the following communication:—

"New Haven, June 18th, 1851.

"HON. HERMAN D. GOULD, DELHI, N. Y.—

"DEAR SIR:—The analysis of the water sent by you for that purpose, has been completed, so far as we are able to complete it, from the quantity sent.

"The specific gravity of the water at 60 Fahrenheit is   1.0180
The number of grains of fixed constituent parts
   in one gallon is,   826.0598
   The composition of this amount is as follows:
      Organic matter, Silica and iron,   2.2715
      Chlorine,   505.9472
      Sodium,   265.6001

Calcium,	42.7886
Magnesium,	6.9682
Carbonic acid and Gas,	2.4842
	826.0598

"You can depend upon the accuracy of these results, which are all, the mean of two concurring trials. This may be shown by calculating the amount of chlorine necessary to combine with the three cases mentioned above, sodium, calcium and magnesium.

"Thus the whole amount of chlorine is 505.9472 grains: 265.600 grains of sodium, require chlorine 407.9176, forming chloride of sodium, or common salt; 42.7886 grains of calcium, require chlorine 75.8577 grains, forming chloride of calcium. 6.9682 grains magnesium, require chlorine 19.5773/505.3526 grains, forming chloride of magnesium.

"The difference between the amount thus calculated, and the amount really found, is but .5966, or little more than half a grain.

"You will see that 674½ grains of the whole are common salt. The water would make a salt more than commonly pure. The iron present is proto-carbonate, and is kept in solution by carbonic acid. The quantity is very small.

"After the above analysis was completed, the remaining liquid was carefully examined, and small quantities of bromine and iodine were found. The determination of the accurate proportions of these cannot be made, unless upon a fresh sample of not less than 12 or 15 gallons.

"For medicinal purposes the determination of these substances would be quite important, but their proportions are so small that much water is required. If you desire it, these determinations shall be made, as soon as you can send on some water. If you would like the results in the per centage form, I can have it done for you.

"I am sir, yours,
"JOHN P. NORTON."

THE DELAWARE LITERARY INSTITUTE

Was incorporated by an Act of the legislature, April 23d, 1836, with twenty-four trustees. The first building erected is of stone, eighty-six feet in length, forty in breadth, and four stories in height. It was opened under the care of Rev. Wm. Fraser, and two assistants, with 103 pupils. For some reason, though an able scholar, and an excellent man, he resigned his post in 1838, and was succeeded by Rev. Silas Fitch, Jr., who continued at the head of the school till May, 1846. The highest number of students, in any one year of his term of office, was 211.

His successor was Rev. George Kerr, L.L.D., with 186 students, during the first year. Under his administration, which continues to the present time, the school has realized more than the most sanguine hopes of its founders. Selecting, for his associates in the department of instruction, college graduates of high standing as scholars, and of peculiar aptness to teach, he soon placed the institution on higher ground than it ever occupied before. Two new and well arranged buildings have been erected, one for the especial accommodation of young ladies, with a boarding department, and the other for young men, with a spacious chapel on the lower floor, and with a large lecture room, and laboratory in the basement, to illustrate chemistry in its application to the arts, and to agriculture. Connected with the institution are several choice libraries, amounting already to nearly 2500 volumes, to which considerable additions are made every year. The *classical* studies are conducted to any extent desired, receiving, as they deserve, a very earnest attention. The *mathematical* course is nearly equal in extent, and fully so in *thoroughness,* to that pursued in our best colleges.

The greatest number of students, during any one year, and since Dr. Kerr has had the seminary in charge, is 414; and this is about the *present* number, with gratifying prospects of increase in the time to come.

The *aim* of this institution, is to take higher ground than that occupied by the common academy; not merely to prepare young men for the ordinary round of duty, but for any advanced standing in college, that they may desire; to prepare them for public life, not only by the *drill,* which imparts the requisite intellectual strength, but by rousing the consciousness of what life and its weighty responsibilities are.

And the *great* peculiarity of this school, which strikes the writer of this notice, is the *unflagging enthusiasm* of its head, which, in its outflow upon the students, can hardly fail to develop whatever sensibility or strength may lie dormant in their souls.

So far as experience enables us to judge, we do not hesitate to say, that the education of the sexes in the same classes, and course of study, is for their mutual benefit; the gentler sex gathering more strength, and the rougher, more polish.

The *grounds* around the institute are laid out in good taste, and adorned by the thrifty growth of several varieties of trees, which from year to year will put on fresh and additional beauty and attractiveness.

FERGUSONVILLE BOARDING ACADEMY.

This institution was founded in 1848, by the Rev. Samuel D. Ferguson, and Sanford I. Ferguson, A. M. It is located in the valley of the Charlotte, a section of the country distinguished for the salubrity of its climate and the beauty of its scenery.

The establishment of a boarding academy, so remote from large cities, in a region of country but sparsely settled, and where but little interest had been manifested in educational matters, was considered a scheme of very doubtful expediency. The success however, which has attended this enterprise, has not only surpassed the expectations of its patrons and friends, but has formed an essential element in the educational interests in this county, and marks an important era in the history of the literary institutions of central New York.

With a mild but strict discipline, and a thorough and efficient course of instruction, it has risen to an elevated position among the seminaries of the State.

Connected with its almost unparalleled success, there are three points worthy of observation:

1st. Its location is such, that students are not exposed to the corrupting influences of tippling, gambling, and other collateral vices, which are the usual concomitants of cities and large villages.

2nd. *Physical* education receives its regular and appropriate attention. A systematic course in the instruction and practice of *Gymnastics*, has contributed much to the proper physical health of the students, both male and female.

3rd. Its *social* character. The examining committee in their report add: "The domestic character of this institution produces a parental, a filial, and a fraternal feeling, which gives to it a close resemblance to a well regulated and wisely governed family."

Connected with the institution, there is an excellent and improved farm, containing about two hundred acres, valued at five thousand dollars. The buildings cost $7000, including the Gymnasium, erected a year since, at a cost of $1000. The buildings are commodious, and accommodate one hundred and twenty boarders.

Rev. Samuel D. Ferguson, and Sanford I. Ferguson, A. M., retired from the institution in the summer of 1855, having devoted seven years of arduous and unremitting labor to the educational interests of the community. They were succeeded in the duties and proprietorship of the institution by James Oliver, Esq., whose elevated character, high standing, and well known ability, afford the strongest guarantee of its future destiny, and recommend its earnest efforts to the patronage of all.

The institution is located in the town of Davenport, Delaware county. It is accessible by stage, either from Albany or Catskill, on the Hudson, daily.

The following is a copy of the constitution of the first temperance society formed in Delaware county:

THE SOCIAL LEAGUE.

"As a band of brothers joined,
Peace and safety we shall find!"

To every reputable, honest man, in Meredith, be his religious or political opinions what they may:—

It cannot have escaped observation, that the state of our society, for the last year or two, instead of bettering, has been waxing worse and worse.

Tavern-haunting, intemperate drinking, carousing and high scrapes, horse-jockeying and trafficking in depreciated and suspected bills; enticing and leading away, one and another of our unwary, unsuspecting neighbors, into like excesses and disgrace; and traducing, slandering, threatening and endeavoring to intimidate and awe into silence, all who wish for better things, all who dare to discountenance and denounce the abandoned and the profligate in the mad career of their vices:—

These enormities, at first stealing and crawling covertly and slyly in among us, have, of late, assumed a bolder aspect, and made rapid and gigantic strides, till, at length, grown bold by impunity, they have dared to brave appearances, and even to show their impudent, brazen front, in open day—setting truth, decency, good manners and good morals, at utter defiance.

With these facts staring us in the face, what have we left us, but to yield a pusillanimous and ignominious submission to the insulting empire of the wicked, whose tender mercies are cruelty, or, to unite, and place ourselves in the gap, array our breasts and our faces, as a mound and as a flint against the torrents of vice and the shafts of malice, that threaten to overwhelm us?

And can there be a single good member of society, who will hesitate for a moment, between these alternatives? Impossible. We cannot but choose the latter.

We therefore unite, as a band of brothers, and under the sanctions and obligations of a sacred league, pledge ourselves to each other, to make common cause, in endeavoring, to the utmost of our abilities and opportunities, to check, arrest and suppress the growing evils described.

We engage to stand by each other, and with our whole influence, example and precept, to strengthen one another's hands, and confirm one another's hearts in the good work of staying the progress of infectious vice, and turning back, upon itself, abashed and confounded, the whole phalanx of desperadoes, with their abettors and upholders; who, if left to themselves, would fain run down the good name, ruin the welfare, and even endanger the peace and safety of our common neighborhood! And, as means of bringing about these wished for ends,—

We engage, as much as may be to avoid frequenting the taverns ourselves, and when occasion calls us thither, mean to make a point of discharging our incumbent duties, with all convenient dispatch, and being off about our business, ever designing while there, to demean ourselves civilly and peaceably, and not to drink intemperately; that we may not, by our own sauntering and intemperance, encourage and hold in countenance the lazy herd of tavern-haunters and tipplers, habitually hanging about some of our inns, to the great annoyance of weary, wayworn travellers, as well as to the great disparagement and disgrace of themselves, and distress of their families and friends.

And as to those tavern-keepers among us, who keep reputable houses, and discourage tippling and tavern haunting, especially of towns-people, and who steadily disallow of drunkenness, profanity, high scrapes and immorality, generally, at their houses, and resolutely refuse dealing out liquors, when men have gotten enough for their good, and when more would only hurt them; to tavern-keepers of this description, we tender our best wishes, intending to patronize them, by recommending their houses, and giving them, so far as we conveniently can, the preference of our custom, as often as occasion shall require our visiting public houses; while at the same time, we design, by our influence, and by avoiding, as far as we consistently can, all houses of a different description, to disapprove and discountenance the conduct of those who keep them: and who render themselves unworthy the approbation and support of the respectable part of the community, by encouraging or even allowing of shameful doings and disgraceful carryings-on, at their houses: and by feeding town-tipplers and drunkards with liquor, when they have already gotten enough, and too much; and when they ought to deny, and send them home, to provide for their suffering families; instead of pouring *out,* and being pleased with seeing them pour *down,* dram after dram, and grog after grog, till they are lost to shame, and worse than lost to themselves, their families, friends and society;—till they become a nuisance, a living stench and chastisement, or a very pest and judgment to all about them!

And as to those young men and old, middle-aged, and boys, if of all such ages there be, who have betaken themselves, not to constant, but to occasional, high scrapes, bacchanalian frolics, and drunken carousals,—we counsel them to desist. We do not give them over, indiscriminately, for lost: but recall them, all of them, who are not past recovery, gone, and given over to a reprobate mind, and to believe in a lie, till they plunge headlong into destruction.—All those, not thus irreclaimably gone, insane and lost, we anxiously recall, and kindly invite back, to participate in our company and confidence; assuring them, if they will forsake the husks, whereon, with the swine, they fain would feed, and do but feed;—if they will abandon bad company, and forsake their more hardened, dissolute companions, and return to better deeds, and better things, and better conduct, we are ready to meet them, with open arms, and to welcome their restoration to reputation and to good standing among the good.

But, we have another set of men, let loose upon us, incomparably worse than the foregoing: a thousand times more incorrigible; possessed, as it were, with seven evil spirits; a set, who appear to make a business of mischief; who idle, drink, curse, swear, carouse, and carry on, at a high rate; who beset, molest, often take in, abuse, wrong, and deeply injure, their neighbors; who strike a dread and terror upon the good, and make even the bad blush, at their impieties and baseness; who keep the neighborhood in a blaze, scattering as it were "firebrands, arrows, and death," wherever they go!

As to these, we have but little hopes of them; and we can only admonish them, that we mean to keep a strict watch over them! And, if they shall still dare to outrage decency, trample on the laws of God and man, and set civil authority at defiance, we are determined to unite, as one man, and make common cause, in bringing them to justice; in causing them to be arraigned, convicted, and punished! And, although they may rail at justice, religion, and the laws of the land; and at those who unite in putting them into execution, we can only ask,

> "What rogue e'er felt the halter draw,
> With good opinion of the law?"

We can only do our duty, and leave them, if they will, to avoid the consequences, by avoiding to expose themselves; by facing to the right about, forsaking their bad practices; becoming peaceable, unoffending, and useful citizens! And then they may rest assured, neither the laws, nor those who put them in force, will hurt so much as a hair of their heads. To evil-doers only, are the laws and the civil magistrates a terror.

And if any mischief-makers, or peace-breakers, infesting our neighborhood, not having the fear of God before their eyes, but moved by the instigation of the devil, be they who they will, whether inhabitants, stragglers, or loiterers about among us, shall be discovered, by any of us, plotting or conspiring or purposing mischief, toward any of us, in our persons, reputation, or estates; we pledge ourselves to each other, to give the earliest possible warning to those against whom such mischief shall be meditated; to the intent, that it may be prevented; engaging moreover, that we, ourselves, will also endeavor, as far as in us lies, to prevent it; and, whenever unable to prevent, will unite in approving and encouraging every just and legal measure, to bring the perpetrators to condign punishment, assuring to all, who shall be active in bringing culprits to justice, our united aid, countenance and thanks.

And if there be a man who shall unite with us, in this sacred, social league, by affixing his name hereto; and who shall, notwithstanding, be so far lost to honor, and all else of man, that's worthy of a man, as to disregard and trample on the rights and duties he hereby engages to respect and fulfil;—over him too, will we, the residue of us, have our united and individual watch; and, unless he forsake the evil of his ways, and evidence a better life by better conduct,—toward him too, will we extend our reprehension and our best endeavors that he be brought either to reformation, or to condign punishment!

Every person affixing his name hereto, shall thenceforth, till he either withdraw his name, or remove out of Meredith, be taken to belong to this league; and shall be considered under the sacred obligations of honor, as well as of honesty and good conscience, to endeavor to fulfil the engagements hereby taken upon himself: Accounting the same no other than those obvious and urgent duties, which find at once their injunction and their justification, in that golden rule of him who spake as never man spake: "Whatsoever ye would that men should do unto you, do ye even so unto them."

But if any person shall at any time wish to withdraw his name, and be no longer considered as belonging to this league, he may do it at pleasure, on applying to him who for the time being, may be keeper hereof, and erasing his name.

Any person affixing his name hereto, and residing within half a mile of the centre of the town, may be keeper hereof; with the privilege to all others, who may subscribe, of free access to and perusal thereof.

Meredith, March 6th, 1810.

LIST OF SUBSCRIBERS.

Cyrenus Stilson,
Benjamin Sears,
Elias Griswold,
Abner Pratt,
Josiah D. Wells,
Edward Jones,
Joseph Bassett,
Nathaniel Mitchell,
Josiah Brown,
Nathan Stilson,
Simon Baldwin,
Sylvester Rich,
Pyam Mitchell,
William Cramer,
Mathew Wiard,
Andrew Bill,
John Chapman,
Eldad Jackson,
Jeremiah Cook,
Henry Thornton,
Abner Pratt, Jr.
Joel Carr,
Joel Hunt,
Eleazer Millard,
Daniel Millard,
Oren Canfield,
Selah French,
Wells Spalding,
Anthony Judd,

Amos Bristol,
Isaiah Jackson,
Joseph Porter,
William Bonton,
Samuel A. Law,
Samuel Moody,
Eleazer Wright, Jr.
Is. Burr,
Simeon P. Griswold,
Daniel Smith,
Ezra Thornton,
Elisha Bisbee,
Simeon Crane,
Adam Saunders,
Samuel Shaw,
Samuel Cottrell,
Ira Thornton,
Barton Bisbee,
Joseph Shaw,
Charles Fish,
Bildad Curtis,
Luke Brown,
Josiah Garritt,
Pearce Mitchell,
Samuel Remington,
David North,
Nathaniel Stewart, Jr.,
Horace Jones,
Medad Jackson,

Truman Rowe,
Truman Smith,
John Thornton,
Herman Harwood,
Ariel Denio,
Josiah Shaw,
Joshua Strickland,
Thomas Forbush,
Shelden Bassett,
Orton Thompson,
Elijah Georgey,
Isaac Lake,
Oliver Tuttle,

Daniel Remington,
Edmund Brawhall,
Isaac Benedict,
Nathan Stilson, Jr.,
James Vellentine,
Thomas Fish,
Lewis Brownson,
Moses Stilson,
Joshua Bailey,
John Dibble,
Asahel Baldwin,
Charles P. Price,
Philander Jones.

www.ingramcontent.com/pod-product-compliance
Lightning Source LLC
Chambersburg PA
CBHW021850230426
43671CB00006B/337